W9-AUO-959

5 STEPS TO A

AP TEST CHANGES / 2020 AND BEYOND

Because of school district closures across the U.S. in response to the global COVID-19 pandemic, the 2019/20 AP school year came to an unexpected halt in March 2020. At that point, educators and students across the country had to scramble to finish up the year and prepare for AP exams.

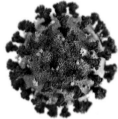

Here at McGraw Hill, the *5 Steps to a 5* team has received numerous questions and concerns about what this means for AP courses and exams moving forward. So, whether your personal test-taking plans in Spring 2020 were directly impacted or you will be sitting for your first AP test in 2021, you are likely experiencing anxiety and uncertainty about the future.

Here are some of the most frequently asked questions regarding 2020/2021 AP Exams:

What happened to the Advanced Placement exams in May 2020?

There were big changes. When the pandemic hit, the College Board (who creates and administers AP exams nationwide) was forced to pivot and administer at-home tests. So, the traditional AP exams did not take place, and new versions were offered online. Prior to testing dates, College Board provided a detailed breakdown of the content that would be covered on each revised exam, allowing for what students were unlikely to have covered in class due to school closures.

How were test-takers impacted? What was the test-taking experience like?

For the first time ever, AP exams were given online. Students took modified 45-minute, web-based, free-response exams, and they were allowed to use their books and notes during the tests. Each test was administered in open book/open note format, and there were no multiple-choice questions at all. Students were able to take the exam on any device (a computer, tablet or a smartphone). Alternatively, students were allowed to submit a photo of their handwritten work.

For the AP European History exam, the following changes took place:

- Testable content was limited to the units that the College Board determined had been covered by most teachers prior to school closures. For AP European History, the testable content was units 1-7.

- The rubric was lightly modified to match the reduced number of documents, awarding 1 point for using 2 documents, and an additional point for using 4 documents. An additional point was awarded for effectively incorporating a second piece of outside knowledge into the argument. Students earned up to 2 points for sourcing (1 point for each document).

Thesis	1 point
Contextualization	1 point
Describe 2 documents	1 point
Use documents to support your argument	1 point (2 docs)
	1 point (4 docs)
Sourcing documents	1 point (1 doc)
	1 point (2nd doc)
Outside evidence to prove thesis	1 point (1 piece of evidence)
	1 point (2nd piece of evidence)
Demonstration of complex understanding	1 point
	10 points total

Is this *5 Steps* guide relevant and up-to-date?

Yes! Everything in this book is reflective of the current course and exam as it was originally designed. The *5 Steps* team strives to keep all information relevant and as up-to-date as possible, both in print and online.

What will happen in May 2021?

Your guess is as good as ours. We're hopeful that next year's test format will return to the complete form as created by the College Board, but at the time of this guide's publication, things remain fairly uncertain. However, whether the AP exams return to the original format, follow the 2020 online model, or something entirely new - we have you covered! We'll be updating our materials whenever any new information becomes available, and will make every effort to revise our digital resources as quickly as possible.

Most importantly, look for regular updates on the College Board website for the latest information on your course at **apcentral.collegeboard.org**. This will be your resource for the most up-to-date information on AP courses.

5 STEPS TO A 5

AP European History

2021

Beth Bartolini-Salimbeni
Wendy Petersen

Mc Graw Hill

New York   Chicago   San Francisco   Athens   London   Madrid
Mexico City   Milan   New Delhi   Singapore   Sydney   Toronto

1 2 3 4 5 6 7 8 9   LHS   24 23 22 21 20

ISBN   978-1-260-46724-6
MHID   1-260-46724-4

e-ISBN   978-1-260-46725-3
e-MHID   1-260-46725-2

McGraw Hill, the McGraw Hill logo, *5 Steps to a 5*, and related trade dress are trademarks or registered trademarks of McGraw Hill and/or its affiliates in the United States and other countries and may not be used without written permission. All other trademarks are the property of their respective owners. McGraw Hill is not associated with any product or vendor mentioned in this book.

AP, Advanced Placement Program, and *College Board* are registered trademarks of the College Board, which was not involved in the production of, and does not endorse, this product.

The series editor was Grace Freedson, and the project editor was Del Franz.

Series design by Jane Tenenbaum.

McGraw Hill products are available at special quantity discounts to use as premiums and sales promotions or for use in corporate training programs. To contact a representative, please visit the Contact Us pages at www.mhprofessional.com.

CONTENTS

Preface ix

Acknowledgments x

About the Authors x

Introduction: The Five-Step Program xi

STEP 1   **Set Up Your Study Program**

1 **What You Need to Know About the AP European History Exam 3**
Background Information 4
Frequently Asked Questions About the AP European History Exam 4

2 **Determine Your Test Readiness 7**
Three Approaches to Preparing for AP Exams 8
Detailed Calendar for Each Plan 8
Setting Up a Study Group 11

STEP 2   **Understand the Skills That Will Be Tested**

3 **The Ways Historians Think 15**
Introduction 16
Reasoning Chronologically 16
Putting Information in Context 18
Arguing from Evidence 19
Developing Your Historical Thinking Skills 21
Rapid Review 22

4 **Take a Diagnostic Exam 23**
AP European History Diagnostic Exam Answer Sheet 24
Section I, Part A: Multiple-Choice Questions 25
Section I, Part B: Short-Answer Questions 38
Section II, Part A: Document-Based Question (DBQ) 40
Section II, Part B: Long-Essay Question 42
Answers and Explanations 43

STEP 3   **Develop Strategies for Success**

5 **The Multiple-Choice Questions 57**
Introduction 58
Passive Knowledge and the Process of Elimination 58
Putting Your Historical Thinking Skills to Use 58
About Guessing 59
Further Practice with Multiple-Choice Questions 59

6 **The Short-Answer Questions 61**
Introduction 62
Putting Your Knowledge and Historical Thinking Skills to Use 62
Further Practice with Short-Answer Questions 63

7 The Document-Based Question (DBQ) 65
Introduction 66
The High-Quality History Essay 66
Five Steps for Creating an Outline for Your Essay 66
Characteristics of the Document-Based Question (DBQ) 68
Applying the Principles of the High-Quality History Essay to
   the Document-Based Question (DBQ) 69
Scoring the Document-Based Question (DBQ) 72
Further Practice for the Document-Based Question (DBQ) 73

8 The Long-Essay Question 75
Introduction 76
Choosing Your Topic 76
Applying the Five Steps to a High-Quality History Essay 76
Scoring of the Essays 77
Further Practice for the Long-Essay Question 77

STEP 4

Review the Knowledge You Need to Score High

9 Major Themes of Modern European History 81
Introduction 82
Interaction of Europe and the World 82
Changes in Wealth and Who Had It 82
Changes in Knowledge Systems and Worldview 82
Changes in Society and Its Institutions 83
The Individual and Society 83
National and European Identity 83
The Organization of the AP Course into Units 83

10 From the Middle Ages to the Renaissance 85
Further Resources 88

11 The Challenge of the Renaissance 89
Introduction 90
Italian Society of the Renaissance 91
Renaissance Values 91
Artistic Achievement of the Renaissance 92
The Renaissance and Scientific Advancements 93
The Spread of the Renaissance 93
Review Questions 94
Rapid Review 96
Further Resources 96

12 The Reformation and the Fracturing of Christianity 97
Introduction 99
The Need for a Religious Reformation 99
The Lutheran Revolt 99
Creation and Spread of the Protestant Movement 100
The English Reformation 101
Reformation in Eastern Europe 102
Calvin and Calvinism 102
Social Dimensions and the Radical Reformation 103
The Catholic Response 103
Review Questions 104
Rapid Review 106
Further Resources 106

13 The Great Voyages of Exploration and Early Colonization 107
Introduction 108
Exploration and Expansion 108
The Spanish Empire in the New World 109
England, France, and the Triangular Trade Networks 110
Review Questions 111
Rapid Review 112
Further Resources 112

14 Economic Change and Political Consolidation 113
Introduction 114
Economic Stress and Change 114
Thirty Years' War 115
Britain: The Rise of Parliament 116
France: The Construction of a State 117
Central and Eastern Europe: Compromise 118
Review Questions 118
Rapid Review 120
Further Resources 120

15 Economic Change and the Expansion of the State 121
Introduction 123
Great Britain: The Triumph of Constitutionalism 123
France: The Triumph of Absolutism 124
Russia: Tsarist Absolutism 124
Breaking the Traditional Cycle of Population and Productivity 124
Market-Oriented Agriculture 125
Rural Manufacturing 125
Technical Innovations in Agriculture and Manufacturing 126
Eastern Ambition 127
War and Diplomacy 127
Review Questions 128
Rapid Review 130
Further Resources 130

16 The Rise of Natural Philosophy, Scientific Revolution, and the Enlightenment 131
Introduction 134
The Traditional View of the Cosmos 134
Alternative Traditions of Knowledge Before the
    Scientific Revolution 135
Development of New Institutions 136
The Rise of Copernicanism 136
Kepler's Laws 137
Galileo and the Value of Empirical Knowledge 137
Advances in Anatomy, Physiology, and Medicine 138
Contributions of Women During the Scientific Revolution 139
Cartesian Skepticism and Deductive Reasoning 139
The Enlightenment 140
The Triumph of Newtonian Science 140
New Ideas About Natural Law, Human Nature, and Society 141
New Political Ideas 142
The *Philosophes* and Enlightened Despotism 143

Salons and Lodges 143
Skepticism, Religion, and Social Criticism 144
The Arts in the Enlightenment 145
The Radical Enlightenment 146
The Other Enlightenment 147
Review Questions 147
Rapid Review 149
Further Resources 149

17 The French Revolution and Empire 151
Introduction 153
The *Ancien Régime* in Crisis 153
The Moderate Phase of the French Revolution (1789–1791) 154
The Radical Phase of the French Revolution (1791–1794) 156
The Final Phase of the French Revolution: Thermidor and the
  Rise of Napoleon (1794–1799) 158
Post-Revolutionary France and the Napoleonic Code 158
Napoleon's Empire 159
The Decline and Fall of Napoleon and His Empire 160
Restoration 161
Review Questions 162
Rapid Review 164
Further Resources 164

18 The Industrial Revolution 165
Introduction 166
The Industrial Revolution Begins in Great Britain 167
The Factory System and the Division of Labor 167
Iron and Steel 168
New Sources of Power 168
The Railway Boom 169
The Reciprocal Nature of Heavy Industry 169
The Spread of Industrialization 170
Social Effects of Industrialization 171
Second Industrial Revolution 172
Science in an Industrial Age 175
Review Questions 176
Rapid Review 178
Further Resources 178

19 Cultural Responses to Revolution and Industrialization 179
Introduction 181
Political Ideologies in the Nineteenth Century 181
Cultural Ideologies in the Nineteenth Century 184
Review Questions 186
Rapid Review 188
Further Resources 188

20 Mass Politics and Nationalism 189
Introduction 190
Nationalism and State-Building 190
The Triumph of Conservative Nationalism 191
The Unification of Italy 191

The Unification of Germany 193
Mass Politics and Nationalism in the Habsburg Empire 195
Mass Politics and Nationalism in France 195
Mass Politics and Nationalism in Russia 196
Mass Politics and Nationalism in Great Britain 196
Review Questions 198
Rapid Review 200
Further Resources 200

21 Mass Politics and Imperialism 201
Introduction 202
Causes of the New Imperialism 202
The Scramble for Africa 203
Dominance in Asia 203
Review Questions 205
Rapid Review 206
Further Resources 207

22 Politics of the Extreme and World War I 209
Introduction 210
Labor Unions Begin in Britain, Then Spread to Other Countries 210
Socialist Parties in Britain, France, and Germany 210
Women's Suffrage Movements and Feminism 211
Anarchist Activity 212
Ultranationalism and Anti-Semitism 212
Zionism 212
The Causes of World War I 212
The Beginning of the War: 1914–1915 213
Total War 214
1916: "The Year of Bloodletting" 215
Russian Revolution and Withdrawal 215
Germany's Disintegration and the Peace Settlement 215
Review Questions 217
Rapid Review 218
Further Resources 219

23 The Interwar Years and World War II 221
Introduction 222
Problems and Challenges After World War I 222
The Weimar Republic in Germany 224
The Soviet Union in Economic Ruins 225
The Great Depression 226
The Rise of Fascism 226
World War II 229
Assessment and Aftermath of World War II 233
Review Questions 234
Rapid Review 236
Further Resources 236

24 The Cold War, Integration, and Globalization 237
Introduction 238
The Development of Nuclear Weapons 239
The Settlement Following World War II 239

The Cold War 240
The European Union 242
The Disintegration of the Iron Curtain and the Soviet Union 243
The Rise of Nationalism in Eastern Europe 245
Social, Economic, and Political Changes in Post–Cold War Europe 246
Challenges to the Welfare State 246
Review Questions 248
Rapid Review 249
Further Resources 250

25 Science and Culture 251

STEP 5   **Build Your Test-Taking Confidence**

AP European History Practice Exam 1 Answer Sheet 257
Section I, Part A: Multiple-Choice Questions 259
Section I, Part B: Short-Answer Questions 273
Section II, Part A: Document-Based Question (DBQ) 275
Section II, Part B: Long-Essay Question 277
Answers and Explanations 279
AP European History Practice Exam 2 Answer Sheet 291
Section I, Part A: Multiple-Choice Questions 293
Section I, Part B: Short-Answer Questions 312
Section II, Part A: The Document-Based Question (DBQ) 313
Section II, Part B: The Long-Essay Question 316
Answers and Explanations 317

Resource Guide 331
Using Literary Works in European History 333
General Websites 335
General Background 337
Resources by Historical Period 339

PREFACE

Welcome to the world of Advanced Placement (AP) European History. Whether you are, or have been, enrolled in an AP European History course at your school or are preparing on your own, this guide will help you to move smoothly and confidently from your individual starting point through a five-step process that will bring you to the level of preparation you desire. Along the way, you will be evaluating your current level of preparation, evaluating your learning strategies, reading widely, analyzing primary documents, taking practice multiple-choice tests, and writing practice essays. As you go, you will be developing the strategies and confidence you need to score a 5 on the AP European History Exam. Each of the content chapters concludes with questions that focus on mastery of content. In general, they follow AP Exam formats, though not strictly as do the practice exams.

The five-step process is described in detail in the Introduction. Here, I simply want to urge you to enter into your preparation with enthusiasm. The intricate story of European history is dramatic, fascinating, and extremely relevant to the world in which you live. The information, understanding, and skills that you will learn by working through this guide will help you to do well on the AP European History Exam, but they will also help you to excel in college and to become a well-informed, critically thinking human being. New to this edition is a section labeled Further Resources at the end of each content chapter. These resources include offerings of fiction and nonfiction, films, music, and artwork that can be used to supplement (though not to supplant) the text.

As you begin, it is important that you not think of this guide as some large book to "get through." This guide is a tool and, like many tools, it can be used in a number of different ways. You can follow it through from beginning to end, or you can jump around, using the information and exercises contained in it in any way that suits you best. So take some time to familiarize yourself with the contents of this guide; get a feel for how it "works." Then, when you are ready, read Chapters 1 and 2; they will help you to choose the mode of preparation that is right for you.

Good luck, and enjoy your journey!

ACKNOWLEDGMENTS

Many thanks to Grace Freedson for putting us in touch with McGraw Hill and to Del Franz for superb editing. We would also like to thank the anonymous outside evaluators for their invaluable guidance.

BBS
WP

ABOUT THE AUTHORS

Beth Bartolini-Salimbeni holds degrees in history, Spanish, Italian, and comparative literature. A former Fulbright scholar and twice a National Endowment for the Humanities (NEH) fellow, she has taught AP World History, AP European History, and AP Art History at the high school level as well as history and languages at the high school and university levels, both in the United States and in Italy.

Wendy Petersen earned undergraduate degrees in political science and French before going to a Master of Arts in political science. Time spent studying in France and England sparked an interest in history, and she began her career teaching world history in southwest Houston in 1997. Since moving to New Mexico in 2000, she has taught a variety of Advanced Placement courses. In 2014, she was selected to be one of the first teachers to pilot the new Advanced Placement Seminar course, part of the College Board's Advanced Placement Capstone program.

INTRODUCTION: THE FIVE-STEP PROGRAM

The Basics

If you are looking at this book, it is because you are considering taking the AP European History Exam. Maybe you are enrolled in an AP European History class in your high school, or maybe you are planning a course of study on your own. Either way, you need some guidance, and you have come to a bookstore or are shopping online to find it. Right now, there are a number of guides either on the shelf or on the screen in front of you, and you are wondering about the differences between them. The fact is all the guides in front of you are similar in a number of ways: each is written by an experienced history instructor who is intimately familiar with the AP European History Exam; each contains a concise review of the material you will need to master in order to do well on the exam; and each contains a number of practice exams and exercises to assist you in that preparation. There is, however, one crucial difference: This book is based upon the highly successful 5 Steps to a 5 program. If you are like the thousands of students who have used the 5 Steps to a 5 program to successfully prepare for AP Exams, it is a difference worth exploring.

Introducing the Five-Step Program

This book is organized as a five-step program to prepare you for success on the AP European History Exam. These steps are designed to provide you with the skills and strategies vital to the exam and the practice that can lead you to that perfect 5. Here are the five steps:

Step 1. Set Up Your Study Program

In Step 1 you will learn the information you need to know about the AP European History Exam itself and be guided through a process to help determine which of the following preparation programs is right for you:

- Full school year: September through May
- One semester: January through May
- Six weeks: Basic training for the exam

Step 2. Understand the Skills That Will Be Tested

In Step 2 you will learn about the various ways in which historians think and discover the historical skills that the AP European History Exam seeks to test, including the following:

- Reasoning chronologically
- Putting information in context
- Arguing from evidence

In this step, you'll will also take a diagnostic exam in AP European History. This pretest should give you an idea of how prepared you are to take the real exam before beginning to study for it.

- Go through the diagnostic exam step by step and question by question to build your confidence level.
- Review the correct answers and explanations so that you see what you do and do not yet understand.

Step 3. Develop Strategies for Success

In Step 3 you will find the strategies that will help you do your best on the exam. These strategies cover all four types of questions asked on the exam. In the four chapters included in Step 3, you will learn the following:

- How to read and answer multiple-choice questions, including whether or not to guess
- How to read and answer short-answer questions
- How to read and answer the document-based question (DBQ)
- How to read and answer the long-essay question

Step 4. Review the Knowledge You Need to Score High

In Step 4 you will learn or review the major themes of modern European history that you will need to know for the exam. You will learn or review the key concepts you will need to know on the exam.

Step 5. Build Your Test-Taking Confidence

In Step 5 you will complete your preparation by testing yourself on a practice exam. This guide contains a complete exam in European history, with full answers and explanations for each multiple-choice and short-answer question, as well as suggestions and possible outlines for answers to the document-based question and the long-essay question. Be aware that these practice exams are *not* reproduced questions from actual AP European History Exams, but they mirror both the material tested by AP and the way in which it is tested.

Introduction to the Graphics Used in This Book

To emphasize particular concepts, strategies, tips, and practice exercises and make them easy to find, several icons are used throughout this book. An icon in the margin will alert you that you should pay particular attention to the accompanying text. The three icons used include the following:

This icon indicates an important concept, fact, or explanation that you should not pass over.

This icon calls your attention to a step-by-step approach you might want to try when attempting to answer a particular type of question.

This icon indicates a suggestion or other helpful information you can use when you prepare for or take the exam.

STEP 1

Set Up Your Study Program

CHAPTER 1   What You Need to Know About the
AP European History Exam

CHAPTER 2   Determine Your Test Readiness

CHAPTER 1

What You Need to Know About the AP European History Exam

IN THIS CHAPTER

Summary: The AP European History program allows students who score well on the AP exam to earn college credits while still in high school. This chapter describes the AP European History program and exam and answers frequently asked questions, including what's on the exam and how it is scored.

Key Ideas:

✪ The exam consists of multiple-choice questions, short-answer questions, a document-based question (DBQ), and a longer essay question.

✪ The exam is scored on a scale of 1 to 5; most schools will give you college credit for a score of 4 or 5, and some will give credit for a 3.

Background Information

The Advanced Placement (AP) Program is overseen by an organization known as the College Board, which is involved in many facets of the college admissions process. The program offers highly motivated high school students the opportunity to take college-level courses while still in high school and the opportunity to earn credit or advanced standing at a college or university by taking the Advanced Placement exams.

Frequently Asked Questions About the AP European History Exam

Why Take the AP European History Exam?

Most students take the exam with the hope of earning college credit. Most schools will give you college credit for a score of 4 or 5, and some will give credit for a 3. However, the policies of individual colleges and universities vary, so you should check with the schools you are interested in attending for their specific policies. The College Board maintains a website that gives you information about all universities' credit policies for all exams: https://apstudent .collegeboard.org/creditandplacement.

One advantage of having college credit in European history is that you are one class closer to graduation; but there are a couple of other good reasons to take the exam:

- First, getting college credit for AP European history means that you will be able to opt out of either a required introductory course in European history or an elective course. Either way, you will have greater flexibility in choosing your courses, and you will be able move on to the more advanced and specific courses (either in history or in some other field) that interest you. Often, arriving at college with credits in your back pocket makes it possible for you to take courses more pertinent to your major, to complete a double major, or to take time to study abroad without worrying about losing credit hours.
- Second, having AP credit on your transcript can increase your chances of getting into the school you want because it tells college admissions officers that you are a serious student who has some experience with college-level work. The director of admissions at a select university put it this way: No matter the score on the AP exam, a student's having taken the exam, and measuring himself/herself against national guidelines, speaks well of him or her.

Do I Have to Take an AP European History Class to Take the Exam?

No. Taking an AP European History class at your high school is a great way to prepare for the exam, but it is not required. The College Board simply urges students to study the kinds of skills and subjects outlined in the AP European History Course Description. The Course Description is available online from the College Board (www.collegeboard.org). The McGraw Hill five-step program is based on both the College Board Course Description for AP European History and on the Exam Guidelines, so working through this guide will help you to develop the relevant skills and to familiarize yourself with the relevant subject material.

Who Writes and Grades the AP European History Exam?

The exam is written by a team of college and high school history instructors called the AP European History Test Development Committee. The Committee is constantly evaluating the test and field-testing potential questions. The exam is graded by a much larger group of college and high school teachers who meet at a central location in early June to evaluate and score exams that were completed by students the previous month.

What Is on the Exam?

Beginning in May 2016, the AP European History Exam adopted a new format. The new format of the AP European History exam is shown in Table 1.1.

Table 1.1   AP European History Exam Format as of May 2016

SECTION	TEST ITEMS	TIME LIMIT	PERCENTAGE OF TOTAL GRADE
I. Multiple Choice	55 questions	55 minutes	40%
II. Short Answer Q1: 1600–2001 Q2: 1600–2001 Q3: periods 1–2 OR Q4: periods 3–4	3 questions	40 minutes	20%
III. Document-Based topics from 1600 to 2001	1 question	60 minutes	25%
IV. Long-Essay: choose from 3 options on same theme. The options include period 1, periods 2–3, periods 3–4.	1 question	40 minutes	15%

Each section of the exam has a set of objectives that fit into the overall scheme of the exam. We will discuss strategies for doing well on the multiple-choice section in Chapter 5, the short-answer questions in Chapter 6, the document-based question (DBQ) in Chapter 7, and the long-essay question in Chapter 8.

How Is the Exam Evaluated and Scored?

The multiple-choice section is scored by computer. The other sections are all scored by "readers" (the college and high school teachers who are hired to do the job), who have been trained to score the responses in accordance with a set of guidelines. The scoring guidelines for each question are drawn up by a team of the most experienced readers. (We will discuss what kinds of things the guidelines tell the readers to look for in Chapters 6 through 8.) Evaluation and scoring are monitored by the Chief Reader, Question Leaders, and Table Leaders, and scoring is periodically analyzed for consistency.

The scores from all sections are combined into a composite score on the AP five-point scale:

- 5 is the highest possible grade; it indicates that you are extremely well qualified to receive college credit.
- 4 indicates that you are well qualified to receive college credit.
- 3 indicates that you are qualified to receive college credit.
- 2 indicates that you are possibly qualified to receive college credit.
- 1 indicates that you are not qualified to receive college credit.

How Do I Register?

Whether you are enrolled in a high school AP course or preparing for the exam on your own, the best thing to do is see your guidance counselor. He or she will direct you to the AP Coordinator for your school. You will need to contact the coordinator because it is this person who will arrange payment for the exam and also give you information about the exact location and date of the exam. If for some reason your school does not have an AP Coordinator, you can test through another school. To find out which schools in your area offer the exam and to find a coordinator, you can check the College Board's website (www. collegeboard.org). You should visit the site, even if your school has an AP Coordinator, as it will always have the latest and most up-to-date information.

In 2019, it cost $94 to take the AP European History Exam. Students who demonstrate financial need may receive a credit or refund to help offset the cost of testing. Registration for the exams you wish to take now happens online, in the fall. See your AP Coordinator or high-school counselor for information specific to your state and school. There are also several optional fees that must be paid if you want your scores rushed to you or if you wish to receive multiple grade reports.

What Should I Bring to the AP Exam?

There are several things that are either required or a good idea to have with you at the exam. They include the following:

- A good supply of #2 pencils with erasers that don't smudge (for the multiple-choice section)
- Several black- or blue-colored ink pens (for the other sections)
- A watch so that you can monitor your time. You never know if the exam room will have a clock, and you won't have a cell phone or other electronic devices (be sure to turn any alarms or chimes off).
- Your photo ID and Social Security number

What Should I NOT Bring to the Exam?

There are a number of things that you are not allowed to use during the exam. Prohibited items you should *not* bring include the following:

- Reference books of any kind, including notebooks, dictionaries, and encyclopedias
- A laptop computer
- Electronic devices, like cell phones, personal digital assistants (PDAs), pagers, and walkie-talkies
- Portable music devices of any kind, including CD players, MP3 players, and iPods
- Mom, dad, and friends (there is no room for them, and you don't need the distraction)

CHAPTER 2

Determine Your Test Readiness

IN THIS CHAPTER

Summary: To do your best on the AP European History Exam, you will need to prepare. Your preparation plan will depend on the time you have available and the way you like to study. This chapter maps out three plans; choose the one that you can most easily adapt to your needs.

Key Idea:
✪ Create a preparation plan adapted to your needs.

Three Approaches to Preparing for AP Exams

What kind of preparation program for the AP exam should you follow? The answer depends on two things: how much time you have and what kind of student you are. Obviously, if you only have one semester or four to six weeks before you intend to take the exam, you can't choose the full-year program. So first decide how much time you have. Then consider what kind of preparation works best for you. No one knows your study habits and learning style better than you do. Consider the three profiles below to see which one most closely describes you and your situation. Then, choose one of the three programs of preparation.

Full-Year Preparation: Approach A

You are a full-year prep student (and should follow Approach A) if:

1. You have a definite love of history.
2. You like detailed planning and preparation.
3. You feel more comfortable and confident when you are thoroughly prepared.
4. You can't wait to get started.
5. You have been successful with this approach in the past.

One-Semester Preparation: Approach B

You are a one-semester prep student (and should follow Approach B) if:

1. You are fairly interested in history.
2. You like to plan but feel there is such a thing as being overprepared.
3. You feel comfortable and confident when you feel you have prepared sufficiently.
4. You have more than one exam you are preparing for and feel one semester is enough time to prepare.
5. You have been successful with this approach in the past.

Four-to-Six-Week Preparation: Approach C

You are a four-to-six-week prep student (and should follow Approach C) if:

1. You are only fairly interested in history, or you are interested only in the exam.
2. You feel like you get stale if you prepare too far in advance.
3. You feel well prepared already and are just looking to sharpen your focus.
4. You are prepping for several exams.
5. You have been successful with this approach in the past.

Detailed Calendar for Each Plan

Calendar for Approach A: Full-School-Year Preparation

September to October (Check off the activities as you complete them.)

_____ Read the Introduction and become familiar with the 5-Step Program.

_____ Read Chapter 1 and become familiar with the AP European History Exam and procedures.

_____ Become familiar with the College Board AP website.

_____ Read Chapter 2 and confer with your AP European History teacher about your preparation program.

_____ Read Chapter 3 and get into the habit of thinking historically.

_____ Take the Diagnostic Exam and get an idea of what you'll need to know to succeed in this course.

November

_____ Read Chapters 5–8, and learn strategies for success for each of the four types of questions asked on the AP European History Exam.

_____ Complete the "Further Practice" sections in each of these chapters.

December

_____ Read Chapters 9–12, along with relevant outside readings and course materials, and become familiar with the events, processes, and key concepts of modern European history covered in those chapters.

_____ Complete the Review Questions at the end of each chapter.

January

_____ Read Chapters 13–16, along with relevant outside readings and course materials, and become familiar with the events, processes, and key concepts of modern European history covered in those chapters.

_____ Complete the Review Questions at the end of each chapter.

February

_____ Read Chapters 17–20, along with relevant outside readings and course materials, and become familiar with the events, processes, and key concepts of modern European history, covered in those chapters.

_____ Complete the Review Questions at the end of each chapter.

March

_____ Read Chapters 21–24, along with relevant outside readings and course materials, and become familiar with the events, processes, and key concepts of modern European history covered in those chapters.

_____ Complete the Review Questions at the end of each chapter.

April

_____ Review Chapters 3–24.

_____ Take the Practice Exams included in this guide.

_____ Evaluate your strengths and weaknesses based on your performance on the Practice Exams.

_____ Study the appropriate chapters and readings to address the areas about which you still feel shaky.

May (First Two Weeks)

_____ Make a list of topics about which you still feel shaky and ask your instructor or study group to help you focus on them.

_____ Answer additional practice questions offered online.

_____ Evaluate your performance.

_____ Review your incorrect answers.

_____ Get a good night's sleep before the exam.

_____ Go to the exam feeling confident; you have prepared well.

Calendar for Approach B: One-Semester Preparation

January (Check off the activities as you complete them.)

_____ Read the Introduction and become familiar with the 5-Step Program.

_____ Read Chapter 1 and become familiar with the AP European History Exam and procedures.

_____ Become familiar with the College Board AP website.

_____ Read Chapter 2 and confer with your AP European History teacher about your preparation program.

_____ Read Chapter 3 and get into the habit of thinking historically.

_____ Take the Diagnostic Exam and get an idea of what you'll need to know to succeed in this course.

February–March

_____ Read Chapters 5–8, and learn strategies for success for each of the four types of questions asked on the AP European History Exam.

_____ Complete the "Further Practice" sections in each of these chapters.

_____ Read Chapters 9–24, along with relevant outside readings and course materials, and become familiar with the events, processes, and key concepts of modern European history covered in those chapters.

_____ Complete the Review Questions at the end of each chapter.

April

_____ Review Chapters 3–24.

_____ Take the Practice Exams included in this guide.

_____ Evaluate your strengths and weaknesses based on your performance on the Practice Exams.

_____ Study the appropriate chapters and readings to address the areas about which you still feel shaky.

May (First Two Weeks)

_____ Make a list of topics about which you still feel shaky and ask your instructor or study group to help you focus on them.

_____ Answer additional practice questions offered online.

_____ Evaluate your performance.

_____ Review your incorrect answers.

_____ Get a good night's sleep before the exam.

_____ Go to the exam feeling confident; you have prepared well.

Calendar for Approach C: Four-to-Six-Week Preparation

April (Check off the activities as you complete them.)

_____ Read Chapters 1–24.

_____ Take the Practice Exams included in this guide.

_____ Evaluate your performance and review as needed.

May (First Two Weeks)

_____ Answer additional practice questions offered online.

_____ Evaluate your performance.

_____ Review your incorrect answers.

_____ Get a good night's sleep before the exam.

_____ Go to the exam feeling confident; you have prepared well.

Setting Up a Study Group

One of the most effective strategies in preparing for the AP European History Exam is to study with other students preparing for the exam; however, not all study groups are equally successful. Here are some important considerations to assist you in the successful planning and implementation of your study group:

Why?

_____ Take advantage of others' strengths and abilities. Different students will have different insights.

_____ Lessen the individual workload by delegating specific topics (a time period, an event, an individual) to each member to present to the group.

_____ Increase your likelihood of following through by making commitments to others.

Who?

_____ Keep the group small. Study groups tend to work best when there are relatively few participants, usually somewhere between two and five people. Groups that are too large are less efficient and more easily distracted.

_____ Consider the composition of the group. Close friends do not necessarily make the best study partners. All members should be committed to the success of the group. Think about students who are interested in the material, willing to ask questions, and are prepared and well organized for class.

_____ Consider, too, how much flexibility members have in their schedules. Students with many commitments may have trouble accommodating the study group sessions.

Where?

_____ Select locations with minimal distractions, where conditions allow for discussions.

_____ Provide seating that is comfortable, preferably with a table for notes and books.

_____ Some libraries have specific rooms for this purpose.

_____ Turn off your cell phones.

_____ Remember that this is a working group, not a potluck. By all means, bring something to drink or eat if you need to; just don't make socializing the focus of the group.

When?

_____ Plan for sessions to last two to three hours. Any longer and students will lose focus and be more likely to become distracted. Much shorter, and it will be difficult to cover material with any degree of depth.

_____ If possible, try to plan study sessions for the same day and time. A regular schedule will help the group remember to meet and make it seem more of a commitment, like a class. It also gives members time to prepare in advance.

How?

_____ For maximum efficiency, have a defined goal or purpose for each session, and ensure that it is clearly communicated to each member in advance. Assign each member specific tasks or responsibilities before meeting. These could include chapters, eras, or historical themes. By doing so, you increase the participation of all members.

_____ Consider assigning a member to be the facilitator, responsible for managing the time and keeping members focused.

STEP 2

Understand the Skills That Will Be Tested

CHAPTER **3**   The Ways Historians Think

CHAPTER **4**   Take a Diagnostic Exam

AP European History Diagnostic Exam Answer Sheet

AP European History Diagnostic Exam Section I

AP European History Diagnostic Exam Section II

AP European History Diagnostic Exam Answers and Explanations

CHAPTER **3**

The Ways Historians Think

IN THIS CHAPTER

Summary: The AP European History Exam requires you to apply the thinking skills historians use. This chapter covers the skills you will need to be proficient in this type of thinking in order to do well on the exam. The second part of the chapter contains a new diagnostic exam, which you can use to determine your strengths and weaknesses.

Answers and explanations follow the exam.

Key Idea:

✪ The skills you will need to be proficient in applying can be grouped into three basic categories: (1) Reasoning chronologically, (2) Putting information in context, and (3) Arguing from evidence.

Introduction

The AP European History Curriculum identifies interrelated sets of "Historical Thinking Skills" and requires students to apply one or more of them in each section of the exam. Your first task is to familiarize yourself with these skills and to understand how historians use them in creating a historical understanding of change over time.

There are many ways in which one might describe and categorize the intellectual skills employed by the historian. The simplest and clearest way for our purposes is to think of them as making up three interrelated thought processes: (1) Reasoning chronologically, (2) Putting information in context, and (3) Arguing from evidence.

Reasoning Chronologically

Chronology is the placing of events in the order in which they occurred. Once an accurate chronology has been constructed, reasoning based on that construction can begin.

Chronology and Causation

All historians seek, in one way or another, to explain change over time. One way to begin to do that is to create a chronology of events and then ponder cause and effect. For example, suppose we know the order of three events that occurred during the first year of World War I (WWI): the Russian Army invaded East Prussia (August 17, 1914); the German Army on the Eastern Front was put under new command and launched an attack against Russian forces (August 23–30, 1914); and Erich von Falkenhayn replaced Helmuth von Moltke as Chief of Staff of the German Army (September 14, 1914). Because we know the chronological order of these events, certain cause-and-effect relationships suggest themselves, whereas others are logically impossible. For example, because the change in command of the German forces on the Eastern Front and the German attack on Russian forces there occurred roughly a week after the Russian Army invaded East Prussia, it is a logical possibility that the Russian attack caused the Germans to react by changing command and counterattacking. Conversely, because the German decisions came roughly a week after the Russian attack, it is simply impossible for the German decisions to have caused the Russian attack.

Notice that, in our example, it is both the order in which the first two events occurred and the close proximity of the two events (both occurred in the same geographical area, and less than a week elapsed between the two events) that make the possibility of a cause-and-effect relationship between the two seem likely. Conversely, while it is possible that the first two events in our example caused the third (the change in overall command of the German Army from von Moltke to von Falkenhayn), the logical argument for a cause-and-effect relationship is weaker because of a lack of close proximity: the general commander was in charge of the entire war, and nearly a month had passed since those two events had occurred on the Eastern Front.

Correlation vs. Causation

Being able to show that a series of events happened in close proximity to one another (both chronologically and geographically) is to show that those events were correlated. However, it is important to understand that correlation does not necessarily imply causation. The fact that two events happened in close geographical or chronological proximity makes a cause-and-effect relationship *possible*, but not *necessary*; the close proximity could have been merely a coincidence. To establish a cause-and-effect relationship between two events, the historian must identify and use evidence. The use of evidence is part of the third set of skills identified by the AP European History Exam and is discussed below.

Multiple Causation

The sophisticated student of history understands that significant events in history usually have many causes. Accordingly, one looks for multiple causes in order to explain events. For example, if the historian discovers evidence (such as correspondence between high-ranking German Army officials) that supports the logical assertion that successful Russian incursions into East Prussia caused both a change in command for the Eastern Front and the decision to launch a counterattack, he or she still asks additional questions and looks for evidence of other contributing causes. What else was happening on the Eastern Front at that time? What did the overall German war effort look like at that time? What other considerations may have gone into those decisions?

Continuity

The historian recognizes that change does not come easily to people or to civilizations. Accordingly, the historian is sensitive to the persistence of certain forms of human activity (social structures, political systems, etc.). Sensitivity to the power of continuity forces the historian to ask questions about the forces that were strong enough to bring about change. For example, sensitivity to the power and importance of continuity in the way in which people live and work reminds the historian that a change from a localized and agriculturally oriented economy to an interconnected, commercial economy was neither inevitable nor even particularly likely. That realization sets the historian looking for the powerful forces that fostered those changes. Likewise, to understand and connect the periods being covered in AP European History, it is useful to look for patterns of cause and effect. Historian Jacques Barzun, in *From Dawn to Decadence*, said that study of the modern world discusses the "desires, attitudes, purposes behind . . . events or movements, some embodied in lasting institutions." He characterized the four periods covered in AP European History as follows: 1450–1648—dominated by the issues of what to believe in religion; 1648–1815—what to do about the status of the individual and the mode of government; 1815–1914—the means by which one achieves social and economic equality; and 1914—present–the mixed consequences of all the previous efforts.

Comparison

When seeking to explain change over time, the historian often looks for patterns. Some patterns can be detected by asking basic questions, such as who, what, where, and when. For example, when seeking to understand the gradual and persistent shift from an agricultural economy to a commercial economy in Europe between the fourteenth and eighteenth centuries, the historian asks: What kinds of people tended to be in the vanguard of such change? Which type of work tended to change first? Did the changes occur simultaneously or follow a geographical progression? What type of economic activity changed first? The next step is to make comparisons. For example, the historian compares the nature of the changes that occurred in Britain to those that occurred in France and in the economies farther to the east. The comparisons reveal both similarities and differences, which the historian then explores, hoping to establish patterns of both change and continuity.

Contingency

Finally, the historian seeking to understand the cause-and-effect nature of historical events understands the role that contingency can play in human events. An event is said to be "contingent" if its occurrence is possible but not certain. The sophisticated student of history understands that there is a profound sense in which all significant events in history are contingent, because their occurrence depends on the action of human beings. For example, one of the most significant events in the history of the French Revolution is the storming of the Bastille on July 14, 1789. On that day, a crowd stormed the notorious fortress in the heart of Paris, killed the guards who defended it, and paraded the severed heads of those guards around the city. Historians seeking to explain this event point to powerful forces, such as the politicization of the urban working people of Paris and their tremendous fear that the armies of their king, Louis XVI, would descend upon the city at any moment. But those same historians know that it was possible that the day could have gone very differently. They know that the crowd believed that there were many prisoners and an enormous amount of weapons inside the Bastille. They also know the crowd was mistaken; the only prisoner was the Marquis de Sade (and he was imprisoned for moral depravity, not political activity), and there were virtually no weapons inside the Bastille. These historians know, therefore, that the situation could have been defused; the guards could simply have abandoned the Bastille (the King's cause would not have been harmed nor the Revolution's cause helped). But the guards were young, inexperienced, and insecure; they panicked and fired into the crowd. Those completely unpredictable actions of the guards are the contingent causes of the storming of the Bastille.

Putting Information in Context

The historian must put every piece of information he or she encounters into its "proper context." That means connecting that information to all of the relevant events or processes occurring at the time and place in which the source of the information was produced.

Constructing a Context for Past Events and Actions

The art of contextualization sounds complicated in the abstract, but in practice, it is really about asking additional, logical questions about a given event or action in the past. For example, one of the most notorious episodes in the history of conflict between England and Ireland is the massacring of the inhabitants of two Irish towns, Drogheda and Wexford, in September and October 1649, respectively. In the context of the English Civil War (1642–1649), Oliver Cromwell and his anti-Royalist army were sent to Ireland by the English Parliament to put down an anti-English rebellion that had been simmering there since 1641. Between September 2 and September 11, 1649, Cromwell and his army laid siege to the town of Drogheda. During the four days *following* Drogheda's surrender, Cromwell oversaw the killing of some 4,000 of its people. Similarly, 2,000 more people were killed *after* the fall and surrender of the town of Wexford in October. Understandably, these events have earned Cromwell a reputation for a level of impulsive cruelty that is practically unintelligible.

But making such actions intelligible (constructing an understanding of how such a thing could occur) is precisely the task of the historian. To do it, the historian has to "put the events in their context," or, more precisely, the historian has to construct a context around the event by asking further questions. In the case of Cromwell, historians have asked: Of the many other towns that Cromwell forced to surrender in his nine-month march through Ireland, how many times did he massacre a town's inhabitants? The answer, interestingly, is none. Did Cromwell view the Irish who resisted merely as military enemies? No, Cromwell was among those within the Parliamentarian faction of the English Civil War who viewed themselves as "Saints," whose mission was to purify the realm of false religions. Accordingly,

Cromwell viewed the Catholic Irish not only as rebellious subjects, but as heretics. Was it unusual to kill large numbers of people after a successful siege? The rules of war at the time called for the inhabitants of a town to be spared, *provided* the governor of the town surrendered without a fight. Conversely, if the governor of a town decided to resist, he knew that he was putting the inhabitants at risk of retribution.

The historian uses the knowledge gained from asking and answering these contextual questions not to condone Cromwell's actions, but to make sense of them. Once the Drogheda and Wexford massacres are put into context, they remain ghastly, but they are no longer unintelligible. Cromwell may indeed have been impulsive and cruel, but he was not insane; there was a rationale behind his actions. He committed no more massacres in Ireland in 1649 because he did not need to. The governors of the other towns had seen the cruel consequences of resistance and surrendered without a fight.

Contextualization of Sources

Another aspect of historical thinking in which contextualization is important is in the use of sources. Historians build their understanding of past events and processes on the use of primary sources: all manner of artifacts that have come down to us from the times and places we wish to study. In order to gain an understanding of those sources—and to use them later as part of an interpretive argument—the historian must first put the sources in context. The process is similar to the one discussed above. The historian begins by asking a number of questions about the sources; the sum total of the answers to those questions makes up the context in which the sources must be interpreted.

For example, in the writing of her remarkable account of the English Civil War, the historian Diane Purkiss uncovered multiple primary sources offering eyewitness testimony to the events that occurred at Barthomley Church in Cheshire, England, in 1643. During the course of the English Civil War, Royalist troops arrived in the town of Barthomley, whose inhabitants were sympathetic to the Parliamentary side. One source that Purkiss uncovered asserts that the Royalist party encircled the church, where about 20 townspeople had taken refuge in the steeple. When the people would not come out, the source asserts, the Royalists set fire to the church, and when the people finally came out to escape the smoke and flames, the Royalists stripped them naked, abused them, and killed them. Another source confirms the report and asserts that it was one of many such instances in the area.

So, Purkiss has primary-source accounts that seem to corroborate each other, but Purkiss knows that even corroborating reports have to be put in context. Both sources, though produced independently of one another, are what is known as "newsbooks." Such newsbooks were penned by Parliamentary sympathizers who were supplying "news" about the conflict. In short, Purkiss knows that such newsbooks were essentially Parliamentary propaganda, and that they cannot, therefore, be counted on as reliable accounts of what happened. Finally, it is frequently easier to place an event in context if you have a visual or literary back-up. At the end of this book, you will find a Resource Guide that contains both artistic and literary resources that will flesh out the historical picture.

Arguing from Evidence

The process of putting sources in context leads the historian directly to the art of arguing from evidence. For example, a historian would initially be tempted to argue that the existence of multiple primary sources asserting that an unprovoked massacre had been carried out by Royalist troops at Barthomley was proof that such a thing had occurred. However, by contextualizing those sources, Purkiss shows that such an argument will not hold up;

the preponderance of evidence that shows that the contents of such newsbooks served as Parliamentary propaganda casts too much doubt on the reliability of those accounts.

But rather than give up on those sources, Purkiss asked herself what the historian *could* reliably learn from Parliamentary propaganda. Purkiss knew that the purpose of propaganda was to cultivate outrage at, and hatred of, the enemy. She knew, in other words, that propaganda aimed to play on the worst fears of its readers. So in order to learn something from those sources, Purkiss changed her question. Rather than asking, "What happened at Barthomley?" she asked, "What do the sources tell us about the fears of Parliamentary readers?" Because all of the newsbook accounts of the incident at Barthomley stressed setting fire to the church, stripping and abusing the people taken prisoner, and the murdering of those people, she concluded that it might be reasonable to assume that the greatest fears of people in that region during the conflict were the desecration of their holy places and the suffering and death of their loved ones at the hands of marauding soldiers. Finally, she went on to show that those fears did, in fact, mirror the major themes of atrocity stories in a large number of Parliamentary newsbooks.

Arguing from Evidence in an Essay

Let's look at an example of how one argues from evidence. Suppose you were faced with the following question:

Explain ONE lasting effect of the Revolutions of 1848 on European political culture.

You might choose to answer with the following assertion:

The ultimate failure of the attempt, in the Revolutions of 1848, to bring about liberal, democratic reform in continental Europe caused a large portion of the European population to put their faith in conservative, rather than liberal, leaders.

Next, you would need to argue from evidence; that is, you would need to support and illustrate the assertion you have made by presenting and explaining events that serve as specific examples of what you have asserted. The result would look something like this:

In February 1848, the decision by King Louis Philippe to ban liberal reformers from holding public meetings led to massive street demonstrations in Paris. Demonstrations soon escalated into revolution, forcing Louis Philippe to abdicate and a new French republic (known as the Second Republic) to be established. The Assembly of the new republic attempted to establish a liberal, democratic constitution for the French Republic. However, in June of the same year, the French Army reestablished conservative control of Paris. An election in December swept the conservative Louis-Napoleon Bonaparte, nephew of Napoleon, to power. Three years later, he staged his own coup d'état, putting an end to the Second Republic.

Similarly, violence broke out in the major cities of the German kingdoms in the first half of 1848. In Berlin, Frederick William IV was forced to order the army out of the city and to agree to the formation of a parliament. In the wake of that victory, liberal leaders from all over Germany formed the Frankfurt Assembly and proclaimed that they would write a liberal, democratic constitution for a united Germany. But in the second half of 1848, Frederick William IV refused the Frankfurt Assembly's offer to be the constitutional monarch of a united, democratic Germany, and instead used military troops to disperse the Assembly and to reassert conservative control in the cities. When, in November, troops moved back into Berlin, they faced little resistance. In the subsequent decades, popular support for German unification was given to Frederick William IV and his conservative chancellor, Otto von Bismarck, rather than to the liberals.

Developing Your Historical Thinking Skills

How do you cultivate and use historical thinking skills? Several steps will help you to do just that. Each one contributes to equipping you with the knowledge and attitudes that evolve into skills.

- **Define terms.** This is critical to understanding both chronology and context. Words change meaning and reflect the values of a given era. They separate fact and opinion.
- **Master the chronology** of the period under study. This may be most easily done by "drawing" or charting things out.

ERA	SOCIETY, DEMOGRAPHICS, ECONOMICS	GOVERNMENT, DOMINANT PHILOSOPHIES	THE ARTS	RELIGION	SCIENCE	INDIVIDUALS
1450–1648						
1648–1815						
1815–1914						
1914–present						

It is important to remember to ask why, or, what leads from one era into the next?

- **Develop guiding questions.** For example, for the first era, you might ask: "How did the Reformation and Catholic (or Counter) Reformation act as an impetus to New World settlement?" "How did the Black Plague disrupt the socioeconomic order?" Or, for all eras: "How does the idea of the heroic change over time? What characteristics remain the same? What characteristics differ?" Try to explain a historical event or movement using only artworks or music or literature and the guiding question of authorial purpose: "How does artwork reflect changing attitudes about revolution or war?"
- **Know the "cast of characters."** Each of the content-based chapters in this book (Chapters 11 to 25) begins with an overview or summary, followed directly by a list of key terms. Following each list are the names of (usually) between five and ten individuals closely associated with each content area. Some chapters have fewer names; some have many more. Your task is to become familiar with these people. Index cards are useful here, perhaps a differently colored one for each of the four AP European eras. For each individual, explain the role played, influence exerted, and legacies. If the person is famous for a written work, add the title of the work. The same holds true for works of art or music.
- **Break the vacuum.** History does not exist in a vacuum. It is made up of events, literature, music, art, philosophy, religion, science, economics, demographics, human and physical geography—in short, of multitudinous elements. At the end of this book, and at the end of each content chapter, are listings of resources to help you round out your command of historical facts. These resources include novels, plays, movies, the visual arts, and even YouTube videos. These can provide a break from your review of your textbook; however, these should supplement your textbook, not replace it.

Rapid Review

The AP European History Curriculum identifies interrelated sets of "Historical Thinking Skills." Those skills can be categorized as follows:

- Reasoning chronologically
- Putting information in context
- Arguing from evidence

Reasoning chronologically is the practice of placing events in the order in which they occurred and then making reasonable inferences from that order about cause and effect. Putting information in context means connecting historical sources to all of the relevant events or processes occurring at the time and place in which the source was produced. Arguing from evidence is the art of making inferences and constructing a logical argument with specific examples.

CHAPTER 4

Take a Diagnostic Exam

IN THIS CHAPTER

Summary: In the following pages you will find a diagnostic exam modeled after the actual Advanced Placement (AP) exam. It is intended to give you an idea of your level of preparation in European History. After you have completed both the multiple-choice and the essay questions, check your multiple-choice answers against the given answers and read over the comments to the possible solutions to the free-response questions:

✪ The Document-Based Question (DBQ) draws on material from all periods.
✪ The long-essay question offers three options.
✪ The multiple-choice questions are equally divided among all the time periods covered in the course.
✪ Rubrics are available for the DBQ and free-response questions on the AP Central website.

Key Ideas:

✪ Practice the kind of multiple-choice and free-response questions you will be asked on the real exam.
✪ Answer questions that approximate the coverage of periods and themes on the real exam.
✪ Check your work against the given answers and the possible solutions to the free-response questions.
✪ Determine your areas of strength and weakness.
✪ Earmark the concepts to which you must give special attention.

AP European History Diagnostic Exam

SECTION I, PART A

ANSWER SHEET

1 (A) (B) (C) (D)	20 (A) (B) (C) (D)	39 (A) (B) (C) (D)
2 (A) (B) (C) (D)	21 (A) (B) (C) (D)	40 (A) (B) (C) (D)
3 (A) (B) (C) (D)	22 (A) (B) (C) (D)	41 (A) (B) (C) (D)
4 (A) (B) (C) (D)	23 (A) (B) (C) (D)	42 (A) (B) (C) (D)
5 (A) (B) (C) (D)	24 (A) (B) (C) (D)	43 (A) (B) (C) (D)
6 (A) (B) (C) (D)	25 (A) (B) (C) (D)	44 (A) (B) (C) (D)
7 (A) (B) (C) (D)	26 (A) (B) (C) (D)	45 (A) (B) (C) (D)
8 (A) (B) (C) (D)	27 (A) (B) (C) (D)	46 (A) (B) (C) (D)
9 (A) (B) (C) (D)	28 (A) (B) (C) (D)	47 (A) (B) (C) (D)
10 (A) (B) (C) (D)	29 (A) (B) (C) (D)	48 (A) (B) (C) (D)
11 (A) (B) (C) (D)	30 (A) (B) (C) (D)	49 (A) (B) (C) (D)
12 (A) (B) (C) (D)	31 (A) (B) (C) (D)	50 (A) (B) (C) (D)
13 (A) (B) (C) (D)	32 (A) (B) (C) (D)	51 (A) (B) (C) (D)
14 (A) (B) (C) (D)	33 (A) (B) (C) (D)	52 (A) (B) (C) (D)
15 (A) (B) (C) (D)	34 (A) (B) (C) (D)	53 (A) (B) (C) (D)
16 (A) (B) (C) (D)	35 (A) (B) (C) (D)	54 (A) (B) (C) (D)
17 (A) (B) (C) (D)	36 (A) (B) (C) (D)	55 (A) (B) (C) (D)
18 (A) (B) (C) (D)	37 (A) (B) (C) (D)	
19 (A) (B) (C) (D)	38 (A) (B) (C) (D)	

AP European History Diagnostic Exam

SECTION I, PART A

Multiple-Choice Questions
Recommended Time—55 minutes

Directions: Each of the questions below is followed by four answer choices. Select the answer choice that best answers the question and fill in the corresponding oval on the answer sheet provided.

Questions 1–3 refer to the image below:

"The Plumb-pudding in danger . . . the great Globe itself and all which it inherit, is too small to satisfy such insatiable appetites."

James Gilray, 1805

1. William Pitt, Prime Minister of England, and the Emperor Napoleon of France, carving up a pudding representing the globe, embody which of the following political ideologies?

   A. Socialism
   B. Absolutism
   C. Imperialism
   D. Conservatism

2. Direct political control is often linked to which of the following practices as shown in the cartoon?

   A. Commercialism
   B. Militarism
   C. Mercantilism
   D. Industrialism

3. The subtitle, "The great Globe . . . is too small to satisfy such insatiable appetites," could be restated as which of the following?

   A. Napoleon and Pitt are all-powerful.
   B. The world grows ever smaller.
   C. There will be no leftovers.
   D. Less is more.

Questions 4–7 refer to the document, shown below:

THE
PEOPLE'S CHARTER;

BEING THE

OUTLINE OF AN ACT

TO PROVIDE FOR THE

JUST REPRESENTATION OF THE PEOPLE OF
GREAT BRITAIN

IN THE

COMMONS' HOUSE OF PARLIAMENT:

EMBRACING THE PRINCIPLES OF

UNIVERSAL SUFFRAGE,
NO PROPERTY QUALIFICATION,
ANNUAL PARLIAMENTS,
EQUAL REPRESENTATION,
PAYMENT OF MEMBERS, AND VOTE BY BALLOT.

PREPARED BY A COMMITTEE OF TWELVE PERSONS,
SIX MEMBERS OF PARLIAMENT AND SIX MEMBERS
OF THE LONDON WORKING MEN'S ASSOCIATION,
AND ADDRESSED TO THE PEOPLE OF THE UNITED
KINGDOM.

May. 1838.
LONDON:
PUBLISHED FOR THE WORKING MEN'S ASSOCIATION,
BY H. HETHERINGTON, 126, STRAND;
SOLD BY CLEAVE, 1, SHOE LANE; WATSON, 15, CITY ROAD;
AND MAY BE HAD OF ALL BOOKSELLERS.

4. Which of the following would be most likely to support the goals of the Chartist movement?

   A. A Tory member of Parliament
   B. A Whig member of Parliament
   C. A working-class man
   D. An aristocrat with land and a title

5. Which of the following protectionist laws was most likely to have contributed to the growth of the Chartist movement?

   A. The Secret Ballot Act of 1872
   B. The Corn Laws of 1815
   C. The Petition of Right (1628)
   D. The Poor Law Amendment Act of 1834

6. The goals of which eighteenth century individuals most closely mirrored those of the Chartists?

   A. Radicals in France
   B. Liberals in Russia
   C. Conservatives in Austria
   D. Neo-Classicists in Italy

7. Which of the Chartist demands never became British law?

   A. Secret ballot
   B. Universal suffrage
   C. Annual Parliamentary elections
   D. No property qualification for voters

Questions 8–11 relate to the following passage:

Upon this a question arises: whether it is better to be loved than feared or feared than loved? It may be answered that one should wish to be both, but, because it is difficult to unite them in one person, it is much safer to be feared than loved, when, of the two, either must be dispensed with. Because this is to be asserted in general of men, that they are ungrateful, fickle, false, cowardly, covetous, and as long as you succeed they are yours entirely; they will offer you their blood, property, life, and children, as is said above, when the need is far distant; but when it approaches, they turn against you. And that prince who, relying entirely on their promises, has neglected other precautions, is ruined; because friendships that are obtained by payments, and not by greatness or nobility of mind, may indeed be earned but they are not secured, and in time of need cannot be relied upon; and men have less scruple in offending one who is beloved than one who is feared, for love is preserved by the link of obligation which, owing to the baseness of men, is broken at every opportunity for their advantage; but fear preserves you by a dread of punishment which never fails.

Niccolò Machiavelli, *The Prince,* 1513

8. Machiavelli's view of the nature of man could be summed up as follows.

    A. Man means well, but lacks willpower.
    B. Man is inherently bad.
    C. Man is loyal.
    D. Man cannot choose his nature.

9. According to Machiavelli, being feared is more desirable than being loved for which particular reason?

    A. Love prompts jealousy, which is destructive.
    B. Fear is an inevitable human condition.
    C. Love makes men weak.
    D. Fear implies the threat of a penalty.

10. What does Machiavelli mean when he says that "men love at their own convenience, but are afraid at the convenience of others"?

    A. Men respond to that which is easiest.
    B. Love is more comfortable than compelling.
    C. Men are afraid of their own desires.
    D. Fear is compelled from without.

11. Which of the following figures in European history most exemplifies Machiavelli's political philosophy?

    A. Elizabeth I of England
    B. Giuseppe Garibaldi
    C. Louis XIV of France
    D. Joseph Stalin

Questions 12–14 refer to the passage below:

The winter of 1788–1789 was extremely cold. In Venice the lagoon froze over . . . There were ice floes in the Seine in Paris . . . France had had a poor harvest the previous summer, and the people were suffering, anxious, and restless. In the provinces there were riots and looting. . . . It was . . . the winter of the aristocratic grasshoppers who had spent the summer ringing and dancing. . . . The luxury and ostentation of . . . the nobility and clergy . . . scandalized the ordinary people in that springtime of scarcity. . . . The humble people . . . were about to make their grievances heard.

Jean Starobinski, *1789: The Emblems of Reason*

12. Climate extremes alone did not lead to the French Revolution, but did give rise to what political action on the part of the people?

    A. The killing of farmers
    B. Removal of the clergy
    C. The Bread Riots
    D. The storming of the Bastille

13. The passage makes clear that the French Revolution included members of which social group?

    A. Merchants
    B. Peasants
    C. Clergy
    D. Bureaucrats

14. Which of the following best summarizes the author's position?

    A. The French Revolution was a rural phenomenon.
    B. The reaction of the nobility contributed to the French Revolution.
    C. The extreme climate was directly responsible for the French Revolution.
    D. The French Revolution was inevitable.

Questions 15–18 relate to the following passage, describing first encounters with native peoples:

It has been a while since I've written . . . but this letter will let you know that about a month ago I returned safe and sound to Seville [Spain], thanks be to God, from the Indies. . . . It seems to me that the opinion of the majority of philosophers that one cannot live in the Torrid Zone is mistaken. During this trip, I found just the opposite to be true. . . . And, let it be said *sotto voce*, practice is worth more than theory.

. . . When we neared land, we saw many people on the beach. They looked on us with great wonder . . . We landed with 22 well-armed men. The people, when they saw us land and realized that we were completely different from them—they don't wear beards, or clothes (men and women alike), and are a different color (they are grey-ish and fawn-colored and we are white)—were afraid and fled to the forest. We learned that they are called cannibals. They live off human meat. I know this for certain: they don't eat each other, but go off in their boats, called "canoes," and hunt on nearby islands or the mainland. They never eat women, unless they are slaves. . . . They are a kind people and handsome. They use bows and arrows. They are terrific shots and very courageous. We established friendly relations with them and they took us to their village, about two leagues from the sea. They gave us lunch, and anything that we wanted, really, either because they were afraid of us or out of friendship. Having spent an entire day with them, we returned to our ships, being good friends.

Amerigo Vespucci, "Letter from Seville," 1500

15. If Vespucci's thoughts are indicative, what was the European reaction to specific indigenous peoples?

    A. Fear
    B. Paternalism
    C. Isolationism
    D. Love

16. According to the passage, what was the indigenous peoples' first reaction to Europeans?

    A. Panic
    B. Pragmatism and caution
    C. Inspiration to learn a new language
    D. Acceptance

17. Why did the Europeans **not** seize property and goods from these particular people?

    A. The Europeans were outnumbered.
    B. The Europeans did not feel provoked, but benevolent.
    C. The natives' weaponry intimidated the Europeans.
    D. The natives hid their property and goods in the forest.

18. Vespucci's letter to his patron is, in general, characterized by which of the following?

    A. A sense of wonder
    B. Opportunism
    C. Idealism
    D. Condescension

Questions 19–22 refer to the document below:

The principal object . . . in these Poems was to choose incidents and situations from common life . . . and, at the same time, to throw over them a certain colouring of imagination, . . . Humble and rustic life was generally chosen, because, in that condition, the essential passions of the heart find a better soil in which they can attain their maturity, are less under restraint, and speak a plainer and more emphatic language; because in that condition of life our elementary feelings coexist in a state of greater simplicity. . . . For all good poetry is the spontaneous overflow of powerful feelings. . . .

[The poet] considers man and nature as essentially adapted to each other, and the mind of man as naturally the mirror of the fairest and most interesting qualities of nature. And thus the Poet . . . converses with general nature with affections akin to those, which, through labour and length of time, the Man of Science has raised up in himself, by conversing with those particular parts of nature which are the objects of his studies. The knowledge both of the Poet and the Man of Science is pleasure; but the knowledge of the one cleaves to us as a necessary part of our existence, our natural and unalienable inheritance; the other is a personal and individual acquisition, slow to come to us, and by no habitual and direct sympathy connecting us with our fellow-beings.

The Man of Science seeks truth as a remote and unknown benefactor; he cherishes and loves it in his solitude: the Poet, singing a song in which all human beings join with him, rejoices in the presence of truth as our visible friend and hourly companion.

William Wordsworth, Preface to *Lyrical Ballads* (1802)

19. Based on the passage, which subject would the author be most likely to write about?

    A. The joys of rural life
    B. The plight of the poor
    C. The bustle of the city
    D. The natural laws of the physical world

20. Which phrase or paraphrase from the passage best supports the response in the previous question?

    A. . . . through labour and length of time, the Man of Science has raised up in himself
    B. . . . For all good poetry is the spontaneous overflow of powerful feelings.
    C. . . . The Man of Science seeks truth as a remote and unknown benefactor;
    D. . . . rustic life was generally chosen, because [there] our elementary feelings coexist in greater simplicity

21. With which artistic or creative movement would these beliefs most be associated?

    A. Baroque
    B. Surrealism
    C. Romanticism
    D. Cubism

22. This creative and artistic movement developed, in part, as a reaction against which of the following historical phenomena?

    A. The Industrial Revolution
    B. Immigration
    C. Imperialism
    D. Mercantilism

Questions 23–26 refer to the image below:

Trade with other EU countries

Balance of trade in goods and services with other EU countries, 2014

Source: Office for National Statistics, The Pink Book 2015, Table 9.3

23. This table most likely provides data from the perspective of which European nation?

   A. Germany
   B. France
   C. Great Britain
   D. Switzerland

24. Based on the graph, with which European Union member nation does the subject have the most favorable balance of trade?

   A. Germany
   B. Ireland
   C. Cyprus
   D. Andorra

25. Which of the following is an economic advantage for members of the European Union (EU)?

   A. All members use a common currency.
   B. There is free movement of goods within the European Union.
   C. They can impose punitive tariffs on other members' goods
   D. There is a standard minimum wage within the European Union.

26. What is the name given to the process of Great Britain's withdrawal from the European Union?

   A. Maastricht
   B. The Geneva Conventions
   C. Brexit
   D. Article 50 Revocation

Questions 27–30 refer to the passages below, from the play by Pierre-Augustin Caron de Beaumarchais that Wolfgang Amadeus Mozart used as the basis for his opera "The Marriage of Figaro" and from the French king's response to the opera generally.

"By an accident of birth,/He's the master, I'm the slave./If some day, wealth should follow worth,/He'd starve, and I'd take all he has./Some will say 'It's nature's balance:/Blood should count for more than talent.'/My lords: Remember, wise men say,/That every dog will have his day."

Beaumarchais, "The Marriage of Figaro," 1786

"It [the opera] is detestable! That shall never be played; it would be necessary to destroy the Bastille before the presentation of this . . . ! This man mocks everything which ought to be respected in a Government!"

King Louis XVI of France, 1786

27. What does Beaumarchais mean by the phrase "Blood should count for more than talent"?

   A. Talent is inborn.
   B. Class rank is a tradition.
   C. Merit outweighs birthright.
   D. Masters will always be strong.

28. According to the king, the Bastille represents what concept?

   A. Equality
   B. Fraternity
   C. Monarchy
   D. Liberty

29. What does the line "every dog will have his day" mean?

   A. Every person will be overcome by animals.
   B. Every being will have moments of success.
   C. Every person will maintain the status quo.
   D. Every being will prove to be opportunistic.

30. In what way are the arts a reliable source for the study of history?

   A. They give a realistic portrait of an age.
   B. They can speak of ideals and desires.
   C. They present a contemporary point of view.
   D. They represent the official voice of an era.

Questions 31–33 relate to the following passage:

"In earlier times, to possess an idea or a fact meant keeping it secret, having the power to prevent others from knowing it. Maps of treasure routes were guarded and the first postal services were designed for the security of the state. Physicians and lawyers locked their knowledge in a learned language. The government helped craft guilds to exclude trespassers from their secrets . . . Europe's ancient institutions of learning, colleges and universities, had been founded not to discover the new but to transmit a heritage."

Daniel J. Boorstin, *The Discoverers*, 1983

31. Guarding knowledge was a standard practice for which of the following reasons?

   A. Prevention of competition
   B. Maintenance of the use of secret languages
   C. Cultivation of xenophobia
   D. Consolidation of power and control

32. Not only physicians and lawyers, but merchants and the clergy used which "learned language"?

   A. Greek
   B. Latin
   C. Hebrew
   D. Arabic

33. The invention of moveable type helped change the status quo because of which long-term effect?

   A. The establishment of the publishing industry
   B. The opening up of possibilities for social advancement
   C. The destruction of financial security
   D. The transmission of established traditions

Questions 34– 38 refer to the image below:

This cartoon by Cham appeared in *Le Chirivari* in 1866. The caption reads, "It is one thing to know how to use a needle, but it is a talent that should not be abused."

34. Which best expresses the author's tone?

    A. Overjoyed
    B. Concerned
    C. Militaristic
    D. Indifferent

35. Who is the most likely figure portrayed in the cartoon?

    A. Tsar Nicholas II
    B. Otto von Bismarck
    C. Napoleon III
    D. Prince Klemens von Metternich

36. The cartoon is most likely from the point of view of which European nation?

    A. Italy
    B. France
    C. Russia
    D. Great Britain

37. Which military conflict most directly resulted from the forces indicated in the cartoon?

    A. The Franco-Prussian War
    B. The Seven Years' War
    C. The Thirty Years' War
    D. World War I

38. Which political philosophy contributed to the events portrayed in the cartoon?

    A. Liberalism
    B. Socialism
    C. Utilitarianism
    D. Nationalism

Questions 39–41 refer to the woodcut below:

Woodcut based on drawing by Walter Crane. It was published in 1889, after May 1 had been declared an international day of worker solidarity.

39. Which of the following is most likely the intended audience of the poster?

    A. Politicians in Europe
    B. Indigenous peoples around the world
    C. Working-class individuals
    D. International capitalists

40. The woman at the top of the image is labeled "Freiheit," which translates to "Freedom." In what sense is the artist advocating for freedom?

    A. Freedom of religion around the world
    B. Universal suffrage
    C. Decolonization in Africa and Asia
    D. Economic independence of workers

41. In which nation or region did these sentiments lead to a political and economic revolution?

    A. Russia
    B. France
    C. Germany
    D. The Balkans

Questions 42–46 refer to the document below:

The following is an excerpt from a speech given in 1895 by Hermann Ahlwardt, author of *The Desperate Struggle between Aryan and Jew*, to fellow members of the Reichstag, in which he advocates closing Germany's borders to Jews:

My political friends do not hold the view that we fight the Jews because of their religion. . . . We would not dream of waging a political struggle against anyone because of his religion. . . . We hold the view that the Jews are a different race, a different people with entirely different character traits. . . . We Teutons are rooted in the cultural soil of labor. . . . The Jews do not believe in the culture of labor, they . . . want to appropriate, without working, the values which others have created . . .

Herr Deputy Rickert here has just expounded how few Jews we have altogether and that their number is steadily declining. . . . Why don't you go to the main business centers and see for yourselves whether the percentages indicated by Herr Rickert prevail there too . . .

It is one thing when a Pole, a Russian, a Frenchman, a Dane immigrates to our country, and quite another thing when a Jew settles here. Once our (Polish, etc.) guests have lived here for ten, twenty years, they come to resemble us. For they have stood with us on the same cultural soil of labor. . . . After thirty, forty years they have become Germans and their grandchildren would be indistinguishable from us. . . . The Jews have lived here for 700, 800 years but have they become Germans? Have they placed themselves on the cultural soil of labor? They never even dreamed of such a thing . . .

How many thousands of Germans have perished as a result of this Jewish exploitation. . . . Is there no one to think of all those hundreds of thousands, nor of those millions of workers whose wages grow smaller and smaller because Jewish competition brings the prices down? . . . What we want is a clear and reasonable separation of the Jews from the Germans. An immediate prerequisite is that we slam the door and see to it that no more of them get in.

42. Which statement best summarizes the argument of Hermann Ahlwardt regarding Jews in Germany?

   A. Jews can be assimilated in Germany, but only after several generations.
   B. Jews enhance the economic strength of Germany.
   C. The Jewish religion leads to immoral behavior.
   D. The Jews are incompatible with the well-being of German workers.

43. Which statement would have served as a counterargument to Hermann Ahlwardt's views?

   A. There were too few Jews in Germany to have much impact.
   B. Jews in Germany had no political power.
   C. The Jewish religion advocates non-violence.
   D. Jewish people obeyed the laws, served in the military, and paid taxes.

44. Which historical incident exemplified anti-Semitism as reflected in this passage?

   A. The XYZ affair
   B. The Dreyfus Affair
   C. The Ems Telegram
   D. The Nuremberg Trials

45. Zionism developed as a response to European anti-Semitism as reflected in this passage. Which statement best articulates this policy?

   A. Use civil disobedience to draw attention to the plight of the Jews.
   B. To ensure their safety, a Jewish state must be established.
   C. To properly assimilate, Jews should convert to Christianity.
   D. Jewish people should engage in armed resistance.

46. Which of the following is true regarding anti-Semitism?

   A. It was only located in Germany.
   B. Government policies eradicated it by World War I.
   C. It was exploited by German politicians in the 1930s.
   D. It was fueled by resentment of Jewish landholdings.

Questions 47–50 refer to the document below:

Pervading all Nature we may see at work a stern discipline, which is a little cruel that it may be very kind. That state of universal warfare maintained throughout the lower creation, to the great perplexity of many worthy people, is at bottom the most merciful provision which the circumstances admit of. The poverty of the incapable, the distresses that come upon the imprudent, the starvation of the idle, and those shoulderings aside of the weak by the strong, which leave so many "in shallows and in miseries," are the decrees of a large, farseeing benevolence. It seems hard that an unskillfulness which with all its efforts he cannot overcome, should entail hunger upon the artisan. It seems hard that a labourer incapacitated by sickness from competing with his stronger fellows, should have to bear the resulting privations. It seems hard that widows and orphans should be left to struggle for life or death. Nevertheless, when regarded not separately, but in connection with the interests of universal humanity, these harsh fatalities are seen to be full of the highest beneficence—the same beneficence which brings to early graves the children of diseased parents, and singles out the low-spirited, the intemperate, and the debilitated as the victims of an epidemic.

Herbert Spencer, *Social Statics*

47. What is the best explanation of author's purpose in referencing Nature in the first sentence?

    A. To reference animals that nurture and care for their weaker members.
    B. To imply that societies are organisms that function similarly to nature.
    C. To imply that we are capable of better than animals in nature.
    D. To demonstrate that social class differences are God's will.

48. Which policies would the author be most likely to favor?

    A. Social insurance for the elderly
    B. Repeal of assistance for the poor
    C. Compulsory religious education in schools
    D. Universal health care

49. On which historical figure's work is the author basing his theory?

    A. Aristotle's classification of the natural world
    B. Freud's theory of the subconscious mind
    C. Rousseau's ideas of the nature of man
    D. Darwin's theory of natural selection

50. Which of the following foreign policies was a logical extension of the author's viewpoint?

    A. Isolationism
    B. Imperialism
    C. Economic interdependence
    D. Containment

Questions 51– 55 refer to the passage below:

Below are excerpts from the speech The Sinews of Peace **given by Winston Churchill on March 5, 1946 to Westminster College in Fulton, Missouri.**

. . . A world organisation has already been erected for the prime purpose of preventing war, UNO [United Nations Organization], the successor of the League of Nations, with the decisive addition of the United States and all that that means, is already at work. We must make sure that its work is fruitful, that it is a reality and not a sham, that it is a force for action, and not merely a frothing of words . . .

From Stettin in the Baltic to Trieste in the Adriatic, an iron curtain has descended across the Continent. Behind that line lie all the capitals of the ancient states of Central and Eastern Europe. Warsaw, Berlin, Prague, Vienna, Budapest, Belgrade, Bucharest, and Sofia, all these famous cities and the populations around them lie in what I must call the Soviet sphere, and all are subject in one form or another, not only to Soviet influence but to a very high and, in many cases, increasing measure of control from Moscow . . . . An attempt is being made by the Russians in Berlin to build up a quasi-Communist party in their zone of Occupied Germany by showing special favours to groups of left-wing German leaders . . . . In Italy the Communist Party is seriously hampered by having to support the Communist-trained Marshal Tito's claims to former Italian territory at the head of the Adriatic. Whatever conclusions may be drawn from these facts—and facts they are—this is certainly not the Liberated Europe we fought to build up. Nor is it one which contains the essentials of permanent peace.

Winston Churchill, 1946

51. Why did Churchill emphasize that the United States would be a member of the new world organization?

   A. Because the United States is the world's policeman.
   B. Because the United States is traditionally an aggressor nation.
   C. The League of Nations was weak because the United States did not join.
   D. Because the United States holds the secret to the atomic bomb.

52. In this speech, Churchill argues for military cooperation with Western democracies in general, and the United States in particular. What Eastern European organization was formed to counter this?

   A. COMECON
   B. The Warsaw Pact
   C. The Ribbentrop-Molotov Pact
   D. The Non-Aligned Movement

53. Which event, foreshadowed in this speech, occurred soon after this speech was given?

   A. Glasnost policies implemented by Gorbachev
   B. The Hungarian Revolution
   C. The Prague Spring
   D. Formal division of Germany into East and West Germany

54. This speech is generally considered to be the beginning of which political phenomenon?

   A. Détente
   B. The Cold War
   C. Isolationism
   D. Perestroika

55. With which group is Marshal Tito, referred to in the speech, most commonly associated?

   A. The North Atlantic Treaty Organization
   B. The Pan-Slavic Movement
   C. The Non-Aligned Movement
   D. The Solidarity Union

Go on to Section I, Part B. ➜

AP European History Diagnostic Exam

SECTION I, PART B

Short-Answer Questions
Recommended Time—40 minutes

Directions: The short-answer section consists of three (of four) questions to be answered in **40 minutes**. Briefly answer ALL PARTS of the questions. Be sure to write in complete sentences; outlines, phrases, and bullets will not be accepted. You must answer questions 1 and 2, but you then may choose to answer **either** question 3 or question 4.

Use the passage below to answer all parts of question 1.

1. "Not until the nineteenth century does the more abstract notion of nationality, of membership in a broad community with shared institutions, traditions, and symbols, get seriously under way. . . . The intellectual historian Isaiah Berlin once called nationalism 'an inflamed condition of national consciousness.' By the later nineteenth century it had metastasized into the philosophy and practice of imperialism."

   100 Ideas That Changed the World, author and editor Richard Lacayo, 2010

   a) Explain the author's use of medical terminology ("inflamed" OR "metastasized") to insert a point of view into his comments.
   b) Explain the evolution of nationalism from nationality, giving ONE example of a European country that followed this path.
   c) Explain the evolution of imperialism from nationalism, giving ONE example of a European country that followed this path.

Read the passage below and answer all parts of question 2.

2. "God so loved the human race that He created man that he might participate, not only in the good that other creatures enjoy, . . . [The devil] inspired his followers to claim that the Indians should be treated as dumb brutes created for our service, pretending that they are incapable of receiving the Catholic faith. We consider, however, that the Indians are truly men . . . We declare that the Indians and all other people who may later be discovered by Christians are by no means to be deprived of their liberty or the possession of their property . . . they may and should, freely and legally, enjoy their liberty and the possession of their property. Nor should they be in any way enslaved."

   Papal Decree, 1537

   a) Identify and explain ONE institutional result in the Spanish conquest that can be traced to this statement.
   b) Identify and explain ONE central concern of the Papacy.
   c) Analyze the effect of this decree on EITHER wars in the New World or on the slave trade.

3. Answer Parts (a), (b), and (c).

   a) Identify and explain the role of globalization in ongoing migration, or, the movement of people from one location to another, whether national or international.
   b) Identify TWO causes for migration to and from European countries in the modern era.
   c) Identify TWO long-term, positive effects of migration to and from European countries in the modern era.

4. Answer Parts (a), (b), and (c).

   a) Identify and explain TWO effects of the invention of the printing press.
   b) Identify and explain TWO effects of the Scientific Revolution.
   c) Identify and explain ONE effect of the establishment of secular (nonreligious) universities.

STOP. End of Section I.

AP European History Diagnostic Exam

SECTION II, PART A

Document-Based Question
Recommended Time—60 minutes

Directions: The following question is based on Documents 1–7 provided below. (The documents have been edited for the purpose of this exercise.) The historical thinking skills that this question is designed to test include contextualization, synthesis, historical argumentation, and the use of historical evidence. Your response should be based on your knowledge of the topic and your analysis of the documents.

Write a well-integrated essay that does the following:

- States an appropriate thesis that directly addresses all parts of the question. Supports that thesis with evidence from all or all but one of the documents *and* your knowledge of European history beyond or outside of the documents.
- Analyzes the majority of the documents in terms of such features as their intended audience, purpose, point of view, format, argument, limitations, and/or social context as appropriate to your argument.
- Places your argument in the context of broader regional, national, or global processes.

Question: Identify and analyze the change in attitudes toward the purpose and value of the education of women between the Renaissance and the early twentieth century.

Document 1

> Source: Erasmus, *Christiani matrimonii institutio*, 1526
>
> "Study busies the whole soul. . . . It is not only a weapon against idleness but also a means of impressing the best precepts upon a girl's mind of leading her to virtue."

Document 2

> Source: Baldassare Castiglione, *The Courtier*, 1528
>
> ". . . while some qualities are common to both and as necessary to man as to woman, there are nevertheless some others that befit woman more than man, . . . but above all, methinks that in her ways, manners, words, gestures and bearing a woman ought to be very unlike a man; for just as it befits him to show a certain stout and sturdy manliness, so it is becoming in a woman to have a soft and dainty tenderness with an air of womanly sweetness in her every movement. . . . For I believe that many faculties of the mind are as necessary to woman as to man; . . . [she] must have not only the good sense to discern the quality of him with whom she is speaking, but knowledge of many things, in order to entertain him graciously; Let her not stupidly pretend to know that which she does not know, but modestly seek to do herself credit in that which she does know. I wish this Lady to have knowledge of letters, music, painting, . . . in everything, she will be very graceful, and will entertain appropriately, and with witticisms and pleasantries befitting her, everyone who shall come before her."

Document 3

Source: Moliere, *The Learned Ladies,* 1672

". . . I don't like all those useless books of yours. Apart from the big Plutarch that keeps my neckbands pressed, you should burn them all. Get rid of this fierce-looking telescope and all the rest of those gadgets. . . . Stop trying to find out what's happening on the moon and mind what's going on in your own house . . . . It's not decent, and there are plenty of reasons why it isn't, for a woman to study and know so much. Teaching her children good principles, running her household, keeping an eye on her servants, and managing her budget thriftily are all the study and philosophy she needs."

Document 4

Source: Mary Wollstonecraft, *Vindication of the Rights of Woman,* 1792

Men and women must be educated, in a great degree, by the opinions and manners of the society they live in. . . . It may then be fairly inferred, that, till society be differently constituted, much cannot be expected from education. . . . The most perfect education, in my opinion, is such an exercise of the understanding as is best calculated to strengthen the body and form the heart. Or, in other words, to enable the individual to attain such habits of virtue as will render it independent. . . . This was Rousseau's opinion respecting men: I extend it to women . . .

Document 5

Source: John Stuart Mill, *The Subjection of Women,* 1869

"The second benefit to be expected from giving to women the free use of their abilities by leaving them free to choose their employments and opening up to them the same range of occupation and the same rewards and encouragements as other human beings have, would be doubling the supply of abilities available for the higher service of humanity. . . . Where there is now one person qualified to benefit mankind . . . as a public teacher or an administrator of some branch of public or social affairs, there would then be a chance of two. . . . This great gain for the intellectual power of our species . . . would come partly through better and more complete intellectual education of women."

Document 6

Source: Emmeline Pankhurst, "Freedom or Death," 1913

"Men make the moral code and they expect women to accept it. They have decided that it is entirely right and proper for men to fight for their liberties and their rights, but that it is not right and proper for women to fight for theirs. . . . We are here, not because we are law-breakers; we are here in our efforts to become law-makers."

Document 7

Source: Virginia Woolf, *Three Guineas,* 1938

"Lock up your libraries if you like; but there is no gate, no lock, no bolt that you can set upon the freedom of my mind. . . . the value of education is among the greatest of all human values."

Go on to Section II, Part B. →

AP European History Diagnostic Exam

SECTION II, PART B

Long-Essay Question
Recommended Time—40 minutes

Directions: Write an essay that responds to ONE of the following three questions.

Question 1: Identify the Industrial and Scientific Revolutions and explain what makes them revolutionary in the context of European history.

Question 2: Identify and analyze TWO major effects of the Reformation and the Counter-Reformation.

Question 3: Identify and compare TWO characteristics of traditional Imperialism (during the sixteenth and seventeenth centuries) and New Imperialism (during the nineteenth century).

End of Diagnostic Exam

❯ Answers and Explanations

Section I, Part A: Multiple-Choice Questions

1. **C.** Imperialism, or the neo-Imperialism of the eighteenth and nineteenth centuries, subscribed to the idea that specific nations were inherently superior to others. England and France spread their influence through military conquest and political and economic control over large parts of the globe. The only absolutist (B) element in this new imperialism was the belief in superiority. Socialism (A) and Conservatism (D) refer to less geopolitical ideologies.

2. **B.** The practice of militarism is what makes it possible to take over all aspects of another nation's government and its social and economic (A, C, D) systems.

3. **C.** "There will be no leftovers" indicates the rapacious, endlessly hungry nature of colonizing nations. While Napoleon and Pitt were exceedingly powerful, or their countries were, they were not alone in the search for new colonies (A). The world was not growing smaller (B); in fact, it must have seemed endless to those nations pursuing power. Less was obviously not enough, much less more for Napoleon, Pitt, and others in search of new colonies (D).

4. **C.** The Chartist movement in Great Britain was intended to secure political rights for working-class Britons. It developed out of anger and resentment over the failure of Parliamentary reforms to extend the vote to those who did not own property, as well as laws intended to drive the poor into workhouses, passed by the middle-class Whigs (B). The Tories tended to be drawn from and support the interests of land-owning elites, not the working class (A, D).

5. **B.** Protectionist laws usually involved using tariffs or price controls to protect particular industries. The Corn Laws protected the landed elites in Great Britain from low corn prices, but at the same time it hurt workers who were hurt by the high prices. The Secret Ballot Act of 1872 occurred after the date on the document (1838) and therefore could not be a cause. It gave men the right to vote using a secret ballot, allowing them to choose to be free from outside influence (A). The Petition of Right limited the King's actions. It was neither a protectionist document, nor was it close enough in time period to be a contributing factor (C). The Poor Law Amendment Act of 1834 forced the poor into hated workhouses. Although it contributed to working-class anger and resentment, it was not a protectionist law, and therefore, is outside the scope of the question (D).

6. **A.** The radicals in France after the French Revolution also demanded universal manhood suffrage and an end to property qualifications. In the eighteenth century, Russia was ruled by a series of absolute monarchs. Liberal ideas did not flourish there (A). Conservatives in Austria would have opposed political and social changes, like expansion of suffrage, as they preferred traditional values and institutions (C). Neoclassicism is an artistic style, and therefore, is not the best choice (D).

7. **C.** Parliament does not have annual elections. Students may have to draw from their knowledge of recent European history to answer this question (for example, the tenure of Prime Ministers like Winston Churchill and Margaret Thatcher do not suggest annual elections). The Secret Ballot Act of 1872 gave men the right to vote using a secret ballot, allowing them to choose to be free from outside influence (A). The Representation of the People Act in 1918 removed property restrictions for males and gave suffrage to men over 21 and to women 30 or older (B, D).

8. **B.** According to Machiavelli, man is "ungrateful, fickle, false, cowardly, covetous," and thus cannot be dependable. This is man's means of dealing with the world and it overrides willpower (A), loyalty (C), and his very nature (D), as it is stronger than other qualities he may possess.

9. **C.** In general, fear is the great motivator, says Machiavelli. Love (A, B, D) is arbitrary, and fear, though not a basic human condition with its threat of repercussions, engenders assured responses.

10. **D.** Fear is a result of someone else's threats or prompts. Love (B, C) may prompt fear, but it is self-induced. Neither fear nor love (A) evokes an easy response.

11. **D.** While Queen Elizabeth (A), Garibaldi (B), and Louis XIV were all strong political figures in European history, it was Joseph Stalin who embodied the idea of the cunning, scheming, and unscrupulous leader that Machiavelli described in *The Prince*.

12. **C.** The Bread Riots were the most immediate and direct political act in response on the part of the ordinary people to a winter and a "springtime of scarcity," during which the elite classes carried on with displays of "luxury and ostentation." The killing of farmers (A) and removal of priests (B) did not happen until the French Revolution was well launched. The storming of the Bastille (D), the symbol of power, took place later in 1789.

13. **B.** Of all the social classes in prerevolutionary France, it was the peasants who felt most powerless and were the instigators, if indirect, of the French Revolution. Merchants (A), the clergy (C), and bureaucrats (D) would only later become involved.

14. **B.** It was the reaction, or lack of reaction and concern, on the part of the nobility that prompted the French Revolution. The initial concerns of the revolutionaries were based on what they saw as a settling of accounts, past due. While it can be argued that the Revolution began in the provinces (A), peasants were generally without power or means of communication; the climatic extremes (C) could be said to have been only indirectly responsible for the Revolution; and Revolution cannot be called inevitable (D) since it takes a "perfect storm" of elements to begin one and to carry it through. Revolution is almost never the result of one action or element.

15. **B.** The overall tone of the author is indicative of a sense of paternalism, especially as the peoples are described as being filled with a sense of "wonder." This is an obvious reference to the superiority of the Europeans. Isolationism (C)

is hardly at play here since the Europeans are exploring new areas with an eye to conquest. Fear (A) may be displayed by the native peoples; love (D) does not enter in.

16. **B.** The native peoples described here reacted with both pragmatism and caution by cooperating with the Europeans first having fled, then having realized perhaps that the Europeans were not going away, by inviting them into their society and sharing what they had. They did not panic (A), but rather showed curiosity, if only eventually. There is no evidence of either party learning a new language (C) or of acceptance (D).

17. **B.** The Europeans were not provoked by a hostile response from the native peoples and evidently felt benevolently toward them, as witness their statement that the people gave them gifts and were considered "friends." The Europeans were probably outnumbered, though this did not seem to be a consideration (A), given their superior weaponry (C). The natives' goods and property were hidden and thus, not readily available for theft (D).

18. **D.** The overall tone of the letter is one of condescension. There is a sense of allowing inferior peoples to maintain their dignity while believing in European superiority. The sense of wonder (A) is attributed to the native peoples. Neither opportunism (B) nor idealism (C) comes into play, yet.

19. **A.** The author states that he chooses to write about "low and rustic life" and clearly feels positively about it ("in that state the essential passions of the heart . . . can attain their maturity.") He does not reference poor people specifically, except as one might assume that rural people are poor; however, he doesn't feel pity for them, but rather celebrates their lives (B). There is no reference to the city, which is the opposite of his preferred subject (C). The author specifically rejects the subjects of the "Man of Science," as he feels it is a solitary pursuit, whereas, the purpose of poetry is to connect all human beings (D).

20. **D.** "Rustic life" refers to rural life, where our feelings exist in simplicity. Choice B discusses poetry in a general sense, not with respect to the specific subjects selected. Choices A and C both relate to the pursuits of the "Man of Science" whose activities the author claims are distinct and separate from the goal of poetry.

21. **C.** Romanticism developed in the early 1800s as a reaction against the cold logic of the Enlightenment and the mechanical, urban world of the Industrial Revolution. Common themes included nature, emotion, spiritual or fantastical elements, and idealization of the past. Surrealism and Cubism are both twentieth-century movements associated with the visual arts. Surrealism expressed imaginative dreams that weren't rational (B). Cubism tried to portray three dimensions on canvas (D). The Baroque movement occurred much earlier in the 1700s, and was characterized by ornate detail, and contrasting elements to heighten drama or emotion (A).

22. **A.** Romanticism was developed in the early 1800s as a reaction against the cold logic of science, rationalism, and the mechanical, urban world of the Industrial Revolution. Common themes included nature, emotion, spiritual or fantastical elements, and idealization of the past. Although there was immigration at this time, it wasn't on the scale that would be seen later, and thus wasn't much of a force in the Romantics' works (B). Likewise, imperialism occurred later in the nineteenth century and did not play a prominent role in the Romantic movement (C). Although mercantilism existed during the Romantic period, it wasn't a primary source of inspiration for the Romantics.

23. **C.** The graph shows the balance of trade of Great Britain. One can tell this by looking at the currency reported, British pounds. Since no other nation in the European Union uses the pound, neither Germany (A), France (B), nor Switzerland (D) is a logical choice. Also, all of those countries are listed on the graph. The subject would not have been listed.

24. **B.** A favorable balance of trade is one in which the subject country exports more than it imports to another country. In this case, Ireland buys over £10 billion more than it sells to Great Britain. Germany has the least favorable balance of trade from Great Britain's perspective, as they sell £30 billion more to Great Britain than Great Britain buys from them (A). Cyprus appears to sell and import approximately the same amount (C). Andorra is not listed, and therefore, cannot be the correct response (D).

25. **B.** The European Union (EU) acts as a single trading bloc, with mostly free trade among member states, which is the opposite of (C). Not all members use the euro as their currency (the English pound is an example) (A). Most nations within the European Union set their own minimum wage, depending on their internal economic situation (D).

26. **C.** Brexit refers to the referendum held in Great Britain in 2016 on Britain's leaving the European Union. It passed 51 percent to 48 percent. Maastricht was the original treaty that formed the European Union (A). Article 50 is the clause of the Treaty of Lisbon setting out procedures for members to leave the European Union (D).

27. **B.** Beaumarchais was criticizing the aristocracy, which maintained that class rank was inviolable; it was held in place by tradition. Talent (A) and merit (C) were not as important as social position, according to the author. While masters may or may not always be strong (D), in this particular case, they should be.

28. **C.** Monarchy and its hold over the populace is equated with the sheer size, and dominance to the landscape, of the Bastille. Equality (A), liberty (B), and fraternity (D) were the landmarks of the revolutionary motto.

29. **B.** Even the most alienated, marginalized, isolated people can have moments of success. Being overcome by animals is not a given (A). If everyone maintained the status quo (C), there would be no revolutions. Not everyone will be opportunistic (D) in the face of other choices, such as being considerate, benevolent, or altruistic, for example.

30. **C.** The arts can present a contemporary point of view not sometimes otherwise able to be portrayed. Censorship was frequently directed at newspapers or speeches, for example, which, unlike the arts, did not always use nuance or symbolism to get ideas across. The arts can be realistic (A) or idealistic and wishful (B), or they can even present an official point of view (D); but it is the arts especially painting, drawing, music, or theater that can both reach a larger audience, assuming less than 100 percent literacy, and allude to points of view rather than stating them outright.

31. **D.** Knowledge is power, as the saying goes. Prevention of competition (A), the use of secret languages (B), and the cultivation of xenophobia (C) are all side effects of guarding knowledge; but power and control lie with those who know things.

32. **B.** Latin was the *lingua franca* of medieval Europe, the one language held in common by educated classes. Greek (A), Hebrew (C), and Arabic (D), while all used in specialized fields of study, were not as widespread in their use.

33. **B.** Before the invention of moveable type and the resultant publication of books, often in the vernacular, reading was a skill limited to the elite classes; after, books and other publications became affordable and accessible to a larger portion of the population and opened up avenues of social advancement. As a result, formerly dominant social hierarchies began to change and weaken. (A), (C), and (D) are simply incorrect, though the establishment of the publishing industry and transmission of traditions could be considered side effects of the invention of moveable type.

34. **B.** The author's tone can be determined, not by the expression of the cartoon character, but by the caption underneath. Thus, the author is expressing concern that Bismarck might take the unification of German states too far. Neither the image nor the caption indicates joy (A) or indifference (C). Militarism is the support of military action, whereas the author is expressing the opposite (D).

35. **B.** The figure most associated with the unification of the German states is Otto von Bismarck. This is further reinforced by the helmet with the spike, often used to indicate Germany in cartoons. The unification came well after Metternich's major contributions in history at the Congress of Vienna in 1815 (D). As Prussia was a rival, France's Napoleon III would not have tried to strengthen Prussia by unifying the German states (C). Tsar Nicholas II was Russian, and there are no indications in the cartoon that the figure might be Russian (A).

36. **B.** A historical rival of Prussia's for influence in Europe, France was most likely to be alarmed by Bismarck's efforts to unify German states,

as is also indicated by the language of the caption. Since neither Great Britain nor Italy bordered Prussia, its expansion would not have been as critical as it was for France, not to mention that Italy and Prussia were allies against Austria in the Seven Weeks' War in 1866 (A, D). Russia generally had positive relations with Prussia in the 1800s. They were part of the Holy Alliance, and Prussia did not intervene against Russia in the Crimean War, making German unification less of an immediate threat (C).

37. **A.** Prussia goaded France into declaring war on Prussia to provide a cause in support of which the German and Austrian states could unite. This was the Franco-Prussian War. The Seven Years' War occurred much earlier (1756–1763), and involved many more European nations, including Great Britain, France, Austria, Russia, Spain, and Prussia (B). The Thirty Years' War was initially fought between Protestants and Catholics in the German States, before engaging other nations. It too took place substantially earlier (1618–1648) (C). World War I was fought after German unification and is thus out of the specified time period (D).

38. **D.** A feeling of pride in one's nation based on things like common language and culture, nationalism was instrumental in the unification of Germany. In the nineteenth century, liberalism referred to the idea of smaller governments to allow for more individual liberties. Although Bismarck implemented some liberal reforms, these are not referenced in the cartoon. Thus (A) is not the best choice. Socialism refers to the idea that the economy should be managed for the benefit of all, which wasn't possible until workers gained political power. It was not a driving force behind German unification (B). Nor was utilitarianism, which postulates that actions are good if they promote happiness for the "greatest number" (C).

39. **C.** The woodcut has the name Karl Marx on the banner, as well as the word "proletarier," which looks like its translation "proletariat." These should be indications that this is to celebrate the working class. This, together with the absence of any government buildings or fancy people, should also help students reject options (A) and (D).

Although the woodcut has representations of people from all over the globe, the key element is that they are workers or farmers, not that they are indigenous people (B).

40. **D.** In the context of communism, the term *freedom* refers to the freedom of the proletariat from the exploitation of the bourgeoisie around the world. There are no indications of voting rights (B) or religious images (A). In fact, communism rejects religion as a tool to subdue the masses. Finally, despite the fact that there are images of people from Africa or Asia, there is no indication of imperialist nations (C). Additionally, decolonization occurred well after the date of the woodcut.

41. **A.** Only Russia had a revolution that targeted both the political and economic systems, as well as being directly related to the Marxist principles expressed in the banner. France's revolution was much earlier and was primarily political (B). Germany never had a revolution per se (C), and neither did the Balkan region, although they had many ethnic conflicts (D).

42. **D.** The author indicates that German workers are being hurt by Jews in Germany (D). Although Jews in Germany might have some economic success, the author feel that is to the detriment of German workers, not an asset for the nation (B). He also attributes the incompatibility to "racial" characteristics, and distinguishes them from other Europeans who could become "German" after a few generations (A). Finally, he states that he has no quarrel with Jews based on their religion, but only based on their "race" (C).

43. **A.** There is an indication that another member of the Reichstag argued against closing the borders on the grounds that there weren't enough Jews in Germany to have a detrimental effect. With ideas of political equality being advanced throughout Europe in the wake of the French Revolution and liberal reforms, Jews were able to vote, own property, and hold office (like Benjamin Disraeli) (B). The other statements do not directly address the author's claim. Whether the Jewish religion favors nonviolence (C), or whether Jews in Germany paid taxes and followed the law (D) is irrelevant to the author's claim of their presence hurting German workers economically.

44. **B.** The Dreyfus Affair, in which a Jewish soldier in France was accused and convicted of passing secrets to the Germans even after exculpatory evidence surfaced, is often thought to have been partly motivated by anti-Semitism. The XYZ affair was a diplomatic conflict between the United States and France that resulted in a brief, undeclared war (A). The Ems Telegram was sent from Prussia to France, with a little creative editing by Otto von Bismarck intended to incite the French into declaring war. It was unrelated to anti-Semitism (C). Although the Nuremberg Trials were indirectly related to anti-Semitism, they involved the trial of Nazis for war crimes; thus, they redressed problems of anti-Semitism (D).

45. **B.** Zionism refers to the belief that the establishment of a Jewish state in Palestine was necessary for the security of the Jewish people. Because it advocated voluntary relocation, nonviolent responses were not part of the belief (A), nor was armed resistance (D). Since the goal was the protection and preservation of Jews and the Jewish religion, conversion to Christianity would have been the opposite of their goal (D).

46. **C.** While anti-Semitism may have subsided, it certainly hadn't disappeared by World War I (B) and was used by Hitler and the Nazis to redirect German anger and frustration toward the Jews in Germany. Because Jews in the Middle Ages were prohibited from owning land, subsequent generations of Jews were unable to inherit land (D). The Dreyfus Affair, discussed earlier, makes it clear that anti-Semitism was a problem throughout Europe, not only Germany (A).

47. **B.** The author is a supporter of social Darwinism, so his purpose is to compare the cruel but beneficial aspects of nature's "survival of the fittest" to the cruel but societally beneficial aspects of weeding out weaker and "deficient" individuals. (A) is incorrect as nature is referred to as having "stern discipline," which is the opposite of caring for the old and weak. In doing so he argues that we are, and should be, the same as animals in Nature ("harsh fatalities are full of beneficence") (C). Social Darwinists tried to apply scientific, rational principles to society, and therefore, don't typically address the role of God.

48. **B.** Social Darwinists argued that social welfare programs ultimately weakened all of society by propping up those with undesirable traits instead of letting them die out, so their traits are not perpetuated. Both options (A) and (D) provide some form of social policy that would benefit the poor. Religious instruction was not part of the social Darwinist argument (C).

49. **D.** Social Darwinism extended the work of Charles Darwin's theories on evolution and natural selection to social institutions. Aristotle worked with classification of the natural world but did not address mechanisms by which animals adapted and improved (A). Rousseau's theories centered on the idea that man was essentially good, and therefore, republics directed by the general will were optimal governments. It isn't directly connected to the idea that letting some members die would strengthen society (C). Freud's theory of the subconscious mind is wholly unrelated (B).

50. **B.** If individual power and wealth can be justified by arguing that the individual must therefore possess superior qualities, then imperialism is a logical extension, with imperialist nations arguing an inherent superiority over their colonies. Isolationism necessarily implies a lack of contact, unlike social Darwinism which considers individuals in a societal context (A). Economic interdependence is the idea that nations are so economically intertwined that the failure of one will cause others to fail. This is different from social Darwinism, in which death of the weak strengthens the whole (C).

51. **C.** The failure of the United States to join the League of Nations is often cited as a reason for its failure. By emphasizing U.S. cooperation, Churchill is reassuring people as to its likelihood of success. At this time the United States was not seen as an aggressor nation, since they originally stayed out of both World Wars until their interests were directly threatened (B). The Truman Doctrine, which indicated a more proactive role for the United States in world affairs, was announced after this speech in 1947, so the United States did not yet have the reputation as the world's policeman (A). Although Churchill does discuss nuclear capability later in this speech, this excerpt does not contain those references (D).

52. **B.** The Warsaw Pact was a military agreement among Eastern European nations and the Soviet Union, designed to counter the North Atlantic Treaty Organization (NATO). COMECON was an agreement among Eastern bloc nations, but it was economic in nature (A). The Ribbentrop-Molotov Pact is another term for the Nazi-Soviet Non-Aggression Pact, which was signed during World War II (C). The Non-Aligned movement was a coalition of nations who were not aligned for or against either of the major power blocs (D).

53. **D.** In his speech, Churchill references Communist efforts to build up support in the Soviet-occupied zone of Germany. Within three years, Germany was officially divided into the German Democratic Republic (East), run by German communists but controlled by the Soviet Union, and the Federal Republic of Germany (West). The Hungarian Revolution (or Hungarian Uprising) occurred in 1956 and the Prague Spring occurred in 1968. Neither is especially close to the date of the speech; moreover, Churchill doesn't reference possible rebellions in Eastern Europe, only that they are falling under communist sway. Gorbachev and glasnost (political openness) were not implemented until 1985 and do not fit the themes of Churchill's speech (A).

54. **B.** Churchill's description of an iron curtain dividing Western democracies and communist countries in Europe is often cited as one of the beginnings of the Cold War, with an "us against them" mentality. Détente refers to a thawing of relations between the United States and the Soviet Union, which did not begin until the late 1960s and early 1970s (A). It was a period of engagement, with military cooperation among Western nations, and with the United States actively seeking to contain communism (C). Perestroika, referring to economic reforms, was promoted by Gorbachev in the 1980s and 1990s (D).

55. **C.** Marshal Tito (aka Josip Broz), leader of Yugoslavia in 1953, is associated with the Non-Aligned movement. With nations like Egypt, India, and Yugoslavia, this was an association of nations not aligned, for or against, either of the

major world powers. This meant he did not join the NATO alliance (A). The Solidarity Union was formed in Poland, and therefore not connected to Tito in Yugoslavia (D). Pan-Slavism refers to a movement to unify Slavic peoples, many of whom were in the Balkans. Although this is the appropriate region for Marshal Tito, the pan-Slavic movement was most prominent in the 1800s and thus, well before Marshal Tito's time (D).

Section I, Part B: Short-Answer Questions

Strategies

Step 1. Compose a topic sentence that responds to the question and gives you something specific to support and illustrate.

Step 2. Support and illustrate your assertion in the topic sentence with specific examples.

Suggested Responses

Question 1

a) A good response will make clear that the author considers nationalism and imperialism negative outgrowths of nationality.
  - Nationality, or national identity/consciousness, developed around a community based on common language, traditions, institutions, and symbols (a flag, for example).
  - The author makes clear that he considers nationalism, or often extreme patriotism, to be a corruption—infected or inflamed—of nationality.
  - The author uses the word "metastasized," which usually refers to the physical spread of disease, to define imperialism.
  - The author's use of language suggests that both nationalism and imperialism are negative outgrowths of the formation of nation-states and the creation of a national identity.

b) A good response will pick probably either Germany or Italy to show how national identity morphed into the more aggressive nationalism.
  - The newly unified nations of Italy (1861) and Germany (1870) confirmed their national, as opposed to regionally based, identities through the nationwide imposition of a common language in schools, the military, the media, and government.
  - People began to consider themselves Italian or German, and their individual identities were subsumed by national identities and a belief in and loyalty to a larger community.

c) A good response will follow up on the points from the answer to 1b, adding the idea that one's nation was both better and more desirable than another, and that it was almost a duty to promulgate the national identity, culture, and traditions.
  - Both Italy and Germany demonstrated this kind of nationalist and imperialist thought and fervor over the years following the achievement of nationhood.

Question 2

a) A good response might begin with identifying the trinity of goals for conquest: God, gold, and glory. Also, while the *encomienda* or *misiones,* both were designed to protect native peoples and their property (gold and glory), they were ultimately tied to the goal of converting native peoples to Christianity (God).
  - Of all the institutions, governmental or religious, the Church was the one that insinuated itself into every aspect of colonial life, defining legal and social mores.

b) The major focus shown in this Papal decree is on the avoidance of the enslaving of native peoples.
  - Because "Indians" were considered human, and not "brutes" or animals, they were thought to have souls. This made them good candidates for conversion to Christianity.

c) Because natives were considered humans with souls, they could not be enslaved. In order to find a labor supply for the widespread and developing plantation economy, the slave trade grew, bringing Black Africans, who were not considered human or to have souls, to sustain it. This fulfilled the profit motive of conquest without presumably violating the rights of the native peoples.

Question 3

a) A good response will begin with a definition of "globalization." Originally, it was defined as the economic process that inspired worldwide interaction and integration. Now it has come to include social, cultural, diplomatic, and military aspects as well. As a result it has made migration more feasible than ever before.
  - The combined aspects of interaction and integration have led to the exchange not just of tangible goods and products, but of people who migrate,

both nationally (rural to urban migration, for example) and internationally (often from developing to developed countries) to take advantage of improved social or economic opportunities.

b) Possible causes for migration might include, for example, TWO of the following: political upheaval, unemployment, education, or social opportunities.

- Internal upheaval, political or economic, can drive people to migrate in search of a more stable and accommodating place to live. After the disintegration of the Eastern European bloc, migrants made their way west (from Romania and Albania, for example) in search of stability and safety. In the years leading up to World War II, scientists, artists, and ordinary people made their way to safer climates, the most famous perhaps being Albert Einstein.

- Unemployment causes people to migrate in search of work. The southern to northern European migration following World War II is an example of this. Many Spaniards and Italians migrated to more economically secure areas, especially to Germany, Great Britain, and the Scandinavian countries.

- Educational and social opportunities have propelled people to leave more traditional, even hidebound, homelands to places more generally egalitarian.

c) Two long-term positive effects of migration to and from European countries might include both educational and informational exchanges that can contribute to social, cultural, and scientific advances.

- One of the earliest examples of globalization and migration took place in the educational sphere: In the twelfth century, scholars traveled to various universities—Bologna, Paris, Salamanca, Padova—to obtain the kind of training they could not find at home. During the Renaissance, such international migration continued, and many scholars either remained abroad or returned home to enrich and expand education and its institutions.

- In modern times, people seeking employment have migrated both within their own countries (from depressed rural areas to more industrialized centers; southern Italians often went north in search of work) and across borders (from southern to northern Europe, again from more economically depressed areas to more industrialized areas).

Question 4

a) A good response will include any two of the following long-term effects of the invention of the printing press. It would not be an overstatement

to contend that the printing press helped to incite the Reformation and the Counter-reformation as well as destroyed traditional economic and social hierarchies.

- The printed book, beginning with the Bible, led to greater accessibility to scriptural writings for secular society. No longer was religious interpretation the only road to salvation; private (secular) interpretation and conscience assumed equal importance and undercut the control of the Roman Catholic Church over society in general.

- Literacy, with the availability of printed works, increased and provided a means of social advancement. No longer was information completely controlled by an educated few.

- As literacy increased, elite control of economic and social hierarchies decreased. Use of the vernacular replace the use of Latin in religion, commerce, and law, which opened up opportunities to different social classes.

b) The Scientific Revolution could also be called the "Secular Revolution." It sought out justification for political authority and explanation of natural phenomena outside of religion. By using the so-called "scientific method" (hypothesis-observation-experimentation-replication), newly minted scientists produced a long list of advancements.

- Among notable advancements were those in medicine. Diseases and even plagues were shown to have "natural" causes, which could be either avoided or treated.

- Royal academies and societies, like the Royal Society of London and the Royal Academy of Sciences in Paris, demonstrated practical applications of theories.

- Copernicanism, which was originally an effort to coordinate the calendar and the seasons, destroyed the Church's view of the cosmos and restated the laws of physics.

- Innovators like Galileo and Francis Bacon showed the need to use reason, as opposed to faith alone, and to understand the universe and its workings.

- General advances would occur in anatomy and physiology, thanks to hands-on research and experimentation, making modern medicine possible.

c) A good response will make clear the connection between the establishment of nonreligious universities and scientific advances.

- New universities, founded by secular patrons, offered courses of study apart from just canon (church) law and were no longer controlled by the Church.

- One lasting legacy of the new universities was the introduction of courses and degrees in the sciences and philosophy. Theory became shored up by practice.
- Eventually, universities no longer under the control of the Church allowed women access to previously denied or forbidden education, which upset the social status quo permanently.

Section II, Part A: Document-Based Question

Question 1 is based on the accompanying documents, which have been edited or adapted for the purpose of this exercise.

Strategies

Step 1. Read through the prompt and all the documents.

Step 2. Create a historically defensible thesis and outline your reasoning.

Step 3. Compose your topic sentences and make sure that they logically present your thesis.

Step 4. Support your argument by referring to at least six documents.

Step 5. Using what you have learned in AP European History, add at least one piece of historical evidence relevant to the prompt.

Step 6. Explain how or why at least three documents reveal point of view, purpose, historical context, or audience, and how this is relevant to your argument.

Step 7. Use evidence to corroborate your argument or response to the prompt.

Outline

A possible outline to the answer for this question looks like this.

Thesis: From the Renaissance until late in the eighteenth century, the purpose and value of education for women focused on how it affected others or helped to fulfill predetermined societal roles. Following the French Revolution, women's education became a matter of equal rights and natural rights and was seen as valuable to society at large.

Topic Sentence A: All the documents speak to the inherent value of education; there is a sharp divide, however, as to the purpose of education.

  Specific Examples: Moliere, using satire (Document 3), sets the stage by making the value of women's education a reflection of man's, and society's, needs. Castiglione and Erasmus (Documents 1 and 2) follow suit. Each document states that the purpose of educating women is that it increases the standing and comfort of men, and, in the process, maintains the status quo.

Topic Sentence B: Documents 4–7 give a different idea of the value of education, assigning it value and purpose for their own sake.

  Specific Examples: Both Mary Wollstonecraft (Document 4) and John Stuart Mill (Document 5) show themselves to be children of the Enlightenment. Wollstonecraft leans toward Romanticism, encouraging cultivation of both reason and emotion, for both men and women. Mill uses logic and reason to assert the benefits to society of educating women. The purpose becomes one of degree, as it were. By educating women, says Mill, society has double the abilities to better humankind than if only men were educated.

Topic Sentence C: By the twentieth century, as Pankhurst (Document 6) and Woolf (Document 7) make clear, the value of education is undisputed. It is a natural right.

  Specific Examples: The purpose of education by the twentieth century is indistinguishable from its value. Pankhurst and Woolf write more to encourage the use of education to promote gender equality.

Conclusion: Read in chronological order, the documents illustrate the passage from considering women's education as a reflection of male society's needs and wants to find value and purpose in using all resources to better mankind.

Section II, Part B: Long-Essay Question

Strategies

Choose the question for which you can quickly write a clear thesis and three topic sentences that you can illustrate and support with several specific examples. Then follow the formula to construct a history essay of high quality.

Step 1. Find the action words in the question and determine what the question wants you to do.

Step 2. Compose a thesis that responds to the question and gives you something specific to support and illustrate.

Step 3. Describe a broader historical context relevant to the prompt.

Step 4. Compose your topic sentences, and make sure that they add up logically to your thesis.

Step 5. Support and illustrate your thesis with specific examples.

Step 6. *If you have time,* compose a one-paragraph conclusion that restates your thesis.

Remember to avoid these pitfalls:

- **Avoid long sentences with multiple clauses.** Your goal is to write the clearest sentence possible; most often the clearest sentence is a relatively short sentence.

- **Do not get caught up in digressions.** No matter how fascinating or insightful you find some idea or fact, if it doesn't directly support or illustrate your thesis, don't put it in.

- **Skip the mystery.** Do not ask a lot of rhetorical questions, and do not go for a surprise ending. The readers are looking for your thesis, your argument, and your evidence; give it to them in a clear, straightforward manner.

Creating Your Outline: Question 1

Question 1: Identify the Industrial and Scientific Revolutions and explain what makes them revolutionary in the context of European history.

Hint: Begin by defining "revolution." *Revolution*: a fundamental change; often irreversible.

Thesis: The *Industrial Revolution*, which took place during the late eighteenth and early nineteenth centuries, resulted from the introduction of steam-driven machinery, the creation of large factories, the development of new transportation systems, and large-scale iron and steel production. It produced a Western European society that was more urban, less family oriented, and filled with uncertainty. In contrast, the *Scientific Revolution* refers to a process that began in the mid-sixteenth century, with the publication of Copernicus's reformed calendar, and the theory of a "heliocentric universe." It stressed the use of reason—based on observation and experimentation—as the basis for knowledge.

Topic Sentence A: The rise of the centralized factory system that characterized the Industrial Revolution produced a Western European society that was much more urban.

Specific Examples: In the eighteenth century, the majority of the British population lived in the countryside. By the end of the nineteenth century, the majority of the British population lived in cities. Examples include the rise of Manchester, Sheffield, and Birmingham from small villages to industrial cities.

Topic Sentence B: The Industrial Revolution created a Western European society that was less family oriented.

Specific Examples: Eldest sons and daughters moved to cities to seek factory work. With the rise of industrial cities came the rise of working-class slums. Fathers, wives, and children often worked in different factories.

Topic Sentence C: The Industrial Revolution destroyed the certainties of traditional society.

Specific Examples: In the agricultural economy, there was no such thing as unemployment. As more and more machines were introduced, the demand for labor went down, and unemployment became a cyclical phenomenon. The rise of the workhouses and poor houses in Great Britain were responses to that unemployment.

Topic Sentence D: The Scientific Revolution could be said to have aided in creating the Industrial Revolution. It created a society that was less vulnerable to the whims of circumstance; and it led to a general secularization of society at large.

Specific Examples: By emphasizing a society ruled by reason, the Scientific Revolution allowed for possibility to replace the feelings of resignation or acceptance of the ambiance in which people lived.

Conclusion: The Industrial Revolution replaced the traditional, rural, family-oriented society of certainty with a new urban, individualized society of uncertainty. The Scientific Revolution replaced uncertainty with possibility.

Question 2: Identify and analyze TWO major effects of the Reformation and the Counter-Reformation.

Thesis: The Reformation of the sixteenth century challenged what was seen as a corrupt Roman Catholic Church and its failure to meet the needs of an increasingly literate population. It gave rise to Protestantism and also to the Roman Catholic Church's response in the Counter-Reformation.

Major effects continue to be felt today, ranging from theology to wars.

Topic Sentence A: The Reformation was prompted by a belief in the need to reform the Roman Catholic Church, and led to the creation of various new, Protestant ("protest-ing") denominations. This separation between Catholic and Protestant churches is perhaps the most visible and long-lasting effect of the Reformation and Counter-Reformation.

Specific Examples: One central theological difference between Catholicism and Protestantism generally involves church hierarchies. The Roman Catholic Church continues to recognize the Pope as the official head of the church. The Protestant denominations do not have one central authority. The Counter-Reformation, in response to the Reformation, maintained that the Roman Catholic Church was the final arbiter in all matters of faith.

Topic Sentence B: Conflict over religious control and beliefs is nothing new. It has resulted in numerous wars, from the Crusades to present-day clashes around the world.

Specific Examples: The clash between Protestants and Catholics has been if not constant, then frequent, since the sixteenth century. In 1555, the Peace of Augsburg maintained that "whoever rules, his religion," meaning that German princes would not go to war with one another over religion. In France, however, the enmity and skirmishes between Protestants (Huguenots) and Catholics lasted for more than a hundred years. England experienced internal wars depending on who was on the throne. Bloody Mary persecuted Protestants; Elizabeth I advocated tolerance. In Ireland, the country was divided by differing religious beliefs, which led to ongoing war and terrorism. The Thirty Years' War (1618–1648) is known as the last of the religious wars, though it was really a dynastic struggle.

Conclusion: The major effects of the Reformation and Counter-Reformation may center around beliefs that have become personal. A loyalty to one of the other sides of the arguments that originally dealt with spiritual matters and the difference between religious and secular power have resulted in ongoing theological debate and military clashes.

Question 3: Identify and compare TWO characteristics of traditional Imperialism (during the sixteenth and seventeenth century) and New Imperialism (during the nineteenth century).

Thesis: Imperialism of the sixteenth and seventeenth century is called "traditional" Imperialism to distinguish it from the New Imperialism of the nineteenth century. Traditional Imperialism was primarily based on economics. The more modern version, New Imperialism, frequently has demonstrated an ideologically based reason for existence.

Topic Sentence A: "God, gold, and glory" were the motives behind much of the conquest of the New World by the Spaniards. While conversion of native peoples to Christianity was certainly an important goal of establishing a New World empire, the original motivation for "discovery" and conquest was "gold," or the search for goods available only from Asia and Asia Minor.

Specific Examples: Traditional Imperialism was visible in the acquisition of territories during the Golden Age of Exploration and Discovery as a money-making endeavor. Conquerors of the New World immediately put into place controls that allowed the conqueror to make major profits via the system of mercantilism and to keep those conquered from developing (or retaining) their own economic systems. This was direct Imperialism as it accounted not only for control of the economics of a colony, but also for political and social control. Native leaders were not left in place, though some of their institutions survived conquest.

Topic Sentence B: A more indirect Imperialism characterized French and Dutch conquests, mainly in Africa and Asia, and mainly along coastal regions, at least initially.

Specific Examples: The trip to acquire the fabled riches of Asia and Asia Minor was long, and often required ships to stop along the way to replenish supplies. Merchants financed farming communities along the coasts of Africa, for example, for this very reason. Investor-financed companies, like the Dutch East India Company, allowed eventual control of other's economies, but without the political control characteristic of more direct Imperialism.

Topic Sentence C: The New Imperialism of the nineteenth century was both direct, involving political, social, and economic control, and it was ideologically inspired.

Specific Examples: The "white man's burden" of civilizing the rest of the world, or of making it conform to European ideas and ideals of civilization, was characteristic of this new form of Imperialism. The Berlin Conference of 1884–1885, for example, divided up Africa without regard for tribal or governmental boundaries and loyalties, and imposed governments that took over all aspects of daily life: religion, education, society generally. Still, the underlying motivation behind much of the New Imperialism was economic. The gold, diamonds, tea, rubber, and other resources and products made conquest and control all the sweeter for the new imperialists.

Conclusion: Imperialism in all its forms seems to be more economically than ideologically driven. A lasting result was the destruction of native economic infrastructure and the marginalization of conquered countries in today's world.

STEP 3

Develop Strategies for Success

CHAPTER 5   The Multiple-Choice Questions
CHAPTER 6   The Short-Answer Questions
CHAPTER 7   The Document-Based Question (DBQ)
CHAPTER 8   The Long-Essay Question

CHAPTER **5**

The Multiple-Choice Questions

IN THIS CHAPTER

Summary: The multiple-choice questions of the new AP European History Exam are all based on a "visual stimulus," making them a little different from the multiple-choice questions you are used to. This chapter will help you learn what to expect and develop a strategy to successfully approach these questions.

Key Ideas:

✪ Use the process of elimination to find the best answer.

✪ If you can't eliminate all but one answer choice, take a guess. In fact, don't leave any multiple-choice answers blank; there's always a chance you will guess correctly.

Introduction

Section I, Part A, of the AP European History Exam consists of 55 multiple-choice questions to be completed within 55 minutes. The questions come in sets of two to five questions, which are tied to a "visual stimulus." The visual stimulus presents a primary or secondary source, a historian's argument, or a historical problem. We will look at an example in a minute, but first let's remind ourselves of what we already know about multiple-choice questions.

Passive Knowledge and the Process of Elimination

All multiple-choice exams test passive knowledge. The multiple-choice section of the AP European History Exam will test your passive knowledge of European history from roughly 1450 to the present. That is, it will test your ability to recognize the *best* answer out of a group of possible answers to a specific historical question. The word *best* is important. It means that all multiple-choice questions are answered through a process of elimination; you begin by eliminating the one that is most clearly not the "best" and continue until you have a "survivor."

Putting Your Historical Thinking Skills to Use

Remember that the point of each section of the AP European History Exam is to test your ability to use the thinking skills of the historian. Recall that the three main categories of historical thinking skills are reasoning chronologically, putting information in context, and arguing from evidence. Although you won't create your own argument from evidence in the multiple-choice section, you will be asked to identify which answer choice is supported by the evidence in the visual stimulus. That means that you will find the best answers to the questions by using all three of these types of historical thinking skills. Let's look at another example.

Here is a set of multiple-choice questions similar to the ones you will encounter on the AP European History Exam. Following the questions is an explanation of how you would arrive at the best answer.

Questions 1 and 2 relate to the following passage:

> I do not feel obliged to believe that the same God who has endowed us with senses, reason and intellect has intended us to forgo their use and by some other means to give us knowledge which we can attain by them. . . . From these things it follows as a necessary consequence that, since the Holy Ghost did not intend to teach us whether heaven moves or stands still, whether its shape is spherical or like a discus or extended in a plane, nor whether the earth is located at its center or off to one side. . . . I would say here something that was heard from an ecclesiastic of the most eminent degree: "That the intention of the Holy Ghost is to teach us how one goes to heaven, not how heaven goes."

> Galileo Galilei, *Letter to Christina, Grand Duchess of Tuscany*, 1615

1. Galileo was participating in what intellectual and cultural development?
   A. The consolidation of political power in the sixteenth and seventeenth centuries
   B. The rise of natural philosophy and the Scientific Revolution
   C. The Great Voyages of Exploration and early colonization
   D. The Industrial Revolution

Read the passage (the visual stimulus), and scan the four possible answers. *It is possible that you recognize that the correct answer is B, because you know that the historical context with which Galileo is associated is the rise of natural philosophy and the Scientific Revolution.* But suppose for a moment that you were taking the exam and drew a blank on Galileo. You could still answer the question fairly quickly by asking yourself a series of chronological and contextual questions about the possible answers. First, you notice that the passage is dated 1615. Can you eliminate any of the answers based on that chronology? Yes, D can be eliminated because you know the Industrial Revolution was a late eighteenth- and early nineteenth-century phenomenon. C also is improbable because most of the Great Voyages occurred earlier than 1615. Now examine the contexts of the remaining answers. Does the passage seem to have anything to do with the context of sea voyages? No, so C can definitely be eliminated. Does the passage seem to have anything to do with the consolidation of political power? No, so A can be eliminated. Finally, contextual reference to the conflict between the authority of the church and concern for how the heavens move confirms that the context for this passage is the rise of natural philosophy and the Scientific Revolution.

2. Galileo's philosophy has brought him into conflict with which of the following?

   A. The King of France

   B. The barons of industry

   C. The Holy Roman Emperor

   D. The authority of the Catholic Church in Rome

Here again, you may know that natural philosophers like Galileo came into conflict with the Catholic Church in Rome. Conversely, the other choices can be eliminated through a combination of chronological reasoning (industrialization, and therefore, the creation of barons of industry, is a nineteenth-century phenomenon) and contextualization (arguments about the movement of the heavens have no contextual relationship to political rulers like the King of France or the Holy Roman Emperor).

About Guessing

Should you guess? Total scores on the multiple-choice section are based solely on the number of questions you answer correctly. Points are not deducted for incorrect answers, and no points are awarded for unanswered questions. In other words, there is no guessing penalty. If you are unsure of an answer, take a guess.

Further Practice with Multiple-Choice Questions

In this book you'll find test-like multiple-choice questions at the end of each content review chapter in Step 4. Use these to practice your strategy for attacking the multiple-choice section of the AP European History Exam. Use the explanations provided to help you understand any questions you get wrong. It's a good idea to read the explanations, not only for the questions you missed, but also for any that you were unsure of or for which you didn't understand one of the answer choices. Additional practice for the multiple-choice questions can be found in the Practice Exams in Step 5. To gain more practice and become more proficient, access the sample multiple-choice questions provided online at the College Board website (www.collegeboard.org).

CHAPTER 6

The Short-Answer Questions

IN THIS CHAPTER

Summary: The AP European History Exam contains a section composed of short-answer questions. This chapter will help you learn what to expect and develop a strategy to successfully approach these questions.

Key Ideas:
- ✪ A good answer to a short-answer question is only one paragraph, or, in the case of a question that asks for two things, two short paragraphs.
- ✪ For each paragraph, create a topic sentence that answers the question and four or five more sentences that support and illustrate your assertions.

Introduction

On the AP European History Exam, you will answer three short-answer questions and have 40 minutes to respond. Some of the questions may be accompanied by a visual stimulus. The first two questions will deal with the period between 1600 and 2001. For the third question, you will choose between one covering periods 1–2 and one covering periods 3–4. See p. 5.

Putting Your Knowledge and Historical Thinking Skills to Use

The short-answer questions test two things: your knowledge of European history and your historical thinking skills. Recall that the three main categories of historical thinking skills are reasoning chronologically, putting information in context, and arguing from evidence. The short-answer questions do not require you to make an argument from evidence, so that means that you will answer the question by using your knowledge, reasoning chronologically, and contextualizing. Let's look at an example to see how that would work.

Question 1: Using your knowledge of European history, answer Parts A and B below.

A) Briefly explain two significant consequences of the development of market-based agriculture in the eighteenth century.

B) Briefly explain how the traditional population and productivity cycles of Western Europe were broken in the eighteenth century.

Begin by making sure you know what the question is asking. In the short-answer questions, that will be straightforward. In the example above, you are to briefly explain two related events: the development of market-based agriculture and the breaking of the population and productivity cycles. Organize your thoughts by locating the two events chronologically, thereby activating your knowledge of the appropriate era and events. These eighteenth-century developments are covered in Chapter 15 of this text: "Economic Change and the Expansion of the State."

A good answer to the short-answer questions is typically one paragraph, or, in the case of a question that asks for two things, two short paragraphs. So what you need is a topic sentence that answers the question and four or five more sentences that support and illustrate your assertions.

Part A of the Short-Answer Question

Here again is Part A of the question, followed by an example of a good response:

A) Briefly explain two significant consequences of the development of market-based agriculture in the eighteenth century.

Topic sentence (an assertion that answers the question): Two significant consequences of the development of market-based agriculture in the eighteenth century were the advent of the enclosure movement and a wave of technical innovation that increased production.

Body of paragraph 1 (supports and illustrates the first assertion of the topic sentence): The shift to cash crops that characterized market-based agriculture in the eighteenth century created a demand for larger amounts of high-profit crops. Accordingly, traditional land-owning elites abandoned their feudal obligations to the peasantry and adopted the attitude of the merchant class. Specifically, they instituted a process known as "enclosure," in which hedges, fences, and walls were built to deny the peasantry access to the commons, which were now converted to fields for cash crops. Later, the landowners extended enclosure into other arable lands, breaking traditional feudal agreements and gradually transforming much of the peasantry into wage labor.

Body of paragraph 2 (supports and illustrates the second assertion of the topic sentence): The demand for larger amounts of high-profit crops also engendered a wave of technical innovation that produced higher yields. The old three-field system, which left roughly one-third of the land fallow, was replaced with new crops such as clover, turnips, and potatoes, which replenished the soil while producing foodstuffs that could be used to feed livestock in winter. As the century progressed, more highly technical innovations, such as the cotton gin (invented in 1793 by the American Eli Whitney), which efficiently removed seed from raw cotton, increased the speed with which agricultural products could be processed and sent to market.

Part B of the Short-Answer Question

Here again is Part B of the question, followed by an example of a good response:

B) Briefly explain how the traditional population and productivity cycles of Western Europe were broken in the eighteenth century.

Topic sentence (an assertion that answers the question): A combination of market-based agriculture and rural manufacturing broke the traditional cycles of population and productivity by subverting the traditional limits to both.

Body of the paragraph (supports and illustrates the assertion of the topic sentence): Natural limits to both population and economic productivity created a traditional cycle in which population and productivity initially rose together, as an increase in the number of people working in an agricultural economy increased the agricultural yield. Eventually, the agricultural yield reached the maximum amount that could be produced given the land available and the methods in use. For a while, population would continue to rise, but eventually, as the number of people far outstripped the agricultural yield, food became scarce and expensive. Scarcity and high prices eventually caused the population to decline. When the population was safely below the possible productivity, the cycle began again. The advent of market-based agriculture shifted the agricultural system from farming for local consumption to a reliance on imported food sold at markets. The introduction of rural manufacture, where people were paid in currency to work at textile production, put money in people's pockets, allowing them to buy food and making them less dependent on land and agricultural cycles, thereby breaking the natural check on population growth.

Further Practice with Short-Answer Questions

In this book you'll find a test-like short-answer question at the end of each content review chapter in Step 4. Use these to practice the skills necessary to do well on the short-answer section of the AP European History Exam. Compare your work to the answer and explanation provided. Additional practice for the short-answer questions can be found in the Practice Exams in Step 5. To gain more practice and become more proficient, access the sample short-answer questions provided online at the College Board website (www.collegeboard.org).

CHAPTER 7

The Document-Based Question (DBQ)

IN THIS CHAPTER

Summary: The AP European History Exam contains an essay question called the "document-based question" (DBQ), which involves using historical documents of various types. In this chapter you'll find out what to expect and develop a strategy to do well on this task.

Key Idea:

✪ The key to doing well on the DBQ is being able to write a history essay of high quality—one that answers the question, makes an argument, and supports the argument with evidence.

Introduction

Your task for both the document-based question (DBQ) and the long-essay question (see Chapter 8) is to write a history essay of high quality. I have seen a lot of gibberish written about how to "crack" AP essay questions that dwells far too much on "what the graders are looking for" and gives misguided advice, such as "throw in a few big words." In reality, those who grade the AP essay exams are "looking for" the thing that all history instructors look for, and, I dare say, hope for when they read student essays: a reasonably well-written essay that answers the question, makes an argument, and supports the argument with evidence. In short, the key to "cracking" the AP essay questions is to know how to write a short history essay of high quality. Learn that skill now, and you will not only do well on the AP Exam, but you will do well in your history classes in college. And, yes, in this chapter, I *do* discuss the guidelines that are given to those who grade the AP European History Exam essays, but only for you to get a sense of the purpose of the questions and an understanding of how they are scored.

The High-Quality History Essay

There are three basic components to a short history essay of high quality:

- A clear thesis that answers the question
- Three to five topic sentences that, taken together, add up logically to the thesis
- Evidence that supports and illustrates each of the topic sentences

The Thesis

In a short history essay, the thesis is a sentence that makes a clear assertion in response to the question. It is, therefore, also a statement of what your reader will believe if your essay is persuasive.

Topic Sentences

Topic sentences should appear at the beginning of clearly marked paragraphs. Each topic sentence makes a clear assertion that you will illustrate and support in the body of the paragraph. All of your topic sentences together should add up logically to your thesis. That is, if you were to successfully persuade your reader of the truth (or at least plausibility) of your topic sentences, the reader would have no choice but to admit the plausibility of your thesis.

Evidence

This is the part that makes your essay historical. In a history essay, the evidence is made up of specific examples, explained to support and illustrate your claim.

Five Steps for Creating an Outline for Your Essay

Before you begin writing a history essay, you should always make an outline. You probably know that, but when you keep the three components of the high-quality history essay in mind, you can produce an outline quickly and efficiently by following a very simple five-step process:

Step 1. Find the Action Words in the Question and Determine What the Question Wants You to Do

Too many essays respond to the topic instead of the question. In order to answer a question, you must do what it asks. To determine, specifically, what a question is asking you to do, you must pay attention to the action words—the words that give you a specific task. Look at the following question, notice the action words, and go to Step 2.

Sample Question: Compare and contrast the roles played by the various social classes in the unification of Italy and Germany in the 1860s and 1870s.

Step 2. Compose a Thesis that Responds to the Question and Gives You Something Specific to Support and Illustrate

Compare the following two attempts at a thesis in response to the question:

A. The German and Italian unifications have a lot in common but also many differences.

B. The unifications of both Italy and Germany were engineered by the aristocracy.

Alas, attempts at a thesis statement that resemble example A are all too common. Notice how example A merely makes a vague claim about the topic and gives the author nothing specific to do next. Example B, in contrast, makes a specific assertion about the role of a social class in the unifications of Italy and Germany; it is responding directly to the question. Moreover, example B is a thesis because it tells its readers what they will accept if the essay is persuasive. Finally, example B gives the author something specific to do, namely, build and support an argument that explains why we should conclude that the unifications of Italy and Germany were engineered by the aristocracy.

Step 3. Compose Your Topic Sentences and Make Sure That They Add Up Logically to Support Your Thesis

In response to the sample question, three good topic sentences might be the following:

A. The architects of both Italian and German unification were conservative, northern aristocrats.

B. The middle classes played virtually no role in Italian unification, and in the south of Germany, the middle classes initially opposed the unification of Germany.

C. The working classes and the peasantry followed the lead of the aristocracy in the unification of both Italy and Germany.

Notice how the topic sentences add up logically to the thesis. Also notice how each gives you something specific to support in the body of the paragraph.

Step 4. Support and Illustrate Your Topic Sentences with Specific Examples

The sentences that follow a topic sentence should present specific examples that illustrate and support its point. That means that each paragraph is made up of two things: factual information and your explanation of how that factual information supports the topic sentence. When making your outline, you can list the examples you want to use. For our question, the outline would look something like this:

Thesis: The unifications of both Italy and Germany were engineered by the aristocracy.

Topic Sentence A: The architects of both Italian and German unification were conservative, northern aristocrats.

Specific Examples: Cavour, conservative aristocrat from Piedmont; Bismarck, conservative aristocrat from Prussia. Both took leadership roles and devised unification strategies.

Topic Sentence B: The middle classes played virtually no role in Italian unification, and in the south of Germany, the middle classes initially opposed the unification of Germany.

Specific Examples: Italy: mid-century Risorgimento, a middle-class movement, failed and played virtually no role in subsequent events. Germany: middle-class liberals in the Frankfurt Parliament were ineffective. Middle-class liberals in southern Germany were initially wary of Prussian domination; they rallied to the cause only when Bismarck engineered the Franco-Prussian War.

Topic Sentence C: The working classes and the peasantry followed the lead of the aristocracy in the unification of both Italy and Germany.

Specific Examples: In Italy, the working classes played no role in the north. The peasantry of the south followed Garibaldi but shifted without resistance to support Cavour and the king at the crucial moment. The working classes in Germany supported Bismarck and Kaiser William I of Prussia. The socialists, supposedly a working-class party, rallied to the cause of war.

Step 5. *If You Have Time,* Compose a One-Paragraph Conclusion that Restates Your Thesis

A conclusion is *not* necessary, and you will get little or no credit for one. If you have time remaining, and you are happy with all the other aspects of your essay, then you can write a one-paragraph conclusion that supports or places your thesis in a broader context.

Pitfalls to Avoid

There are some things that sabotage an otherwise promising essay and should be avoided. They include the following:

- **Avoid long sentences with multiple clauses.** Your goal is to write the clearest sentence possible; most often the clearest sentence is a relatively short sentence.
- **Do not get caught up in digressions.** No matter how fascinating or insightful you find some idea or fact, if it doesn't directly support or illustrate your thesis, don't put it in.
- **Skip the mystery.** Do not ask a lot of rhetorical questions, and do not go for a surprise ending. The readers are looking for your thesis, your argument, and your evidence; give it to them in a clear, straightforward manner.

Characteristics of the Document-Based Question (DBQ)

The document-based question (DBQ) is simply an essay question about primary sources. It asks you to respond to a question by interpreting a set of excerpts from primary-source documents (typically five to seven) that were written in a particular historical period. The DBQ is the third section of the AP European History Exam. It is administered after the short break that follows the multiple-choice and short-answer sections of the exam. Because the DBQ involves reading and organizing short excerpts from documents, it begins with a 15-minute reading period. Following the reading period, you will have 45 minutes to write your essay.

In their present form, the directions you will encounter are lengthy and complex. Don't let that worry you.

Directions: The following question is based on the accompanying Documents 1–7. (The documents have been slightly edited for use with this exercise.) The purpose of this question is to assess how well you are able to apply several historical thinking skills simultaneously. These skills include the ability to understand and use arguments based on historical interpretation, the ability to assess and use evidence from history, the ability to understand historical context, and the ability to synthesize historical knowledge. In writing your response, base your ideas on your analysis of the documents and on whatever outside knowledge of the topic you may have. Your essay should do the following:

- Present a thesis that addresses all parts of the question.
- Support that thesis with evidence from all of the documents (or all but one of them) AND your own knowledge of European history.
- Analyze and interpret the documents in terms of their intended audience, the author's purpose and point of view, any limitations in the author's perspective, and the historical context within which the document was created.
- Place your thesis within the context of broader national, regional, or global historical trends.

That is a lot of instructions, but the good news is that, basically, it boils down to writing a quality essay and being conscious of demonstrating your knowledge and skill. The only instruction not automatically taken care of by writing a quality essay is to make sure that you use all or all but one of the documents.

Applying the Principles of the High-Quality History Essay to the Document-Based Question (DBQ)

Keeping in mind the need to use all, or all but one, of the sources, the five steps to outlining a history essay explained above can easily be modified for the DBQ. Here are the five steps adapted for the DBQ:

Step 1. As you read the documents, determine what they have in common and how you can group them.
Step 2. Compose a thesis that explains how these documents are linked in the way you have chosen.
Step 3. Compose your topic sentences, and make sure that they add up logically to your thesis.
Step 4. Support and illustrate your thesis with specific examples that contextualize the documents.
Step 5. *If you have time*, compose a one-paragraph conclusion that supports your thesis.

A Sample DBQ

Let's look at a question similar to the one you might see on the AP European History Exam and see how you could approach it.

Question: Discuss the changing attitudes and arguments regarding the basis for knowledge of the natural world in the following documents.

Document 1

Source: Giambattista della Porta, *Natural Magick*, 1584.

"There are two sorts of Magick, the one is infamous, and unhappy, because it has to do with foul spirits and consists of incantations and wicked curiosity; and this is called sorcery. . . . The other Magick is natural; which all excellent, wise men do admit and embrace, and worship with great applause; neither is there anything more highly esteemed, or better thought of, by men of learning. . . . Others have named it the practical part of natural philosophy, which produces her effects by the mutual and fit application of one natural thing to another. Magick is nothing else but the survey of the whole course of nature."

Document 2

Source: Galileo Galilei, "Letter to the Grand Duchess Christina of Tuscany," 1615.

"[Copernicus] stands always upon physical conclusions pertaining to the celestial motions, and deals with them by astronomical and geometrical demonstrations, founded primarily on sense experiences and very exact observations. . . . I think that in discussions of physical problems we ought to begin not from the authority of scriptural passages, but from sense-experiences and necessary demonstrations. . . . Nature . . . is inexorable and immutable; she never transgresses the laws imposed upon her, or cares a whit whether her abstruse reasons and methods of operation are understandable to men."

Document 3

Source: Robert Bellarmine, "Letter on Galileo's Theories," 1615.

"For to say that, assuming the earth moves and the sun stands still, all the appearances are saved better than with eccentrics and epicycles, is to speak well; there is no danger in this, and it is sufficient for mathematicians. But to want to affirm that the sun really is fixed in the center of the heavens . . . is a very dangerous thing, not only by irritating all the philosophers and scholastic theologians, but also by injuring our holy faith and rendering the Holy Scripture false."

Document 4

Source: Francis Bacon, *Novum Organum*, 1620.

"There are two ways, and can only be two, of seeking and finding truth. The one, from sense and reason, takes a flight to the most general axioms, and from these principles and their truth, settled once for all, invents and judges of all intermediate axioms. The other method collects axioms from sense and particulars, ascending continuously and by degrees so that in the end it arrives at the most general axioms. This latter is the only true one, but never hitherto tried."

Document 5

Source: William Harvey, *On the Motion of the Heart and Blood in Animals*, 1628.

"The heart, it is vulgarly said, is the fountain and workshop of the vital spirits, the centre from which life is dispensed to the several parts of the body. Yet it is denied that the right ventricle makes spirits, which is rather held to supply the nourishment to the lungs.... Why, I ask, when we see that the structure of both ventricles is almost identical, there being the same apparatus of fibres, and braces, and valves, and vessels, and auricles, and both in the same way in our dissections are found to be filled up with blood similarly black in colour, and coagulated—why, I say, should their uses be imagined to be different, when the action, motion, and pulse of both are the same?"

Document 6

Source: Johannes Agricola, *Treatise on Gold*, 1638.

"All true chymists and philosophers write that common corporeal gold is of not much use in man's body if it is only ingested as such, for no metallic body can be of use if it is not previously dissolved and reduced to the *prima materia*. We have an example in corals. The virtue of corals is not in the stone or the body but in their red color. If the corals are to release their power, a separation must first occur through a dissolution, and the redness must be separated from the body.... Consequently, whoever wants to do something useful in medicine must see to it that he first dissolve and open his metallic body, then extract its soul and essence, and the work will then not result in no fruit."

Document 7

Source: Isaac Newton, *Principia Mathematica*, 1687.

"Rule I. We are to admit no more causes of natural things than such as are both true and sufficient to explain their appearances.
"Rule II. Therefore to the same natural effects we must, as far as possible, assign the same causes.
"Rule III. The qualities of bodies, which admit neither intension nor remission of degrees, and which are found to belong to all bodies within reach of our experiments, are to be esteemed as universal qualities of all bodies whatsoever."

Getting Started

Remember the first step to a history essay of high quality adapted to the DBQ:

Step 1. As you read the documents, determine what they have in common and how you can group them.

For this question, the documents display a wide array of positions, so a good strategy would be to try to identify a central dividing issue. In these documents, you can notice that some seem to take some sort of position on the senses and observation; some believe that all knowledge of nature must start with direct sense experience, whereas others argue that starting with sense experience is a mistake. Focus your essay on that central divide and then see if you can form a few groups based on the similarities and differences between the approaches used in these pieces.

Creating the Outline for the DBQ

Recall that the next steps in creating your essay in response to the DBQ include the following:

Step 2. Compose a thesis that explains how these documents are linked in the way you have chosen.

Step 3. Compose your topic sentences and make sure that they add up logically to your thesis.

Step 4. Support and illustrate your thesis with specific examples that contextualize the documents.

An outline for your essay in response to this DBQ could look like this:

Thesis: These documents show that arguments regarding the basis for knowledge of the natural world have often hinged on assumptions about the reliability of sense experience.

Topic Sentence A: Documents 1 and 6 illustrate the faith in direct, trial-and-error experience that developed in the "alchemy" and "natural magic" traditions.

Specific Examples: della Porta places emphasis on "practical application"; Agricola places emphasis emphasis on handling the materials, making "dissolutions" and "combinations," and recording results carefully

Topic Sentence B: Documents 4 and 5 illustrate the emphasis on observation as the correct starting place for knowledge of the natural world.

Specific Examples: Bacon outlines two approaches and argues for the superiority of the one that begins with observed particulars; Harvey illustrates how the method should work.

Topic Sentence C: Documents 2 and 7 refine the process to include the goal of finding general laws.

Specific Examples: Galileo discusses sense experiences and very exact observations. Begin not from the authority of scriptural passages, but from sense experiences and necessary demonstrations. Nature never transgresses the laws imposed upon her. Newton codifies the approach into "rules."

Topic Sentence D: Document 3 dissents from the view that sense experience is a valid foundation for knowledge of the natural world.

Specific Examples: Bellarmine discusses the dangers of contradicting scholastic and church authority.

Now you are ready to write your essay based on this outline. If you have time, you can go on to step 5, but remember a conclusion isn't actually necessary. Here's a sample topic sentence for a short concluding paragraph:

Conclusion: The variety of attitudes and positions regarding knowledge about the natural world depended upon the amount of faith one put in the reliability of sense experience.

Scoring the Document-Based Question (DBQ)

Although I encourage you not to get too concerned with how the graders go about scoring the exams (writing a quality essay is the best way to ensure a good score), it is worth mentioning that the scoring of essays on the AP European History Exam is now done with an "analytical rubric" as opposed to a "holistic rubric." What that means is that instead of awarding a single score for the overall quality of the essay, the high school and college instructors scoring your essay will be awarding points for particular aspects of a response. That is, they will be awarding points for each of the historical thinking skills you demonstrate. So it is worth remembering that, in their most basic forms, the historical thinking skills are reasoning chronologically, contextualizing, and arguing from evidence. Accordingly, you can look at the essay you have constructed and ask yourself if you have done all three of those things. If you have constructed a good thesis, created a good argument, and supported the argument with evidence, you will have automatically demonstrated the three categories of historical thinking.

Further Practice for the Document-Based Question (DBQ)

To practice creating an outline and writing a response to a DBQ question, you can use the Practice Exams provided in Step 5 of this book. Give yourself 60 minutes to create your essay for the DBQ. Then compare your work to the answer and explanation provided. To gain more practice responding to a DBQ, go to the College Board website (www.collegeboard.org).

CHAPTER 8

The Long-Essay Question

IN THIS CHAPTER

Summary: The AP European History Exam contains a long-essay question that involves using your European history knowledge to create a historical argument. In this chapter you'll find out what to expect and how to develop a strategy to do well on this task.

Key Idea:

✪ The key to doing well on the long-essay question is being able to write a history essay of high quality—one that answers the question, makes an argument, and supports the argument with evidence.

Introduction

The long-essay question tests your ability to use your knowledge of European history to create a historical argument. On the AP European History Exam, you will choose one of three available long-essay questions and have 40 minutes to respond. All three questions will focus on the same theme and skill, but give you a choice of three periods for consideration (periods 1, 2–3, 3–4). The keys to success are choosing properly and following the five steps to writing a history essay of high quality.

Choosing Your Topic

You can choose which one of the topics you want to write about. The key to choosing properly is to understand that you are *not* looking for the "easiest" question to answer; each of the questions you encounter on the exam will take equal amounts of knowledge and effort. The key is to recognize the question for which you are best prepared to respond. Keep in mind the five-step process to writing a history essay of high quality. That means that you should look at each question and ask yourself: "For which of these questions can I most quickly write a clear thesis and three topic sentences that I can illustrate and support with several specific examples?" Then choose your question based on this analysis.

Applying the Five Steps to a High-Quality History Essay

Once you have chosen your question, simply follow the five-step formula to constructing a history essay of high quality:

Step 1. Find the action words in the question, and determine what the question wants you to do.

Step 2. Compose a thesis that responds to the question and gives you something specific to support and illustrate.

Step 3. Compose your topic sentences, and make sure that they add up logically to support your thesis.

Step 4. Support and illustrate your topic sentences with specific examples.

Step 5. *If you have time*, compose a one-paragraph conclusion that supports your thesis.

Also, remember the pitfalls to avoid:

- **Avoid long sentences with multiple clauses.** Your goal is to write the clearest sentence possible; most often the clearest sentence is a relatively short sentence.
- **Do not get caught up in digressions.** No matter how fascinating or insightful you find some idea or fact, if it doesn't directly support or illustrate your thesis, don't put it in.
- **Skip the mystery.** Do not ask a lot of rhetorical questions, and do not go for a surprise ending. The readers are looking for your thesis, your argument, and your evidence; give it to them in a clear, straightforward manner.

Sample Question

Let's look at a question similar to the one you'll encounter on the AP European History Exam and see how you could approach it.

Question: Discuss the relative successes and failures of seventeenth-century monarchs' attempts to consolidate political power within their kingdoms.

Outlining Your Essay

Formulate a thesis statement such as the one below:

Thesis: The success or failure of seventeenth-century monarchs to consolidate political power within their kingdoms rested on their ability to form an alliance with a rising commercial class.

Then you outline between three and five topic sentences that build a logical case for your thesis. Note specific examples you will use to support and illustrate the points asserted in the topic sentences:

Topic Sentence A: The French monarchy built the most absolutist government by cementing an alliance with both the clergy and middle class, and by using the great administrative expertise of both to build a powerful centralized bureaucracy.

Specific Examples: Richelieu's division of France into 30 administrative districts, each under the control of an *intendent*, an administrative bureaucrat, usually chosen from the middle class.

Topic Sentence B: In England, the Parliament successfully resisted the absolutist designs of the Stuart monarchy because the English Parliament of the seventeenth century was a pre-existing alliance of nobles and well-to-do members of a thriving merchant and professional class that saw itself as a voice of the "English people."

Specific Examples: Social composition of the two camps in the English Civil War; the traditional landed nobility and the high church sided with the king; the newer, commercial-based nobles and the merchant class fought for Parliament.

Topic Sentence C: In those areas where the commercial class was less developed, a political standoff between monarch and landed nobility was the norm.

Specific Examples: Brandenburg-Prussia, the independent German states, Austria, and Poland all lacked a well-developed commercial class, and all were characterized by a political compromise between monarchy and traditional elites.

Now you write your essay, beginning with the thesis and starting a new paragraph for each topic sentence. As you write the body of each paragraph, make sure to identify the example you are using and explain why it supports and illustrates your topic sentence. If you have time, you can write a concluding paragraph, but this isn't actually necessary.

Scoring of the Essays

Like the DBQs, the long-essay questions are scored on a point system, but, again, there are no tricks to the scoring, and the best way to get the highest score is to simply write a history essay of high quality. If your essay answers the question with a clear thesis, and develops and supports your thesis with paragraphs made up of clear topic sentences and specific examples, you will get the maximum number of points.

Further Practice for the Long-Essay Question

To practice creating an outline and writing a response to a long-essay question, you can use the practice exam provided in Step 5 of this book. Give yourself 40 minutes. Then compare your work to the answer and explanation provided. To gain more practice responding to this type of question, go to the College Board website (www.collegeboard.org).

STEP **4**

Review the Knowledge You Need to Score High

CHAPTER **9** Major Themes of Modern European History

CHAPTER **10** From the Middle Ages to the Renaissance

CHAPTER **11** The Challenge of the Renaissance

CHAPTER **12** The Reformation and the Fracturing of Christianity

CHAPTER **13** The Great Voyages of Exploration and Early Colonization

CHAPTER **14** Economic Change and Political Consolidation

CHAPTER **15** Economic Change and the Expansion of the State

CHAPTER **16** The Rise of Natural Philosophy, Scientific Revolution, and the Enlightenment

CHAPTER **17** The French Revolution and Empire

CHAPTER **18**   The Industrial Revolution

CHAPTER **19**   Cultural Responses to Revolution and Industrialization

CHAPTER **20**   Mass Politics and Nationalism

CHAPTER **21**   Mass Politics and Imperialism

CHAPTER **22**   Politics of the Extreme and World War I

CHAPTER **23**   The Interwar Years and World War II

CHAPTER **24**   The Cold War, Integration, and Globalization

CHAPTER **25**   Science and Culture

CHAPTER 9

Major Themes of Modern European History

IN THIS CHAPTER

Summary: The AP History course is focused on six broad themes of European history. All of the questions on the AP European History Exam involve one or more of these themes. In this chapter you'll learn more about those six themes.

Key Idea:

The six themes of the AP European History course and exam are as follows:

- ✪ Interaction of Europe and the World
- ✪ Changes in Wealth and Who Had It
- ✪ Changes in Knowledge Systems and Worldview
- ✪ Changes in Society and Its Institutions Before the Individual and Society
- ✪ The Individual and Society
- ✪ National and European Identity

Introduction

The AP European History Exam identifies six main themes in modern European history. These themes are explored throughout the curriculum of AP European history courses. In fact, *all* of the various kinds of questions posed on the AP European History Exam refer to one or more of these themes. The particulars of each theme will be discussed in detail in Chapters 11 through 25. For now, just become familiar with these broad themes, as such familiarity will allow you to take the first step in contextualizing the visual prompts from each question on the exam.

Interaction of Europe and the World

By the fifteenth century, increased wealth flowing into the economies of Western European kingdoms from reviving trade with Eastern civilizations made both the monarchies and the merchant class of Western Europe very wealthy. Beginning in the fifteenth century, the combined investment of those monarchies and merchant classes funded great voyages of exploration across the globe, establishing new trade routes and bringing European civilization into contact with civilizations previously unknown to Europeans. The effects of this exploration and interaction on both the civilization of Western Europe and on those they encountered were profound.

Changes in Wealth and Who Had It

From the fifteenth through the nineteenth centuries, the economies of Western European civilization expanded and changed. The new wealth that flowed into those economies from their trading empires and colonies fostered a shift in the very nature of wealth and in who possessed it. At the outset of the fifteenth century, wealth was land, and it was literally in the hands of those who had the military ability to hold and protect it. Gradually, over the next four centuries, wealth became capital (money in all of its forms), whereas land became simply one form of capital—one more thing that could be bought and sold. The wealthy, those who had and controlled capital, became a larger and slightly more diverse segment of society, ranging from traditional landholders who were savvy enough to transform their traditional holdings into capital-producing concerns, to the class of merchants, bankers, and entrepreneurs who are often referred to as the bourgeoisie.

Changes in Knowledge Systems and Worldview

Throughout the course of modern European history, intellectuals were engaged in the pursuit of knowledge. In traditional or medieval European society, knowledge was produced by church scholars whose abilities to read and write allowed them access to ancient texts. From those texts, they chose information and a worldview that seemed compatible with Christian notions of revealed knowledge and a hierarchical order. Accordingly, traditional Christian scholars found knowledge in texts they believed to be divinely inspired and which presented a worldview in which humans sat in the middle (literally and figuratively) of a cosmos created especially for them by a loving God.

Beginning in the sixteenth century, increased wealth allowed European elites to create secular spaces for intellectual pursuits. This development bred a new type of secular scholar who stressed the use of observation and reason in the creation of knowledge, and who, in due course, successfully challenged the notion of a theocentric universe. This change resulted in a large variety of cultural responses.

Changes in Society and Its Institutions

Beginning in the fifteenth century, the expansion and increasing complexity of the European economy and a corresponding growth in the size of its populations put great stress upon the traditional social structures and institutions of European society. Changes in the means of production and exchange both fostered and benefitted from dramatic changes in where and how the population lived and worked.

The Individual and Society

The economic and social changes occurring from the fifteenth through the twentieth centuries created demands for corresponding changes in the nature of the social hierarchy. Traditional European elites found themselves contending with newer, commercial elites for political power. The pre-industrial period saw women participating in sociocultural change. In the nineteenth century, women, along with industrial and urban workers began to agitate for access to, and sometimes participation in, the wielding of political power.

National and European Identity

The idea of national, and eventually European, identity was often based on shared language, geography, and political consolidation of power. The Reconquest of Spain, the creation of a parliamentary monarchy in England, the unification of Italy and Germany in the late nineteenth century are all examples of states united in their shared beliefs in social, political, cultural, and/or religious values. The idea of a European identity remains in flux, depending on changing economic, political, social, cultural, and legal frameworks.

The Organization of the AP Course into Units

To organize the content relating to these major themes of European history, the College Board has defined four "units," or time periods. These units form the basic structure of the AP course—but don't worry, you won't have to memorize these time periods. They are only a behind-the-scenes organizational structure for the course and won't be part of the AP exam. It may be useful, however, to see what these four units are and to know how they correspond to the review chapters in this book, especially if, besides using this book, you are also using the College Board website to review for the AP exam. The table below provides this information.

UNIT	TIME PERIOD		CHAPTERS IN THIS BOOK
Unit 1	1450–1648	Chapter 11	The Challenge of the Renaissance
		Chapter 12	The Reformation and the Fracturing of Christianity
		Chapter 13	The Great Voyages of Exploration and Early Colonization
		Chapter 14	Economic Change and Political Consolidation
Unit 2	1648–1815	Chapter 15	Economic Change and the Expansion of the State
		Chapter 16	The Rise of Natural Philosophy, Scientific Revolution, and The Enlightenment
		Chapter 17	The French Revolution and Empire
Unit 3	1815–1914	Chapter 18	The Industrial Revolution
		Chapter 19	Cultural Responses to Revolution and Industrialization
		Chapter 20	Mass Politics and Nationalism
		Chapter 21	Mass Politics and Imperialism
Unit 4	1914–Present	Chapter 22	Politics of the Extreme and World War I
		Chapter 23	The Interwar Years and World War II
		Chapter 24	The Cold War, Integration, and Globalization
		Chapter 25	Science and Culture

From the Middle Ages to the Renaissance

The Middle Ages used to be called the "Dark Ages," a term that traditionally (and arbitrarily) encompassed the period from the fall of the Western Roman Empire (476 CE) to either the height of the Black Plague (1347–1349) or until the fall of Christian Constantinople to the Turks in 1453. Then, seemingly full-blown, came the Renaissance. But history is not so neatly divided. Arbitrary, dated divisions ignore cause and effect, frequently stressing chronology at the expense of continuity.

To understand Europe from the fifteenth century onward, it becomes necessary to look at the foundations upon which it was built, and to recognize that the Renaissance, or "rebirth," implies a former birth. The medieval period in Europe was initially characterized by nothing so much as chaos. The Western Roman Empire was brought to its knees by "barbaric" invasions. The resultant supposed loss of classical Greek and Roman learning and culture ignores the rise of another culture, one that would affect the creation of today's Europe: Christianity. By 800 CE, with the establishment of the Holy Roman Empire, feudalism became the dominant social structure at the highest levels, binding church and state, often uncomfortably, in their attempts to control the political, economic, social, religious, and cultural evolution of a modernizing society. Christianity, though a unifying force, did not result in political unity. Political unity, based on nation-states, would be a long time coming.

Feudalism, at its most elemental, established a social hierarchy that affected these political, economic, religious, and cultural elements for centuries. Essentially a pyramidal structure, feudal society had at the very top a king. Everyone below pledged allegiance to the king and to God. Nobles or feudal lords acted to enforce the will of the king. The clergy controlled education and, to a large degree, cultural activity. Knights (the first standing armies) maintained order and fought on behalf of their lords as necessary. Merchants worked for the feudal lords. They held trade fairs and paid fees and taxes. That is, they paid to gain access to towns where they could sell their goods, a fee to set up booths, and a "tax" of sorts on everything sold. Serfs (peasants) worked the land to the benefit of everyone higher in the social pyramid and in return received protection, initially from barbarian raiders (including the Vikings), and then from other feudal lords intent on expanding their fiefdoms. Two events, or series of events, in particular would introduce irreparable cracks in this pyramidal structure: the Crusades and the Black Plague.

The Crusades included eight major and several minor wars that began in 1095 and continued until nearly the end of the fifteenth century. They did not simply extend the reach of Christianity. Neither did they enrich solely the Roman Church. The Crusades resulted in an exchange of scientific and cultural ideas, goods, traditions, and even diseases, and they led to the establishment of transportation and trade networks across continents. Manufacture of goods, from weaponry to foodstuffs, and an increase in industry (for example, shipbuilding) were equally noteworthy. As goods made their way between Asia and Europe, the merchant class began to expand. It held expanded trade fairs and promoted the growth of cities.

The Black Plague weakened the pyramidal structure by empowering the serfs. The plague did not discriminate, wiping out as much as 50 percent of Europe's population at all levels. As a result, some feudal lords lost their labor pool and had to recruit workers from elsewhere. For the first time, serfs could bargain and get paid for their labor. Control was no longer absolutely in the hands of feudal lords. A middle class began to form, led by merchants and artisans and guilds, and sustained by the peasant class.

These changes should sound familiar. They echo what had happened millennia before when the domestication of animals and agriculture led to settlement, which led to differentiated social roles, division and specialization of labor, and to some standardization of produced goods.

One of the great ironies of history is that during the Middle Ages, when the Crusades represented the Christian attempt to reclaim the Holy Land from the "infidel" Muslim, a sort of proto-Renaissance was taking place on the Muslim-dominated Iberian Peninsula. Between 711 and 1492, the Iberian Peninsula was under the control of the Umayyad Dynasty. The Muslim government established hospitals (open to all), public libraries, and schools of translation; these last provided alternate versions of classical science and philosophy, rescued a great deal of classical literature from oblivion, and provoked new directions of scholarship. It established universities. It introduced chess. It introduced irrigation systems; some are still in use today. Literature flourished in the form of the first multicultural poetry, primarily love poetry written in Arabic and Ibero-Romance.

The attempts by Christians to retake the peninsula gave us the *chansons de geste,* epics that told the history of the Reconquest of the Iberian Peninsula. As had the epics of classical times, they continued the tradition of teaching history to the general public. Literature and artwork often revealed or recreated historical events and frequently stressed the importance of the heroic individual. Emphasis on the individual would in turn lead to a less theocentric, more human-centered vision of the universe, a decidedly Renaissance trait. Architecture, however, perhaps most reflects the changes in attitude between medieval and renaissance thought. The secular Alhambra in Granada and the religious Great Mosque of Córdoba both made use of ancient architectural elements—like the arch—that would enable Europe's medieval architecture to produce Gothic wonders. Besides physical changes reflected in such architecture, the resurgence of a belief in man's ability to contemplate the divine through human endeavor characterized the modernizing world. It allowed people to explore potential and possibility instead of resigning themselves to their position in the social hierarchy.

Language as well would play no small role in this change. The vernacular(s) replaced Latin as the language of trade and education and paved the way for the Reformation and Counter-Reformation of the High Renaissance.

One last element to consider as laying the foundations for the Renaissance is warfare. Technological advances resulting from medieval Asian–European interactions (the use of gunpowder, cannons, and the longbow) led to the "impersonalization," almost the "dehumanization," of war. No longer was combat primarily face-to-face. Cannons and the longbow made it possible to kill "the enemy" more efficiently and from a distance. The word "enemy" is critical here as it represents a nameless, faceless opponent. Changes in weaponry would also lead to changes in political organization and to a militarily based social hierarchy.

As the Renaissance would have southern and northern European manifestations, so did the Middle Ages. Northern Europe, the British Isles, France, Kievan Russia, and Sicily were changed forever by the Vikings and their descendants, the Normans: by their military and trade excursions, expansion and settlement, and conversion to Christianity. It was the Normans, after all, who under the leadership of William the Conqueror conquered England at the Battle of Hastings in 1066, ending Saxon rule and paving the way for the subsequent ruling dynasties (especially the medieval Plantagenets) that would have profound cultural, political, and juridical effects.

In order to understand how the medieval foundations allowed the building of the Renaissance, students should focus on two words: legacies and purpose. Legacies encompass the ideas of continuity, action/reaction, and cause and effect. Purpose is one way to respond to the most basic of questions: why?

A good example of continuity can be seen by looking at the reign of King Henry II of England. Henry's legacies include groundbreaking work in establishing the jury system, replacing Roman law with common law in England, and gaining some control over powerful feudal lords. He is best known, however, for the following things: first, his marriage to Eleanor of Aquitaine and his attempts to expand England's control in France. The latter resulted in almost 400 years of war. He is also known for his friendship with Thomas à Becket. Henry's friend and drinking companion, Thomas à Becket studied theology at the University of Bologna in Italy, where, among other things, he evidently grew a conscience. Home in England, and elected Archbishop of Canterbury, he defied the king by defending the rights of the Church. In response to Henry's exasperation over not gaining juridical control of the church, four of Henry's knights rode to Canterbury and murdered Becket in the cathedral. Two hundred years later, Geoffrey Chaucer would set his fictional pilgrims, who came from all social classes, on their trek to Thomas à Becket's shrine. Chaucer wrote in the vernacular. He matched style and literary form to characters who came from all walks of life. King Henry's legacies are obvious and long lasting: elimination of trial by ordeal, the use of judges and juries, and the change from a feudal monarchy to one with a bureaucracy made up of professionals, which would eventually lead to the establishment of a representative parliament.

The Renaissance was not a brand-new creation, but the culmination of changes begun before and during the Middle Ages. History is not contained or defined by isolated eras. It reflects the actions and reactions, the innovations and the adaptations of everything that has come before. As you study Europe's history, you might consider the following guiding questions:

- What are the roots of something seemingly new? For example, compare the Magna Carta, the United States Bill of Rights, and the French *Declaration of the Rights of Man*.
- What is the "climate of opinion" of a given era? If the Middle Ages were theocentric, as visible in university curricula, literature, art, and architecture, what characterized the Renaissance and made it more "humanistic"?

- What events or ideas made possibility, potential, freedom, individuality, and responsibility important? What did these elements make possible? How, for example, might Renaissance thought have influenced exploration, discovery, and settlement of new worlds?
- What is the role of the arts in reference to either instigating change or reflecting contemporary issues and manners? Were the arts idealistic or realistic? In other words, what is the *purpose* of the arts at any given moment?
- How did the power or status of the individual change over time? How did merchants become a dominant power during the Renaissance? How did women seek to define themselves within the confines of a changing society? What was the role of demographic shifts in these changes?

History is more than a linear chronology. It is a consideration of causes and effects, of connections, of changes, adaptations, and innovations over time. History **is** time.

Further Resources

Novels

Michael Crichton, *Timeline*

Ildefonso Falcones, *The Cathedral of the Sea*

Ken Follett, *Pillars of the Earth*

Edith Pargeter, *A Bloody Field by Shrewsbury*

Various mysteries, including *Sister Fidelma* by Peter Tremayne and *The Chronicles of Brother* Cadfael series by Ellis Peters (pen name of Edith Pargeter). A television adaptation titled *Cadfael* is available on DVD and streaming media.

Films

El Cid (1961)

Becket (1964)

The Lion in Winter (1968)

The Name of the Rose (1986)

Henry V (with Laurence Olivier, 1944; with Kenneth Branagh, 1989)

CHAPTER 11

The Challenge of the Renaissance

IN THIS CHAPTER

Summary: The Renaissance refers to the revival of commerce, the renewal of interest in the classical world, and the growing belief in the potential of human achievement that occurred on the Italian peninsula between 1350 and 1550. This chapter describes the society, values, and artistic achievements of the Italian Renaissance and their spread to northern Europe.

Key Terms:

- ☼ **Guilds** Exclusive organizations that monopolized the skilled trades in Europe from the medieval period until broken by the development of cottage industries in the eighteenth century.
- ☼ **Humanism** In the Renaissance, both a belief in the value of human achievement and an educational program based on classical Greek and Roman languages and values.
- ☼ *Studia humanitas* The educational program of the Renaissance, founded on knowledge of the classical Latin and Greek languages and literatures.
- ☼ *Oration on the Dignity of Man* One of the best articulations (1486) of the belief in the dignity and potential of humans that characterized Renaissance humanism, authored by Giovanni Pico della Mirandola.
- ☼ *The Prince* The book by Niccolò Machiavelli (1513), which marks the shift from a "civic ideal" to a "princely ideal" in Renaissance humanism. The princely ideal is focused on the qualities and strategies necessary for attaining and holding social and political power.

- **Neoplatonism** In the Renaissance and Early Modern period, a philosophy based on that of Plato, which contended that reality was located in a changeless world of forms and which, accordingly, spurred the study of mathematics. It also refers to the attempt to reconcile pagan and Christian ideals, and the artistic idea that contemplation of beauty led to contemplation of the divine.
- **Florentine Academy** An informal gathering of humanists devoted to the revival of the teachings of Plato, founded in 1462 under the leadership of Marsilio Ficino and the patronage of Cosimo de' Medici. One of the leading lights of the Florentine Academy, besides Marilio Ficino, was Pico della Mirandola.
- **Frescos** Paintings done either on wet or dry plaster; an important medium of art during the Renaissance.
- **Michelangelo's *David*** Sculpted by Michelangelo Buonarroti (1504), this sculpture of the biblical hero is characteristic of the last and most heroic phase of Renaissance art. Sculpted from a single piece of marble, it is larger than real life and offers a vision of the human body and spirit that is more dramatic than real life, an effect that Michelangelo produced by making the head and hands deliberately too large for the torso.
- **Treaty of Lodi/Peace of Lodi** The treaty (1454–1455) that established a mutual defensive pact among Venice, Milan, Florence, Naples, and the Papal States. It lapsed after the French invasion of 1494.
- ***Colloquies*** Dialogues written (beginning in 1519) by the most important and influential of the northern humanists, Desiderius Erasmus, for the purpose of teaching his students both the Latin language and how to live a good life.
- **Lay piety** A tradition in the smaller, independent German provinces, flourishing in the fifteenth and sixteenth centuries, whereby organized groups promoted pious behavior and learning outside the bureaucracy of the church.
- **Patronage** The support of artists and artisans, frequently by both aristocrats and the newly emergent middle class merchant; also, the awarding of noble titles and government appointments as a means of gaining political support.

Key Individuals:
- Machiavelli
- Castiglione
- Palladio
- Leonardo da Vinci
- El Greco
- Rubens
- Erasmus
- Bruegel
- Shakespeare

Introduction

KEY IDEA

The word *Renaissance* means "rebirth." Historically, it refers to a time in Western civilization (1350–1550) that was characterized by the revival of three things: commerce, interest in the classical world, and the belief in the potential of human achievement. For reasons that are geographic, economic, and social, the Renaissance began in Italy, where expanded trade with the East flowed into Europe via the Mediterranean Sea and, therefore, through the Italian city-states. With the invention of the printing press, both ideas and commerce spread north from Italy and led to the Northern Renaissance, characterized by a more religious (as opposed to a secular, or humanist) slant and credited with directly influencing the Protestant Reformation. The Renaissance flowered for approximately 200 years, and, as a result of increased military, economic, and cultural interactions with the rest of Europe, made its way north.

Italian Society of the Renaissance

The society of the Italian peninsula between 1350 and 1550 was unique in Western civilization. The most outstanding characteristic of Italian society was the degree to which it was urban. By 1500, seven of the ten largest cities in Europe were in Italy. Whereas most of Western Europe was characterized by large kingdoms with powerful monarchs and increasingly centralized bureaucracies, the Italian peninsula was made up of numerous independent city-states, such as Milan, Florence, Venice, and Genoa. These city-states were, by virtue of their location, flourishing centers of commerce in control of reviving networks of trade with Eastern empires.

Social status within these city-states was determined primarily by occupation, rather than by birth or the ownership of land, as was common in the rest of Europe during this period. The trades were controlled by government-protected monopolies called guilds. Members of the manufacturing guilds, such as clothiers and metalworkers, sat at the top of the social hierarchy. The next most prestigious were the professional groups that included bankers, administrators, and merchants. They were followed by skilled laborers, such as the stone masons.

Because the city-states of Italy developed as commercial centers, wealth was not based on the control of land as it was in the rest of Europe during this period. Instead, wealth was in the form of capital, and power was the ability to lend it. Accordingly, the traditional landed aristocracy of the Italian peninsula was not as politically powerful as their other European counterparts. Rather, powerful merchant families dominated socially and politically. Their status as the holders of capital also made the commercial elites of Italy powerful throughout Europe, as the monarchs of the more traditional kingdoms had to come to them when seeking loans to finance their wars of territorial expansion.

The city-states of Renaissance Italy were set up according to a variety of models. Some, like Naples, were ruled by hereditary monarchs; others were ruled by powerful families, such as the Medicis of Florence; still others, specifically Venice, were led by the *doge*, the elected civil, ecclesiastical, and military head of the Venetian Republic.

Renaissance Values

Before the Renaissance, the values of European civilization reflected the beliefs of Christianity and the social relations of traditional feudal hierarchy. During the Renaissance, these traditional values were transformed to reflect both the ambition and pride of the commercial class that dominated Renaissance Italian society. In contrast to traditional European noblemen, who competed for prestige on the battlefield or in jousting and fencing tournaments, successful Renaissance men competed via displays of civic duty, which included patronage of philosophy and the arts.

At the center of the Renaissance system of values was humanism. Renaissance humanism combined an admiration for classical Greek and Roman literature with a newfound confidence in what modern men could achieve. Accordingly, Renaissance humanism was characterized by the *studia humanitas*, an educational program founded on knowledge of the classical Latin and Greek languages and scholarship. Once the languages had been mastered, the Renaissance humanist could read deeply in the classical works of the ancient Greek and Roman authors, absorbing what the philosophers of the last great Western civilizations had to teach them about how to succeed in life and how to live a good life.

To the Renaissance humanist, the ancient Greek and Roman philosophers were guides, but guides whose achievements could be equaled and eventually improved upon. The ultimate goal of the Renaissance humanist program was the truly well-rounded citizen, one who excelled in grammar, rhetoric, poetry, history, politics, and moral philosophy. These scholarly achievements were valued in their own right, as a testament to the dignity and ability of man, but also for the way in which they contributed to the glory of the city-state.

Prime examples of early Renaissance humanists were Petrarch, who celebrated the glory of ancient Rome in his *Letters to the Ancient Dead*, and Boccaccio, who compiled an encyclopedia of Greek and Roman mythology. The best articulation of the belief in the dignity and potential of man that characterized Renaissance humanism was Pico della Mirandola's *Oration on the Dignity of Man* (1486). In the *Oration*, della Mirandola argued that God endowed man with the ability to shape his own being and that man has the obligation to become all that he can be.

By the late Renaissance, humanism lost some of its ideal character, where scholarly achievements were valued for their own sake, and took on a more cynical quality that promoted only individual success. This shift is sometimes characterized as a shift from a "civic ideal" to a "princely ideal," as texts like Castiglione's *The Book of the Courtier* (1513–1518) and Machiavelli's *The Prince* (1513) focused on the qualities and strategies necessary for attaining and holding social and political power.

Artistic Achievement of the Renaissance

The unique structure of Renaissance society and the corresponding system of Renaissance values combined to give birth to one of the most amazing bursts of artistic creativity in the history of Western civilization. The wealthy and powerful elites of Renaissance society patronized the arts for the fame and prestige that it brought them. The competitive spirit of the elites both within and among the Italian city-states meant that artists and craftsmen were in almost constant demand.

For example, Lorenzo de' Medici, who led the ruling family of Florence from 1469 until his death in 1492, commissioned work by almost all of the great Renaissance artists. As an art patron, he was rivaled by Pope Julius II, whose patronage of the arts during his papacy (1503–1513), including the construction of St. Peter's Basilica, transformed Rome into one of Europe's most beautiful cities.

The artists themselves usually hailed not from the elite class but from the class of guild craftsmen. Young men with skill were identified and apprenticed to guild shops run by master craftsmen. Accordingly, there was no separation between the "artistic" and "commercial" sides of the Renaissance art world. All works were commissioned, and the artist was expected to give the patron what he ordered. The Renaissance artist demonstrated his creativity within the bounds of explicit contracts that specified all details of the work.

Another aspect of the guild culture that contributed to the brilliant innovations of the Renaissance period was the fact that the various media—such as sculpture, painting, and architecture—were not viewed as separate disciplines; instead, the Renaissance apprentice was expected to master the techniques of each of these art forms. As a result, mature Renaissance artists were able to work with a variety of materials and to apply ideas and techniques learned in one medium to projects in another.

Whereas medieval art had been characterized by religious subject matter, the Renaissance style took from its Greek and Roman forebears the human being and the human form as its subject. The transition can be seen in the series of frescos painted by Giotto in the fourteenth century. Although he still focused on religious subject matter (i.e., the life of St. Francis), Giotto depicted the human characters in realistic detail and with a concern for their psychological reaction to the events of St. Francis's life. The Renaissance artist's concern for the human form in all its complexity is illustrated by two great sculptures, each nominally depicting the biblical character of David:

- One is Donatello's version (completed in 1432), which was the first life-size, free-standing, bronze nude sculpture since antiquity. The sculpture depicts David as a young Florentine gentleman. Goliath was understood to be the Papacy.
- The second version was sculpted by Michelangelo Buonarroti (completed in 1504) and is characteristic of the last and most idealistic phase of Renaissance art. Sculpted from a single piece of marble, Michelangelo's *David* is larger than life and offers a vision of the human body and spirit that is more dramatic than real life, an effect that Michelangelo produced by making the head and hands deliberately too large for the torso. Upon its completion, the rulers of Florence originally placed Michelangelo's *David* at the entrance to the city hall as a symbol of Florentine strength.

Not to be overlooked during this century was the introduction of the printing press, which allowed more rapid dissemination of ideas. Also, the use of the vernacular language gave access to documents, fiction, and religious texts and began to reach a growing audience.

The Renaissance and Scientific Advancements

Using a scientific method, or proceeding through the stages of hypothesis, observation, experimentation, and replication, individuals like Copernicus and Galileo challenged the accepted wisdom of the day by developing the heliocentric ("sun-centered") vision of the universe. Physicians followed a similar form of inquiry and used anatomical studies as well to put to rest the idea that human health was governed by the four humors. Such advances often contradicted Church teachings and led to punishment (including excommunication) of early scientists.

The Spread of the Renaissance

In the late fifteenth century and throughout the sixteenth century, the Renaissance spread to France, Germany, England, and Spain. The catalyst for this spread was the breakup of the equilibrium that characterized the politics of the Italian peninsula. An internal balance of power had been established by the Treaty of Lodi (1454–1455), which brought Milan, Naples, Florence, Venice, and the Papal States into a mutual defense alliance. The balance of power was shattered in 1494, when Naples, supported by both Florence and the pope, prepared to attack Milan. The Milanese despot, Ludovico il Moro, appealed to the French king, Charles VIII of France, for help. Ludovico invited the king to lead French troops into Italy and to revive his old dynastic claims to Naples, which the French had ruled from 1266 to 1435. French troops invaded the Italian peninsula in 1494 and forced Florence, Naples, and the Papal States to make major concessions. In response, the pope and the Venetians persuaded the Holy Roman Emperor, King Ferdinand of Aragon, to bring troops to Italy to help resist French aggression. From the late 1490s through most of the sixteenth century, Italy became a battleground in a war for supremacy between European monarchs.

Once the isolation of the Italian peninsula was shattered, the ideals and values of the Renaissance spread from Italy through a variety of agents:

- Artisans, teachers, theatrical troupes, and musicians migrating out of Italy
- Students who came to study in Italy and then returned home
- European merchants whose interests now penetrated the peninsula
- Various lay groups seeking to spread their message of piety
- The use of the vernacular, as opposed to Latin, for religious, economic, and socio-cultural writings

However, the major cause of the spread of Renaissance ideals and values was the printing press. Invented by Johannes Gutenberg in the German city of Mainz in about 1445 in response to increased demand for books from an increasingly literate public, the moveable-type printing press allowed for faster, cheaper, mass-produced books to be created and distributed throughout Europe. By 1500, between fifteen and twenty million books were in circulation. Among the ideas that spread with the books were the thoughts and philosophies of the Renaissance humanists, which were both adopted and transformed in northern Europe.

The most important and influential of the northern humanists was Desiderius Erasmus, sometimes referred to as "the prince of the humanists." Spreading the Renaissance belief in the value of education, Erasmus made his living as an educator. He taught his students both the Latin language and lessons on how to live a good life from Latin dialogues that he wrote himself. Published under the title of *Colloquies*, Erasmus's dialogues also displayed the humanist's faith in both the power of learning and the ability of man by satirizing the old scholastic notions that the truth about God and nature could be discerned only by priests. Erasmus argued instead that, by mastering ancient languages, any man could teach himself to read both the Bible and the works of an array of ancient philosophers, thereby learning the truth about God and nature for himself.

In France, England, and Spain, the existence of strong monarchies meant that the Renaissance was centered in the royal courts. In the smaller, independent German provinces, the characteristics of the Renaissance were absorbed into a tradition of lay piety, where organized groups, such as the Brethren of Common Life, promoted pious behavior and learning outside the bureaucracy of the church. In that context, German scholars, such as Martin Luther, who were educated in a context that combined the humanistic and lay piety traditions, would be prominent in the creation of the Reformation.

Review Questions

Multiple Choice

Questions 1 through 3 refer to the following passage:

[Considering the origin of] grace, I find one universal rule concerning it, which seems to me worth more in this matter than any other in all things human that are done or said: and that is to avoid affectation to the uttermost and as it were a very sharp and dangerous rock; and, to use possibly a new word, to practice in everything a certain nonchalance [*sprezzatura*] that shall conceal design and show that what is done and said is done without effort and almost without thought. From this I believe grace is in large measure derived, because everyone knows the difficulty of those things that are rare and done well, and therefore facility in them excites the highest admiration.

[And] I wish to discuss another matter, which I deem of great importance and therefore think our Courtier ought by no means to omit: and this is to know how to draw and to have acquaintance with the very art of painting. . . . And truly he who does not esteem this art, seems to me very unreasonable; . . . [For] the ancients greatly prized both the art and the artists, which thus attained the summit of highest excellence; very sure proof of which may be found in the antique marble and bronze statues that yet are seen. . . .

Baldassare Castiglione, *The Book of the Courtier,* 1508–1513

1. In what way is the passage indicative of the "princely ideal" of the late Renaissance?
   A. It promotes individual achievement.
   B. It is by the author of *The Prince.*
   C. It describes the manner in which a prince should behave.
   D. It focuses on the value of personal achievement for individual success rather than the civic good.

2. How does the passage illustrate the transformation of traditional values into Renaissance values?
   A. It stresses the pursuit of excellence.
   B. It extols the virtue of skill in the visual arts rather than the martial arts.
   C. It stresses the changing social status of the artist.
   D. It values grace.

3. In what way does the passage illustrate the values of Renaissance humanism?
   A. It instructs the individual to pay attention to personal appearance.
   B. It argues that reason should be the measure of all things.
   C. It looks to the ancients for guidance in matters of taste and accomplishment.
   D. It encourages all men to aspire to be Courtiers.

Short Answer

4. Briefly explain and illustrate the difference between the "civic ideal" in Renaissance humanism and the "princely ideal" that supplanted it.

Answers and Explanations

1. **D** is correct because the "princely ideal" of the late Renaissance focused on the value of achievements, such as grace and nonchalance (*sprezzatura*) in promoting individual success, rather than the civic good. A is incorrect because it is too general; all Renaissance ideals promoted individual achievement. B is incorrect because Machiavelli is the author of *The Prince,* not Castiglione. C is incorrect because *The Courtier* offers advice to all would-be gentlemen, not just princes.

2. **B** is correct because, during the Renaissance, skill in the visual arts was more highly valued than skill in the martial arts. A and D are incorrect because individual achievement and grace were valued in both traditional and Renaissance culture. C is incorrect because the passage makes no reference to the social status of artists.

3. **C** is correct because Renaissance humanism looked backward to the accomplishments of ancient Greece and Rome for guidance and inspiration. A is incorrect because attention to personal appearance was not unique to Renaissance humanism. B is incorrect because neither Renaissance humanism nor the passage argued that reason should be the measure of all things. D is incorrect because neither Renaissance humanism nor the passage encouraged all men to be Courtiers.

4. Suggested answer:

Thesis: The "civic ideal" in Renaissance humanism valued individual achievement in scholarship and the arts for its own sake, as a fulfillment of God's gift and as a part of good citizenship. The "princely ideal" that supplanted it was less idealistic, valuing individual achievement in scholarship and the arts as a tool for individual success.

Paragraph Outline:

I. Pico della Mirandola's *Oration on the Dignity of Man* (1486) as an example of the belief in the dignity and potential of man that characterized Renaissance humanism.

II. Castiglione's *The Book of the Courtier* (1513–1518) and Machiavelli's *The Prince* (1513) as examples of individual achievement and refinement for the purpose of attaining and holding social status and political power.

Rapid Review

The revival of commerce, interest in the classical world, and belief in the potential of human achievement that occurred on the Italian peninsula between 1350 and 1550 is known as the Renaissance. Within the independent, urban city-states of Renaissance Italian society, the successful merchant class sought a well-rounded life of achievement and civic virtue, which led them to give their patronage to scholars and artists. Accordingly, both scholarship and artistic achievement reached new heights, and new philosophies like humanism and Neoplatonism were fashioned. In 1494, mounting jealousy and mistrust between the Italian city-states caused the leaders of Milan to invite intervention by the powerful French monarchy, thereby breaking a delicate balance of power and causing the Italian peninsula to become a battleground in a war for supremacy among European monarchies. The destruction of the independence of the Italian city-states caused the spread and transformation of Renaissance ideals and values. A northern European humanism, less secular than its Italian counterpart, developed and served as the foundation of the Reformation.

Further Resources

Machiavelli, *La Mandragola* ("The Mandrake Root"). This play is the source of the line "the end justifies the means."

Irving Stone, *The Agony and the Ecstasy*, which is also a film

A Season of Giants, a made-for-television movie about the life of Michelangelo

Michelangelo and Petrarch, various poems

Boccaccio, Decameron (excerpts)

Erasmus, *In Praise of Folly*

Various films appeared to commemorate the 500th anniversary of the death of Leonardo da Vinci.

CHAPTER 12

The Reformation and the Fracturing of Christianity

IN THIS CHAPTER

Summary: In the sixteenth century, the preoccupation of the Roman Church with worldly matters and its failure to meet the needs of an increasingly literate population led to challenges to its doctrine and authority. This chapter describes the rise of Protestant churches in northern Europe and the Catholic Church's response in the Counter-Reformation.

Key Terms:

- ✪ **Papal States** A kingdom in central Italy, ruled directly by the pope until Italian unification (1861–1870).
- ✪ **Indulgences** Certificates of absolution sold by the church forgiving people of their sins, sometimes even before they committed them, in return for a monetary contribution. The selling of indulgences was one of the practices that Martin Luther objected to.
- ✪ **Millenarianism** The belief that one is living in the last days of the world and that the judgment day is at hand (originally tied to the belief that the end would come in the year AD 1000).
- ✪ **Salvation by Faith Alone** One of the central tenets of Martin Luther's theology: the belief that salvation is a gift from God given to all who possess true faith.

- **Scripture Alone (*Sola Scriptura*)** One of the central tenets of Martin Luther's theology: the belief that scripture is the only guide to knowledge of God. (In contrast, the Catholic Church holds that there are two guides to knowledge of God: scripture and Church tradition.)
- **Priesthood of All Believers** One of the central tenets of Martin Luther's theology: the belief that all who have true faith are "priests," that is, they are competent to read and understand scripture.
- ***The Ninety-Five Theses*** The 95 propositions or challenges to official Church theology posted by Martin Luther on the door of Wittenberg castle church in the autumn of 1517.
- **Peace of Augsburg** The treaty, signed in 1555, that established the principle of "whoever rules, his religion" and signaled to Rome that the German princes would not go to war with each other over religion.
- **Peasantry** The class of rural, agricultural laborers in traditional European society.
- **Huguenots** The sixteenth- and seventeenth-century term for French Protestants.
- **Edict of Nantes** A royal edict that established the principle of religious toleration in France, proclaimed in 1598 and revoked in 1685.
- **Anglican Church** The state church of England, established by Henry VIII in the early sixteenth century when he decided to break from the Church in Rome.
- **Dissenters** The collective name for Protestant groups who refused to join the Anglican Church in England.
- **Predestination** The Calvinist belief that asserts that God has predetermined which people will be saved and which will be damned.
- **The elect** The name given in Calvinist theology to the group of people who have been predestined by God for salvation.
- **Anabaptists** A sect of radical Protestant reformers in Europe in the sixteenth century who considered true Protestant faith to require social reform.
- **Council of Trent** The Counter-Reformation council of the Catholic Church that began its deliberations in 1545. Despite its reformist aims, it continued to insist that the Catholic Church was the final arbiter in all matters of faith.
- **Inquisition** An institution within the Catholic Church, created in 1478 to enforce the conversion of Muslims and Jews in Spain. It was revived and expanded during the Reformation to combat all perceived threats to orthodoxy and the Church's authority.
- **St. Bartholomew's Day Massacre** King Charles IX's massacre of Huguenots in August 1572.
- **Thirty Years' War (1618–1648)** The "last of the religious wars," but actually a European-wide struggle for dominance among the Bourbon and Habsburg dynasties and the Holy Roman Empire.

Key Individuals:

- Sir Thomas More
- King Henry VIII (England)
- Henri IV (France)
- Elizabeth I (England)

Introduction

The Reformation in sixteenth-century Europe began as an effort to reform the Catholic Church, which many believed had become too concerned with worldly matters. Soon, however, the Church found itself facing a serious challenge from a brilliant German theologian, Martin Luther, and his followers. What began as a protest evolved into a revolution with social and political overtones. At stake was secular as opposed to religious political control. By the end of the century, a Europe that had been united by a single Church was deeply divided, as the Catholic and Protestant faiths vied for the minds and hearts of the people.

The Need for a Religious Reformation

By the onset of the sixteenth century, the Catholic Church of Europe was facing a serious set of interconnected problems. Concern was growing that the Church had become too worldly and corrupt in its practices. The Church, and particularly the papacy in Rome, was widely seen to be more concerned with building and retaining worldly power and wealth than in guiding souls to salvation. The pope was not only the head of a powerful Church hierarchy, but he was the ruler of the Papal States, a kingdom that encompassed much of the central portion of the Italian peninsula. He collected taxes, kept an army, and used his religious power to influence politics in every kingdom in Europe.

The selling of indulgences (which allowed people to be absolved of their sins, sometimes even before they committed them, by making a monetary contribution to the Church) is just one example of the way in which the Church seemed more concerned with amassing power and wealth than with guiding the faithful to salvation. To many common people who yearned for a powerful, personal, and emotional connection with God, the Church not only failed to provide it but worked actively to discourage it in the following ways:

- By protecting the power of the priesthood
- By saying the mass in Latin, a language understood by only the educated elite
- By refusing to allow the printing of the Bible in the vernacular

The Lutheran Revolt

Martin Luther was an unlikely candidate to lead a revolt against the Church. The son of a mine manager in eastern Germany, Luther received a humanistic education, studying law before being drawn to the Church and being ordained as a priest in 1507. Continuing his education, Luther received a doctorate of theology from the University of Wittenberg and was appointed to the faculty there in 1512.

The revolutionary ideas that would come to define Lutheran theology were a product of Luther's personal search. Luther believed that he was living in the last days of the world and that God's final judgment would soon be upon the world. This view, now referred to as millenarianism and widespread in sixteenth-century Europe, led Luther to become obsessed with the question of how any human being could be good enough to deserve salvation. He found his answer through the rigorous study of scripture, and he formulated three interconnected theological assertions:

- Salvation by Faith Alone, which declared that salvation came only to those who had true faith

- Scripture Alone, which stated that scripture was the only source of true knowledge of God's will
- The Priesthood of All Believers, which argued that all true believers received God's grace and were, therefore, priests in God's eyes

Each of Luther's assertions put him in direct opposition to the Church's orthodox theology:

- Salvation by Faith Alone contradicted the Church's assertion that salvation was gained both by having faith and by performing works of piety and charity.
- Scripture Alone contradicted the Church's assertion that there were two sources of true knowledge of God: scripture and the traditions of the Church.
- The Priesthood of All Believers contradicted the Church's assertion that only ordained priests could read and correctly interpret scripture.

Creation and Spread of the Protestant Movement

In the autumn of 1517, Luther launched his protest by tacking 95 theses, or propositions, that ran contrary to the theology and practice of the Church to the door of the Wittenberg castle church. His students quickly translated them from Latin into the German vernacular and distributed printed versions throughout the German-speaking kingdoms and provinces. With the aid of the printing press, Luther attracted many followers, but the survival of a Protestant movement was due to the political climate. Had the papacy moved quickly to excommunicate Luther and his followers, the movement might not have survived. However, Luther found a powerful protector in Frederick of Saxony, the prince of Luther's district. Frederick was one of seven electors, the princes who elected the Holy Roman Emperor to whom the princes of the German districts owed their allegiance. Frederick's protection caused the pope to delay Luther's excommunication until 1520. By that time, it was too late; Luther and his followers had established throughout Germany congregations for the kind of Christian worship that, after 1529, would be known as Protestant.

Luther promoted his theology to both the nobility and common people. To the nobility, he wrote an "Address to the Christian Nobility of the German Nation" (1520), which appealed both to the German princes' desire for greater unity and power and to their desire to be out from under the thumb of an Italian pope. To the common people, he addressed "The Freedom of the Christian Man" (1520), in which he encouraged common men to obey their Christian conscience and respect those in authority who seemed to possess true Christian principles. Through this strategy, Luther offered the noble princes of Germany an opportunity to break with the Roman Church and papacy without losing the obedience of the common people. It was an opportunity that was too good to pass up. By 1555, the German princes made it clear that they would no longer bow to Rome; they signed the Peace of Augsburg, which established the principle of "whoever rules, his religion" and signaled to Rome that the German princes would not go to war with each other over religion.

Once it gained a foothold in northern Germany, Protestantism tended to flourish in those areas where the local rulers were either unwilling or not strong enough to enforce orthodoxy and loyalty to Rome. Accordingly, the Protestant movement spread with success to the Netherlands, Scandinavia, Scotland, and England, but it encountered more difficulty and little or no success in southern and eastern Europe. The site of the most bloodshed was France, where Protestantism was declared both heretical and illegal in 1534. Initially French Protestants, known as Huguenots, were tolerated, but a civil war pitting Catholics against Protestants erupted in 1562. Peaceful coexistence was briefly restored by the Edict of Nantes in 1598, which established the principle of religious toleration in France, but the edict would be revoked in 1685.

The English Reformation

The English Reformation was unique. England had long traditions of dissent and anti-clericalism that stemmed from a humanist tradition. In that context, Protestantism in England grew slowly, appealing especially to the middle classes, and by 1524, illegal English-language Bibles were circulating. But as the English monarch Henry VIII tried to consolidate his power and his legacy, he took the existence of a Protestant movement as an opportunity to break from Rome and create a national church, the Church of England, or, the Anglican Church.

Henry needed a divorce from his wife, Catherine of Aragon, because she could not provide him with a male heir to the throne. He also needed money and land with which to buy the loyalty of existing nobles and to establish loyalty in new ones who would owe their position to him. In 1534, he officially broke with the Church in Rome and had himself declared the head of the new Church of England. In 1536, he dissolved the English monasteries and seized church lands and properties, awarding them to those loyal to him. English humanist Sir Thomas More, friend and counselor to Henry, refused to swear allegiance to Henry and was subsequently executed. It soon became apparent, however, that the Church that Henry had created was Protestant only in the sense that it broke from Rome. In terms of the characteristics opposed by most Protestant reformers—its episcopal or hierarchical nature, the existence of priests, and the retention of the sacraments and symbols of the traditional Roman church—the Church of England was hardly Protestant at all.

For the rest of the century, the unfinished Reformation left England plagued by religious turmoil. During the reign of Edward VI, the son of Henry and Jane Seymour, England was officially Anglican, but communities who wished to organize themselves along more Protestant lines grew to sufficient numbers to be known collectively as Dissenters. Upon the accession of Mary I (the daughter of Henry and his first wife, Catherine of Aragon), England was returned to Catholicism and Protestants were persecuted. Under the subsequent reign of Elizabeth I (the daughter of Henry and Anne Boleyn), England was again Anglican. Elizabeth was moderate in her religious views and a political pragmatist. To secure her throne, she would need the support of influential nobles and bishops, many of whom were Catholic. At the same time, upon her ascent to the throne in 1558, throngs of Protestants (including more radical Puritans), who had fled to Europe to avoid persecution under Mary I, returned to England expecting Elizabeth to stamp out Catholicism and elevate Protestantism. As part of the Elizabethan Religious Settlement, the Act of Supremacy in 1559 declared Queen Elizabeth Supreme Governor of the Church of England and required an oath of loyalty from all public officials. She also passed the Act of Uniformity (1559), which made both attendance at Anglican services and use of a Common Book of Prayer (revised to include some elements acceptable to Catholics) mandatory, though in practice she overlooked private Catholic worship from those who were loyal.

Unfortunately, religious conflict in England was not so easily settled. In 1570 a Papal Bull labeled Elizabeth a heretic and usurper, and absolved Catholics of all allegiance to her. Mary, Queen of Scots, remained a focal point for Catholic plots to reinstate a Catholic on England's throne, especially since Elizabeth had no heir, resulting in her imprisonment in the Tower of London for years. Geopolitics and religion were intertwined, as Catholic Spain brutally suppressed Protestant revolts in the Netherlands, right on England's doorstep. This prompted Elizabeth I to provide military support to the Netherlands, albeit half-heartedly. An enraged Philip II of Spain then ordered the Spanish Armada into the English Channel in 1588, only to see them defeated by the English. These events served to erode Elizabeth's patience for religious toleration. During this period, Jesuits and Catholic priests were expelled (1585), Mary Queen of Scots was beheaded for plotting against Elizabeth (1587), and commissions were established to seek "recusants," or those who refused to worship at

Anglican services. Although Elizabeth never engaged in religious repression to the extent Mary I did, her later reign was less tolerant than the early years.

Reformation in Eastern Europe

Poland-Lithuania's reformation got underway when university students began to spread ideas of religious reform. Although pockets of Lutheranism developed in a few German communities, antipathy toward Germany meant the Polish people were more likely to follow other reformers, like Ulrich Zwingli, Jan Hus, and especially John Calvin. In addition, many Jewish refugees found a home in Poland, while Lithuania was primarily Orthodox, with a small Islamic Tatar population. Though diverse Protestant sects were able to gain a foothold in Poland, in the end their divisions prevented them from mounting a unified opposition to a rejuvenated Catholic presence. A concerted effort by the Jesuits to restore Catholicism to respectability, together with the support of the poor, who had never really adopted the Calvinist beliefs favored by local nobility, resulted in the eventual dwindling of Protestant numbers.

The progress of the Reformation in Hungary was complicated by the invasion of the Ottoman Turks. In 1526, at the Battle of Mohács, Ottoman forces led by Suleiman I defeated Habsburg armies, resulting in the division of Hungary into three parts: the southern plains became part of the Ottoman empire, Eastern Hungary/Transylvania was governed by Hungarian Magyars as Ottoman vassal states, and the Northwest was governed by the Habsburgs, ruling as Kings of Hungary. The Ottomans practiced religious toleration and were more accommodating to Protestants than to Catholics, who would be likely to support the Catholic Habsburgs. Christians paid a head tax but weren't forced to convert. Among the Magyar, Calvinism became popular. For the next 150 years or more, Hungary was plagued by intermittent border conflicts until the Ottomans were driven out in the late seventeenth century. Afterward, the Habsburgs engaged in an aggressive Counter-Reformation campaign to restore Catholicism as the dominant faith.

Calvin and Calvinism

Once the break from the Roman Church was accomplished, Protestant leaders faced the task of creating new religious communities and systematizing a theology. The most influential of the second-generation Protestant theologians was John Calvin. Converting to Protestantism around 1534, Calvin was forced to leave his native France and flee to Switzerland, whose towns were governed by strong town councils that had historically competed with the Church bishops for local power. Calvin settled in Geneva where, in 1536, the adult male population had voted to become Protestant. For the next 40 years, Calvin worked in Geneva, articulating the theology and structure for Protestant religious communities that would come to be known as Calvinism.

Calvinism accepted both Martin Luther's contentions that salvation is gained by faith alone and that scripture is the sole source of authoritative knowledge of God's will. But on the subject of salvation, Calvin went further, developing the doctrine of Predestination, which asserted that God has predetermined which people will be saved and which will be damned. Those who are predestined to salvation are known as "the elect," and, although their earthly behavior could not affect the status of their salvation, Calvin taught that the elect would be known both by their righteous behavior and by their prosperity, as God would bless all their earthly enterprises.

In Calvinist communities, the structure and discipline of the congregation were integrated into those of the town. In place of the hierarchical structure of the Roman church, Calvinist churches were organized by function:

- Pastors preached the gospel.
- Doctors studied scripture and wrote commentaries.
- Deacons saw to the social welfare of the community.
- Elders governed the church and the community in moral matters and enforced discipline.

Geneva soon became the inspirational center of the Protestant movement.

Social Dimensions and the Radical Reformation

The Protestantism of Martin Luther and John Calvin appealed to the industrious and prosperous commercial and merchant classes. At these higher rungs of the social hierarchy, people could read and react to criticism of both the doctrine and practice of the orthodox Roman Church. The strict discipline of the Calvinist communities mirrored the self-discipline their own professions demanded, and the promise that God would bless the worldly endeavors of the elect provided a self-satisfying justification for the wealth and prosperity that many were enjoying. Further down the social ladder, among the artisan and peasant classes, a more radical reformation was being shaped.

The religious beliefs of the poorer and less-educated classes were always less uniform than those of the elite. Their knowledge of Christian theology tended to be superficial and wedded to older folklore that deified the forces of nature. What they cared about was that the suffering they endured in this life would be rewarded in the next. Accordingly, leaders of Protestant movements among the artisan and peasant classes interpreted the doctrines of justification by faith alone and predestination to mean that God would never abandon the poor and simple people who suffered, and that they could have direct knowledge of their salvation through an inner light that came to them directly from God. In some circles, this was combined with millenarian notions that the judgment day was near, to create a belief that the poor had a special mission to purge the world of evil and prepare it for the second coming of Christ.

The first and largest group of such radical reformers was known as "the Anabaptists." In 1534, proclaiming that judgment day was at hand, a group of them captured the German city of Münster, seized the property of nonbelievers, and burned all books except the Bible. To Protestant and Catholic elites alike, the Anabaptists represented a threat to the social order that could not be tolerated. Their rebellion was subsequently put down by an army led by the Lutheran Prince Philip of Hesse, and the Anabaptist movement was violently repressed and driven underground.

The Catholic Response

Although it was slow to believe that Protestantism could pose a threat to its power, the Roman Church—which was increasingly referred to as "catholic" (meaning one, true, and universal)—began to construct a response by the middle of the sixteenth century. Although sometimes referred to as the Counter-Reformation, the Catholic response actually had two dimensions: one aimed at reforming the Catholic Church and another aimed at exterminating the Protestant movement.

At the center of both dimensions was the Society of Jesus. Founded in 1534 by Ignatius Loyola, the Jesuits (as they came to be known) were a tightly organized order who saw themselves as soldiers in a war against Satan. Strategically, the Jesuits focused on education, building schools and universities throughout Europe. The Jesuits also served as missionaries, and they were often among the first Europeans to visit the new worlds that the Age of Exploration was opening up, thereby establishing a beachhead for Catholicism. Internally, they preached a new piety and pushed the Church to curb its worldly practices and to serve as a model for a selfless, holy life that could lead to salvation.

The Catholic reform movement reached its peak with the Council of Trent, which began its deliberations in 1545. Over many years, the Council passed reforms abolishing the worst of the abuses that had led to Protestant discontent. However, the Council of Trent also symbolized a defeat for Protestants who hoped for reconciliation, as the Council refused to compromise on any of the key theological issues and continued to insist that the Catholic Church was the final arbiter in all matters of faith.

At the heart of the Catholic Church's efforts to defeat Protestantism was the office known as "the Inquisition." An old institution within the Church that investigated charges of heresy, its duties were revived and expanded to combat all perceived threats to orthodoxy and the Church's authority. Those who ran afoul of the Inquisition ran the risk of imprisonment, torture, and execution. The Church's other main weapon in its aggressive response to the Reformation was censorship. Books that were considered unorthodox or at odds with the Church's teachings were placed on the *Index of Banned Books*.

Review Questions

Multiple Choice

Questions 1–3 refer to the following passage:

The covenant of life not being equally preached to all, and among those to whom it is preached not always finding the same reception, this diversity discovers the wonderful depth of the Divine judgment. Nor is it to be doubted that this variety also follows, subject to the decision of God's eternal election. If it be evidently the result of the Divine will, that salvation is freely offered to some, and others are prevented from attaining it—this immediately gives rise to important and difficult questions, which are incapable of any other explication, than by the establishment of pious minds in what ought to be received concerning election and predestination . . . that . . . some should be predestinated to salvation, and others to destruction. . . . His eternal election, which illustrates the grace of God by this comparison, that He adopts not all promiscuously to the hope of salvation, but gives to some what He refuses to others. . . .

We affirm that this counsel, as far as concerns the elect, is founded on his gratuitous mercy, totally irrespective of human merit; but that to those whom he devotes to condemnation, the gate of life is closed by a just and irreprehensible, but incomprehensible, judgment. In the elect, we consider calling as an evidence of election, and justification as another token of its manifestation, till they arrive in glory, which constitutes its completion. As God seals his elect by vocation and justification, so by excluding the reprobate from the knowledge of his name and the sanctification of his Spirit, he affords an indication of the judgment that awaits them.

John Calvin, *Institutes of the Christian Religion*, 1536

1. From the passage, one may conclude that Calvin asserted as true which of the following?
   A. God does not offer salvation to everyone.
   B. Man is incapable of understanding salvation.
   C. One can "elect" to be saved or refuse to be saved.
   D. Only Protestants are saved.

2. Calvin believed that the fact that some souls are predestined to eternal condemnation resulted from which of the following?
   A. Sins committed by those souls on Earth.
   B. Sins committed in a previous life.
   C. It is not open to human understanding.
   D. It is open to interpretation.

3. Calvin asserted that finding a "calling" led to which of the following?
   A. Finding a "calling" or vocation earns one salvation.
   B. Finding a "calling" or vocation is evidence that one is predestined to salvation.
   C. Finding a "calling" or vocation can save the previously damned.
   D. Finding a "calling" or vocation offers consolation to the damned.

Short Answer

4. Briefly explain TWO ways in which Protestant theology differed from Catholic theology and ONE way in which Lutheran theology differed from Calvinist theology.

Answers and Explanations

1. **A** is correct because the passage clearly states that, where salvation is concerned, God "gives to some what He refuses to others." B is incorrect because the passage does offer an explanation of salvation and how it comes to some. C is incorrect because, in the passage, the word "election" refers to God's choosing to elect (or predestine) some souls for salvation. D is incorrect because the passage does not say that all Protestants are saved or that non-Protestants are damned.

2. **C** is correct because the passage asserts that the condemnation of some souls is due to God's "just" but "incomprehensible" judgment. A is incorrect because the passage states that salvation or condemnation is "totally irrespective of human merit." B is incorrect because the passage makes no mention of previous lives. D is incorrect because the passage states that God's judgment is incomprehensible, not open to interpretation.

3. **B** is correct because the passage states that Calvin and his followers "consider calling as an evidence of election." A is incorrect because the passage does not say that finding a calling earns one salvation. C is incorrect because the passage indicates that nothing can save those to whom salvation has been denied. D is incorrect because the passage says nothing about consolation for the damned.

4. Suggested answer:

   Thesis: Protestant theology differed from Catholic theology in its assertion of the doctrine of Scripture Alone and in its denial that good works could earn one's soul salvation. Calvinist theology differed from Lutheran theology in its insistence on the doctrine of Predestination.

   Paragraph Outline:

   I. The Protestant doctrine (articulated by Luther) of *Sola Scriptura* (Scripture Alone), which stated that only scripture provides reliable knowledge of God's will, contradicted the Catholic Church's assertion that both scripture and the traditions of the Church provide reliable knowledge of God's will.

   II. The Protestant doctrines of Faith Alone (Luther) and Predestination (Calvin) contradict the Catholic Church's assertion that good works can earn one salvation.

   III. Luther's doctrine of Faith Alone asserts that anyone who has true faith (thereby receiving God's grace) can be saved. Calvin's doctrine of Predestination asserts that God has predestined some to salvation and some to damnation; no one not elected by God can achieve salvation by developing true faith.

Rapid Review

By the sixteenth century, the Christian Church was faced with mounting criticism of its preoccupation with worldly matters. In Germany in 1517, Martin Luther charged that the Church had abandoned scripture and strayed from its mission. He offered an alternative and simplified theology that asserted that salvation came by having faith alone, and that scripture alone was the source of all knowledge about salvation. In England, the powerful monarch Henry VIII used the existence of a Protestant movement to break with Rome in 1524, confiscating church lands and creating the Church of England, which retained the hierarchy and trappings of the Catholic Church. By mid-century, the Protestant movement had diversified and fragmented, as second-generation Protestant theologians faced the task of articulating the specific beliefs and structures of the new Church they were building.

The Catholic response to the Protestant movement, the Counter-Reformation, was two-pronged. The Church carried out many internal reforms that addressed the grievances of the faithful; it also enhanced the role of the Inquisition, which was aimed at stamping out Protestantism.

Further Resources

Films

The Borgias (1981, PBS/BBC miniseries in 10 episodes)

Martin Luther (1953)

A Man for All Seasons (1988)

Elizabeth (1998)

CHAPTER 13

The Great Voyages of Exploration and Early Colonization

IN THIS CHAPTER

Summary: In the fifteenth century, a more secular and ambitious culture emerged as European nations began to explore and exploit new areas of the globe, including Africa, the Americas, and the East. This chapter describes the growth of global trade, the establishment of European colonies in new regions of the world, and the severe stress on the traditional economic and social organization of Europe caused by the new sources of wealth and power.

Key Terms:

- **Spice trade** The importation of spices from Asia into Europe, revived during the Renaissance. The need to find shorter, more efficient routes gave impetus to the great voyages of exploration of the fifteenth and sixteenth centuries.
- *Haciendas* The large estates that produced food and leather goods for the mining areas and urban centers of the Spanish Empire in the New World.
- *Encomiendas* Lands given to conquering soldiers as a reward for service to the Spanish monarchs. In return for Christianizing, educating, and providing food, shelter, and other necessities to conquered natives, *encomenderos* received tribute and labor from those placed in their care and under their protection.
- **Triangular Trade Networks** The system of interconnected trade routes that quadrupled foreign trade in both Britain and France in the eighteenth century.
- **The Middle Passage** The leg of the triangular trade networks in which African slaves were transported in brutal conditions across the Atlantic Ocean on European trade ships.

○ **Plantations** The large estates in the West Indies, which produced sugar for export to Europe.

○ **Mercantilism** Economic theory that held that money (gold and silver, especially) is the only form of wealth. Mercantilism led to the quashing of any incipient industry in colonized areas, leaving economic control strictly in the hands of the colonizer.

Key Individuals:

○ The Catholic Kings (Ferdinand and Isabella)
○ Prince Henry the Navigator
○ Bartolomeo de las Casas
○ Christopher Columbus

Introduction

Around the middle of the fifteenth century, European civilization began to recover from a series of calamities that had destroyed much of the culture that characterized the High Middle Ages. What emerged was a more secular, ambitious culture that began to explore and exploit new areas of the globe, including Africa, the Americas, and the East, thanks in large part to technological advances in navigation (the compass being perhaps the most notable), cartography, and weaponry. The influx of trade, wealth, and new cultural influences put severe stress on the traditional economic and social organization of Europe.

Exploration and Expansion

The marriage of Isabella of Castile and Ferdinand of Aragon in 1469 united two previously unruly Spanish kingdoms. With the resources of the joint kingdoms at their disposal, Isabella and Ferdinand increased Spain's power first, by completing the reconquista, or definitively retaking the Iberian peninsula from the Moors (1492) and uniting the Kingdom of Spain, and second, by promoting overseas exploration. They sponsored the voyages of the Genoese explorer Christopher Columbus, who, sailing west in 1492 in search of a shorter route to the spice markets of the Far East, reached the Caribbean, thereby "discovering" a "New World" for Europeans and setting in motion a chain of events that would lead to the establishment of a Spanish Empire in Mexico and Peru.

Spain was not alone in the fifteenth century in sponsoring seafaring exploration. The Portuguese prince Henry the Navigator sponsored Portuguese exploration of the African coast. By the end of the fifteenth century, Portuguese trading ships were bringing in gold from Guinea. Soon, European powers came to understand that there was also gold to be had in the selling of spices imported from India that were used both to preserve and flavor food. The search for gold and competition for the spice trade combined to inspire an era of daring exploration and discovery:

- In 1487, Bartholomew Dias rounded the Cape of Good Hope at the southern tip of Africa, thereby opening Portuguese trade routes in the East.
- In 1498, Vasco da Gama extended Portuguese trade by reaching the coast of India and returning with a cargo that earned his investors a 60 percent profit.
- The Portuguese formed trading colonies in Goa and Calcutta on India's Malabar Coast.
- Amerigo Vespucci, an Italian sailing for Spain in 1499 and for Portugal in 1501, helped to show that the lands discovered by Columbus were not in the Far East, but rather a new continent, which the German cartographer Martin Waldseemüller dubbed "America" in his honor.

- In 1519, Hernán Cortés landed at what is today Veracruz in Mexico and began the conquest of the Aztec Empire; this would be the beginning of more than 300 years of Spanish domination in the New World. Also in 1519, a Spanish expedition led by the Portuguese sailor Ferdinand Magellan sailed west in search of a new route to the Spice Islands of the East. Rounding the tip of South America in 1520, the expedition sailed into the Pacific Ocean and arrived at the Spice Islands in 1521. In 1522, the expedition completed the first circumnavigation of the globe, returning to Spain without Magellan, who had been killed in the Philippines.

Exploration and colonization were made possible in no small way thanks to technological advances. Until the Portuguese development of the caravel (1450s), ships used for exploration and trade were primarily a kind of barge that was difficult to control and limited in navigational prowess. The caravel incorporated more masts, used lateen sails to increase maneuverability, and made speed and power the elements by which the Spaniards and Portuguese were able to carry out trade and exploratory missions. The use of guns and horses in warfare, while not precisely new, gave European colonizers of the New World a decided and obvious advantage over cultures that had neither.

The Spanish Empire in the New World

Spain led the way in exploiting the economic opportunities of the New World. The process of exploitation got underway in 1519, when Hernán Cortés landed on the coast of what is now Mexico with 600 troops. Soon thereafter, Cortés marched on the Aztec capital of Tenochtitlán and imprisoned their leader, Montezuma. By 1521, the Aztecs were defeated, and the Aztec Empire was renamed New Spain.

In 1531, Francisco Pizarro landed on the western coast of South America with 200 well-armed men and proceeded into the highlands of what is now Peru to encounter and conquer the Inca civilization. By 1533, the Incas were subdued. Internal divisions within the conquering force initially made conquest difficult, but by the late 1560s, effective control by the Spanish Crown was established.

The major economic components of the Spanish Empire in the New World, based on the ideas espoused in mercantilism, included the following:

- Mining, primarily silver from Peru and northern Mexico that was exported to Spain
- Agriculture, through large landed estates called *haciendas*, which produced food and leather goods for the mining areas and urban centers of the New World, and plantations in the West Indies, which produced sugar for export

A second source of agricultural products, mainly for local consumption, can be traced to the establishment of the *encomienda*. This system would also prove race and ethnicity to be the primary determinants of political and economic power.

The *encomienda* derived from the Spanish practice, initiated during the reconquest of the Iberian Peninsula from the Moors, of giving soldiers lands and entrusting them with Christianizing those Moors who remained. The system was modified under the so-called New Laws of the Indies (1546). Subsequently, natives could not be forced into personal service or domestic servitude, though *encomenderos* could still collect tribute. Some *encomiendas* evolved into large estates that were maintained until well into the nineteenth century.

One side effect was the reinforcement of social strata. Society was labeled according to ethnic, national, and racial criteria and divided into four main classes:

- *Peninsulares*, colonists born in Spain of Spanish parents, held the highest social and political (and, as a result, economic) positions in the New World.

- *Criollos* (Creoles), colonists born in the New World of European parents. Well educated and financially secure, criollos could hold a limited number of positions, but never those at the top of the political or social ladders. Eventually, they would be among the organizers of colonial independence movements.
- *Mestizos*, those with European and native ancestry, were further limited in what they could do and what rights they held.

Mulatos (Mulattos), people of mixed European and African ancestry. Along with the *Mestizos*, Mulattos, as well as slaves, occupied the lowest political and social position in Spanish-American society.

In both the mining and the agriculture sectors, ownership was in the hands of Spanish-born or Spanish-descended overlords, while labor was coerced from the native population. Native populations could not, however, be enslaved unless taken as captives in a "just war"; this in turn led to the importation of African (black) workers, who could be enslaved, especially in plantation economies.

The establishment of an exploitative foreign empire in the New World had several lasting results on the civilizations of the New World, particularly in Central and South America:

- The establishment of Roman Catholicism in the New World
- The establishment of economic dependence between the New World and Europe
- The establishment of a European-style hierarchical social structure in the cultures of the New World

It also had lasting effects on Spain and, eventually, the rest of Europe:

- A steady rise in prices, eventually produced inflation, due to the increase in available wealth and coinage
- An eventual rise of a wealthy merchant class that sat uneasily in the traditional feudal social structure of Europe
- Raised expectations for quality of life throughout the social structure of Europe

England, France, and the Triangular Trade Networks

By 1600, England and France were endeavoring to form their own colonies in the New World. They founded settler colonies in North America through the formation of joint stock companies (which allowed private investment combined with investment by the Crown). These colonies soon thrived, initially with considerable help from, and later at the expense of, the indigenous populations.

In the eighteenth century, England and, to a lesser extent, France surpassed Spain, Portugal, and Holland as the dominant economic powers in Europe and in the New World. They did so by controlling the majority of the increasingly lucrative Triangular Trade Networks that connected Europe to Africa and the Americas. The phrase "Triangular Trade Networks" refers to a system of interconnected trade routes that quadrupled foreign trade in both Britain and France in the eighteenth century. Here are three characteristics of the Triangular Trade Networks:

- Manufactured goods (primarily guns and gin) were exported from Europe to Africa.
- Slaves were exported to serve as labor in European colonies in North America, South America, and the Caribbean.
- Raw materials (especially furs, timber, tobacco, rice, cotton, indigo dye, coffee, rum, and sugar) were exported from the colonies to Europe in exchange for slaves and manufactured goods.

Before the eighteenth century, the primary destination of Africans taken into slavery by their rivals had been either the Mediterranean basin or Asia. The eighteenth-century expansion of the European colonies greatly increased the demand for African slaves and reoriented the slave trade to the West. The majority of slaves were destined for the West Indies and Brazil, with about 10 percent going to colonies in North America. The transportation of African slaves across the Atlantic Ocean on European trade ships was known as "the Middle Passage." As many as 700 slaves per ship were transported, chained below deck in horrific conditions. It is estimated that somewhere between 50,000 and 100,000 Africans were transported each year during the height of the eighteenth-century slave trade.

Review Questions

Multiple Choice

Questions 1–3 refer to the following passage:

The great city of Tenochtitlan is built on the salt lake. . . . [C]onsidering that these people were barbarous, so cut off from the knowledge of God and other civilized peoples, it is admirable to see to what they attained in every respect. . . .

It happened . . . that a Spaniard saw an Indian . . . eating a piece of flesh taken from the body of an Indian who had been killed. . . . I had the culprit burned, explaining that the cause was his having killed the Indian and eaten him which was prohibited by Your Majesty, and by me in Your Royal name. I further made the chief understand that all the people . . . must abstain from this custom . . . I came . . . to teach them that they were to adore but one God . . . that they must turn from their idols, and the rites they had practiced until then, for these were lies and deceptions which the devil . . . had invented. . . . I, likewise, had come to teach them that Your Majesty, by the will of Divine Providence, rules the universe, and that they also must submit themselves to the imperial yoke, and do all that we who are Your Majesty's ministers here might order them.

Hernán Cortés, *Letters to Charles V, King of Spain*, 1521

1. Cortés saw the people of Tenochtitlán in what way?

   A. As more technologically advanced than the Spanish

   B. As disadvantaged by the absence of Christianity in their culture

   C. As ready to convert to Christianity

   D. As morally superior to Europeans

2. From the passage, Cortés maintained which of the following points of view?

   A. He believed that God had chosen him to conquer the people of Tenochtitlán.

   B. He doubted the morality of his mission in the New World.

   C. He believed that the Spanish had complete authority over the people of Tenochtitlán.

   D. He intended to set himself up as the God of the people of Tenochtitlán.

3. From the passage, which of the following best informs the conqueror's goals?

   A. Cortés intended to impose the laws of Christianity and Spain on the people of Tenochtitlán.

   B. Cortés intended to exterminate the people of Tenochtitlán.

   C. Cortés's main mission was to educate the people of Tenochtitlán.

   D. Cortés thought that the people of Tenochtitlán were devil worshipers and needed to be converted to Christianity.

Short Answer

4. Briefly explain TWO ways in which Spanish colonization changed life in the New World.

Answers and Explanations

1. **B** is correct because the passage indicates that Cortés was impressed by the technical accomplishments of the people of Tenochtitlán, *despite* their "barbarous" state, "so cut off from the knowledge of God." A is incorrect because nothing in the passage indicates that Cortés saw the people of Tenochtitlán as *more* advanced than the Spanish. C is incorrect because nothing in the passage indicates that Cortés saw the people of Tenochtitlán as "ready to convert" to Christianity. D is incorrect because the passage indicates that Cortés saw the people of Tenochtitlán as morally *inferior* to Europeans.

2. **C** is correct because both Cortés's willingness to outlaw the eating of flesh and to order the natives to turn away from idols indicate that Cortés believed that he had complete authority over the people of Tenochtitlán. A is incorrect because there is nothing in the passage that indicates that Cortés believed that he had been personally chosen by God. B is incorrect because nothing in the passage indicates that Cortés doubted the moral correctness of his mission. D is incorrect because nothing in the passage indicates that Cortés intended to set himself up as the God of the people of Tenochtitlán.

3. **A** is correct because the banning of cannibalism and the "turning away" from idols referred to in the passage allow one to infer that Cortés intended to impose the laws of Christianity and Spain on the people of Tenochtitlán. B is incorrect because nothing in the passage indicates that Cortés intended to exterminate the people of Tenochtitlán. C is incorrect; despite the reference to "teaching" the people of Tenochtitlán, the passage makes it clear that Cortés's primary mission was to rule the people of Tenochtitlán. D is incorrect because the passage allows one to infer nothing in regard to the worship practices of the people of Tenochtitlán; rather, the passage gives inferences of the ways in which Cortés interpreted those practices.

4. Suggested answer:

Thesis: Spanish colonization changed life in the New World by creating a new agricultural system and by shifting ownership of both the agricultural and mining sectors away from local populations.

Paragraph Outline:

I. Spanish colonization created a new agricultural system in which large estates called *haciendas* produced food and leather goods for the mining areas and urban centers of the New World, and plantations in the West Indies produced sugar for export.

II. In both the mining and agriculture sectors, ownership was in the hands of Spanish-born or Spanish-descended overlords, while labor was coerced from the native population.

Rapid Review

In the fifteenth century, Isabella and Ferdinand used the resources of the newly united kingdom of Spain to promote overseas exploration. Other European kingdoms followed suit. This led to an unprecedented era of exploration and discovery in the sixteenth and seventeenth centuries, and to the building of a Spanish empire in the New World. In the eighteenth centuries, Britain and France came to dominate the lucrative Triangular Trade Networks that imported valuable raw materials from North America and the Caribbean to Europe in exchange for the selling of manufactured goods to colonies and for slaves acquired from Africa.

Further Resources

Film
The Mission (1986)

CHAPTER 14

Economic Change and Political Consolidation

IN THIS CHAPTER

Summary: In the first half of the seventeenth century, the traditional, hierarchical social structure of European kingdoms came under new pressures. This chapter describes the economic, social, and political changes as economies underwent a transformation from an agrarian base to a more complex economic system, which included expanding the trade that had begun in the later Middle Ages, compliments of the Black Plague and the Crusades, and the growth of a middle class of merchants and professionals.

Key Terms:
- ✪ **Peasantry** The class of rural, agricultural laborers in traditional European society.
- ✪ **Nobility** The class of privileged landowners in traditional European society.
- ✪ **Monarchs** The hereditary rulers of traditional European society.
- ✪ **Divine Right of Kings** The theory that monarchs received their right to rule directly from God.
- ✪ **Absolutism** A theory of government that a rightful ruler holds absolute power over his or her subjects.
- ✪ **English Civil War** (1642–1646) The war in which forces loyal to King Charles I fought to defend the power of the monarchy, the official Church of England, and the privileges and prerogatives of the nobility, while forces supporting Parliament fought to uphold the rights of Parliament, to bring an end to the notion of an official state church, and for the ideals of individual liberty and the rule of law.

- ◆ **The Commonwealth (1649–1660)** The period during which England was ruled without a monarch, following the victory of the Parliamentary forces in the English Civil War and the subsequent execution of King Charles I.
- ◆ **Constitutional monarchy** A theory of government that contends that a rightful ruler's power is limited by an agreement with his or her subjects.
- ◆ *Intendent* An administrative bureaucrat in absolutist France of the seventeenth century, usually chosen from the middle class, who owed his position and, therefore, his loyalty directly to the state.
- ◆ **Edict of Nantes (1598)** Decree by King Henry IV of France granting Protestants religious tolerance and marking the end of France's Religious Wars. Revoked in 1685.

Key Individuals:

- ◆ James I (England)
- ◆ Peter the Great (Russia)
- ◆ Catherine the Great (Russia)
- ◆ Philip II, III, and IV (Spain)

Introduction

In the first half of the seventeenth century, the traditional hierarchical structure of European society came under new pressures. This structure was one in which a large class of poor agricultural laborers (the peasantry) supported a small and wealthy class of elites (the nobility). As the monarchs of Europe fought wars to expand their kingdoms and created larger state bureaucracies to manage them, the pressure to raise greater sums of money through taxes stretched the economies and social structures of European societies to the breaking point. Meanwhile, a continuous increase in trade and in the diversification of the economy was creating a new class of people: a middle class made up of merchants and professionals, which did not fit comfortably into the traditional hierarchy.

Economic Stress and Change

The first half of the 1600s was characterized by an economic contraction, precipitated by a variety of factors. At the same time as new European nations began Atlantic exploration, colonization, and trade, the amount of silver extracted from Spanish mines in the Americas declined. This drop-off in the silver trade, coupled with a shift away from Mediterranean trade routes toward the Atlantic, resulted in both Italy and Spain becoming less economically dominant.

A series of unusually harsh winters that characterized the "little ice age" of the 1600s led to a series of poor harvests, which, in turn, led to malnutrition and disease. In an effort to cope with increasing poverty, members of the besieged agricultural class opted to have smaller families. While the smaller family unit would, over time, contribute to a higher standard of living, this adjustment took time. The immediate impact of the combination of famine, poverty, and disease was a significant decrease in the population during this period.

The problems of the European peasantry were exacerbated during this period by increasing demands from the nobility that ruled them. As warfare and military might became increasingly necessary for a ruler's power and influence, the importance and nature of the military changed. New military tactics (including the salvo, in which all lines of infantry fired simultaneously, rather than row by row) and equipment necessitated a more professional, trained army. Standing armies were formed, growing ever larger, in part through conscription. These military changes further decimated the agricultural population, both through conscription and death, as warfare took its inevitable toll. Funding the military and wars required money, which monarchs raised through increased taxations. Because the nobility was largely exempt from taxes, the peasantry bore the brunt of this new economic burden.

These economic and social pressures, together with simmering religious tensions that had never been fully resolved, strained the fabric of traditional society. Poverty forced increasing numbers of peasants into begging and vagrancy. Rebellions flared across Europe, led by nobles resisting erosion of their position and privilege, and by peasants protesting their extreme poverty. In many communities, religious, social and economic instability found its expression in a series of witch hunts. Economic and personal hardships were attributed to the workings of the devil through witches. Often located in regions where religious upheaval was greatest, the accusations caused a form of mass hysteria, in which people feared both witchcraft and the accusation of witchcraft. Frequently, the targets of these accusations were women, for whom the decline in typical forms of charity was most dire, and who were easy targets. Long thought to be both intellectually and morally weaker than men, women were seen as more susceptible to evil influences, and confessions of "consorting" with the devil were common, often elicited through torture.

Thirty Years' War

The instability and upheaval of this period is probably best illustrated by the Thirty Years' War. Though the Peace of Augsburg in 1555 tamped down the fires of religious conflict in Germany, it did not remove them altogether. German Catholic and Lutheran principalities continued to jockey for power. Additionally, the Peace of Augsburg failed to legitimize the Calvinist sect, which was increasingly popular in some areas. In 1617, the Austrian Archduke Ferdinand, a member of the powerful Catholic Habsburg family, became ruler of predominantly Calvinist Bohemia, and later emperor of the Holy Roman Empire. As he took measures to centralize royal power and the Catholic faith in Bohemia, Calvinist nobles expressed their displeasure by defenestrating (throwing out a window) a few of Ferdinand's key advisers. The Calvinist rebels appealed to other Protestant states for assistance, while Ferdinand sought help from other German Catholics, Spain, and the papacy. Ultimately the Catholic forces prevailed, giving Spain access to a coveted trade route from Italy to the Netherlands, and solidifying the position of both the Catholics and the Habsburgs in Germany.

In 1625, the Danish king Christian IV, fearing that a powerful Holy Roman Empire threatened his sovereignty, came to the aid of the Protestant state of Saxony, invading northern Germany. The imperial forces were led by Albrecht von Wallenstein, a Bohemian nobleman whose wealth came from confiscated Protestant land. Though Denmark had gained some marginal support from France and Britain, it wasn't enough. Devastating the land as it went, Wallenstein's army defeated the Danish forces, giving the Holy Roman Empire control of Baltic ports such as Hamburg, and ending Denmark's supremacy in that area.

Later, King Gustavus Adolphus of Sweden, motivated by the same desires and fears as King Christian but with a stronger military acumen, successfully invaded northern Germany and the Holy Roman Empire but was eventually killed in battle. With his death and the return of Wallenstein at the head of the imperial forces, the Swedish army was defeated, and negotiations among the Holy Roman Empire and Protestant German states began. German princes were no longer able to negotiate alliances among themselves or with other nations, and the German armies were incorporated into one large force under the Holy Roman Empire.

This turn of events alarmed the Bourbon regime in France, which, although Catholic, feared the growing strength of the Habsburgs surrounding them, both in Spain and in the Holy Roman Empire. This prompted them to set aside religious loyalties in favor of political realities and ally with Sweden against Spain and the Holy Roman Empire in 1635. Although Spain enjoyed some initial successes, eventually the tide turned in favor of the French and Swedes, partly because Spain's attention was diverted by local rebellions (rebellions which had been encouraged by France's Cardinal Richelieu). Eventually tiring of protracted warfare and (in the case of France) needing to attend to domestic matters, all parties signed a series of agreements in 1648 known as the Peace of Westphalia, which marked the end of the Thirty Years' War.

The impact of this conflict on Europe was significant. It marked the end of religion as the primary factor in international alignments and conflicts. Power and authority remained decentralized in German central Europe. The power of the Holy Roman Empire was much reduced, and German unification wouldn't occur for another two hundred years. Calvinism was included as a legitimate option for German states. The Dutch Netherlands gained independence, while the power of the papacy in political affairs declined. Finally, the impact on German states was devastating. Estimates of population losses range from 20 percent to 50 percent in some areas, and the disruption to farming and commerce was incalculable.

Britain: The Rise of Parliament

In Britain, these tensions came to a head in the form of a struggle between the monarchs of the Stuart dynasty and the English Parliament. Already an old and important institution by 1600, the English Parliament was an assembly of elites who advised the king. But it differed from its counterparts in the other European kingdoms in several important ways:

- Its members were elected by the property-holding people of their county or district.
- Eligibility for election was based on property ownership, so its members included wealthy merchants and professional men, as well as nobles.
- Members voted individually, rather than as an order or class.

As a result, the English Parliament of the seventeenth century was an alliance of nobles and well-to-do members of a thriving merchant and professional class that saw itself as a voice of the "English people." It soon clashed with the monarch it had invited to succeed the heirless Elizabeth I.

Although the Tudor monarchs (Henry VII, Henry VIII, Edward VI, Mary I, and Elizabeth I) were generally inclined toward absolutism, they recognized the Parliament's utility in legitimizing their actions and took care to operate within a constitutional framework. In turn, Parliament generally supported the actions of the monarchy, with a few exceptions. Henry VII rarely convened Parliament, preferring to use alternative means of obtaining money for the royal treasury, rather than ask Parliament for taxes (their primary power). Though Parliament sometimes acted as a rubber stamp for Henry VII, passing tariffs and reinstating Crown lands, the legislative patterns were being set. Under King Henry VIII, the Reformation Parliament was the longest-sitting Parliament to date, addressing royal succession, establishing King Henry VIII as the Supreme Head of the Church, giving royal proclamations the force of law, and assigning ecclesiastical taxes to the royal treasury.

Despite this, when Parliament balked at a 20-percent property tax to support a war with France, Henry VIII eventually compromised, settling on a 10-percent tax. Mary I similarly found Parliament acquiesced on matters like canceling the annulment of her mother Catherine of Aragon's marriage, and Mary's proposed marriage to Philip II of Spain, but she wasn't able to get Parliament's agreement for the restoration of Church property.

A believer in absolutism, Elizabeth was nevertheless careful not to push Parliament too far. She called Parliament into session only 13 times in a 45-year rule, primarily for taxes, and could limit the topics Parliament could discuss. When Parliament pressured her to marry and name an heir, she resisted, stating that issues relating to her marriage, succession, and foreign affairs were outside their purview. Over time, Parliament (particularly the Puritans) became more assertive, arguing against her restrictions on their speech and debate in religious affairs, prompting Elizabeth to imprison for a month one of the key agitators. Toward the end of her reign, Elizabeth garnered money from selling monopoly licenses. Resentment over the resulting price increases prompted Parliament to withhold taxes until Elizabeth withdrew the monopolies, a compromise she made in a speech that both flattered and gratified Parliament. By working with Parliament and compromising where necessary, Tudor monarchs legitimized their role in English government.

When James Stuart, the reigning king of Scotland (known there as James VI), agreed to take the throne of England as James I (r. 1603–1625), he was determined to rule England in the manner described by the theory of absolutism. Under this theory, monarchs were viewed as having been appointed by God (an appointment known as the "Divine Right of Kings"). As such, they were entitled to rule with absolute authority over their subjects. Despite the tension between Parliament and the monarchy, James I's reign was characterized by a contentious but peaceful coexistence with Parliament.

A religious element was added when James's son and successor, Charles I (r. 1625–1649), married a sister of the Catholic king of France. That, together with his insistence on waging costly wars, led to a confrontation with Parliament. Having provoked the Scots into invading England by threatening their religious independence, Charles I was forced to call on the English Parliament for yet more funds. Parliament responded by making funds contingent on the curbing of monarchical power. This led to a stalemate, which degenerated into the English Civil War (1642–1646). Forces loyal to the king fought to defend the power of the monarchy, the official Church of England, and the privileges and prerogatives of the nobility; forces supporting Parliament fought to uphold the rights of Parliament, to bring an end to the notion of an official state church, and for notions of individual liberty and the rule of law. The victory of the Parliamentary forces led to the trial and execution of Charles I for treason and to the establishment of the Commonwealth period (1649–1660), in which Britain was governed without a king.

France: The Construction of a State

Several key differences allowed for a far different outcome in France. A series of religious and dynastic wars in the sixteenth century produced a kingdom in which the religious issue had been settled firmly in favor of the Catholic majority, though the Edict of Nantes (1598) which ended the religious wars, granted French Protestants religious tolerance and freedom to worship. The lack of religious turmoil in the seventeenth century allowed the French monarchy to cement an alliance with both the Catholic clergy and the merchant class, and to use the great administrative expertise of both to begin to build a powerful centralized government. Both Louis XIII (r. 1610–1643) and Louis XIV (r. 1643–1715) relied on well-connected Catholic cardinals to oversee the consolidation of royal power by transferring local authority from provincial nobility to a bureaucracy that was both efficient and trustworthy.

As chief minister to Louis XIII, Cardinal Richelieu used the royal army to disband the private armies of the great French aristocrats and to strip the autonomy granted to the few remaining Protestant towns. More significantly, he stripped provincial aristocrats and elites of their administrative power by dividing France into some 30 administrative districts and putting each under the control of an *intendent*, an administrative bureaucrat who owed his position, and therefore his loyalty, directly to Richelieu.

Central and Eastern Europe: Compromise

Whereas the contests for power and sovereignty in Britain and France had clear winners and losers, similar contests in the European kingdoms farther to the east resulted in a series of compromises between monarchs and rival elites. In general, European kingdoms in eastern and central Europe, such as Brandenburg-Prussia, the independent German states, Austria, and Poland, were less economically developed than their western counterparts.

The economies of Britain and France in the seventeenth century were based on an agricultural system run by a free and mobile peasantry and supplemented by an increasingly prosperous middle class consisting of artisans and merchants in thriving towns. In contrast, the landholding nobility of the kingdoms in central and eastern Europe during this period managed to retain control of vast estates worked by serfs, agricultural laborers who were bound by the land. By doing so, they were able to avoid the erosion of wealth that weakened their counterparts in Britain and France.

Review Questions

Multiple Choice

Questions 1–3 refer to the following passage:

The only way to erect . . . a Common Power, as may be able to defend them from the invasion of [foreigners] and the injuries of one another, and thereby to secure them in such sort, as that by their own industry, and by the fruits of the Earth, they may nourish themselves and live contentedly is, to confer all their power and strength upon one Man, or upon one Assembly of men, that may reduce all their Wills, by plurality of voices, unto one Will . . . and therein to submit their Wills, everyone to his Will, and their judgments, to his judgment. This is more than Consent, or Concord; it is a real Unity of them all, in one and the same Person, made by Covenant of every man with every man, in such manner, as if every man should say to every man, I Authorize and give up my Right of Governing myself to this Man, or to this Assembly of men, on this condition, that thou give up thy Right to him, and Authorize all his Actions in like manner. . . . [And] being thereby bound by Covenant . . . cannot lawfully make a new Covenant, amongst themselves, to be obedient to any other, in anything whatsoever, without his permission.

Thomas Hobbes, *Leviathan,* 1651

1. Hobbes was an advocate of which form of governance?
   A. Absolutism
   B. Constitutionalism
   C. Socialism
   D. Millenarianism

2. Hobbes proposed a system of government based on which of the following?
   A. Conditional consent between the governing and the governed
   B. A limited concord between the governing and the governed
   C. An unbreakable covenant between the governing and the governed
   D. The concept of representational democracy
3. Hobbes was primarily which of the following?
   A. He was an advocate of representative democracy.
   B. He was opposed to the deposing of Charles I and the establishment of the Commonwealth government in England.
   C. He was opposed to the centralization of power in government.
   D. He was an advocate of an unwritten constitution.

Short Answer

4. Briefly explain ONE similarity and TWO differences between the English and French experience of the consolidation of political power in the seventeenth century.

Answers and Explanations

1. **A** is correct because the phrases "confer all their power and strength," "submit their Wills," and "I Authorize and give up my Right of Governing myself" all indicate an advocacy of absolutism. B is incorrect because the passage makes no mention of limiting the power of the sovereign by a constitution. C is incorrect because the passage makes no reference to the collectivist principles of socialism. D is incorrect because the passage makes no reference to the millennial belief in the imminent end of the world.

2. **C** is correct because the passage explicitly calls for an unbreakable "Covenant of every man with every man, in such manner, as if every man should say to every man, I Authorize and give up my Right of Governing." A is incorrect because the covenant discussed in the passage is not conditional in any way. B is incorrect because the covenant discussed in the passage is not limited in any way. D is incorrect because the passage makes no reference to any kind of democracy.

3. **B** is correct because the passage establishes that Hobbes was an advocate of an unbreakable political covenant, and one may therefore infer that he was opposed to the deposing of the reigning monarchy and the establishment of a commonwealth based on conditional consent. A is incorrect because the passage makes no mention of any kind of democracy. C is incorrect because the passage indicates the advantages of centralized power. D is incorrect because the passage establishes Hobbes's opposition to any kind of constitution because it would limit the power of the sovereign.

4. Suggested answer:

Thesis: In the seventeenth century, the people of both England and France experienced attempts by their kings to consolidate political power around the monarchy. In the English situation, that effort was complicated by religious differences and was ultimately unsuccessful. In the French case, the power of a dominant Catholic Church was used in the service of the monarchy, and the effort was ultimately successful.

Paragraph Outline:

I. Efforts by the monarchs of England (James I and Charles I) and the monarchs of France (Louis XIII and XIV) to consolidate power in the seventeenth century

II. Split between the monarchists' advocacy of the Church of England and the Parliamentarians' advocacy of further Protestant reform in England. Bourbon use of the Church as a bureaucratic mechanism for the consolidation of political power in France.

III. English Civil War and defeat of the monarchists' efforts to consolidate power in England. Successful consolidation of political power by the Bourbon monarchy in France.

Rapid Review

During the period from 1600 to 1648, the dynamics of the traditional, hierarchical social structure of European kingdoms came under new pressures. As their economies underwent a transformation from a purely agricultural base to a more complex system that included expanding trade and the uneven growth of a middle class of merchants and professionals, European monarchs attempted to solidify their claims to sovereignty.

In both Britain and France, the power struggle between the monarch and the elites was won by the side who managed to form an alliance with the wealthy merchant and professional classes. In the European kingdoms farther east, however, these classes failed to gain in wealth and numbers as their counterparts in Britain and France had done. As a result, the stalemate between royal and aristocratic wealth and power remained more balanced, necessitating compromise.

Further Resources

Films

The Last Valley (1970)

Cromwell (1970)

CHAPTER 15

Economic Change and the Expansion of the State

IN THIS CHAPTER

Summary: In the eighteenth century, the influx of capital generated by colonial trade in Great Britain and France spurred changes in agricultural and manufacturing production that destroyed the last vestiges of feudalism and converted the peasantry and guildsmen into wage laborers, a process that began as early as the fourteenth century with the demographic changes resulting from the Black Plague. This chapter describes these economic changes, the resulting social and political changes in Great Britain and France, and the efforts of other European powers to catch up.

KEY IDEA

Key Terms:

- ✪ **The Commonwealth** The period (1649–1660) during which England was ruled without a monarch, following the victory of the Parliamentary forces in the English Civil War and the subsequent execution of Charles I.
- ✪ **The Restoration** The period of English history (1660–1688) following the Commonwealth and preceding the Glorious Revolution. It encompassed the reigns of Charles II (1660–1685) and James II (1685–1688).
- ✪ **The Glorious Revolution** The quick, nearly bloodless uprising (1688) that coordinated Parliament-led uprisings in England with the invasion of a Protestant fleet and army from the Netherlands and led to the expulsion of James II and the establishment of a constitutional monarchy in England under William and Mary.

- **Constitutional monarchy** A theory of government that contends that a rightful ruler's power is limited by an agreement with his or her subjects.
- *Two Treatises on Government* A philosophical work (1690) by the Englishman John Locke, which became the primary argument for the establishment of natural limits to governmental authority.
- **Versailles** The great palace of the French monarchs, located 11 miles outside of Paris, which was the center of court life and political power in France from 1682 until the French Revolution in 1789.
- **Tsars** The hereditary monarchs of Russia.
- **Law Code of 1649** Legislation in Russia that converted the legal status of groups as varied as peasants and slaves into that of a single class of serfs.
- **Manorial system** The traditional economic system of Europe, developed in the medieval period, in which landowning elites (lords of the manor) held vast estates divided into small plots of arable land farmed by peasants for local consumption.
- **Cash crops** Crops grown for sale and export in the market-oriented approach that replaced the manorial system during the Agricultural Revolution of the eighteenth century.
- **Enclosure** The building of hedges, fences, and walls to deny the peasantry access to traditional farming plots and common lands, which had been converted to fields for cash crops during the Agricultural Revolution of the eighteenth century.
- **Putting-out system (also "cottage industry")** A system in which rural peasants engaged in small-scale textile manufacturing. It was developed in the eighteenth century to allow merchants, faced with an ever-expanding demand for textiles, to get around the guild system.
- **Guilds** Exclusive organizations that monopolized the skilled trades in Europe from the medieval period until broken by the development of cottage industry in the eighteenth century.
- **Flying shuttle** A machine invented in 1733 by John Kay that doubled the speed at which cloth could be woven on a loom, creating a need to find a way to produce greater amounts of thread faster.
- **Spinning jenny** A machine invented in the 1760s by James Hargreaves that greatly increased the amount of thread a single spinner could produce from cotton, creating a need to speed up the harvesting of cotton.
- **Cotton gin** A machine invented in 1793 by an American, Eli Whitney, that efficiently removed seed from raw cotton, thereby increasing the speed with which it could be processed and sent to the spinners.
- **Diplomatic Revolution** The mid-eighteenth-century shift in European alliances, whereby the expansionist aims of Frederick II of Prussia caused old enemies to become allies. Prussia, fearful of being isolated by its enemies, forged an alliance in 1756 with its former enemy Great Britain; Austria and France, previously antagonistic toward one another, responded by forging an alliance of their own.
- **The Seven Years' War (1756–1763)** A conflict that pitted France, Austria, Russia, Saxony, Sweden, and (after 1762) Spain against Prussia, Great Britain, and the German state of Hanover in a contest for control of both the European Continent and the New World in North America.

Key Individuals:
- ✪ King Charles II (England)
- ✪ King James II (England)
- ✪ Cardinal Richelieu
- ✪ Cardinal Jules Mazarin
- ✪ King Louis XIV (France)
- ✪ Catherine the Great (Russia)
- ✪ Frederick II (Prussia)
- ✪ Oliver Cromwell

Introduction

In the second half of the seventeenth century and into the eighteenth century, Great Britain and, to a lesser extent, France, surpassed Spain, Portugal, and Holland as the dominant economic and political powers in Europe. As they did so, the political struggle among the elites reached their respective climaxes.

Great Britain and France rose to prominence by controlling the majority of the increasingly lucrative Triangular Trade Networks that connected Europe to Africa and the Americas (see Chapter 13). The resulting wealth and prosperity set in motion a series of innovations that radically changed European agricultural and manufacturing production, which in turn produced changes in the social structure of Europe. Competition between Great Britain and France, and the desire of their eastern European rivals to catch up, led to innovations in diplomacy and war—the twin processes by which eighteenth-century European rulers built and expanded their states.

Great Britain: The Triumph of Constitutionalism

The Commonwealth (1649–1660) deteriorated into a fundamentalist Protestant dictatorship under the rule of the Parliamentary army's leading general, Oliver Cromwell. Upon Cromwell's death in 1658, English Parliamentarians worked to establish a Restoration (1660–1688) of the English monarchy, inviting the son of the king they executed to take the throne as Charles II (1660–1685).

The relative peace of the Restoration period broke down when Charles's brother, a Catholic, ascended the throne as James II (1685–1688). James was determined to establish religious freedom for Catholics, to avenge his father's death, and to restore absolute monarchy to Great Britain. To thwart James's plans, Parliament enlisted the aid of the king's eldest daughter, Mary, the Protestant wife of William of Orange of the Netherlands. The quick, nearly bloodless uprising that coordinated Parliament-led uprisings with the invasion of a Protestant fleet and army from the Netherlands led to the quick expulsion of James II in 1688. This is known as the Glorious Revolution. The reign of William and Mary marks the clear establishment of a constitutional monarchy, a system by which the monarch rules within the limits of the laws passed by a legislative body. The text written by the leading legal spokesman of the Parliamentary faction, John Locke's *Two Treatises on Government* (1690), is still read today as the primary argument for the establishment of natural limits to governmental authority.

France: The Triumph of Absolutism

The policies of Cardinal Richelieu were continued by his successor, Cardinal Jules Mazarin, and perfected by Louis XIV (r. 1643–1715) when he took full control of the government upon Mazarin's death in 1661. To the intimidation tactics practiced by Richelieu and Mazarin, Louis added bribery. Building the great palace at Versailles, 11 miles outside of Paris, Louis presented the nobility of France with a choice: oppose him and face destruction or join him and be part of the most lavish court in Europe. In choosing to spend most of their time at Versailles, French nobles forfeited the advantages that made their English Parliamentary counterparts so powerful: control of both the wealth and loyalty of their local provinces and districts. As a result, Louis XIV became known as "the Sun King," because all French life seemed to revolve around him as the planets revolved around the sun.

Russia: Tsarist Absolutism

The seventeenth-century kingdom farthest to the east proved to be an exception to the rule. Its monarchs, the *tsars*, managed to achieve a high degree of absolutism despite an agricultural economy based on serfdom and the lack of an alliance with a thriving middle class.

Beginning in 1613 and reaching its zenith with the reign of Peter the Great (1689–1725), the Romanov tsars consolidated their power by buying the loyalty of the nobility. In return for their loyalty, the Romanov tsars gave the nobility complete control over the classes of people below them. A prime example is the Law Code of 1649, which converted the legal status of groups as varied as peasants and slaves into that of a single class of serfs. Under the Romanov tsars, the Russian nobility also enjoyed the fruit of new lands and wealth acquired by aggressive expansion of the Russian empire eastward into Asia.

With the nobility firmly tied to the tsar, opposition to the tsar's power manifested itself only periodically in the form of revolts from coalitions of smaller landholders and peasants angered by the progressive loss of their wealth and rights. Such revolts, like the revolts of the Cossacks in the 1660s and early 1670s, were ruthlessly put down by the tsar's increasingly modern military forces. The smaller landholders and peasants were controlled thereafter by the creation of a state bureaucracy modeled on those of Western Europe, and by encouraging the primacy and importance of the Russian Orthodox Church, which taught that the traditional social hierarchy was mandated by God.

Breaking the Traditional Cycle of Population and Productivity

The enormous wealth generated by the British and French colonies and the Triangular Trade Networks created pressure for social change that eventually affected the whole populations of both Great Britain and France. The effects were felt more strongly in Great Britain and led to changes that, taken together, constituted the first phase of the Industrial Revolution, which began in Great Britain and then spread eastward throughout Europe. This Industrial Revolution broke the traditional cycle of population and productivity.

The traditional cycle of population and productivity worked like this:

- Population and productivity rose together, as an increase in the number of people working in an agricultural economy increased the agricultural yield.
- Eventually, the agricultural yield reached the maximum amount that could be produced given the land available and the methods in use.

- For a while, population would continue to rise, but eventually, as the number of people far outstripped the agricultural yield, food became scarce and expensive.
- Scarcity and high prices eventually caused the population to decline.
- When the population was safely below the possible productivity, the cycle began again.

In the eighteenth century, several developments related to new wealth combined to break this cycle:

- Agriculture became market oriented.
- Rural manufacturing spread capital throughout the population.
- Increased demand led to technical innovation.

The new market orientation of agriculture created a shift from farming for local consumption to a reliance on imported food sold at markets. The introduction of rural manufacturing put larger amounts of currency into the system and made the working population less dependent on land and agricultural cycles, thereby breaking the natural check on population growth.

Market-Oriented Agriculture

The increase in population created more mouths to feed. The existence of a vast colonial empire of trade created an increasingly wealthy merchant class of individuals who both bought land from, and affected the behavior of, traditional landholding elites. The result was the destruction of the traditional manorial system in which landowning elites (lords of the manor) held vast estates divided into small plots of arable land farmed by peasants for local consumption and vast grounds, known as "commons," where peasants grazed their livestock. That system was slowly replaced by a market-oriented approach in which cash crops were grown for sale and export.

The shift to a cash-crop system created pressure that led to the reorganization of the social structure of the countryside. The traditional landowning elites abandoned their feudal obligations to the peasantry and adopted the attitude of the merchant class. Cash crops created a demand for larger fields. Landowners responded by instituting a process known as "enclosure," because of the hedges, fences, and walls that were built to deny the peasantry access to the commons, which had been converted to fields for cash crops. Later, the landowners extended enclosure into other arable lands, breaking traditional feudal agreements and gradually transforming much of the peasantry into wage labor. By the middle of the eighteenth century, three-quarters of the arable land in England was enclosed informally or "by agreement" (though the peasantry had not, in fact, been given any choice); after 1750, the process continued more formally as land was enclosed via acts of Parliament.

Rural Manufacturing

The increase in population also created greater demand for the other necessities of life, particularly clothing. In the feudal system, all aspects of textile production had been under the control of guilds (which were organizations of skilled laborers, such as spinners and weavers), which enjoyed the protection of town officials. Membership in a guild was gained only through a lengthy apprenticeship. In that way, the guilds kept competition to a minimum and controlled the supply of textiles, thereby guaranteeing that they could make a decent living. In the eighteenth century, merchants faced with an ever-expanding demand for textiles had to find a way around the guild system; the result was a system of rural manufacturing, known variously as "cottage industry" or "the putting-out system."

In the putting-out system, merchants went into the countryside and engaged the peasantry in small-scale textile production. Each month, a merchant would provide raw material and rent equipment to peasant families. At the end of the month, he would return and pay the family for whatever thread or cloth they had produced. Initially, peasant families supplemented their agricultural income in this way; eventually, some of them gave up farming altogether and pooled their resources to create small textile mills in the countryside. As the system grew, the guilds of the town were unable to compete with the mills, and cottage industry replaced the urban guilds as the center for textile production.

The new system of rural manufacturing went hand in hand with the shift to market-oriented agriculture; the destruction of the manorial system could not have been accomplished if the cash flowing into the economy did not find its way into the hands of the rural population. The creation of cottage industries provided the cash that enabled rural families to buy their food, rather than having to grow it themselves.

However, the social change that accompanied the destruction of both the manorial system and the guilds also brought hardship and insecurity. The enclosure movement meant that thousands of small landholders, tenant farmers, and sharecroppers lost their land and their social status. Forced to work for wages, their lives and those of their families were now at the mercy of the marketplace. The destruction of the guilds produced similar trauma for the artisans whose livelihood had been protected by the guilds and their families. For both the peasantry and the artisans, the economic and social changes of the eighteenth century meant the destruction of their traditional place and status in society; they were now faced with both new opportunity and great insecurity.

Technical Innovations in Agriculture and Manufacturing

It is important to remember that technical innovations are always responses to new challenges. The people of earlier centuries did not fail to innovate because they were less intelligent; they simply had no need for the innovations. The ever-growing population and demand for food and goods in the eighteenth century created a series of related demands that eventually led to technical innovations in both agriculture and manufacturing. Single innovations often created a need for further innovation in a different part of the process.

The key technical innovation in the agricultural sector in the eighteenth century was the replacement of the old three-field system (in which roughly one-third of the land was left fallow to allow the soil to replenish itself with the necessary nutrients to produce crops) with new crops, such as clover, turnips, and potatoes, which replenished the soil while also producing foodstuffs that could be used to feed livestock in winter. More and healthier livestock contributed to the creation of products as varied as dairy and leather.

In the manufacturing sector, a number of interconnected technical innovations greatly increased the pace and output of the textile industry:

- In 1733, John Kay invented the flying shuttle, which doubled the speed at which cloth could be woven on a loom, creating a need to find a way to produce greater amounts of thread faster.
- In the 1760s, James Hargreaves invented the spinning jenny, which greatly increased the amount of thread a single spinner could produce from cotton, creating a need to speed up the harvesting of cotton.
- In 1793, the American Eli Whitney invented the cotton gin, which efficiently removed seed from raw cotton, thereby increasing the speed with which it could be processed and sent to the spinners.

These technical innovations greatly increased the pace and productivity of the textile industry. The need to supervise these larger, faster machines also contributed to the development of centralized textile mills, which replaced the scattered putting-out system by the end of the eighteenth century.

Eastern Ambition

The prosperity and power of Great Britain and France caused their eastern European rivals to try to strengthen and modernize their kingdoms.

Prussia

In Prussia, Frederick William I built a strong centralized government in which the military, under the command of the nobles, played a dominant role. In 1740, his successor Frederick II (the Great) used that military to extend Prussia into lands controlled by the Habsburgs. Challenging the right of Maria Theresa to ascend the throne of Austria (which was a right guaranteed her by a document known as "the Pragmatic Sanction"), Frederick II marched troops into Silesia. In what came to be known as the War of the Austrian Succession (1740–1748), Maria Theresa was able to rally Austrian and Hungarian troops to fight Prussia and its allies, the French, Spanish, Saxons, and Bavarians, resulting in a standoff.

Russia

In Russia, the progress toward modernization and centralization made under Peter the Great had largely been undone in the first half of the eighteenth century. However, under the leadership of Catherine the Great, Russia defeated the Ottoman Turks in 1774, thereby extending Russia's borders as far as the Black Sea and the Balkan Peninsula. In 1775, Russia joined with Prussia and Austria to conquer Poland and to divide its territories among the three of them.

War and Diplomacy

In eighteenth-century Europe, state-building was still primarily conducted through war and diplomacy. The competition between Great Britain and France in the Triangular Trade Networks meant that they would contend militarily for control of colonies in North America and the Caribbean; in addition, the desire to weaken one another also led them to become entangled in land wars in Europe.

The expansionist aims of Frederick II of Prussia led to a shift in diplomatic alliances, which is now referred to as the Diplomatic Revolution:

- Prussia, fearful of being isolated by its enemies, forged an alliance in 1756 with its former enemy, Great Britain.
- Austria and France, previously antagonistic toward one another, were so alarmed by the alliance of Prussia and Great Britain that they forged an alliance of their own.

Colonial and continental rivalries combined to bring all of the great European powers into conflict during the Seven Years' War (1756–1763). Land and sea battles were fought in North America (where the conflict is sometimes referred to as "the French and Indian War"),

Europe, and India. The European hostilities were concluded in 1763 by a peace agreement that essentially reestablished prewar boundaries. The North American conflict, and particularly the fall of Quebec in 1759, shifted the balance of power in North America to the British. The British had similar success in India.

As the eighteenth century progressed, the nature of European armies and wars changed in ways that would have profound implications for the ruling regimes:

- The size of the standing armies increased.
- The officer corps became full-time servants of the state.
- Troops consisted of conscripts, volunteers, mercenaries, and criminals who were pressed into service.
- Discipline and training became harsher and more extensive.

At the same time, weapons and tactics changed to accommodate the new armies:

- Muskets became more efficient and more accurate.
- Cannons became more mobile.
- Wars were now decided not by a decisive battle, but by a superior organization of resources.
- Naval battles were now often more crucial than land battles.

Review Questions

Multiple Choice

Questions 1–3 refer to the following passage:

The political dominance of large landowners determined the course of enclosure. . . . [I]t was their power in Parliament and as local Justices of the Peace that enabled them to redistribute the land in their own favor.

A typical round of enclosure began when several, or even a single, prominent landholder initiated it . . . by petition to Parliament. . . . [T]he commissioners were invariably of the same class and outlook as the major landholders who had petitioned in the first place, [so] it was not surprising that the great landholders awarded themselves the best land and the most of it, thereby making England a classic land of great, well-kept estates with a small marginal peasantry and a large class of rural wage laborers.

Joseph R. Stromberg, "English Enclosures and Soviet Collectivization: Two Instances of an Anti-Peasant Mode of Development," 1995

1. Stromberg sees the seventeenth-century English Parliament and justices of the peace as primarily which of the following?
   A. Protectors of the rights of agricultural laborers
   B. Political innovations
   C. A check on agricultural innovation
   D. Instruments of the landowning class
2. Which statement best describes the petitioning process by which enclosure was carried out?
   A. It favored the interests of urban industry.
   B. It favored the interests of the landowning class.
   C. It was fair and balanced.
   D. It promoted cottage industry.

3. The enclosure movement made England into a society characterized by
   A. great economic inequity.
   B. great economic opportunity.
   C. industrialization.
   D. urbanization.

Short Answer

4. Briefly explain the rise of technical innovation in eighteenth-century agriculture. Illustrate your explanation with THREE examples.

Answers and Explanations

1. **D** is correct as the passage asserts that Parliament and local justices of the peace "enabled [large landowners] to redistribute the land in their own favor." A is incorrect as the passage indicates that Parliament and local justices of the peace looked out for the interests of the landowning classes, not of the agricultural laborers. B is incorrect because nothing in the passage refers to political innovation. C is incorrect because the passage indicates that Parliament and local justices of the peace helped to bring about enclosure, which was an agricultural innovation.

2. **B** is correct because the passage indicates that the commissioners who oversaw the petitioning process were of the landowning class and "awarded themselves the best land and the most of it." A is incorrect because the passage makes no reference to urban industry. C is incorrect because the passage clearly indicates that the process favored the landowning class. D is incorrect because the passage makes no reference to cottage industry.

3. **A** is correct because the last sentence of the passage indicates that enclosure created an England in which the landowning classes had great, landed estates, while the peasantry was "marginal," and the rest of the population were reduced to being "wage laborers." B is incorrect because the passage makes no reference to enclosure furthering economic opportunity. C and D are incorrect because the passage makes no reference to industrialization or urbanization.

4. Suggested answer:

   Thesis: The rise of technical innovation in eighteenth-century agriculture was a response to the rising demand for food and goods created by an increasing population. The process of innovation was spurred on by its reciprocal nature, as innovation in one sector of the process created a demand for innovation in other sectors.

   Paragraph Outline:

   I. For example, the increasing population created an increased demand for textile production. That demand created a need for faster ways to process larger amounts of wool and cotton goods. As a response, the flying shuttle was developed in 1733 to increase the speed at which cloth could be woven; the spinning jenny was developed in the 1760s to increase the amount of thread that could be spun by a single spinner; and the cotton gin was developed in 1793 to increase the speed with which seeds could be removed from cotton.

   II. The process of innovation in one aspect of textile production created a demand for innovation in other aspects. By doubling the speed at which cloth could be woven, the flying shuttle created a demand for greater amounts of thread. That demand was met by the spinning jenny, which increased the amount of thread that could be produced by a single spinner, but that in turn created a demand for faster, more efficient harvesting of cotton. That demand was met by the cotton gin.

Rapid Review

In the eighteenth century, Great Britain and France continued down their respective paths toward constitutionalism and absolutism. Concurrently, they came to dominate the lucrative Triangular Trade Networks, which allowed valuable raw materials from North America and the Caribbean to be imported to Europe in exchange for serving as a market for manufactured goods and for slaves acquired from Africa. The influx of capital generated by the colonial trade served as a spur for unchecked population growth made possible by an agricultural revolution and the creation of a system of rural manufacturing. The changes in agricultural and manufacturing production destroyed the last vestiges of an economic system (manorialism) and a social system (feudalism) that dated back to the medieval period. In that process, both the traditional European peasantry and the guildsmen were converted to wage labor.

The intensifying rivalry between Great Britain and France, and the growing ambition of their Eastern European counterparts, led to a series of mid-century wars, including the War of the Austrian Succession and the Seven Years' War. Rivalries also led to a series of innovations in diplomacy and warfare.

Further Resources

Films

The Return of Martin Guerre (1982)

Ivan the Terrible (1982)

Peter the Great (1986) TV mini series

Catherine the Great (1986) TV mini series

CHAPTER 16

The Rise of Natural Philosophy, Scientific Revolution, and the Enlightenment

IN THIS CHAPTER

Summary: By the mid-sixteenth century, the spirit of Renaissance human-ism fused with other traditions to create a Platonic-Pythagorean point of view that sought to identify the fundamental mathematical laws of nature. This culminated in Newton's discovery of the laws of physics. Inspired by Newton's achievements, many of the educated elite in France and England tried to apply reason and logic to discover the "natural laws" for social and political order. These scientific and philosophic developments had serious political and reli-gious ramifications. This chapter examines some of the significant contributions in astronomy, medicine, and mathematics, and then looks at the beliefs of the most influential thinkers of the Enlightenment. It then discusses how the more egalitarian and democratic thought of this period contributed to an atmos-phere of political and social revolution that flourished in Europe at the end of the century.

KEY IDEA

Key Terms:

- ✪ **Celestial realm** The realm, in the Aristotelian view of the cosmos, above the orbit of the moon.
- ✪ **Elements** The basic components of matter in Aristotelian physics; there were five: earth, water, air, fire, and ether.
- ✪ **Qualities** A term, in Aristotelian physics, for the tendencies of matter; that is, Earth sinks, air floats, etc.
- ✪ **Geocentric** Earth-centered; the Aristotelian model of the cosmos.

- **Scholasticism** A term for the pre-Renaissance system of knowledge characterized by the belief that everything worth knowing was written down in ancient texts.
- **Hermeticism** A tradition of knowledge that taught that the world was infused with a single spirit that could be explored through mathematics, as well as through magic.
- *Two Treatises on Government* Philosophical treatise (1690) by the Englishman John Locke, which became the primary argument for the establishment of natural limits to governmental authority.
- **Civil society** The society formed when free individuals come together and surrender some of their individual power in return for greater protection.
- *The Spirit of Laws* The Baron de Montesquieu's treatise of 1748, in which he expanded on John Locke's theory of limited government and outlined a system in which government was divided into branches in order to check and balance its power.
- *An Essay Concerning Human Understanding* John Locke's treatise of 1689–1690, which argued that humans are born *tabula rasa* (as "blank slates"), contradicting the traditional Christian notion that humans were born corrupt and sinful, and implying that what humans become is purely a result of what they experience.
- *The Wealth of Nations* Adam Smith's treatise of 1776, which argued that there are laws of human labor, production, and trade that stem from the unerring tendency of all humans to seek their own self-interest.
- *Invisible hand* A phrase, penned by Adam Smith in *The Wealth of Nations* (1776), to denote the way in which natural economic laws guide the economy.
- *Vindication of the Rights of Woman* Mary Wollstonecraft's treatise of 1792, in which she argued that reason was the basis of moral behavior in *all* human beings, not just in men.
- **Salons** Places where both men and women gathered, in eighteenth-century France, to educate themselves about and discuss the new ideas of the Enlightenment in privacy and safety.
- *Philosophe* Public intellectual of the French Enlightenment who believed that society should be reformed on the basis of natural law and reason.
- **Masonic lodges** Secret meeting places established and run by Freemasons, whose origins dated back to the medieval guilds of the stonemasons. By the eighteenth century, the lodges were fraternities of aristocratic and middle-class men (and occasionally women) who gathered to discuss alternatives to traditional beliefs.
- **Deism** The belief that the complexity, order, and natural laws exhibited by the universe were reasonable proof that it had been created by a God who was no longer active.
- **Enlightened despotism** The hope shared by many philosophes that the powerful monarchs of European civilization, once educated in the ideals of the Enlightenment, would use their power to reform and rationalize society.
- *Candide* Voltaire's sprawling satire of European culture, penned in 1759, which has become the classic example of Enlightenment-period satire.
- *Encyclopedia* Produced by the tireless efforts of its coeditors, Denis Diderot and Jean le Rond d'Alembert (1751–1772), the entries of the *Encyclopedia* championed a scientific approach to knowledge and labeled anything not based on reason as superstition.

- *System of Nature*   The Baron Paul d'Holbach's treatise of 1770, which was the first work of Enlightenment philosophy to be openly atheist and materialist.
- *The Social Contract*   Jean-Jacques Rousseau's treatise of 1762, in which he wrote, "Man is born free; and everywhere he is in chains." Rousseau argued that a virtuous citizen should be willing to subordinate his own self-interest to the general good of the community and that the government must be continually responsive to the general will of the people.
- **Almanacs**   Popular eighteenth-century texts that incorporated much of the new scientific and rational knowledge of the Enlightenment.
- **Philosophical texts**   The underground book trade's code name for banned books, which included some versions of philosophical treatises and bawdy, popularized versions of *the philosophes*' critique of the Church and the ruling classes.
- **Neoplatonism**   In the Renaissance and the Early Modern period, a philosophy based on that of Plato, which contended that reality was located in a changeless world of forms and that, accordingly, spurred the study of mathematics. It also refers to the attempt to reconcile pagan and Christian ideals, and the artistic idea that contemplation of beauty led to contemplation of the divine.
- **Platonic–Pythagorean tradition**   A tradition of philosophy that developed in the sixteenth and seventeenth centuries, which embraced the works of Plato and Pythagoras and which had as its goal the identification of the fundamental mathematical laws of nature.
- **Heliocentric**   Sun-centered; the model of the cosmos proposed by Nicolas Copernicus in 1534.
- **Copernicanism**   The theory, following Nicolas Copernicus, that the sun is at the center of the cosmos and that the Earth is the third planet from the sun.
- **Kepler's laws**   Three laws of planetary motion developed by Johannes Kepler between 1609 and 1619.
- *The Starry Messenger*   Galileo's treatise of 1610, in which he published his celestial observations made with a telescope.
- *Dialogue on the Two Chief Systems of the World*   Galileo's treatise of 1632, in which he dismantled the arguments in favor of the traditional, Aristotelian view of the cosmos and presented the Copernican system as the only alternative for reasonable people.
- *Discourse on Method*   René Descartes's treatise of 1637, in which he established a method of philosophical inquiry based on radical skepticism.

Key Individuals:
- Copernicus
- Kepler
- Galileo
- Descartes
- Paracelsus
- Andreas Vesalius
- William Harvey
- Margaret Cavendish
- Maria Sibylla Merian
- Maria Winkelmann

- ✪ Cesare Beccaria
- ✪ David Hume
- ✪ Diego Velásquez
- ✪ Gian Bernini
- ✪ J. S. Bach
- ✪ Rembrandt
- ✪ Vermeer
- ✪ Jacques-Louis David
- ✪ Jane Austen
- ✪ René Descartes
- ✪ William Hogarth

Introduction

Natural philosophy is a term that refers to the attempt of intellectuals to understand the natural world. The Scientific Revolution is the term given to the rise of a particular kind of natural philosophy that stressed empirical observation and reason. While it is hard to know where to cite the beginning of such a development, many historians point to a key publication by Nicolas Copernicus in 1543 and to Galileo Galilei's challenge to the old Aristotelian view of the cosmos and the authority of the Catholic Church in 1610. "The Enlightenment" refers to an eighteenth-century cultural movement whose proponents argued that society and its laws should be based on human reason, rather than on custom, religion, or tradition. Its roots can be traced to the late seventeenth century, when thinkers and writers began praising the method of inquiry and the accomplishments of Sir Isaac Newton. Following Newton, political writers like John Locke began suggesting that there were natural laws that govern human behavior and that these laws could be discovered through reason. In the eighteenth century, intellectuals known as *philosophes* developed a program for reforming society along the lines of reason, which they initially hoped to implement by educating the powerful rulers, or "enlightened despots," of Europe. Later in the century, when enlightened despotism seemed to have failed, Enlightenment ideals began to be applied in more revolutionary contexts.

The Traditional View of the Cosmos

The traditional view of the cosmos in European civilization was one that it inherited from the ancient Greek philosopher Aristotle. The Aristotelian cosmos was based on observation and common sense. Because the Earth appeared, to all of one's senses, to stand still, Aristotle believed the Earth was the unmoving center point of the cosmos. The moon, the planets, and the stars were understood to move in concentric circular orbits around the Earth because that is what they appeared to do. The stars were conceived of as "fixed" into a single sphere because they do not move relative to each other.

The Aristotelian cosmos was divided into two realms:

- The terrestrial realm, which contained the Earth and all matter inside the orbit of the moon
- The celestial realm, or the realm of the heavens, which existed beyond the orbit of the moon

In the Aristotelian cosmos, there were five basic elements, each of which was defined by its qualities:

1. Earth, which was heavy and tended to sink toward the center of the cosmos
2. Water, which was slightly lighter and accumulated on top of the solid Earth
3. Air, which was lighter still
4. Fire, which was the lightest of all and tended to try to rise above all the others
5. Ether, which was perfect matter that existed only in the celestial realm and which moved in uniform circular motion

The qualities of the five types of matter served as the basis of Aristotelian physics. The motion of terrestrial matter was understood to be the result of its composition. For example, if you threw a rock, its motion described a parabola because the force of the throw gave its motion a horizontal component, while its heaviness gave it a vertical component toward the Earth. If you filled an air-tight bag with air and submerged it in water, it would float to the top because the air was lighter than Earth or water. The planets and stars of the celestial realm moved at a uniform rate in perfect circles around the Earth because they were composed purely of ether.

To the medieval church scholars who rediscovered and translated the writings of Aristotle, this Earth-centered, or "geocentric," model of the cosmos made logical sense. It confirmed the Christian theological doctrine that the perfect kingdom of God awaited in the heavens for those humans who could transcend the corruption of the world.

Alternative Traditions of Knowledge Before the Scientific Revolution

Although the dominant tradition of knowledge in European civilization before the Scientific Revolution was scholasticism, which derived its knowledge from ancient texts like those of Aristotle, there were other traditions upon which the Scientific Revolution drew.

Natural Magic, Alchemy, and Hermeticism

One was the tradition of natural magic and alchemy that understood the natural world to be alive with latent power, just waiting to be tapped by those who could learn its secrets. One strain of magical thought drew inspiration from a corpus of texts erroneously attributed to a supposed ancient Egyptian priest, Hermes Trismegistus. Hermeticism taught that the world was infused with a single spirit that could be explored through mathematics as well as through magic.

Neoplatonism

The most powerful and potent of the alternative traditions was developed by Renaissance humanists who rediscovered and revered the work of the ancient Greek philosopher Plato. Plato's writings distinguished between a changeless and eternal realm of being or form and the temporary and perishable world we experience. To the Neoplatonists, mathematics was the language with which one could discover and describe the world of forms. Like the

Hermetic tradition, Neoplatonism taught that mathematics described the essential nature and soul of the cosmos, a soul that was God itself. The use of mathematics to discover and describe the world of forms was reflected in both the use of perspective in art and the reconciliation of pagan and Christian symbols.

The Platonic–Pythagorean Tradition

By the advent of the seventeenth century, these alternative traditions had fused into an approach to gaining knowledge of the natural world that has come to be known as the Platonic–Pythagorean tradition (after Plato and the ancient mathematically oriented school of Pythagoras), which had as its goal the identification of the fundamental mathematical laws of nature.

Development of New Institutions

Because the curricula of traditional universities were devoted to the teaching of Aristotle and other authorities in the scholastic tradition, new institutions were required for the alternative traditions to flourish. New institutions that emerged to fill that role included the following:

- Royal courts, where kings, dukes, and other ruling nobles were determined to show off both their wealth and their virtue by patronizing not only great artists and musicians but also natural philosophers
- Royal societies and academies, like the Royal Society of London and the Royal Academy of Sciences in Paris, both established in the 1660s, where organized groups of natural philosophers sought and received the patronage of the Crown by emphasizing both the prestige and the practical applications of their discoveries
- Smaller academies under the patronage of individual nobles, like the *Accademia dei Lincei*, founded in Italy in 1603 by Federico Cesi, the oldest scientific academy in the world
- New universities, particularly in Italy, which were funded by the civic-minded merchants in the Renaissance tradition and which were outside the control of the Church

The Rise of Copernicanism

The central challenge to the traditional view of the cosmos was made in the context of the Church's own effort to reform the calendar and, therefore, the science of astronomy. The annual changes in the position of the sun, the moon, and the planets with respect to the constellations of stars are the means by which human beings construct calendars that keep track of time and predict seasonal climate patterns. In keeping with the philosophy of scholasticism, European Church scholars constructed calendars based on ancient astronomical tables that dated back to the ancient Greek astronomer Claudius Ptolemy. Though amazingly accurate, the multiplication over thousands of years of small errors in the Ptolemaic astronomical tables led to a situation in the early sixteenth century in which the calendars were dramatically out of sync with the actual seasons.

In 1515, a church council appointed to consider calendar reform summoned the Polish churchman and astronomer Nicolas Copernicus to remedy the situation. Educated in a Neoplatonic academy and a proponent of the Platonic–Pythagorean tradition, Copernicus proposed to reconcile the calendar and the actual movements of the heavens by introducing a new sun-centered, or "heliocentric," astronomical model of the cosmos.

Copernicus's proposal alarmed Church authorities for several reasons:

- It questioned the authority of the Aristotelian tradition on which scholasticism relied.
- It contradicted the physical principles that served as the foundation of physics.
- It destroyed the theological coherence of the cosmos.
- It required the Church to admit it had been in error.

Shortly before Copernicus's death in 1543, the Church allowed his theory to be published in a work titled *De revolutionibus orbium coelestium* (*On the Revolutions of the Heavenly Bodies*), provided that it be accompanied by a preface stating that the theory was only being presented as a useful hypothetical model, not as a true account of the physical nature of the cosmos. Because Copernicus's great work was written in Latin (which was the language of educated scholars) and because it was a highly technical work, its publication created no great stir. But slowly, over the course of the next seventy years, Copernicanism (as the theory came to be known) spread in circles of men educated both within the Church and in the newer academies and societies.

Kepler's Laws

By the seventeenth century, a loose network of Copernicans championed the new world view as part of a new empirical and mathematical approach to the study of the natural world. One was a German mathematician working in the Hermetic and Neoplatonic traditions, Johannes Kepler, who devoted his life to finding the mathematical harmonies of the cosmos. Between 1609 and 1619, he developed three laws of planetary motion that would come to be known as Kepler's laws:

1. The first law broke with the tradition of conceiving of the planets as moving in uniform circles, suggesting that the planetary orbits took the form of an ellipse, with the sun as one of their foci.
2. The second law abandoned the notion that planetary motion was uniform and asserted that a planet's velocity varied according to its distances from the sun, sweeping out equal areas in equal times.
3. The third law gave a mathematical description for the physical relationship between the planets and the sun, asserting that the squares of the orbital periods of the planets are in the same ratio as the cubes of their average distance from the sun.

Galileo and the Value of Empirical Knowledge

Although Kepler worked in obscurity, Galileo Galilei was an ambitious self-promoter. Dubbing himself a "mathematical philosopher," Galileo championed an approach to knowing the natural world that emphasized the need to apply reason to observational and mathematical data. Also, following the English philosopher Francis Bacon, Galileo combined his approach with an appeal to the practical and pragmatic value of such knowledge.

Having dismantled and analyzed a spyglass he bought from Dutch merchants, Galileo drew up schematics for a larger, more powerful version. The result was the world's first telescope, and Galileo immediately turned his new invention on the heavens. In 1610, Galileo published his findings in a pamphlet titled *Sidereus Nuncius* (*The Starry Messenger*). There, he announced several discoveries, which, although they did not explicitly promote the Copernican theory, did implicitly call into question the veracity of the Aristotelian model. These discoveries included the following:

- The existence of countless stars previously unseen, suggesting that there was much about the cosmos that was not known.
- The rugged, crater-filled surface of the moon, suggesting that it was not created of perfect celestial matter.
- Four moons orbiting the planet Jupiter, suggesting that it would not be so strange for Earth to have a moon as well.

Unfortunately, Galileo mistakenly believed that both a combination of his growing fame and his value to his powerful patron (the Grand Duke of Tuscany, Cosimo de' Medici) would protect him from the wrath of the Catholic Church. Because of this mistaken belief, Galileo began to promote more boldly both the Copernican theory and his method of knowing nature through the application of reason to empirical observations. In 1615, he was summoned to Rome, where he narrowly escaped being branded a heretic only because he had a powerful friend, Cardinal Maffeo Barberini, who interceded on Galileo's behalf and managed to convince the Church to brand the Copernican theory "erroneous" rather than "heretical." Galileo was set free with a stern warning. In 1623, Barberini became Pope Urban VIII. The following year, Galileo returned to Rome for a series of discussions with the pope. He left having been given permission to teach Copernicanism as a theory, but not as a true account of the cosmos.

Over the next decade and a half, Galileo continued to promote his particular brand of natural philosophy. In 1632, chafing against the constrictions put upon him, Galileo effectively took his case to the public by abandoning the Latin prose of the scholarly elite for the vernacular Italian of the masses and publishing a thinly veiled attack on what he considered to be the absurdity of the Church's defense of the Aristotelian model. His *Dialogue on the Two Chief Systems of the World* dismantled the arguments in favor of the traditional, Aristotelian view of the cosmos and presented the Copernican system as the only alternative for reasonable people. Early the following year, Galileo was summoned before the Inquisition and forced to recant. He was sentenced to spend the rest of his life under house arrest and forbidden ever to publish again. The long-term effect of Galileo's condemnation was to shift the locus of the Scientific Revolution to the Protestant countries of Europe.

Advances in Anatomy, Physiology, and Medicine

During the sixteenth century, the fields of anatomy, physiology, and medicine were heavily influenced by the work of a Greek physician Galen, whose ideas were derived from observation and dissection of animals. He postulated that there were two vascular (blood) systems: muscular, with bright red blood in arteries; and digestive, with darker blood located in veins. He also believed humans had four "humors," or liquids in the body whose balance was integral to health. An imbalance of blood, yellow bile, black bile, or phlegm would be diagnosed through observation of the urine.

Galen's views were rejected by Paracelsus (an adopted name, meaning "greater than Celsus"). Influenced in part by his childhood in a mining town where he observed that metals "grow" in the earth, he developed an interest in alchemy, chemistry, and metallurgy, specifically that illness resulted from chemical imbalance. He also placed great weight in the folk remedies and wisdom of commoners. Due to his irascible and egotistical nature, his ideas were not widely adopted. He did identify metals as the cause of silicosis (through inhalation) and goiter (through drinking water), and used combinations of metals in treatment of diseases like syphilis and others. His advances laid the foundations for using chemistry in drug therapies and homeopathy.

The study of anatomy in the mid-sixteenth century typically consisted of a butcher dissecting a human cadaver while the instructor read aloud from the relevant historical text, without actually participating in the dissection. Andreas Vesalius, unusually, performed his own dissections, developing such skill that he moved quickly from assistant, to doctor, to anatomy professor. His greatest work is *De humani corporis fabrica—The Structure of the Human Body*, an anatomical text with over 200 illustrations, based on his personal observations through dissection of human cadavers. In it, he corrected many misconceptions, like his assertion that the largest blood vessels originate in the heart, rather than the liver. Though he had fewer illustrations of women, he did note that women have the same number of ribs and teeth as men.

Following in the observational tradition of Vesalius, William Harvey relied on his own dissections of humans and animals to write *Anatomical Studies on the Motion of Heart and Blood in Animals (De Moto Cordis)*. In this book he identified the vascular system as completing a circuit within the body, the locus of which was located in the heart.

Contributions of Women During the Scientific Revolution

Women in the sciences during the sixteenth and seventeenth centuries endured tremendous challenges. Many of them were noblewomen—who were informally taught through interactions with or assistance of male relatives—such as Margaret Cavendish, Duchess of Newcastle-on-Tyne, a poet, playwright, and natural philosopher. She and her husband had a small salon, whose attendees included Thomas Hobbes and René Descartes. Though permitted to attend a meeting of the Royal Society, she was denied membership. Through her writings, she popularized many of the scientific theories of the day. She challenged the scientific establishment, claiming that, for example, observations via microscope could be misleading, resulting in false interpretations of the world. She also argued that theology and the cosmos were beyond the scope of scientific inquiry and man's control.

Another avenue for scientific study for middle-class women was through family trades. Such was the case in Germany of Maria Sibylla Merian, whose father and stepfather were an illustrator and an artist, respectively. Starting as an assistant to her stepfather, she collected plants and insects for his works, eventually studying their life cycles and documenting them, both in words and images. Eventually she began publishing her works, which became known for their detail and accuracy, especially those in an exhaustive study of the insects and plants of Surinam. Similarly, Maria Winkelmann assisted first her father and later her husband, Gottfried Kirch, with their study of astronomy. With her husband, she observed and recorded the movement of stars and the weather and compiled the data to be used in calendars and almanacs. In 1702, Winkelmann discovered a comet, and was the first woman to do so, but it was not acknowledged until eight years later. After her husband's death, the Royal Academy of Sciences in Berlin rejected her application to take her husband's place. Winkelmann continued working in the field of astronomy, even predicting a comet, but still struggled with being recognized in her own right.

Cartesian Skepticism and Deductive Reasoning

Although many of those who took the lead in the Scientific Revolution in the second half of the seventeenth century were born in Protestant countries, René Descartes had been a citizen of Catholic France. But upon hearing of Galileo's condemnation, Descartes relocated to the Netherlands, where he published (in 1637) a challenge to both the authority of scholasticism and to the validity of the Galilean approach. In *Discourse on Method*, Descartes began by sweeping away all previous claims to knowledge by skeptically asserting that "received knowledge"—that is, information that you do not learn for yourself—amounted to nothing more than "opinion." But rather than proceed from observation, Descartes extended his skepticism to the senses, which, he asserted, could easily be fooled; instead, he sought the "clear and distinct idea"—that is, one that could not reasonably be doubted.

The first idea that Descartes could not doubt was that he was thinking, and that if he was thinking, then he must really exist. From that famous formulation—"I think, therefore I am"—Descartes proceeded to deduce a variety of truths, including the existence of God and a cosmos made up of only two things: matter and motion. Putting the sun in the center (as Copernicus had done), Descartes described a solar system in which the planets were simply large chunks of matter that were caught in swirling vortices of smaller matter. This Cartesian approach of deducing the details of nature from a set of clearly defined general propositions appealed to those who sought an intelligible explanation of the cosmos, rather than the mathematical calculations of the Platonic–Pythagorean tradition.

The Enlightenment

"The Enlightenment" refers to an eighteenth-century cultural movement whose proponents argued that society and its laws should be based on human reason, rather than on custom, religion, or tradition. Its roots can be traced to the late seventeenth century, when thinkers and writers began praising the method of inquiry and the accomplishments of Sir Isaac Newton. Following Newton, political writers like John Locke began suggesting that there were natural laws that govern human behavior and that these laws could be discovered through reason. In the eighteenth century, intellectuals known as *philosophes* developed a program for reforming society along the lines of reason, which they initially hoped to implement by educating the powerful rulers, or "enlightened despots," of Europe. Later in the century, when enlightened despotism seemed to have failed, Enlightenment ideals began to be applied in more revolutionary contexts.

The Triumph of Newtonian Science

Isaac Newton was an Englishman who was educated at Cambridge University at a time when its faculty was committed to the advancement of Neoplatonism and to the rejection of Cartesianism. As a fellow of Trinity College, Cambridge, Newton lived a solitary life and was driven by the notion that God had left clues to His true nature in the laws that governed the natural world. Newton was intensely focused on solving the mystery of planetary motion. Using a mathematical system of his own creation, which he called "fluxions" (and which we now refer to as calculus), and following Kepler's suggestion that the paths of planetary orbits were elliptical, Newton was able to calculate the orbits of the planets precisely by assuming that each particle of matter, no matter how large or small, was drawn to every other piece of matter by a force that he called "universal gravitation."

Newton published his results in 1687 in his great work, the *Principia Mathematica* (*The Mathematical Principles of Natural Philosophy*), in which he stated, "Every particle of matter in the universe attracts every other particle with a force varying inversely as the square of the distance between them and directly proportional to the product of their masses." The *Principia* not only provided the correct calculations for planetary motion, it set out "definitions" and "laws of motion," which demonstrated how mathematical philosophy was henceforth to be done.

For the rest of the seventeenth century, the methods of Newton and Descartes served as competing models, with Newtonianism reigning in Great Britain and Cartesianism dominating in continental Europe. But by the dawn of the eighteenth century, Newtonianism had won out and served as a model not just for natural philosophy, but for an approach to the understanding of human society—an approach that would come to be known as "the Enlightenment."

New Ideas About Natural Law, Human Nature, and Society

Isaac Newton had shown that, through the rigorous application of empirical observation and reason, humans could discern the laws that God had created to govern the natural world. His eighteenth-century successors, the *philosophes*, argued that the same process could lead to knowledge of the natural laws that govern human behavior. Accordingly, the Enlightenment view of society rested upon certain assumptions about the "natural state" of human beings.

Thomas Hobbes

One assumption about human nature that was foundational to Enlightenment thought was the belief that human beings could discern and would naturally follow their own self-interest. Thomas Hobbes, the author of *Leviathan* (1651), asserted that self-interest motivated nearly all human behavior. Specifically, Hobbes argued that human beings were naturally driven to quarrel by competition, diffidence, and glory. Hobbes therefore concluded that "without a common power to keep them in awe," the natural state of man was one of war.

John Locke

More typical of Enlightenment thought about human nature were the ideas of John Locke. In his *Essay Concerning Human Understanding* (1689–1690), Locke argued that humans are born *tabula rasa* (as "blank slates"). This contradicted the traditional Christian notion that humans were born corrupt and sinful, and it implied that what humans become is purely a result of what they experience. Accordingly, Locke argued that educational and social systems that taught and rewarded rational behavior would produce law-abiding and peaceful citizens.

Locke shared Hobbes's belief in self-interest, and its importance in Locke's thought can be seen in his influential theory of private property, which appeared in his *Two Treatises on Government* (1690). Locke argued that God created the world and its abundance so that humans might make it productive. To ensure that productivity, God established a natural right to property. Private property is created, Locke argued, when an individual mixes a common resource with his individual labor. For example, when an individual does the work of cutting down a tree and crafting the wood into a chair, he has mixed a common resource with his individual labor to create something that did not exist before. That creation is his private property and, therefore, his incentive to be productive.

Adam Smith

A typical eighteenth-century example of self-interest as natural law can be seen in the work of Adam Smith, who applied Enlightenment ideals to the realm of economics. In *The Wealth of Nations* (1776), Smith argued that there were laws of human labor, production, and trade that stemmed from the unerring tendency of all humans to seek their own self-interest.

The economic laws that Smith identified, such as the law of supply and demand, are all by-products of human self-interest. Smith asserted that the sum total of these natural economic laws functioned like an "invisible hand" that guided the economy. Though the prevailing economic theory, mercantilism, encouraged government intervention in the economy through tariffs, subsidies for domestic industry, and a favorable balance of trade, Smith challenged this view. Efforts by governments to alter the natural laws of an economy, such as putting a tax or tariff on foreign products, would ultimately fail, Smith argued. Accordingly, Smith and his followers advocated a hands-off, or *laissez-faire*, economic policy, exemplified by free markets and free trade.

Mary Wollstonecraft

In 1792, the English *philosophe* Mary Wollstonecraft published *Vindication of the Rights of Woman*, in which she argued that reason was the basis of moral behavior in all human beings (not just men). From that basis, she went on to assert that the subjugation of women in European society was based on irrational belief and the blind following of tradition, and she challenged all men of reason to acknowledge the equality and human rights of all men and women.

New Political Ideas

Enlightenment ideals about natural law, human nature, and society led Enlightenment thinkers to ponder the question of the origin and proper role of government. Both Locke and Hobbes wrote in the context of the English Civil War that pitted Royalists against Parliamentarians. The Royalists supported the traditional power and privilege of the aristocracy and the king. In contrast, the Parliamentarians were seeking to limit the power and privilege of the aristocracy and the king.

Thomas Hobbes

Hobbes was a Royalist. From his point of view, the Parliamentarians had brought chaos to England by naively ignoring the fact that the natural state of humanity was war. Peace, Hobbes argued in *Leviathan*, required a government capable of simultaneously striking the fear of death in its subjects and guaranteeing that lawful subjects would attain a good quality of life. In order to accomplish these tasks, the government required absolute power, which it acquired by entering into an unbreakable contract, or sacred covenant, with the people.

John Locke and Cesare Beccaria

Locke, a Parliamentarian, agreed that men were often ruled by their passions. But in *Two Treatises*, he argued that in civil society, men settled disputes dispassionately and effectively by creating a system of impartial judges and communal enforcement. In such a system, the power of government came from the consent of the people, and its use was limited to protecting the people's natural rights, particularly their right to property. Any government that did not use its power to protect the rights of its people was no longer legitimate and both could and should be deposed. In this way, he repudiated not only the idea of the divine right of kings, but also the concept of absolutism.

In the eighteenth century, it was Locke's vision of government and law that came to dominate the Enlightenment. The Italian philosopher Cesare Beccaria carried Locke's line of thinking about the proper function of government further, arguing in *Crime and Punishment* (1764) that the purpose of punishment should be to rehabilitate and reintegrate the individual into society. Accordingly, the severity of the punishment should reflect the severity of the crime.

Baron de Montesquieu

The Baron de Montesquieu was a French aristocrat and judge who expanded on Locke's theory of limited government by investigating the effects of climate and custom on human behavior. In *The Spirit of Laws* (1748), he stressed the importance of the rule of law and outlined a system in which government was divided into branches in order to check and balance its power.

Thomas Jefferson

Thomas Jefferson established the notion that the only legitimate role of a government was to guarantee its citizens the "inalienable rights to life, liberty, and the pursuit of happiness," which became the philosophical justification for the American Declaration of Independence from the rule of George III and Great Britain in 1776.

The *Philosophes* and Enlightened Despotism

The term *philosophe*, originally just the French term for *philosopher*, came to identify a new breed of philosopher, one dedicated to educating the broader public. Many were popularizers of the ideas of others, looking to spread an ideal of a society governed by reason. To reach the broadest possible audience, they wrote in many different genres: histories, novels, plays, pamphlets, and satires, as well as traditional philosophical treatises.

The phrase "enlightened despotism" referred to the hope shared by many *philosophes* that the powerful monarchs of European civilization, once educated in the ideals of the Enlightenment, would use their power to reform and rationalize society. To one degree or another, many eighteenth-century European monarchs instituted reforms, but within limits:

- Frederick II (the Great) of Prussia abolished serfdom, instituted a policy of religious toleration, and attracted French Protestants and dissidents, such as Voltaire, to his kingdom. But Prussia remained a militaristic state under an absolutist regime, and Voltaire eventually became disenchanted.
- Joseph II of Austria legislated religious toleration for Lutherans and Calvinists, abolished serfdom, and passed laws that liberalized the rules governing the press. But when pamphlets about the French Revolution appeared, he reimposed censorship.
- Catherine II (the Great) of Russia read the works of the *philosophes*; befriended Voltaire, Beccaria, and Diderot; and called for a legislative commission to study reform. But she dismissed the commission before most of its findings had even been reported and had no intention of departing from absolutism.

In the final analysis, enlightened despotism was the use of select Enlightenment ideals to help monarchs modernize and reform certain government and social institutions for the purpose of centralizing and strengthening their grasp on power. In the end, the interests of a ruling monarch ran counter to the more democratic and egalitarian ideals of the Enlightenment.

Salons and Lodges

The development and spread of an intellectual movement required places for people to congregate and share ideas. While *philosophes* could be found in most major European cities, the culture of salons flourished in Paris, making it the center of the Enlightenment.

Originally, the term *salon* had referred to the room in aristocratic homes where the family and its guests gathered for leisure activities. During the Enlightenment, however, aristocratic and, eventually, upper middle-class women transformed such rooms (and the term) by turning them into a place where both men and women gathered to educate themselves about and discuss the new ideas of the age in privacy and safety. In the more prestigious houses, the leading *philosophes* were often invited to give informal lectures and to lead discussions.

It was through the salons that women made their most direct contribution to the Enlightenment. As hostesses, they controlled the guest list and enforced the rules of polite conversation. They were, therefore, in control of what ideas were discussed in front of which influential men, and were somewhat able to affect the reception that those ideas were given. Additionally, they controlled an extensive international correspondence network, as they decided which letters from *philosophes* in other cities were to be read, discussed, and replied to.

Another eighteenth-century home of Enlightenment thought was the Masonic lodge. The lodges were established and run by Freemasons, whose origins dated back to the medieval guilds of the stonemasons. By the eighteenth century, the lodges had become fraternities of aristocratic and middle-class men (and occasionally women) who gathered to discuss alternatives to traditional beliefs. Following the customs of the old guilds, the Masonic fraternities were run along democratic principles, the likes of which were new to continental Europe. Linked together by membership in the Grand Lodge, the lodges formed a network of communication for new ideas and ideals that rivaled that of the salons. Some of the most influential men of the eighteenth century were Masons, including the Duke of Montagu in England, Voltaire and Mozart in France, and Benjamin Franklin in America. In Berlin, Frederick the Great cultivated the Masonic lodges as centers of learning.

Skepticism, Religion, and Social Criticism

Skepticism

Skepticism, or the habit of doubting what one has not learned for oneself, was also a key element of the Scientific Revolution that was developed more widely during the Enlightenment. A particular target of Enlightenment skeptics was religion. In his *Historical and Critical Dictionary* (1697), the French religious skeptic Pierre Bayle included entries for numerous religious beliefs, illustrating why they did not, in his opinion, stand the test of reason. More generally, Bayle argued that all dogmas, including those based on scripture, should be considered false if they contradicted conclusions based on clear and natural reasoning.

Deism

The most prevalent form of religious belief among the *philosophes* was deism. The deists believed that the complexity, order, and natural laws exhibited by the universe were reasonable proof that it had been created by a God. But reason also told them that once God had created the universe and the natural laws that govern it, there would no longer be any further role for Him in the universe. A typical deist tract was John Toland's *Christianity Not Mysterious* (1696). There, Toland argued that the aspects of Christianity that were not compatible with reason should be discarded and that Christians should worship an intelligible God.

Hume

Some *philosophes* went further with their skepticism. The Scottish philosopher David Hume rejected Christianity, arguing that Christianity required a belief in miracles and that the notion of miracles was contradicted by human reason. Hume also attacked the deist position, arguing that the order humans perceived in the universe was probably the product of human minds and social conventions, concluding that all religion was based on "hope and fear." In the final analysis, Hume contended that reason must be the ultimate test and that belief should be in proportion to evidence.

Voltaire

The most famous skeptic of the Enlightenment wrote under the pen name of Voltaire. He raised satire to an art form and used it to criticize those institutions that promoted intolerance and bigotry. For his criticism of the French monarchy, aristocracy, and the Church, he was briefly imprisoned in the Bastille. While in exile in England, he became an admirer of Newton and Locke. In *Lettres philosophiques (Philosophic Letters on the English)* (1734), he compared the constitutional monarchy, rationalism, and toleration that he found in England with the absolutism, superstition, and bigotry of his native France. Later, he produced a sprawling satire of European culture in *Candide* (1759). For a time he lived and worked with the most accomplished female *philosophe*, Madame du Châtelet, who made the only French translation of *Newton's Principia*.

Pascal

Not all philosophers of the Enlightenment were so quick to separate Christianity from science. Many tried to reconcile the two, including French mathematician Blaise Pascal. Pascal's contributions are many, from an early version of the calculator, to the foundations of probability theory. He is probably best known, though, for *Pensées*, an unfinished book published posthumously as a collection of his thoughts. In it, he attempted to unite religion and reason. He claimed men without religion are an odd mixture of greatness and lowliness and that philosophy alone could not explain this contradiction. To convince skeptics, he offered his famous wager: it is rational to believe in God. If there is no God, one loses nothing. If there is a God, one gains eternal paradise.

Spinoza

Benedict Spinoza took an alternative approach to those who separated the laws of nature and of God. To his mind, God and Nature were not separate at all, but two aspects of the same thing. A sort of pantheistic approach, he argued that God is everywhere and everything is God. Accordingly, he contended that God was not separate from the world but existed as the system of the world in all its aspects. This led him to conclude that the system was deterministic and that man did not have free will. Rather, his actions, as all actions within the system, were driven by necessity. Since the world system is perfectly ordered and predetermined by God, moral ideas of good and evil are, therefore, arbitrary and artificial constructs of men. As such, Spinoza was a proponent of moral relativism.

The Arts in the Enlightenment

During the seventeenth century and even into the early eighteenth century, the arts were dominated by the Baroque style, characterized by dramatic uses of light and shadow, emotion, and tension, and whose religious and sometimes grandiose themes were often supported by elites, especially in predominantly Catholic nations. Later, the eighteenth century saw the creation of new opportunities for artists, as the rise of a wealthy middle class broke the aristocratic monopoly on artistic patronage. The tastes of middle-class or bourgeois patrons were simpler than those of their aristocratic counterparts; the art produced for them was, consequently, less grand and less stylized. The middle class particularly patronized the visual arts and demanded genre paintings that depicted more realistic scenes and themes from everyday life. The paintings and engravings of William Hogarth, such as the series titled *Marriage à la Mode* (c. 1744), are examples of this genre.

By the end of the Enlightenment, the artistic world saw a resurgence of interest in the classical Greek and Roman art forms. The neoclassical movement was sparked in part as a reaction against the sometimes frivolous art of the Rococo period (early eighteenth century), but also due to the renewed interest in classical philosophy, particularly the ideas of civic virtue and democracy. Following the classical values of reason and moderation, these paintings were often cerebral rather than emotional. In architecture, this movement saw these ideals reflected in the construction of public buildings with columns based on ancient Greek and Roman buildings.

The Radical Enlightenment

Diderot

As the monarchs and ruling regimes of Europe showed the limits of enlightened despotism, the elements of Enlightenment thought came together in increasingly radical ways. The multi-volume *Encyclopedia* (1751–1772), containing 28 volumes, was produced by the tireless efforts of its coeditors, Denis Diderot and Jean le Rond d'Alembert. Their stated goal was to overturn the barriers of superstition and bigotry, and to contribute to the progress of human knowledge. The entries of the *Encyclopedia* championed a scientific approach to knowledge and labeled anything not based on reason as superstition. Its pages were strewn with Enlightenment thought and the rhetoric of natural rights that was egalitarian and democratic. King Louis XV of France declared that the *Encyclopedia* was causing "irreparable damage to morality and religion," and twice banned its publication.

d'Holbach

Another more radical position was that of the German-born French *philosophe*, the Baron Paul d'Holbach, whose philosophy was openly atheist and materialist. In *System of Nature* (1770), d'Holbach offered the eighteenth-century reader a view of the world as a complex system of purely material substances, acting and developing according to purely mechanical laws of cause and effect, rather than having been imposed by a rational God.

Rousseau

Perhaps the most influential radical voice emerged at mid-century, articulating a view of human nature that differed from Locke's *tabula rasa* and that suggested different political implications. In *Émile* (1762), Jean-Jacques Rousseau argued that humans were born essentially good and virtuous but were easily corrupted by society. Accordingly, Rousseau argued that the early years of a child's education should be spent developing the senses, sensibilities, and sentiments.

Politically, Rousseau agreed with his predecessors that individuals come together to form a civil society and give power to their government by their consent. But where Locke and Montesquieu were content with a constitutional monarchy, Rousseau's model was the ancient Greek city-state in which citizens participated directly in the political life of the state. He expressed his discontent with the political state of affairs in *The Social Contract* (1762): "Man is born free; and everywhere he is in chains." Accordingly, Rousseau believed that the virtuous citizens should be willing to subordinate their own self-interest to the general good of the community, and he argued that a lawful government must be continually responsible to the general will of the people. Toward the end of the century, as the ruling regimes of continental Europe mobilized to protect their power and privilege, it would be Rousseau's version of the Enlightenment that resonated with an increasingly discontented population.

To be clear, though Rousseau was concerned about issues of equality and the education of man, these concerns did not extend to the equality and education of women. For Rousseau, women were clearly the weaker sex. While men desired women, they did not need women in the same way he believed women were dependent on men. Women's education, therefore, was to support their primary purpose, as wife and mother. Interestingly, though he perceived women as incapable of reason, in Rousseau's *Émile*, women serve as educators.

The Other Enlightenment

The Enlightenment of the *philosophes*, with their salons and lodges, was primarily a cultural movement experienced by aristocrats and upper middle-class people. But further down the social hierarchy, a version of the Enlightenment reached an increasingly literate population in the following ways:

- Excerpted versions of the *Encyclopedia*
- Popular almanacs, which incorporated much of the new scientific and rational knowledge
- "Philosophical texts," the underground book trade's code name for banned books, which included some versions of philosophical treatises, and bawdy, popularized versions of the *philosophes'* critique of the Church and the ruling classes

In these texts the most radical of Enlightenment ideals—particularly those of Rousseau and d'Holbach—together with satirical lampooning of the clergy and the ruling class, reached a broad audience. They helped to undermine respect for and the legitimacy of the ruling regimes.

Review Questions

Multiple Choice

Questions 1–3 refer to the following passage:

The political liberty of the subject is a tranquility of mind, arising from the opinion each person has of his safety. In order to have this liberty, it is requisite the government be so constituted as one man need not be afraid of another.

When the legislative and executive powers are united in the same person, or in the same body of magistrates, there can be no liberty; because apprehensions may arise, lest the same monarch or senate should enact tyrannical laws, to execute them in a tyrannical manner.

Again, there is no liberty, if the power of judging be not separated from the legislative and executive powers. Were it joined with the legislative, the life and liberty of the subject would be exposed to arbitrary control, for the judge would then be the legislator. Were it joined to the executive power, the judge might behave with all the violence of an oppressor. . . .

The executive power ought to be in the hands of a monarch; because this branch of government, which has always need of expedition, is better administered by one than by many:

Whereas, whatever depends on the legislative power, is oftentimes better regulated by many than by a single person.

The Baron Montesquieu, *The Spirit of the Laws*, 1748

1. Montesquieu was an advocate of what political ideology born during the Enlightenment?
   A. Classical conservatism
   B. Classical liberalism
   C. Absolutism
   D. Deism

2. The author of the passage argues that tyranny is best avoided by which means?
   A. Direct representation of the people in government
   B. Virtual representation of the people in government
   C. The consolidation of power within the government
   D. A division of power within the government

3. According to the passage, who is best qualified to hold and implement the law?
   A. A king or queen
   B. An assembly
   C. A judiciary
   D. The people

Short Answer

4. Briefly explain the concept of enlightened despotism and illustrate, with TWO examples, why it ultimately failed.

Answers and Explanations

1. **B** is correct because the passage's emphasis on individual liberty identifies its author as an advocate of classical liberalism. A is incorrect because nothing in the passage advocates the conservative reverence for tradition and traditional institutions. C is incorrect because the emphasis on individual liberty and on the limited nature of political power is in opposition to absolutism. D is incorrect because nothing in the passage allows you to infer anything about the religious beliefs of the author.

2. **D** is correct because the passage proposes to protect liberty by dividing power between the legislative, executive, and judicial branches of government. A and B are incorrect because the passage makes no reference to representation. C is incorrect because the passage argues that power should be split between branches of the government, not consolidated into one branch as absolutism would recommend.

3. **A** is correct because the passage states that the executive power (the power to implement a law) "ought to be in the hands of the monarch." B is incorrect because the passage states that the executive power (the power to implement a law) "ought to be in the hands of the monarch" and because it states that such power "is better administered by one than by many." C is incorrect because the passage states that the executive power (the power to implement a law) "ought to be in the hands of the monarch." D is incorrect because the passage states that the executive power (the power to implement a law) "ought to be in the hands of the monarch" and because it makes no mention of "the people."

4. Suggested answer:

   Thesis: The approaches of Galileo and Descartes were similar in that they both began with skepticism. The approaches were different in two ways: (1) Galileo relied on empirical observation, whereas Descartes considered the senses unreliable. (2) Galileo tended to employ an inductive method, gathering facts and then generalizing from them, while Descartes preferred to deduce general principles and then explain the facts based on those principles.

Paragraph Outline:

I. Galileo's rejection of the Aristotelian model of the cosmos and the scholastic approach. Descartes's skeptical assertion that "received knowledge"—that is, information that you do not learn for yourself—amounted to nothing more than "opinion."

II. Galileo's observations of the moon and his inductive argument that those observations refute the claims of Aristotle. Descartes's rejection of observation on the grounds that our senses can be fooled and his deduction of his own existence by the fact that he cannot doubt that he is thinking about the question of his existence.

Rapid Review

By the mid-sixteenth century, the spirit of Renaissance humanism fused with other reviving traditions, such as Hermeticism and Neoplatonism, to create a Platonic–Pythagorean tradition that sought to identify the fundamental mathematical laws of nature. Nicolas Copernicus was the first to challenge the traditional scholastic view of the cosmos by suggesting that the sun—not the Earth—was at the center of the system. But it was in the seventeenth century that Copernicus's successors promoted new ways of knowing about nature:

- Galileo promoted both the Copernican system and an observationally based inductive method in increasingly bold ways until he was silenced by the Inquisition in 1633.
- René Descartes developed and promoted an alternative method that began with radical skepticism and went on to deduce knowledge about nature by seeking clear and distinct thought.
- Near the end of the seventeenth century, Isaac Newton showed, through empirical observation and reason, that one could discern the laws that God had created to govern the cosmos. In the eighteenth century, writers known as *philosophes* developed and popularized a vision of society based on Newton's emphasis on reason. They wrote philosophical treatises, histories, novels, plays, pamphlets, and satires critical of traditional social and political conventions and institutions, like absolute monarchy and the Church. Hoping to reform society by educating the powerful monarchs of European kingdoms, when enlightened despotism waned, *philosophes* found new venues, like salons, to discuss and promote the more egalitarian and democratic aspects of Enlightenment thought, contributing to an atmosphere of political and social revolution that flourished in modern Europe at the end of the eighteenth century.

Further Resources

Victor Hugo, *Les Misérables*

Mary Shelley, *Frankenstein*

Charles Dickens, *A Tale of Two Cities*

Mary Wollstonecraft, *Maria, or the Wrongs of Woman*

Any of the Romantic poets, but especially Shelley's "To a Skylark," Byron's "Childe Harold" and "Don Juan," and Wordsworth's "The Prelude"

For satire, look at the works of William Hogarth (1697–1764) and James Gilray (1792–1810), caricaturists who specialized in political and social satire. Later, but perhaps better known, is Honoré Daumier (1808–1879). All gave rise to political and editorial cartooning.

CHAPTER 17

The French Revolution and Empire

IN THIS CHAPTER

Summary: In France in 1789, bourgeois representatives of the Third Estate, influenced by the Enlightenment, launched a revolution aimed at curbing the power and privilege of the nobility and clergy and establishing a constitutional monarchy. This chapter reviews the various phases of the French Revolution as it moved further to the left toward the Reign of Terror and then back to the right (Thermidor). It also describes the rise of Napoleon Bonaparte and the creation of a Europe-wide French Empire.

Key Terms:

KEY IDEA

- **Bourgeoisie** A term for the merchant and commercial classes of eighteenth- and nineteenth-century France. In Marxist social critique, the class that owns the means of production and exploits wage laborers.
- *Ancien Régime* **(also Old Regime)** The traditional social and political hierarchy of eighteenth-century France.
- **Estates-General** The representative body of eighteenth-century France. Members representing each of the three Estates met to hear the problems of the realm and royal requests for new taxes. In return, they were allowed to present a list of their own concerns and proposals, called *cahiers*, to the Crown.
- **National Assembly** The name taken by the representatives of the Third Estate on June 17, 1789, declaring themselves to be the legislative body of France. This event is often seen as the beginning of the French Revolution's moderate phase.

- **"Declaration of the Rights of Man and of the Citizen"** A declaration adopted by the National Assembly of France on August 27, 1789, espousing individual rights and liberties for all citizens.
- *Sans-culottes* The working people (bakers, shopkeepers, artisans, and manual laborers) who asserted their will in the radical phase of the French Revolution (1791–1794). They were characterized by their long working pants, hence, *sans-culottes* (literally "without short pants").
- **Girondins** Active during the National Assembly, the Girondins, primarily drawn from the provincial bourgeoisie, supported the Revolution, and advocated war with Europe as a means of uniting France behind the revolutionaries. During the National Convention phase, they became concerned with the increasing violence and the power of the sans-culottes, whose economic demands they opposed. They also opposed execution of the king. Thus they evolved into the moderate faction of the National Convention, especially when compared to their more radical counterparts, the Jacobins.
- **Jacobins** Members of a political club who were active in the National Assembly, the Jacobins intended to secure support for the Revolution. During the National Convention phase, the group was dominated by more radical elements who called for the execution of the king, opposed war with Europe, advocated a republic, and allied with the sans-culottes and the Paris commune. After purging the Girondins, the Jacobin faction was responsible for instituting the Reign of Terror.
- **Committee of Public Safety** A twelve-man committee created in the summer of 1793 and invested with nearly absolute power in order that it might secure the fragile French Republic from its enemies.
- **Reign of Terror** The period of the French Revolution during which Robespierre, the leader of the Committee of Public Safety, created tribunals in the major cities of France to try individuals suspected of being enemies of the Revolution. During the Reign of Terror, between September 1793 and July 1794, between 200,000 and 400,000 people were sentenced to prison; between 25,000 and 50,000 of them are believed to have died either in prison or at the guillotine.
- **Directory** A five-man board created to handle the executive functions of the government during Thermidor, the third and final phase of the French Revolution (1794–1799).
- **Napoleonic Code (also known as the Civil Code of 1804)** A system of uniform law and administrative policy that Napoleon created for the empire he was building in Europe.
- **Continental System** A system established by Napoleon in order to weaken Britain by forbidding the continental European states and kingdoms under French control from trading with Great Britain.
- **Concert of Europe** The alliance created in November 1815 that required important diplomatic decisions to be made by all four great powers—Austria, Russia, Prussia, and Great Britain—"in concert" with one another.

Key Individuals:

- King Louis XVI (France)
- Georges Danton
- Jean-Paul Marat
- Maximilien Robespierre

○ Napoleon Bonaparte
○ Lazare Carnot
○ the Duke of Wellington

Introduction

Between 1789 and 1799, the Kingdom of France underwent a political revolution that unfolded in three phases:

- A moderate phase (1789–1791), in which the politically active portions of the bourgeoisie, or merchant class, attempted to curb the power and privilege of the monarchy, the aristocracy, and the clergy, and to create a limited constitutional monarchy similar to that which existed in Great Britain.
- A radical phase (1791–1794), in which the politicized urban working class of Paris seized control and attempted to create a democratic republic and a more materially, politically, and socially egalitarian society.
- An end phase, known as "the Thermidor" (or Thermidorian Reaction), after the name of the month of the revolutionary calendar in which it occurred. In this phase, members of the Committee of Public Safety turned on Robespierre, who was executed. The resulting power vacuum led to the resurgence of the moderates and bourgeoisie who, after purging the radical elements from power, began dismantling Robespierre's reforms by removing price controls and printing more money.

The National Convention then wrote a new constitution, guarding against both dictatorship and republicanism, and favoring the propertied middle classes. This system had representative legislative bodies, but became known as "the Directory," after the five-man executive committee. Politically weak, by 1799, the Directory's power over foreign policy was usurped by military generals, including Napoleon Bonaparte, who staged a coup d'état in November of that year. Napoleon embarked on an ambitious campaign to create a French Empire that would span most of Europe. Upon his defeat in 1815, by a coalition of European powers, the French monarchy was restored, and the Kingdom of France was returned to its traditional boundaries.

The *Ancien Régime* in Crisis

The phrase *Ancien Régime*, or Old Regime, refers to the traditional social and political hierarchy of eighteenth-century France. It was composed of three "Estates":

- The First Estate, made up of the clergy, included all ordained members of the Catholic Church in France.
- The Second Estate, made up of the nobility, included all titled aristocrats.
- The Third Estate, made up of the citizenry, included everyone who was not either clergy or nobility and whose membership accounted for 96 percent of the population of France.

Together, the clergy and the nobility wielded enormous power and enjoyed tremendous privilege. The various groups that made up the Third Estate, however, bore the tax burden.

The Catholic Church in France functioned as a branch of the government bureaucracy. It registered births, marriages, and deaths; collected certain kinds of agricultural taxes; and oversaw both education and poverty relief. The Church owned approximately 10 percent of all the land in France, but paid no taxes to the government; instead, it made an annual gift to the Crown in an amount of its own choosing. The clergy who populated the hierarchical structure of the Catholic Church in France ranged from poor, simple parish priests to the powerful cardinals, who were connected to the pope in Rome, and who often served as chief advisors in the government of the French king.

The nobility were the traditional landowning elite of France, though by this period they often supplemented their fortunes through banking and commerce. They owned somewhere between 25 and 33 percent of the land in France, but were exempt from most taxes despite the fact that they still collected various types of manorial dues from peasant farmers. Members of the nobility held most of the high offices in the French government, army, and Church.

The citizenry can roughly be divided into three social groups:

- The bourgeoisie, including merchants, manufacturers, bankers, lawyers, and master craftsmen
- The peasantry, including all agricultural laborers, ranging from very prosperous land owners to poor sharecroppers and migrant workers
- Urban laborers, including journeymen craftsmen, mill and other small-scale manufacturing workers, and all wage laborers who populated the cities and towns of France

By 1787, the government of King Louis XVI was in financial crisis. When he took the throne in 1774, Louis XVI had inherited a huge and ever-increasing national debt, most of it incurred by expansion of the bureaucracy, and by borrowing money to finance wars and maintain an army. With interest on the debt mounting and bankers refusing to lend the government more money, Louis XVI and his ministers attempted to reform the tax system of France and to pry some of the vast wealth out of the hands of the nobility. When the nobility resisted, he was forced to do something that had not been done since 1614; he called into session the Estates General. The Estates General was the closest thing to a legislative assembly that existed in eighteenth-century France. Members representing each of the three Estates met to hear the problems of the realm and to hear pleas for new taxes. In return, they were allowed to present a list of their own concerns and proposals, called *cahiers*, to the Crown. When the representatives arrived at Versailles, the palace of Louis XVI, in April 1789, the representatives of the Third Estate presented a series of proposals that were revolutionary in nature.

The Moderate Phase of the French Revolution (1789–1791)

The representatives of the Third Estate, in reality all members of the bourgeoisie, demanded that the number of representatives for the Third Estate be doubled in order to equal the number of representatives in the other two Estates combined and that representatives of all three Estates meet together and vote by head rather than by Estate. These demands were designed to give the Third Estate a chance to pass resolutions by persuading a single member of the nobility or clergy to side with them. The demands of the Third Estate posed a dilemma for Louis XVI; granting their demands would give the Third Estate unprecedented power, and that power would come at the expense of the nobility and the clergy, but could perhaps be used to achieve the tax reforms that Louis XVI and his ministers needed to address France's financial crisis.

Demand for a New Constitution

While Louis XVI considered his options, the representatives of the Third Estate grew bolder. Arguing that they were the voice of the nation, on June 17, 1789, they declared themselves to be the National Assembly of France. When they were locked out of their meeting hall three days later, they pushed their way into the indoor tennis court of Louis XVI and vowed that they would not disband until a new constitution had been written for France. This proclamation became known as "the Tennis Court Oath." On June 27, Louis XVI decided in favor of the Third Estate, decreeing that all members should join the National Assembly.

Fear Causes Parisians to Storm the Bastille

While the bourgeois leaders of the new National Assembly worked on writing a constitution for France, the uncertainty of the situation created an atmosphere of fear and mistrust. Nervous nobles began to demand that Louis XVI break up the new Assembly, which in turn demanded an explanation for the arrival of new regiments of mercenary troops in Versailles. By July 1789, much of the urban population of Paris, which now looked to the Assembly as its champion, believed that the nobility and, perhaps, the king intended to remove the Assembly by force. Their fears focused on the infamous Bastille, a prison fortress in Paris, which they wrongly believed housed the guns and ammunition that would be needed for the job.

On July 14, an angry crowd marched on the Bastille. The nervous governor of the Bastille ordered the crowd to disperse; when they refused, he had his guard fire into the crowd. The crowd responded by storming the Bastille. By the time it was over, 98 people had been killed and 73 wounded. The governor and his guard were killed, and their heads were paraded on pikes through the city. In the aftermath, the king's advisors urged him to flee Versailles and raise an army to crush the Assembly and restore order to Paris. Louis XVI decided to try to soothe the city instead, and he promised to withdraw the mercenary troops.

Rural Unrest Emboldens the Assembly

While order was restored in Paris, it was disintegrating in the countryside, where peasants, aware that the nobility had been weakened and fearful that they would soon reassert their power with a vengeance, seized the opportunity to act. They raided granaries to ensure that they would be able to have affordable bread and attacked the *chateaux* of the local nobility in order to burn debt records. In the context of that rural unrest, sometimes known as "the Great Fear," the Assembly passed "the August Decrees," in which most of the traditional privileges of the nobility and the clergy were renounced and abolished. In an attempt to assure all citizens of France of their intention to bring about a new, more just society, on August 27, 1789, the Assembly adopted "The Declaration of the Rights of Man and of the Citizen," a document that espoused individual rights and liberties for all citizens.

By the end of the summer of 1789, severe economic stress, in the form of high bread prices and unemployment, again caused the people of Paris to take action. Prompted by rumors that the nobility in Louis's court were plotting a coup, and spurred on by an active tabloid press, the people of Paris rioted on October 5, 1789. This event came to be known as "the October Riot." The next day, a contingent of Parisian women organized an 11-mile march from Paris to the king's palace at Versailles. Along the way, they were joined by the Paris Guards, a citizen militia, and together they forced their way into the palace and insisted that Louis XVI accompany them back to Paris. He did, and within two weeks the

National Assembly itself had relocated from Versailles to Paris. "The March to Versailles," as it came to be known, demonstrated two important things:

- First, the crowds of Paris did not yet look upon Louis XVI as their enemy; they had marched to Versailles to retrieve him because they believed that if he were with them in Paris, rather than isolated in Versailles where he was surrounded by his aristocratic advisors, he would side with them and support the Assembly's efforts.
- Second, the crowd of Paris, and their willingness to do violence, had become a powerful political force.

The relocation of both the king and the National Assembly to Paris, within easy reach of the Parisian crowd, set the stage for the radical phase of the Revolution.

The Radical Phase of the French Revolution (1791–1794)

The end of the October Riot marked the beginning of a two-year period of relative calm. A gradual improvement in the economy eased the tension in Paris, and the Assembly's most determined aristocratic enemies either fled to the countryside or emigrated. The Assembly used this period of relative calm to complete the constitution and to draft and pass the Civil Constitution of the Clergy, a piece of legislation that turned clergymen into employees of the government and turned Church property into property of the state. The Assembly soon sold off the confiscated property to pay off part of the national debt, but the attack on the clergy and the Church turned many faithful Catholics against the Assembly.

When Louis XVI signed the new constitution into law on September 15, 1791, the goals of the bourgeois leaders of the Assembly had been fulfilled: the power of the nobility and the Church had been diminished, and France was now a constitutional monarchy. Four developments conspired to send the Revolution into a more radical phase (each of which is reviewed in the sections that follow this list):

- The king's attempt to secretly flee Paris in June 1791
- The outbreak of war with Austria and Prussia in April 1792
- The division of the National Assembly into political factions
- The rise of a politicized laboring faction, known as the *sans-culottes* because of the long work pants they wore

The King's Attempt to Secretly Flee Paris

The king's attempt to flee Paris and head north to rally supporters, an event that came to be known as "the Flight to Varennes," was disastrous. He and the royal family were apprehended and forcibly returned to Paris. He was officially forgiven by the Assembly, but he had forever lost the trust of the people of Paris.

The Outbreak of War with Austria and Prussia

The war with Austria and Prussia came about partly because French aristocratic émigrés had been urging the Austrian and Prussian monarchies to come to the aid of the embattled Louis XVI. But both Louis XVI and the Assembly wanted the war—the king because he believed that the country would have to turn to him to lead it in a time of war, and the Assembly because they believed it would unite the people of France in a common cause. However, when the combined forces of the Austrian and Prussian armies invaded France, the French army collapsed, and the country went into a panic.

The Division of the National Assembly into Political Factions

The development of political factions within the Assembly revealed the differing opinions about the goals and aims of the French Revolution that had always lurked under the surface of its united front against the nobility and the clergy. In October 1791, an attempt to defuse factional rivalries by dissolving the National Assembly and electing a new Legislative Assembly failed to solve the problem.

The Rise of a Politicized Laboring Faction: The *Sans-Culottes*

From the beginning, the Parisian crowd and its willingness to do violence had been a factor in the Revolution. But it had been a force with essentially traditional and conservative aims, insisting that the king pay attention to, and take proper care of, his people. By 1792, the crowd was different; the working people (bakers, shopkeepers, artisans, and manual laborers, characterized by their long working pants) were now seen attending meetings of political clubs and discussing the reforms that were still needed, reforms that would bring about true equality.

Once the men and women of the *sans-culottes* began to assert themselves, political power belonged to whomever they supported. This fact became evident on August 10, 1792, when a crowd stormed first the royal palace and then the hall of the Assembly. Unable to resist the crowd, the leaders of the Assembly voted to depose and imprison the king and to immediately convene a new National Convention to deal with the crises facing the country.

The Vote to End the French Monarchy

The membership of the National Convention was elected by universal manhood suffrage, where each adult male was entitled to a single vote. Accordingly, the members of the National Convention, particularly the Jacobin faction, were more radical than their predecessors. In September 1792, the Convention voted to abolish the monarchy and to proclaim France a republic. It also managed to reorganize the French army and push the invading Austrian and Prussian forces back across the border. When the Convention proclaimed the war an extension of the Revolution and vowed to carry it anywhere people yearned for liberty and freedom, the monarchies of Europe responded by forming a coalition to crush the Revolution.

In January 1793, the Convention put Louis XVI on trial for treason. The debate that followed his conviction revealed a split between two powerful factions within the Convention. The Girondins, drawn from the provincial bourgeoisie, were concerned by growing extremism and violence of the Revolution, illustrated by the September massacres, in which mobs of Parisians killed prisoners feared to be planning counterrevolutionary action. Accordingly, they mostly opposed execution of the king. The Jacobins, whose members came from the lower strata of the bourgeoisie, were adamant that he must die. The vote was close, but the Jacobins prevailed, and Louis XVI was sent to the guillotine on January 21, 1793.

A New Constitution and Robespierre's Reign of Terror

The execution of the king, combined with a decision to increase the number of men conscripted into the army, caused large anti-Convention uprisings throughout France. In Paris, the Jacobins used the revolt as an opportunity to purge the Girondins from the Convention. In June 1793, a Jacobin-led mob occupied the Convention hall and refused to leave until the Girondins resigned. Those Girondins who refused to resign were arrested. The purged Convention then passed "the Law of the Maximum" to cap the price of bread and other essentials, and drafted a new constitution that guaranteed universal manhood suffrage, universal education, and subsistence wages. In order to secure the egalitarian, democratic republic espoused by the new constitution, the Convention created a twelve-man Committee of Public Safety and invested it with almost total power in order that it might secure the fragile republic from its enemies. Within the Committee, a young lawyer from the provinces, Maximilien Robespierre, gained control through his ability to persuade both his fellow Jacobins and the *sans-culottes* crowd to follow him.

Under Robespierre's leadership, the Committee instituted what has come to be known as the Reign of Terror. Arguing that, in times of revolution, terror was the necessary companion to virtue, Robespierre created tribunals in the major cities of France to try individuals suspected of being enemies of the Revolution. During the period of the Terror, between September 1793 and July 1794, between 200,000 and 400,000 people were sentenced to prison; between 25,000 and 50,000 of them are believed to have died either in prison or at the guillotine.

Among the victims of the Reign of Terror were those who rivaled Robespierre for power. In April 1794, when Robespierre had the popular and influential Jacobin leader, Georges-Jacques Danton, arrested and executed for daring to suggest that it was time to reassess the Reign of Terror, he lost the support of both the Jacobins and the crowd. In July 1794, Robespierre was arrested, tried, and executed by the same Terror machine that he had created. The execution of Robespierre marked the end of the radical phase of the Revolution, as an exhausted Paris, devoid of its radical leaders, succumbed to a reassertion of power by the propertied bourgeoisie.

The Final Phase of the French Revolution: Thermidor and the Rise of Napoleon (1794–1799)

For several months following the execution of Robespierre, the revolutionary terror was replaced by the Thermidor Reaction, so named after the month of the revolutionary calendar in which Robespierre was executed. What followed was a terror of reaction characterized by a purge of the remaining Jacobins, and a reversal of Robespierre's policies. In the Convention, the moderates wrote a new constitution limiting political suffrage to propertied middle classes, eliminating price controls, and printing currency to handle debts. The resulting inflation hurt lower socioeconomic classes, but any unrest was quickly subdued. The executive functions of the government were placed in the hands of a five-man board known as the Directory. Increasingly, the Directory relied on the military to keep order and to protect it from both the *sans-culottes*, who stormed the Convention in May 1795, and from the Royalists, who attempted a coup five months later.

When the war against the European coalition began to go badly, conservative factions within the Convention conspired with the ambitious and popular army general, Napoleon Bonaparte, to overthrow the Directory. On November 9, 1799, the conspirators staged a successful coup, and Napoleon acquired the powers necessary to govern as "first consul." By 1804, Napoleon had rid himself of his coconspirators and had France proclaimed an "empire" and himself "emperor." He governed France with a mixture of reform and traditionalism, and oversaw the military expansion of the French Empire until his defeat at the hands of coalition forces at the Battle of Waterloo in 1815.

Post-Revolutionary France and the Napoleonic Code

By the time Napoleon had himself declared emperor in 1804, he was well on his way to completing the process, begun by the Revolution, of creating a strong central government and administrative uniformity in France. To solidify his position, Napoleon took the following measures:

- Suppressed Royalists and Republicans through the use of spies and surprise arrests
- Censored and controlled the press
- Regulated what was taught in schools
- Reconciled France with the Roman Church by signing the Concordat of 1801, which stipulated that French clergy would be chosen and paid by the state but consecrated by the pope

To provide a system of uniform law and administrative policy, Napoleon created the Civil Code of 1804, more widely known as the Napoleonic Code. It incorporated many principles that had been espoused during the Revolution, some revolutionary and some reactionary. In accordance with revolutionary principles, the Code:

- Safeguarded all forms of property
- Upheld equality before the law
- Established the right to choose a profession
- Guaranteed promotion on merit for employees of the state

In accordance with reactionary principles, the Code:

- Upheld the ban on working men's associations
- Upheld the patriarchal nature of French society by granting men extensive rights over their wives and children

As Napoleon conquered Europe, he spread the Code across the continent. The overall effect of the Code on Europe was to erode the remnants of the old feudal system by further weakening the traditional power of the nobility and clergy.

Napoleon's Empire

Between 1805 and 1810, Napoleon's forces won a series of battles that allowed France to dominate all of continental Europe, except the Balkan Peninsula. These key victories included the following:

- The Battle of Austerlitz (December 1805), defeating Russo-Austrian forces
- The Battle of Jena (October 1806), defeating Prussian forces
- The Battle of Friedland (June 1807), defeating Russian forces

The resulting French Empire consisted of some states that were annexed directly into the French Empire, including the following:

- Belgium
- Germany to the Rhine
- The German coastal region to the western Baltic
- West-central Italy, including Rome, Genoa, and Trieste

Also included in the Empire were five satellite kingdoms ruled by Napoleon's relatives:

- Holland, ruled by his brother Louis
- Westphalia, ruled by his brother Jérôme
- Spain, ruled by his brother Joseph
- The Kingdom of Italy, ruled by his stepson Eugène
- The Kingdom of Naples, ruled by his brother-in-law Joachim Murat

The remaining portions of the Empire consisted of a series of subservient states and confederations, which included the following:

- The Confederation of the Rhine, eventually consisting of eighteen German states that had been part of the now-defunct Holy Roman Empire
- The nineteen cantons of the Swiss Confederation
- The Duchy of Warsaw, carved out of Prussia's Polish lands

Those European states that remained independent from France were reluctant allies that simply had no choice but to bow to Napoleon's power. Such states included the following:

- Austria, where Francis II ruled a kingdom diminished by the disintegration of the Holy Roman Empire
- Prussia, now much smaller for losing its Polish lands and other areas to the Confederation of the Rhine
- Russia, which, following the defeat at Friedland, signed the Treaty of Tilsit on July 7, 1807, recognizing France's claims in Europe
- Sweden
- Denmark

The one European nation that still threatened Napoleon was Great Britain, whose superior naval power, as exemplified by its victory over the combined French and Spanish fleets at the Battle of Trafalgar on October 21, 1805, made it unconquerable. In order to weaken Great Britain, Napoleon established what came to be known as the Continental System, whereby the Continental European states and kingdoms under French control were forbidden to trade with Great Britain.

The Decline and Fall of Napoleon and His Empire

The decline and fall of Napoleon and his empire were due to a combination of flawed policies and growing resistance to his rule. The trade restrictions of the Continental System failed to weaken Great Britain and succeeded instead in being a constant source of resentment amongst the conquered states of Europe. The British responded with a counter-blockade that damaged the French economy and engaged in a lively smuggling enterprise with the rest of Europe. The combination of the restrictions of the Continental System and general resentment of French rule led to the growth of a new national spirit in many parts of continental Europe.

Spain

In Spain, popular resistance to the rule of Napoleon's brother Joseph was immediate. There were demonstrations and riots in Madrid. The brutal repression with which Napoleon's troops met these demonstrations only stiffened opposition, the spirit of which was captured forever in Francisco de Goya's painting titled *The Third of May, 1808*, which depicts a French firing squad executing helpless Spanish protestors. Opposition to French domination grew into what has been called the first example of guerrilla warfare, as loosely organized pockets of opposition carried out raids throughout Spain in a sporadic and unpredictable way, which the French could do little to prevent.

Germany

In Germany a new sense of nationalism grew in response to French domination. The sense of independence that was once a source of pride in the independent principalities and duchies was now perceived as a fatal weakness that had made Germany vulnerable to the French. In response, opposition forces in Germany began to work together, and many looked to Prussia for leadership. For its own part, Prussia quietly modernized its civil institutions and its army, and waited for an opportunity to rise up against its French overlords.

Russia

In Russia, the competing ambitions of Tsar Alexander I and Napoleon led to renewed hostilities. In June 1812, Napoleon invaded Russia with a *Grande Armée* ("Great Army") of over 600,000 troops. The Russian army retreated, stripping towns of supplies and burning croplands as they went. In September, the Russian army turned on the tired and hungry French troops at Borodino, some 70 miles east of Moscow, and fought one of the bloodiest battles of the nineteenth century. The Russians withdrew, opening the way to Moscow, but the French army lost over 40,000 men. On September 14, Napoleon led his army into Moscow to find that the Russians had deserted it and set it aflame. Napoleon reluctantly retreated, but it was too late. In November and December, the Russian winter and advancing Russian troops eventually finished off the Grande Armée, undersupplied and too far from home. Nearly 500,000 French troops were lost in all; Napoleon abandoned them and dashed back to Paris.

Exile to Elba

News of the defeat of the Grande Armée in Russia galvanized resistance to Napoleon's rule throughout Europe. Napoleon raised a new army, but it lacked the supplies and veterans lost in Russia. In October 1813, a coalition of forces from Austria, Russia, Prussia, and Sweden defeated Napoleon's forces at Leipzig. In November, a combined force of British and Spanish troops crossed the Pyrenees into France and took Paris. The victorious coalition exiled Napoleon to the island of Elba, off the coast of Italy.

The Battle of Waterloo

In 1815, Napoleon staged one last comeback, known as "the Hundred Days," returning to France and raising one last army. He was defeated at the Battle of Waterloo in Belgium by coalition forces led by the Duke of Wellington. Napoleon was finished. He was captured and imprisoned on the island of St. Helena in the South Atlantic, where he died six years later.

Restoration

In November 1814, representatives from the four major powers that had combined to defeat Napoleon—Great Britain, Russia, Prussia, and Austria—met for a peace conference, known as "the Congress of Vienna." Those representatives—Lord Castlereagh, Tsar Alexander I, Baron Hardenberg, and Prince Klemens von Metternich—were all conservative members of the aristocracy. Accordingly, the goal of the conference was to reestablish the foundations of aristocratic dominance that had been challenged by the French Revolution. They were guided by the twin principles of legitimacy and stability. Their concept of legitimacy dictated that all European territories should be returned to the control of the aristocratic house that had governed before Napoleon had redrawn the map. But the concept of stability meant a restoration of a balance of power in Europe. Accordingly, the important elements of the resulting settlement consisted of both tradition and innovation. The important components of the settlement included the following:

- The restoration of the monarchy in Spain under Ferdinand VII
- The restoration of the monarchy in France under Louis XVIII
- The reconstitution of France inside borders that were nearly those of 1789
- The ceding of parts of Saxony, Westphalia, and the Rhine to Prussia
- The unification of the Austrian Netherlands (Belgium) and the Dutch Republic to form a single kingdom of the Netherlands under the House of Orange
- The placing of the kingdoms of Lombardy and Venetia in Italy, and of the states in the German Confederation, under the control of Austria

In an attempt to secure the balance of power created by the Vienna Settlement, the leaders of Austria, Russia, Prussia, and Great Britain entered into a military alliance designed to make aggression by individual states or kingdoms impossible. The alliance, created in November 1815, came to be known as "the Concert of Europe," for the way in which it required important diplomatic decisions to be made by all four great powers "in concert" with one another. In 1818, France, having paid its war indemnities, joined the alliance.

Review Questions

Multiple Choice

Questions 1–3 refer to the following passage:

> But, to found and consolidate democracy, to achieve the peaceable reign of the constitutional laws, we must end the war of liberty against tyranny and pass safely across the storms of the revolution: such is the aim of the revolutionary system that you have enacted. Your conduct, then, ought also to be regulated by the stormy circumstances in which the republic is placed; and the plan of your administration must result from the spirit of the revolutionary government combined with the general principles of democracy.
>
> Now, what is the fundamental principle of the democratic or popular government—that is, the essential spring which makes it move? It is virtue; I am speaking of the public virtue which . . . is nothing other than the love of country and of its laws. . . .
>
> If the spring of popular government in time of peace is virtue, the springs of popular government in revolution are at once virtue and terror: virtue, without which terror is fatal; terror, without which virtue is powerless. Terror is nothing other than justice, prompt, severe, inflexible; it is therefore an emanation of virtue; it is not so much a special principle as it is a consequence of the general principle of democracy applied to our country's most urgent needs.
>
> It has been said that terror is the principle of despotic government. Does your government therefore resemble despotism? Yes, as the sword that gleams in the hands of the heroes of liberty resembles that with which the henchmen of tyranny are armed.
>
> Maximilien Robespierre, "Speech of February 5, 1794"

1. Based on the passage, what was the goal of the Revolution for Robespierre?
   A. To create a tyranny of the virtuous
   B. To create a constitutional monarchy
   C. To create a democratic republic governed by the rule of law
   D. To create an absolute monarchy

2. How did Robespierre feel about the use of terror?
   A. It was immoral and indicative of tyranny.
   B. It was a necessary means to a just end.
   C. It was fatal to the Revolution.
   D. It was an indication of powerlessness.

3. How would Robespierre have responded to the charge that his revolutionary government had become despotic?
   A. That the resemblance to despotism was superficial.
   B. That despotism was necessary to establish a virtuous monarchy.
   C. That, as a hero, he was entitled to despotic rule.
   D. Despotism was inevitable.

Short Answer

4. Briefly give TWO illustrations of the existence of a "radical phase" of the French Revolution and explain ONE cause of the shift to that phase.

Answers and Explanations

1. **C** is correct because the passage argues that a war of liberty is being fought in order to bring about a democracy and "the peaceable reign of the constitutional laws." A is incorrect because the passage argues that tyranny is a tool, not a goal of the Revolution. B and D are incorrect because the passage makes no reference to a monarchy as a goal of the Revolution.

2. **B** is correct because the passage states that virtue without terror is powerless against tyrannical enemies. A is incorrect because the passage argues that terror is a tool and that the morality of its usage depends upon the goal of the user. C is incorrect because the passage argues that terror is necessary for the success of the Revolution, not fatal to it. D is incorrect because the passage states that it is virtue that is powerless in times of revolution, unless it is paired with terror.

3. **A** is correct because the passage states that his government resembles despotism only as "the sword that gleams in the hands of the heroes of liberty resembles that with which the henchmen of tyranny are armed"; that is, only superficially. B is incorrect because the passage states that the redemptive goal of the Revolution is the institution of a virtuous *republic*, not monarchy. C is incorrect because the passage disputes the notion that his government has become despotic. D is incorrect because the passage argues that the Revolution can be successful in its battle against despotism if it is willing to use terror.

4. Suggested answer:

   Thesis: The existence of a radical phase of the French Revolution can be detected in the passage of the Civil Constitution of the Clergy in July 1790 and in the vote to abolish the monarchy in September 1792. One explanation for the advent of this phase was the rise of the *sans-culottes*.

   Paragraph Outline:

   I. The passage of the Civil Constitution of the Clergy in July 1790 is evidence of a radical phase because its subordination of the clergy to the new French state was not a goal of the original, moderate leaders of the Revolution, who wanted only to curb the privileges of the clergy.

II. The vote to abolish the monarchy in September 1792 is evidence of a radical phase because the abolition of the French monarchy was not a goal of the original, moderate leaders of the Revolution, who wanted only to curb the absolutist tendencies of the king and his government.

III. One explanation for the shift to a radical phase is the rise of the *sans-culottes*, the working people (bakers, shopkeepers, artisans, and manual laborers) of Paris. They helped to cause the radical phase because they had the willingness and the numerical strength to violently impose the more radical agenda of Convention members like Robespierre.

Rapid Review

When Louis XVI was forced by financial difficulties to call the seldom-used Estates General into session in 1789, the bourgeois representatives of the Third Estate launched a revolution aimed at curbing the power and privilege of the nobility and the clergy, and they attempted to turn France into a constitutional monarchy. Supported by the Paris crowd, the leaders of the newly formed National Assembly nearly succeeded, but foreign intervention, persistent resistance from the nobility, the indecisiveness of Louis XVI, and the development of factions within the Assembly allowed new, more radical leaders to win over the *sans-culottes* who now made up the Parisian crowd and set the Revolution on a more radical course. Besieged by a coalition of European powers and beset with factional strife, the radicals resorted to a Reign of Terror, which eventually consumed them.

By 1794, the propertied bourgeoisie reasserted itself and concentrated on restoring order and repealing the gains made by the radicals. In 1799, their executive organ, known as the Directory, was overthrown by a military general, Napoleon Bonaparte. He gradually assumed dictatorial powers and attempted to create a Europe-wide French Empire. Upon his defeat in 1815 by coalition forces, the French monarchy was restored, and the Kingdom of France was restored to its pre-Revolutionary boundaries.

Further Resources

The Broadway musical version of *Les Miserables*, from the novel by Victor Hugo

CHAPTER 18

The Industrial Revolution

IN THIS CHAPTER

Summary: Between 1815 and 1914, the increasing demand for goods was met by the creation of the factory system, which standardized and increased industrial production. This chapter reviews the Industrial Revolution in Great Britain, its uneven spread across Europe, and the social effects of industrialization, including urbanization, standardization of work, and changes to the class system. The chapter also describes new modes of scientific explanation, such as the kinetic theory of gases and Darwin's theory of evolution by natural selection.

Key Terms:

- ✪ **Industrial Revolution** The phase of the industrialization process, lasting roughly from 1820 to 1900, characterized by the advent of large-scale iron-and-steel production, the application of the steam engine, and the development of a railway system.
- ✪ **Factory system** A system of production created in order to better supervise and centralize labor, increasing efficiency. In the factory system, workers came to a central location and worked with machines under the supervision of managers.
- ✪ **Division of labor** A technique whereby formerly complex tasks that required knowledge and skill were broken down into a series of simple tasks, aided by machines.

- **Bessemer process** A process, invented in the 1850s by English engineer Henry Bessemer, that allowed steel to be produced more cheaply and in larger quantities.
- **Steam engine** A power source that burns coal to produce steam pressure. First used in the early eighteenth century to pump water out of coal mines, it came to be used to drive machinery as diverse as the bellows of iron forges, looms for textile manufacture, and mills for grain, and, in the nineteenth century, as a source of locomotive power.
- **Internal combustion engine** Developed in 1886 by two German engineers, Gottlieb Daimler and Karl Benz, an engine that burns petroleum as fuel. When mounted on a carriage, it was used to create the automobile.
- **The Railway Boom** The rapid development of a railway system, beginning in Great Britain in the 1830s. The development of railway systems further spurred the development of heavy industry, as railroads facilitated the speedy transportation of iron and steel while simultaneously consuming large quantities of both.
- **Class consciousness** A sense of belonging to a "working class" that developed among European workers during the Industrial Revolution of the nineteenth century. It developed partly due to their working together in factories and living together in isolated slums.
- **Garden cities** An urban planning movement that endeavored to balance urban and residential areas with greenspaces and agricultural countryside.
- **Zollverein** An economic organization comprised of German states, led by Prussia, to promote free trade among members and impose protective tariffs on imports.

Key Individuals:
- Charles Darwin
- Henry Bessemer
- Thomas Newcomen
- James Watt
- Gottlieb Daimler
- Karl Benz
- Friedrich List
- Sergei Witte
- Rudolf Clausius
- James Maxwell
- Thomas Edison and Nikolai Tesla
- Louis Pasteur
- Robert Owen
- Joseph Lister

Introduction

During the eighteenth century, the development of a more diverse economy propelled by a system of rural manufacturing (sometimes referred to as proto-industrialization or even the "First Industrial Revolution") radically increased the demand for manufactured goods. In response, nineteenth-century entrepreneurs and inventors created a new, more mechanized system of production, known as "the factory system." This new system of production, coupled with the introduction of new sources of power, led to what is termed the Industrial Revolution (or sometimes the "Second Industrial Revolution"). This process of heavy, concentrated industrialization, lasting roughly from 1870 to 1914, was characterized by the advent of large-scale iron and steel production, the application of the steam engine, and the development of a railway system. The Industrial Revolution of the nineteenth century transformed almost every aspect of European life.

The Industrial Revolution Begins in Great Britain

In Great Britain, a number of variables fostered the emergence of new industries and modes of production, well before the rest of continental Europe. First, new agricultural methods in the eighteenth century resulted in a production boom that lowered prices and the demand for agricultural labor, while also increasing available money for families to purchase manufactured goods. Great Britain's mercantilist traditions and extensive colonies resulted in surplus capital for investment, additional markets for manufactured goods, and credit and banking institutions to finance industrial enterprises, as well as a culture that embraced wealth, commerce, and the associated risks. Great Britain enjoyed geographic advantages, too, including ample supplies of key natural resources (coal, iron), compact territory that made creation of transportation networks easier, and access to navigable ports and rivers. Political conditions were also favorable, with a stable government that supported private enterprise, few internal trade barriers, and isolation from wars on the European continent. The Crystal Palace, made of glass and steel, constructed for "The Great Exhibition of the Works of Industry of All Nations," the first industrial fair in 1851, was a symbol of Great Britain's industrial achievements.

Despite Great Britain's remarkable progress, there were occasional barriers to industrialism. For example, Great Britain made some limited attempts at protective tariffs, most notably imposing the Corn Laws of 1815, which were intended to protect British landowners from cheap imported grain (not just corn) that flooded the market after Great Britain's blockade of Europe when the Napoleonic Wars ended. These laws benefited the nobility, who owned the bulk of the fertile land, but hurt both the lower classes now spending most of their income on grain, as well as the manufacturers who suffered a decline in demand as disposable income declined. When the Reform Act of 1832 extended suffrage to the merchant class, Parliament became more sympathetic to those opposing the Corn Laws, and eventually repealed them in 1846. As industrialism and manufacturing matured in Great Britain, its success spurred other European nations to encourage industrialism within their own borders.

The Factory System and the Division of Labor

The factory system was created in order to better supervise labor. In the old, rural manufacturing system (or cottage industry) that characterized European proto-industrialization, peasants were left on their own to work at the spinning wheel or the loom. Both the quality and the efficiency of their work depended on factors that were beyond the entrepreneur's control. Beginning in the textile industry, new more efficient machines, like the spinning jenny and the water frame, were cost-prohibitive for individuals and required power sources. This led to the development of factories, where workers came to a central location and worked with machines under the supervision of managers.

The factory system employed a technique known as "the division of labor," whereby formerly complex tasks that required knowledge and skill were broken down into a series of simple tasks, aided by machines. Additionally, larger, centralized factories allowed entrepreneurs to take advantage of power sources required to operate new machines. With the division of labor, skilled craftsman were replaced with unskilled labor, thereby increasing the supply of labor and decreasing the wages that needed to be paid. At the same time, the volume that manufacturers could produce increased, thereby allowing them to sell products for less and still increase profits. As machines did more and more of the work, the number of workers needed decreased, which created unemployment and competition for jobs.

Iron and Steel

The iron and steel industry helped to drive the Industrial Revolution of the nineteenth century. The new machines of the textile industry created increased demand for the iron from which they were partly constructed. New, larger armies demanded more iron for guns, cannons, and ammunition. The growing population required even more iron for nails and tools.

Traditionally, the fuel for the iron-smelting process was charcoal, which came from wood. By the eighteenth century, dwindling forests limited the charcoal supply, and steel was smelted in blast furnaces, using coal as the fuel. In the 1850s, Henry Bessemer, an English engineer, discovered a way to manufacture steel more cheaply and in larger quantities. The use of the Bessemer process (as it came to be called), together with the use of the steam engine to power smelting furnaces, increased the supply of iron and steel to the point at which it could meet ever-growing demand. In 1860, Great Britain, France, Germany, and Belgium produced approximately 125,000 tons of steel. By 1913, they produced nearly 32 million tons.

New Sources of Power

Coal

Coal mines provided the most important fuel of the Industrial Revolution. Initially, coal was used to heat homes and to fuel the blast furnaces of the expanding iron and steel industry. Later, demand increased even further as steam engines devoured mass quantities of coal for fuel. Wherever there were natural deposits of coal, huge mining industries grew up around them; agricultural production in these areas was largely abandoned, and the peasants were drawn by the thousands to subterranean work in the mines.

Steam

The perfection of the steam engine increased both the scale and the pace of heavy industry by replacing human muscle and hydropower. The steam engine was first used in the early eighteenth century to pump water out of coal mines. It was perfected and made more efficient by Thomas Newcomen and James Watt. The improved version was used to drive machinery as diverse as the bellows of iron forges, looms for textile manufacture, and mills for processing grain. The shift to steam power allowed entrepreneurs to relocate their mills away from water sources. During the 1820s, entrepreneurs began to exploit the potential of the steam engine as a source of locomotive power; its first use in this way was to power ships. In the 1830s, it was adapted to power railway locomotives.

Electricity

Toward the end of the nineteenth century, the Second Industrial Revolution received another boost from the widespread application of electrical power. More versatile and more easily transported than steam engines, electrical generators were used to power a wide variety of small- and large-scale factories and mills. By 1881, the first large-scale public power plant was constructed in Great Britain, and over the next two decades, plants were built and lines were run to illuminate houses across Europe.

Petroleum and the Internal Combustion Engine

In 1886, two German engineers, Gottlieb Daimler and Karl Benz, perfected the internal combustion engine, which burned petroleum as fuel, and mounted it on a carriage to create the first automobile. The early German automobiles were luxury items. But in 1908, the American engineer Henry Ford produced the "Model T," an automobile for the common man, which he began to mass-produce, creating yet another large factory-based industry. The internal combustion engine, along with its cousin the diesel engine, made transportation and travel cheaper and, therefore, more widely available.

The Railway Boom

In the 1820s, the British inventor George Stephenson developed a railway line with trains pulled by steam-powered locomotives. The Stockton and Darlington Line opened in 1825, and by 1830, another major line traveled between Liverpool and Manchester. The speed and reliability of the new locomotives made them a huge success, which led to what would come to be known as "the Railway Boom of the 1830s and 1840s," as competitors quickly developed their own systems. The development of railway systems further spurred the development of heavy industry, as railroads facilitated the speedy transportation of iron and steel while simultaneously consuming large quantities of both.

The Reciprocal Nature of Heavy Industry

The four major components of the Second Industrial Revolution—the iron and steel industry, the coal industry, steam power, and the railways—had a reciprocal effect on one another:

- The iron and steel industry required improvements in the steam engine to run its blast furnaces, greater amounts of coal to fuel the engines, and railways to transport both the coal and the smelted iron and steel.
- The coal industry required more and improved steam engines to pump water out of the mines and to power digging machinery; it also required railways to transport the coal.
- The steam power industry required iron and steel to forge the engines, coal to run them, and railways to transport them.
- The railways required huge amounts of steel and iron for the construction of the engines, cars, and tracks; steam engines to drive the locomotives; and coal to fuel the engines.

Working together, these four industries created an ever-increasing cycle of supply and demand that drove the Second Industrial Revolution of the nineteenth century.

The Spread of Industrialization

As described earlier, the Industrial Revolution began in Great Britain, but did not take hold immediately in continental Europe, as those nations did not possess the same favorable conditions. Transportation in continental Europe was problematic, with few good roads and many customs barriers across its rivers and borders. Guilds were more powerful there, acting to protect traditional craft systems from industrial change. Particularly in France, wars created political and economic turmoil, limiting access to new technologies from Great Britain. This was exacerbated by Great Britain's attempts to maintain its advantage by restricting access to its engineers, technology, and industrial equipment.

A key factor in the spread of industrialism was the development of new commercial banking enterprises. As continental Europe tried to "catch up" with Great Britain, the scale and cost of industrial equipment had increased beyond individual financing. New commercial banks in continental Europe held small deposits from numerous customers, allowing them to amass huge amounts of capital, which then invested in new industrial enterprises. Like joint-stock corporations, the liability of shareholders was limited to the original investment. This helped make industry feasible in continental Europe. Slowly, industrialization spread from west to east. As it did, the pace and degree of government intervention increased.

France and Belgium

Belgium was one of the first to follow Great Britain, having access to its own reserves of natural resources and the advantage of a compact territory. The Belgian government undertook construction of a railroad to integrate the nation. France's transition to industrialism was more gradual than Great Britain's. Though the medieval guilds were ended by France's Revolution, doing so limited France's population and strengthened the position of the peasantry. During Napoleon's reign, he sponsored huge infrastructure projects, including roads, canals, and ports. The French government also encouraged the construction of railroads through public-private partnerships in which the government paid for much of the construction costs. With the Bourbon Restoration came tariffs on inexpensive British goods to protect French industries.

German States

Although the German states had access to large coal and iron deposits, there were numerous barriers to industrialization, including limited access to ports serving the Atlantic trade routes. Traditional institutions, like serfdom and guilds, continued, which impeded free movement of labor and establishment of industry. Also, political fragmentation limited Germany's economic impact. Prussia emerged as an industrial leader, creating *Zollverein*, a protective customs union formed by a coalition of German states. This was influenced by German economist Friedrich List, who argued that nations should reduce internal trade barriers but employ protective tariffs to foster the development of fledgling domestic industries. When private capital proved to be insufficient, the governments of the German states took action; they financed railway construction, subsidized locomotive industry, and even nationalized railways altogether. The economic and transportation integration of the German states helped facilitate their eventual unification under Prussia. Later, government investments in heavy industry and technical education made Germany a world industrial power in the Second Industrial Revolution, also known as the "Technological Revolution."

Eastern Europe and Russia

In Eastern Europe, traditional economic systems persisted, including a conservative and powerful landed aristocracy supported by an agricultural peasantry, including serfs. These powerful elites lacked the incentive to invest in modern industries, which might threaten the status quo. In Russia, a military defeat in the Crimea highlighted the weakness of its economy. Reforms implemented by Alexander II included creating a mobile labor force by ending serfdom, and agricultural reforms to improve output. The government, under the direction of Count Sergei Witte, Minister of Ways and Means, then Minister of Finance, and finally Prime Minister, built railroads to connect resources, factories, and markets, including the Trans-Siberian Railway. Witte also provided incentives for foreign investment, stabilized the currency, and funded development of telegraph lines and electrical plants. By 1900, Russia was the fourth-largest producer of steel in the world.

Social Effects of Industrialization

Rural Areas

The Industrial Revolution transformed European life across all demographic groups, but not always in the same way or evenly. A general change was population growth, more due to the reduction in wars, famines, and epidemics than to increased birth rates. Ending serfdom created large classes of landless peasants who had to pay rents, regardless of the harvest. In some rural areas, this overcrowding meant smaller plots of land for families. In Ireland, the potato required a relatively small space to sustain a family, making millions of rural Irish dependent on them. Crop failures led to widespread starvation among the Irish, some of whom emigrated to the United States. In other rural areas, migration of labor to the cities created different problems.

Urbanization

Cities transformed from centers of government and trade to manufacturing centers. Factories were located in cities for access to transportation, energy, and labor. Millions of people migrated to cities in search of work. Not designed to accommodate such a huge influx of people, cities struggled with overcrowding. Housing was scarce. Human waste and refuse were thrown in the streets. The waste ran into local water supplies. As a result, outbreaks of diseases, like cholera, were common. Crime and fraud were widespread. City governments were unwilling or unable to step in to improve conditions, never having had to in the past.

Working Class

For many members of the working class, the nature of their work, and therefore their lives, fundamentally changed. In agriculture, there are busy periods, but there are also long stretches of inactivity, and the workers could often set their own pace. Factory owners couldn't afford to let machines sit idle, so the workers were expected to work constantly for the duration of their shift.

Discipline was harsh and unforgiving. No social insurance laws existed to protect workers in case of injury or unemployment, or to guarantee wages. Initially, in coal mines and factories, entire families worked side by side as they had done when farming. Child labor was common, and often preferable, as children's small size afforded them some advantages in mines and around machines, but they typically earned less than a third of a man's wages. Pauper children—orphaned or abandoned by parents—were "apprenticed" by parish authorities to factories or mines, where they received miserable housing and board for hours of unrelenting labor. Eventually, in Great Britain, government inquiries into working conditions led to the passage of a minimum age of nine years for child labor (the Factory Act of 1833) and the limitation of work hours for child and female labor (the Ten Hours Act of 1847), though these applied mainly to textile and coal industries.

Industrial workers were particularly vulnerable to the volatility of business cycles and market forces. If an economic downturn was severe enough, an entrepreneur could lose his entire business. But before that, he would fire workers or reduce wages, as necessary. In England, to guard against a potentially radicalized poor like that which contributed to the Revolution in France, "Anti-Combination Laws" were passed to limit workers from organizing. Despite this, workers formed trade unions, using collective actions like strikes to improve their position.

Middle Class

The economic benefits of the Industrial Revolution were not evenly distributed, but one clear winner was the growing middle class. This included owners and managers of factories and mines, bankers, lawyers, doctors, and skilled artisans, among others. Though investing in industry carried risks, the profits for successful enterprises were sizeable. Members of the middle class were able to move out from the cities to suburbs, employ servants, and even purchase large estates alongside traditional aristocrats. These wealthy professionals and businessmen became known as "the *bourgeoisie*." Eventually they sought political power to match their economic and social status. Some artisans and craftspeople who were members of traditional guilds resisted industrialism. They feared competition from cheap, factory-produced goods. One resistance group in the early 1800s, the Luddites, destroyed machines in textile factories in a futile attempt to prevent mechanization of the industry.

Women and Family Life

As previously mentioned, families worked side by side in early factories and mines, as they had in the agriculture fields. Eventually, the responsibilities and hours of parents no longer coincided with the hours of their children. With restrictions on child-labor hours, parents and children no longer had the same schedules. These restrictions also resulted in changes for women, as they needed to be home to care for their children.

Laws were passed limiting women's factory hours. This had implications for female labor. As reform movements examined factory and mining labor practices, the role of women was also examined. Much was made about new opportunities for women in the workplace, but most women in factories were unmarried. People feared that women and men working together would result in immoral behavior, so it was discouraged.

Family life evolved, with the focus shifting to a nuclear family. As living standards increased, especially in the middle class, marriage was seen less as an economic imperative, and more as a romantic arrangement. Women were perceived as caretakers of the home and family, again, especially in the middle class. Thus, female employment, particularly for working-class women, centered on domestic service or work that could be done in the home, like laundry or sewing. For the most economically vulnerable women, prostitution was a means of survival.

Second Industrial Revolution

New Technology

Beginning around 1870, the Second Industrial Revolution was not characterized by innovations in heavy industry, but rather by new technologies that improved upon existing methods. Based on the work of Thomas Edison and Nikolai Tesla, electricity was distributed across a public grid, transforming both economic and social life. Combined with the smaller internal combustion engine, electricity extended the use of labor-saving machinery into previously artisanal industries; this expanded the mass production of goods. These cheaper factory-produced goods and new labor-saving devices began making their way into newly prosperous middle-class homes.

Improvements in the Bessemer process made refining iron into more durable steel more efficient, and it reduced the price of steel substantially. Railways expanded dramatically as a result. The discovery of petroleum not only changed the fuel needed to run machines, but it also led to the development of new materials—like vulcanized rubber, plastics, and fertilizers. Refrigerated rail cars, ice boxes, and canning processes dramatically changed the way food could be stored and consumed. Steamships provided faster transport of goods across oceans. Communications were also revolutionized, first with the telegraph and later with the telephone. These new technology combined to create a truly global marketplace, with the communications systems available to handle international orders for raw materials and manufactured goods, and the distribution networks available to fulfill them.

Medical Advances

Louis Pasteur demonstrated the importance of microorganisms in natural processes. His work improved food safety through the pasteurization of food, in which food is heated to kill bacteria. His work also resulted in the development of vaccines for diseases like cholera, diphtheria, and typhoid. Joseph Lister pioneered the use of antiseptics, reducing post-surgical mortality, and anesthesia, which later broadened the scope of surgical interventions. These advances gave rise to medical schools with rigorous, scientifically based curricula, including some for women. The London School of Medicine for Women was founded in 1874 by Elizabeth Garrett Anderson (although Dorothea Erxleben of Germany had been granted an MD more than a hundred years earlier).

Urban Reforms

As cities became more crowded and the problems associated with urbanization grew more acute, reformers attempted to ameliorate the problems. The British, who were at the forefront of industrialism, were also the pioneers of many reforms. Often driven by a self-interested middle class concerned about the spread of crime, filth, and disease, these reform movements were responsible for public works projects like sewers, water purification, and plumbing, as well as the gradual assumption of responsibility for public health by government entities. Sir Edwin Chadwick was one such reformer; he was partly responsible for "the modern administrative state." Whether in his 1842 report *The Sanitary Conditions of the Labouring Population*, which demonstrated a causal link between poor sanitation and disease, or in the Poor Law Commission report, which argued for consistent but draconian conditions in poorhouses, Chadwick advocated for centralized, efficient public administration of social programs.

Internal combustion engines and petroleum made automobiles, street cars, street trolleys, and other forms of mass transit possible, which in turn changed residential patterns as middle classes moved from cities to suburbs. Early forms of urban planning began with "the garden city movement," pioneered by Sir Ebenezer Howard of Great Britain, which sought to balance greenspaces and countryside with urban areas. Model villages were created like New Lanark (by Robert Owen) and Port Sunlight, based on the idea that providing quality housing and pastoral environments would result in increased productivity. Though these towns charged comparatively low rents, wages were also low and residents were often subject to paternalistic rules set by the industrialist or landowner. Government authorities eventually addressed the lack of affordable housing, through local taxes used to build cheap public housing in Great Britain, and through generous credit terms in France.

In France, Napoleon III chose Georges-Eugène Haussmann to renovate Paris by removing medieval walls; widening streets; filling city centers with museums, parks, theaters, and government buildings; and lining streets with new glowing gas lamps. Haussmann's vision included apartment buildings with a homogenous, coherent exterior that became part of the urban landscape. Former residents relocated to the suburbs, using new mass transit systems to commute to work.

Business Changes

Although there wasn't a worldwide depression during this time, volatility in the business cycles led to periods of economic hardship in different places and at different times. Protective tariffs were imposed to protect emerging domestic industries from competition by cheap foreign goods. Economic zones emerged, with distinctions between industrial producers of manufactured goods (Western Europe) and agricultural exporters of raw materials (Southern and Eastern Europe). In Germany, cartels, or groups of businesses, coordinated with each other to impose production quotas and to fix market prices. Germany, as a later industrializing nation, also took advantage of economies of scale and new machinery to create mega-sized factory plants, which allowed goods to be produced more cheaply and with less labor.

Wage-based workers were especially vulnerable to market pressures, as they could be easily fired and hired in response to market fluctuations. Efforts to unionize had mixed success, particularly in England where attempts to create a national federation of unions failed, but local trade unions persisted. Economic historians Karl Marx and Friedrich Engels saw these struggles as a continuation of historic clashes of socioeconomic classes, in this case with the capitalist bourgeoisie exploiting the labor of the workers, or the proletariat. Articulated in the *Communist Manifesto* in 1848, this theory helped explain the development of class consciousness, especially among the working class.

Social Changes

That each social class now lived and worked together facilitated class consciousness. An elite class developed, merging aristocratic landholders with newly wealthy industrialists, partly due to changing views on marriage and partly due to elite schools that both groups attended. This upper class often pursued government or military jobs, reinforcing their influence. Middle classes often worked to create a semblance of an upper-class lifestyle.

Men provided income and women were viewed as the guardians of the perfect family. The cult of domesticity envisioned beautiful, gentle mothers who kept a perfect home, sang and played piano, excelled at domestic arts, and raised perfectly behaved children. Often the reality was much different, and many middle-class wives who couldn't afford enough domestic servants toiled behind the scenes to create the illusion of perfection.

In addition, being excluded from most workplaces served to keep women dependent on fathers and husbands for their economic security. This caused them to be relegated to marginalized forms of work, like piecework sewing in sweatshops. Later, opportunities opened up for middle-class women as teachers, nurses, or shop clerks, but these were low-wage positions. For some women, who lacked family or marital protection, prostitution was the only viable option. It is important to note that Eastern European nations followed a different pattern. Though some implemented land reforms intended to liberate the serfs and create a mobile workforce, they were met with resistance. Landowners, often members of the new local assemblies, retained the best land. Peasants were obliged to repay the landowners, which was difficult given the infertility of their new land. This situation made it difficult for them to leave while they still owed money to the landowners.

Mass Culture

As standards of living increased and prices declined, a consumer culture developed. Department stores, which aggregated a variety of goods, were created to make shopping easier and more enticing. Mass marketing was used to attract new customers. Advertising found a home in newspapers with mass circulation, as well as on radio shows, which captured the public's imagination.

With the advent of public education systems, beginning as voluntary elementary education in France in 1833 and later spreading to most Western European nations in the form of compulsory education for boys and girls, literacy rates soared. Public education served to reinforce patriotism, reflected liberal beliefs in science and progress, and created a literate, disciplined workforce. With the standardization of working hours came the standardization of leisure hours. Leisure became commercialized, as mass transit allowed people to travel to entertainment venues. Spectator sports, beaches, recreation centers, dance halls, theaters, and amusement parks all flourished. This created a mass culture through a commonality of shared experiences.

Science in an Industrial Age

Advances in gas theory and a spirit of scientific realism dominated the physical sciences in the nineteenth century. Physicists in this period concentrated on providing a scientific understanding of the processes that drove the engines of the Industrial Revolution. In the middle of the nineteenth century, the German physicist Rudolf Clausius and the Scottish physicist James Clerk Maxwell developed the Kinetic Theory of Gases. Their theory envisioned gas pressure and temperature as resulting from a certain volume of molecules in motion. Such an approach allowed them to analyze, and therefore to measure and predict, pressure and temperature statistically. Later in the century, physicists such as Julius Robert von Mayer, Hermann von Helmoltz, and William Thomson, Lord Kelvin, pursued this kind of statistical analysis to articulate the laws of thermodynamics.

The success of "matter-in-motion" models in physics created a wider philosophical movement that argued that all natural phenomena could and should be understood as a result of matter in motion. The movement, known as "scientific materialism," was first articulated by a trinity of German natural philosophers: Karl Vogt, Jakob Moleschott, and Ludwig Büchner. By the end of the nineteenth century, scientific materialism had become the foundational assumption of the scientific view of the world.

The natural sciences of the nineteenth century were dominated by Charles Darwin's theory of evolution by natural selection. As a young man, Darwin had sailed around the globe as a naturalist for the *H. M. S. Beagle*. During the *Beagle*'s five-year voyage, commencing December 27, 1831, and ending on October 2, 1836, Darwin collected specimens for shipment home to England and made observations on the flora and fauna of the many continents he explored. Twenty-three years later, he published a book titled *On the Origin of Species by Means of Natural Selection, or the Preservation of Favoured Races in the Struggle for Life*. In *On the Origin of Species,* Darwin offered an answer to the two questions at the heart of nineteenth-century natural science: Why was there so much diversity among living organisms? and Why did organisms seem to "fit" into the environments in which they lived? Darwin's answer, unlike earlier answers that referred to God's will and a process of creation, was materialist. He argued that both the wide range of diversity and the environmental "fit" of living organisms to their environment were due to a process he termed "natural selection." The fact that many more organisms were born than could survive led, Darwin explained, to a constant "struggle for existence" between individual living organisms. Only those individuals who survived the struggle passed their physical characteristics onto their offspring. Over millions of years, that simple process had caused populations of organisms to evolve in ways that produced both the amazing diversity and the environmental "fit."

On the Origin of Species went through six editions, and Darwin's theory became the central organizing principle of the science of biology, which developed in the late nineteenth and early twentieth centuries. In 1871, Darwin published *The Descent of Man*, which explained Darwin's views on how human beings had come into existence through the process of natural selection.

Review Questions

Multiple Choice

Questions 1–3 refer to the following two passages:

The blessings which physio-mechanical science has bestowed on society, and the means it has still in store for ameliorating the lot of mankind, have been too little dwelt upon. . . . [I]n the factory, every member of the loom is so adjusted, that the driving force leaves the attendant nearly nothing at all to do, certainly no muscular fatigue to sustain, while it procures for him good, unfailing wages, besides a healthy workshop gratis: whereas the non-factory weaver, having everything to execute by muscular exertion, finds the labor irksome, makes in consequence innumerable short pauses, separately of little account, but great when added together; earns therefore proportionally low wages, while he loses his health by poor diet and the dampness of his hovel. . . .

The constant aim and effect of scientific improvement in manufactures are philanthropic, as they tend to relieve the workmen either from niceties of adjustment which exhaust his mind and fatigue his eyes, or from painful repetition of efforts which distort or wear out his frame.

Andrew Ure, *The Philosophy of the Manufacturers*, 1835

Any man who has stood at twelve o'clock at the single narrow door-way, which serves as the place of exit for the hands employed in the great cotton-mills, must acknowledge, that an uglier set of men and women, of boys and girls, taking them in the mass, it would be impossible to congregate in a smaller compass. Their complexion is sallow and pallid—with a peculiar flatness of feature, caused by the want of a proper quantity of adipose [fatty] substance to cushion out the cheeks. Their stature low—the average height of four hundred men, measured at different times, and different places, being five feet six inches. Their limbs slender, and playing badly and ungracefully. A very general bowing of the legs. Great numbers of girls and women walking lamely or awkwardly, with raised chests and spinal flexures. Nearly all have flat feet, accompanied with a down-tread, differing very widely from the elasticity of action in the foot and ankle, attendant upon perfect formation. . . . A spiritless and dejected air, a sprawling and wide action of the legs, and an appearance, taken as a whole, giving the world but "little assurance of a man."

P. Gaskell, *The Manufacturing Population of England*, 1833

1. Based on the two passages, what can one logically conclude about Great Britain in the 1830s?
   A. There was general consensus about the benefits of industrialization for British laborers.
   B. There was scientific evidence for the detrimental effects of industrialization on British laborers.
   C. There was a wide difference of opinion about the benefits of industrialization for British laborers.
   D. There was a general consensus about the detriments of industrialization for British laborers.

2. Based on the two passages, what was the most likely source of disagreement between Ure and Gaskell?
   A. The degree to which British labor has become industrialized
   B. The physical effects of industrial production on the industrial worker
   C. The effect of industrialization on the wages of industrial workers
   D. The economic benefits of industrialization for Great Britain

3. Which of the following can one conclude about Great Britain in the 1830s?
   A. It was being widely argued that industrial production was physically detrimental to industrial workers.
   B. Efforts to reform working conditions in factories were underway.
   C. It was being widely argued that women and children should not be working in factories.
   D. It was being widely argued that industrial production was economically beneficial to industrial workers.

Short Answer

4. Briefly explain the reciprocal nature of industrial production in this period and give TWO examples that illustrate the point.

Answers and Explanations

1. **C** is correct because the two passages could be used as evidence for the existence of a wide difference of opinion about the benefits of industrialization for British laborers. A and D are incorrect because the differing opinions expressed in the two passages argue against there being any consensus of opinion on the benefits of industrialization for British laborers. B is incorrect because neither passage offers scientific evidence.

2. **B** is correct because Ure states that industrial work leaves the worker "nearly nothing at all to do" and causes "no muscular fatigue," while Gaskell details the numerous detrimental physical effects of industrialized work. A is incorrect because the two passages offer no evidence of disagreement over the degree to which British labor had become industrialized. C is incorrect because only Ure addresses the effects of industrialization on wages. D is incorrect because neither passage addresses the effects of industrialization on the economy of Great Britain.

3. **A** is correct because the fact that Gaskell explicitly makes the argument, while Ure (a defender of industrial production) feels it necessary to refute the charge, allows one to infer that it was an argument that was fairly widely made. B is incorrect because neither passage refers to the existence of a reform movement. C is incorrect

because Ure makes no mention of women and children, and Gaskell's implication is not sufficient to infer that such a view was widely held. D is incorrect because Gaskell makes no mention of it and Ure's assertion is insufficient to infer that it was widely held.

4. Suggested answer:

Thesis: The four major components of the Industrial Revolution—the iron and steel industry, the coal industry, steam power, and the railways—had a reciprocal effect on one another because each developed in response to a demand created by the others, and each stimulated further demand for the others.

Paragraph Outline:

I. The iron and steel industry required improvements in the steam engine to run its blast furnaces, greater amounts of coal to fuel the engines, and railways to transport both the coal and the smelted iron and steel.

II. The coal industry required more and improved steam engines to pump water out of the mines and to power digging machinery; it also required railways to transport the coal.

Rapid Review

Between 1815 and 1914, the demand for goods on the part of a steadily increasing population was met by entrepreneurs who created the factory system. The new system standardized and increased industrial production. As the century went on, the development of four interrelated heavy industries—iron and steel, coal mining, steam power, and railroads—combined to drive Europe's economy to unprecedented heights, constituting an industrial revolution. The urbanization, standardization of work, and effects of the class system wrought by the Second Industrial Revolution significantly transformed social life in Europe.

The changes wrought by the Industrial Revolution led to the development of materialist modes of scientific explanation. This was manifested in the physical sciences by the kinetic theory of gases and in the natural sciences by Darwin's theory of evolution by natural selection.

Further Resources

Charles Dickens, *Oliver Twist*

Jane Austen, *Pride and Prejudice*

Novels about imperialism/colonialism:

Africa: Chinua Achebe, *Things Fall Apart*, and be sure to read the Yeats poem "The Second Coming"

India: Kamala Markandaya, *Nectar in a Sieve*, and J. G. Farrell, *The Siege of Krishnapur*

CHAPTER 19

Cultural Responses to Revolution and Industrialization

IN THIS CHAPTER

Summary: In the nineteenth century, intellectuals developed various ideologies in order to make sense of a rapidly changing world. Among the political and cultural ideologies explained in this chapter are conservatism, liberalism, anarchism, utopian socialism, scientific socialism or communism, romanticism, nationalism, and social Darwinism. At the lower level of the social hierarchy, the laboring classes violently resisted innovations that threatened their livelihood. Literature, art, and music played major roles in disseminating ideologies (see the Resource Guide at the end of this book).

Key Terms:

- ✪ **Conservatism** A nineteenth-century ideology that held that tradition was the only trustworthy guide to social and political action.
- ✪ **Liberalism** An eighteenth- and nineteenth-century ideology that asserted that the task of government was to promote individual liberty and active participation in governance by all social classes.
- ✪ **Socialism** An ideology that sought to reorder society in ways that would end or minimize competition, foster cooperation, and allow the working classes to share in the wealth being produced by industrialization.
- ✪ **Utopian socialism** A form of socialism that envisioned, and sometimes tried to establish, ideal communities (or utopias) where work and its fruits were shared equitably.

- **Psychological socialism** A variety of nineteenth-century utopian socialism that saw a conflict between the structure of society and the natural needs and tendencies of human beings. Its leading advocate was Charles Fourier, who argued that the ideal society was one organized on a smaller, more human scale.
- **Technocratic socialism** A variety of nineteenth-century utopian socialism that envisioned a society run by technical experts who managed resources efficiently and in a way that was best for all. The most prominent nineteenth-century advocate of technocratic socialism was the French aristocrat Henri Comte de Saint-Simon.
- **Scientific socialism/communism** An ideology dedicated to the creation of a class-free society through the abolition of private property.
- **Anarchism** A nineteenth-century ideology that saw the modern state and its institutions as the enemy of individual freedom and recommended terrorism as a way to disrupt the machinery of government.
- **Romanticism** A nineteenth-century ideology that urged the cultivation of sentiment and emotion by reconnecting with nature and with the past.
- **Nationalism** A nineteenth-century ideology that asserted that a nation was a natural, organic entity whose people shared a cultural identity and a historical destiny.
- **Social Darwinism** A nineteenth-century ideology that asserted that competition was natural and necessary for the evolutionary progress of a society.

Key Individuals:

Because of the nature of this chapter, there are a great many individuals mentioned; some are political thinkers, some are artists or musicians. All play a role in this extremely important period.

- Adam Smith
- Charles Fourier
- Edmund Burke
- Ernst Moritz Arndt
- Eugène Delacroix
- Francisco Goya
- Frédéric Chopin
- Friedrich Engels
- Georg Wilhelm Friedrich Hegel
- Georges Sorel
- Gioacchino Rossini
- Giuseppe Verdi
- Grimm Brothers
- Henri Comte de Saint-Simon
- Herbert Spencer
- Jeremy Bentham
- Johann Gottlieb Fichte
- John Locke
- Johann Wolfgang von Goethe
- John Constable
- John Stuart Mill
- Joseph de Maistre
- Lord Byron

- Ludwig von Beethoven
- Mary Shelley
- Mikhail Bakunin
- Prince Klemens von Metternich
- Pyotr Ilyich Tchaikovsky
- Richard Wagner
- Robert Owen
- Rosa Luxemburg
- Samuel Taylor Coleridge
- Victor Hugo
- William Wordsworth

Introduction

The French Revolution had challenged Europeans' beliefs in and assumptions about society; the Industrial Revolution seemed to be transforming society at a dizzying pace. In order to cope with these changes, and to answer the questions posed by them, nineteenth-century Europeans offered a number of significant cultural responses.

Political Ideologies in the Nineteenth Century

One such response was the creation of a number of political ideologies. Each claimed to hold the key to creating the best society possible.

Conservatism

In the nineteenth century, conservatism was the ideology that asserted that tradition was the only trustworthy guide to social and political action. Conservatives argued that traditions were time-tested, organic solutions to social and political problems. Accordingly, nineteenth-century conservatives supported monarchy, the hierarchical class system dominated by the aristocracy, and the Church. They opposed innovation and reform, arguing that the French Revolution had demonstrated that reform led directly to revolution and chaos. Supporters of the conservative position originally came from the traditional elites of Europe, the landed aristocracy.

The British writer and statesman Edmund Burke is often considered "the father of conservatism," as his *Reflections on the Revolution in France* (1790) seemed to predict the bloodshed and chaos that characterized the radical phase of the revolution. His work prompted responses from Thomas Paine. But perhaps more famous were the reactions of Mary Wollstonecraft in *Vindication of the Rights of Man* and *Vindication of the Rights of Woman* (1790); this latter is a model of thought and ideas for later feminists. The French writer Joseph de Maistre's *Essay on the Generative Principle of Political Constitutions* (1814) is a prime example of nineteenth-century conservatism's opposition to constitutionalism and reform.

The Congress of Vienna, convened by the major European powers in 1815 after Napoleon's defeat at Waterloo and led by Prince Klemens von Metternich of Germany, was another conservative response to the liberal and radical forces created by the French

Revolution. The Congress of Vienna's purpose was to maintain a balance of power in Europe and to strengthen traditional institutions like hereditary monarchy.

Liberalism

Liberalism was the nineteenth-century ideology asserting that the task of government was to promote individual liberty. Liberals viewed many traditions as impediments to that freedom and, therefore, campaigned for reform. Pointing to the accomplishments of the Scientific Revolution, nineteenth-century liberals asserted that there were God-given, natural rights and laws that individuals could discern through the use of reason. Accordingly, they supported innovation and reform (in contrast to conservatives), arguing that many traditions were simply superstitions. Liberals promoted constitutional monarchy over absolutism, and they campaigned for an end to the traditional privileges of the aristocracy and the Church in favor of a meritocracy and middle-class participation in government. Supporters of liberalism originally came from the middle class.

Two British philosophers, John Locke and Adam Smith, are usually thought of as the fathers of liberalism. In *The Two Treatises of Government* (1690), Locke made the argument for the existence of God-given natural rights and asserted that the proper goal of government was to protect and to promote individual liberty. In *Wealth of Nations* (1776), Smith made the case for the existence of economic laws that guided human behavior like an "invisible hand." Smith also promoted the notion of *laissez-faire* ("let it be") governance, which stated that governments should not interfere with the natural workings of an economy, a notion that became one of the basic tenets of liberalism in the nineteenth century.

Late-eighteenth- and early-nineteenth-century thinkers extended and cemented Smith's ideas. In *An Essay on the Principle of Population* (1798), Thomas Malthus asserted that free and constant competition would always be the norm in human societies because the human species would always reproduce at a greater rate than the food supply. By mid-century, liberal economic thinkers alleged that there was an "iron law of wages," which argued that competition between workers for jobs would always, in the long run, force wages to sink to subsistence levels. This "law" is sometimes attributed to the English economist David Ricardo, but it was promoted most prominently by the German sociologist Ferdinand LaSalle.

As the nineteenth century progressed, liberalism evolved. The followers of the English philosopher Jeremy Bentham espoused utilitarianism, which argued that all human laws and institutions ought to be judged by their usefulness in promoting "the greatest good for the greatest number" of people. Accordingly, they supported reforms to sweep away traditional institutions that failed the test and to create new institutions that would pass it. Utilitarians tended to be more supportive of government intervention than other liberals. For example, they drafted and supported new legislation—like the First Reform Bill of 1832, the Factory Act of 1833, and the Ten Hours Act of 1847—to limit the hours that women and children could work in factories and to regulate the sanitary conditions of factories and mines.

Early-nineteenth-century liberals had been leery of democracy, arguing that the masses had to be educated before they could usefully contribute to the political life of the country. But by mid-century, liberals began advocating democracy, reasoning that the best way to identify the greatest good for the greatest number was to maximize the number of people voting. The best example of mid-century utilitarian thought is John Stuart Mill's *On Liberty* (1859), which argued for freedom of thought and democracy, but also warned against the tyranny of the majority. Together, Mill and his companion, Harriet Taylor, led the liberal campaign for women's rights, Taylor publishing *The Enfranchisement of Women* (anonymously in 1851) and Mill publishing *The Subjection of Women* (1869).

Utopian Socialism

Socialism in the nineteenth century was the ideology that emphasized the collective over the individual and challenged the liberal notion that competition was natural. Socialists sought to reorder society in ways that would end or minimize competition, foster cooperation, and allow the working classes to share in the wealth being produced by industrialization.

The earliest forms of socialism have come to collectively be called utopian socialism for the way in which they envisioned, and sometimes tried to establish, ideal communities (or utopias) where work and its fruit were shared equitably. In the nineteenth century, there were three distinct forms of utopian socialism (described in the following sections).

Technocratic Socialism

This type of utopian socialism envisioned a society run by technical experts who managed resources efficiently and in a way that was best for all. The most prominent nineteenth-century advocate of technocratic socialism was a French aristocrat, Henri Comte de Saint-Simon, who renounced his title during the French Revolution and spent his life championing the progress of technology and his vision of a society organized and run by scientifically trained managers or "technocrats."

Psychological Socialism

This type of utopian socialism saw a conflict between the structure of society and the natural needs and tendencies of human beings. Its leading nineteenth-century advocate was Charles Fourier, who argued that the ideal society was one organized on a smaller, more human scale. He advocated the creation of self-sufficient communities, called "phalansteries," consisting of no more than 1,600 people, in which the inhabitants did work that suited them best.

Industrial Socialism

This type of utopian socialism argued that it was possible to have a productive, profitable industrial enterprise without exploiting workers. Its leading advocate was a Scottish textile manufacturer, Robert Owen. Owen set out to prove his thesis by setting up industrial communities, like the New Lanark cotton mill in Scotland and, later, a larger manufacturing community in New Harmony, Indiana, which paid higher wages and provided food, shelter, and clothing at reasonable prices.

Scientific Socialism and Communism

By the middle of the nineteenth century, the exploitation of European workers had grown more evident, and the dreams of the utopian socialists seemed less plausible. In their place arose a form of socialism based on what its adherents claimed was a scientific analysis of society's workings. The most famous and influential of the self-proclaimed scientific socialists was the German revolutionary Karl Marx. In *The Communist Manifesto* (1848), a slim pamphlet distributed to workers throughout Europe, Marx and his collaborator, Friedrich Engels, argued that "all history is the history of class struggle." In the *Manifesto*, and later in the much larger *Capital* (vol. 1, 1867), Marx argued that a human being's relationship to the means of production gave him a social identity. In the Industrial Age of the nineteenth century, Marx argued, only two classes existed: the bourgeoisie, who controlled the means of production, and the proletariat, who sold their labor for wages. The key point in Marx's analysis was that the bourgeoisie exploited the proletariat because competition demanded it; if a factory owner chose to treat his workers more generously, then he would have to charge more for his goods, and his competitors would drive him out of business. (That, in short, is what happened to Robert Owen as a result of his experiments.)

Marx's analysis led him to adopt a position that came to be known as communism, which declared that the only way to end social exploitation was to abolish private ownership of the means of production. If no one could claim to own the means of production, then there could be no distinction between owner and worker; all class distinctions would disappear, and the workers would be free to distribute the benefits of production more equally.

Anarchism

Anarchism was the nineteenth-century ideology that saw the state and its governing institutions as the ultimate enemy of individual freedom. Early anarchists drew inspiration from the writings of Pierre Joseph Proudhon, who argued that man's freedom had been progressively curtailed by industrialization and larger, more centralized governments. Proudhon famously suggested that "property is theft" since it promoted inequality. Anarchy had the greatest appeal in those areas where governments were most oppressive; in the nineteenth century, that meant Russia. There, Mikhail Bakunin, the son of a Russian nobleman, organized secret societies whose goal was to destroy the Russian state forever. Throughout Europe, nineteenth-century anarchists engaged in acts of political terrorism, particularly attempts to assassinate high-ranking government officials.

Cultural Ideologies in the Nineteenth Century

Other ideologies developed in the nineteenth century that sought to reach beyond "mere politics." Two of the most influential were Romanticism and nationalism.

Romanticism

Romanticism was a reaction to the Enlightenment and industrialization. The nineteenth-century Romantics rebelled against the Enlightenment's emphasis on reason, considering it an act of intellectual hubris, and urged the cultivation of imagination and emotion. They suggested that knowledge was reached through intuition. Fittingly, Romantics tended to avoid political tracts and expressed themselves mostly through art, music, and literature, which frequently captured history in creative ways. They stressed the purity of nature, as compared to the corruption of society.

The roots of Romanticism are often traced back to the works of Jean-Jacques Rousseau, because in *Émile* (1762), he had argued that humans were born essentially good and virtuous but were easily corrupted by society, and that the early years of a child's education should be spent developing the senses, sensibilities, and sentiments. Another source of Romanticism was the German *Sturm und Drang* ("Storm and Stress") movement of the late eighteenth century, exemplified by Johann Wolfgang von Goethe's *The Sorrows of Young Werther* (1774), which glorified the "inner experience" of the sensitive individual.

In response to the rationalism of the Enlightenment (and to some degree, of liberalism), the Romantics offered the solace of nature. Good examples of this vein of nineteenth-century Romanticism are the works of the English poets George Gordon, Lord Byron (who once wrote, "I love not man the less, but Nature more"), Percy Bysshe Shelley, William Wordsworth, and Samuel Taylor Coleridge, the last two of whom extolled the almost mystical qualities of the lake country of northwest England.

It is important to note, however, that the Romantics did not avoid politics completely. Frequently, Romanticism is defined as the period between 1789, the year the French Revolution began, and 1832, the year of the passage of the First Reform Bill in Great Britain, the deaths of Sir Walter Scott and Johann Wolfgang von Goethe, and the independence of Greece from the Ottoman Turks after almost 400 years.

Romantic influence is clearly evident in the liberal, revolutionary, and nationalistic movements of this time period. William Wordsworth described the joy he felt as he witnessed the beginning of the French Revolution ("Bliss it was that dawn to be alive, but to be young was very Heaven."). Mary Wollstonecraft, considered the mother of modern feminism, returned to Great Britain from the French Revolution and wrote *A Vindication of the Rights of Women*, urging equality of educational and thus economic opportunity. These and other writers embraced the idea that humans are inherently good, though corrupted by society. They all advocated release from the status quo.

Lord Byron went so far as to help the Italian *Carbonari* in their quest to establish a republican Italy, and he died in Greece, where he had gone to fight for Greek independence. He and other Romantics agreed that "it is not one man, nor the million, but the spirit of liberty which must be spread."

Romantic painters—like John Constable in England, Francisco Goya in Spain, and Karl Friedrich Schinkel in Germany—offered inspiring landscapes, a record of historical events, and images of a romanticized past. Beethoven, Chopin, Rossini, and Wagner expressed the imaginative, intuitive spirit of Romanticism in music. It is instructive to compare, thematically speaking, the operas of Mozart, who represented the Enlightenment as seen in his portrayal of social classes and revolution (*The Marriage of Figaro*), and those of Rossini, a Romantic of the first order (*The Barber of Seville*), who focused on human nature and emotions.

Nationalism

In the nineteenth century, nationalism was the ideology that asserted that a nation was a natural, organic entity whose people were bound together by shared language, customs, and history. Nationalists argued that each nation had natural boundaries, shared cultural traits, and a historical destiny to fulfill. Accordingly, nineteenth-century nationalists in existing nation-states like Britain and France argued for strong, expansionist foreign policies. Nationalists in areas like Germany and Italy argued for national unification and the expulsion of foreign rulers.

In the early nineteenth century, nationalism was allied to liberalism. Both shared a spirit of optimism, believing that their goals represented the inevitable, historical progress of humankind. In the non-unified lands of Germany and Italy, occupation by Napoleonic France had helped to foster a spirit of nationalism. Under Napoleon's rule, Germans and Italians came to think of their own disunity as a weakness. The best early examples of this kind of nationalism are the works of German writers Johann Gottlieb Fichte, whose *Addresses to the German Nation* (1808) urged the German people to unite in order to fulfill their historical role in bringing about the ultimate progress of humanity, and Georg Wilhelm Friedrich Hegel, who argued that every nation had a historical role to play in the unfolding of the universe and that Germany's time to take center stage in that drama had arrived.

Like the Romantics, early-nineteenth-century nationalists emphasized the role that environment played in shaping the character of a nation and sentimentalized the past. A good example of Romantic nationalism is the work of Ernst Moritz Arndt, who urged Germans to unify through a shared heritage and through love of all things German. In a similar vein, the Grimm brothers compiled traditional German folk stories to celebrate the beliefs and traditions of ethnic Germans. Strains of Romanticism can also be seen in the work of the great Italian nationalist of the early nineteenth century, Giuseppe Mazzini, whose nationalist movement, Young Italy, made appeals to unity based on natural affinities and a shared soul.

Social Darwinism

The socialist notion that competition was unnatural was countered by yet another nineteenth-century ideology that came to be known as social Darwinism. In 1859, the

British naturalist Charles Darwin published *On the Origin of Species*, which argued that all living things had descended from a few simple forms. In *On the Origin of Species*, Darwin described a complex process in which biological inheritance, environment, and competition for resources combined over millions of years to produce the amazing diversity in living forms that exists in the world.

The philosopher Herbert Spencer argued that Darwin's theory proved that competition was not only natural, but necessary, for the progress of a society. Spencer coined the phrase "survival of the fittest" (a phrase adopted by Darwin in the sixth and final edition of *On the Origin of Species*) and argued along liberal lines that government intervention in social issues interfered with natural selection and, therefore, with progress. By the last decades of the nineteenth century, social Darwinism was being used to argue that imperialism, the competition between nations for control of the globe, was a natural and necessary step in the evolution of the human species. Eugenics, the notion that a progressive, scientific nation should plan and manage the biological reproduction of its population as carefully as it planned and managed its economy, also flourished in the last decades of the nineteenth century.

Violent Resistance of the Laboring Classes

When the increased use of machines in industrial and agricultural production threatened the livelihood of skilled laborers, workers responded with violent resistance. In Britain, textile workers resisted the introduction of stocking frames, spinning frames, and power looms by destroying the machines, giving birth to what became known as the Luddite movement. In the countryside, workers resisted the introduction of threshing machines by burning hayricks in what became known as the Swing Riots.

Review Questions

Multiple Choice

Questions 1–3 refer to the following passage:

> WHERE is the German's fatherland?
> The Prussian land? The Swabian land?
> Where Rhine the vine-clad mountain laves?
> Where skims the gull the Baltic waves?
> Ah, no, no, no!
> His fatherland's not bounded so!
> Where is the German's fatherland?
> Bavarian land? or Stygian land?
> Where sturdy peasants plough the plain?
> Where mountain-sons bright metal gain?
> Ah, no, no, no!
> His fatherland's not bounded so! . . .
> Where is the German's fatherland?
> Then name, oh, name the mighty land!
> Wherever is heard the German tongue,
> And German hymns to God are sung!
> This is the land, thy Hermann's land;
> This, German, is thy fatherland.

Ernst Moritz Arndt, *The German Fatherland*, c. 1812

1. Arndt was a supporter of which nineteenth-century ideology?
   A. Conservatism
   B. Liberalism
   C. Nationalism
   D. Anarchism

2. What is the most-likely purpose of the poem?
   A. To celebrate the unification of Germany
   B. To urge German-speaking people to seek unity
   C. To indicate the superiority of Prussian culture
   D. To celebrate the beauty of Germany

3. According to the poem, Arndt believed what about the German kingdoms of Prussia, Swabia, and Bavaria?
   A. They were German nation-states.
   B. They were part of a German empire.
   C. They were part of the French Empire.
   D. They were part of the true Germany.

Short Answer

4. Briefly define Romanticism and illustrate your definition with TWO examples.

Answers and Explanations

1. **C** is correct because the passage indicates that Arndt believed that the true boundaries of a nation were shared language and culture. A is incorrect because the passage does not extol the virtues of tradition as a nineteenth-century conservative would. B is incorrect because the passage does not extol the virtues of individual liberty as a nineteenth-century liberal would. D is incorrect because the passage does not identify the state as the enemy of liberty as a nineteenth-century anarchist would.

2. **B** is correct because the passage urges German-speaking people to ignore the political divisions and provincialism of their current situation and to understand that a German fatherland exists wherever German is spoken and German customs are observed. A is incorrect because the passage cannot be celebrating a unification that would not come until 1871. C is incorrect because the passage is praising German-ness, not Prussia. D is incorrect because the poem does not speak of beauty.

3. **D** is correct because the passage indicates that all of the customary German and German-speaking kingdoms are really part of the true Germany. A is incorrect because the passage says that one will not find a fatherland in those kingdoms, and because those kingdoms are not nation-states. B is incorrect because nothing in the passage indicates that Arndt thought in terms of a German empire. C is incorrect because nothing in the passage refers to the French Empire.

4. Suggested answer:

   Thesis: Romanticism was the nineteenth-century ideology that reacted against the rationalism of the Enlightenment by urging the cultivation of imagination and emotion by reconnecting with nature and with the (idealized) past. Two examples of Romantic works in the nineteenth century are Goethe's *The Sorrows of Young Werther* and the works of English lake poets.

Paragraph Outline:

I. Johann Wolfgang von Goethe's *The Sorrows of Young Werther* (1774) illustrates the Romantic cultivation of sentiment by the way in which it glorified the "inner experience" of its young protagonist.

II. The works of the lake poets, such as William Wordsworth and Samuel Taylor Coleridge, illustrate the Romantic call to reconnect with nature by the way in which they extolled the almost mystical qualities of the lake country of northwest England.

Rapid Review

In the nineteenth century, intellectuals articulated numerous ideologies in order to make sense of a rapidly changing world. By the end of the century, a thinking person could choose from a spectrum of ideologies, which included and can be categorized and summarized as follows:

Political Ideologies

- Conservatism: championing tradition
- Liberalism: urging reform
- Anarchism: scheming to bring down the state
- Utopian socialisms: emphasizing the collective over the individual good and well-being
- Scientific socialism and communism: espousing the abolition of the private ownership of the means of production

Cultural Ideologies

- Romanticism: encouraging the cultivation of sentiment and emotion
- Nationalism: preaching ethnic, linguistic, and cultural unity
- Social Darwinism: advocating the benefits of unfettered competition

Further Resources

Jane Austen, *Pride and Prejudice*

Charles Darwin, *Origin of Species*

Charles Dickens, almost anything, but especially *Oliver Twist*

Mountains of the Moon (1990)

CHAPTER 20

Mass Politics and Nationalism

IN THIS CHAPTER

Summary: In the nineteenth century, increased political participation by the masses supported the growth of nationalism, encouraged by some in the Romantic movement who idealized traditional culture and nationalist struggles. This resulted in the establishment of the nation-state as the dominant unit of European political organization. The unifications of Germany and Italy by the conservative aristocracy, the nationalities problem of Austria-Hungary, the fall of the Second Empire in France, and the growth of democracy in Great Britain are among the topics reviewed in this chapter on the effects of growing political participation and nationalism.

Key Terms:

- ✪ *Carbonari* Secret groups of Italian nationalists active in the early part of the nineteenth century. In 1820, the *Carbonari* had briefly succeeded in organizing an uprising that forced King Ferdinand I of the Kingdom of the Two Sicilies to grant a constitution and a new Parliament.
- ✪ *Risorgimento* The mid-nineteenth-century Italian nationalist movement composed mostly of intellectuals and university students. From 1834 to 1848, the *Risorgimento* attempted a series of popular insurrections and briefly established a Roman Republic in 1848.
- ✪ *Junkers* A powerful class of landed aristocrats in nineteenth-century Prussia who supported Bismarck's plan for the unification of Germany.

○ *Realpolitik* A political theory, made fashionable by Bismarck in the nineteenth century, which asserted that the aim of any political policy should be to increase the power of a nation by whatever means and strategies were necessary and useful.

○ **The nationalities problem** The name given to the conflict between the ten distinct linguistic and ethnic groups that lived within the borders of Austria-Hungary and their German-speaking rulers.

○ **Russianization** Alexander III's attempt, in the 1880s, to make Russian the standard language and the Russian Orthodox Church the standard religion throughout the Russian Empire.

○ **Chartism** A movement in Britain (1837–1842) in support of the People's Charter, a petition that called for universal manhood suffrage, annual Parliaments, voting by secret ballot, equal electoral districts, the abolition of property qualifications for Members of Parliament, and the payment of Members of Parliament.

○ **Nationalism** This term is often conflated with patriotism, but the differences are both subtle and important. Nationalism means a strong sense of national identity based on commonalities like language, culture, ethnicity, and traditional homeland. It can be either a unifying force (Italy, Germany) or a fragmenting one (Greece, Austrian Empire). In its later usage, nationalism is distinguished from patriotism in that, though both entail love of country, nationalism has connotations of national superiority, sometimes manifesting in aggression.

Key Individuals:

○ Otto von Bismarck
○ Count Camillo Benso di Cavour
○ Giuseppe Garibaldi
○ Emperor Franz Joseph
○ Charles-Louis Napoleon Bonaparte (Napoleon III)
○ Tsar Alexander II
○ Tsar Alexander III
○ Benjamin Disraeli
○ William Gladstone

Introduction

In the hundred years following the fall of Napoleon's empire, classes of people who were traditionally left out of the politics of Europe's nations and empires demanded participation in a variety of ways. One context in which the advent of mass politics contributed to significant change was in the triumph of the nation-state as the primary unit of political organization.

Nationalism and State-Building

Over the course of the nineteenth century, nationalism triumphed over all other competing ideologies. In areas where people lived under foreign domination, nationalism was used by conservative statesmen to bring about the unification of Italy and Germany. In the

Habsburg Empire, the nationalist aspirations of ethnic minorities worked to undermine Austrian domination. In France and Russia, the force of nationalism was used to end the remaining dreams of liberals and to strengthen the hold of autocratic rulers.

The Triumph of Conservative Nationalism

In the first half of the nineteenth century, liberals and nationalists tended to ally themselves against the forces of conservatism. Both believed that political sovereignty resided in the people, and they shared an optimistic belief that progress toward their goals was inevitable. Campaigns for liberal reform (which attempted to break the conservative aristocracy's grip on political power and to promote individual rights) tended to merge with the struggle for national rights or self-determination. Accordingly, most liberals supported the idea of free and unified nation-states in Germany and Italy, the rebirth of Poland, and Greek independence; most conservatives opposed these ideas.

However, both partial victory and eventual defeat drove a wedge between liberals and nationalists. When liberals won temporary victories over conservative aristocrats between 1830 and 1838, fundamental differences between the agendas of liberal reformers and nationalists began to emerge. The emphasis on individual liberty and limited government did not mesh well with the nationalist emphasis on the collective national tribe or with the desire of nationalists for a strong national government. In short, liberals believed in promoting the rights of *all peoples*; nationalists cared only about promoting their nation's interests.

When, in 1848, the more radical liberal agenda of democratic reform emerged as a wave of revolutions across Europe, the conservative tendencies of nationalism came to the fore. Nationalists not only shared the conservatives' belief in the value of historical traditions, they tended to mythologize the past and dream of a return to an era of national glory. Ultimately, however, what drove a wedge between liberals and nationalists was the failure of liberals to hold the power they had temporarily seized. As the conservative reaction in the second half of 1848 smashed liberal movements and revolutions everywhere in Europe, nationalists dreaming of a strong, unified country free from foreign rule increasingly turned to conservative leaders. Both the unification of Italy and the unification of Germany were primarily engineered by and for the conservative aristocrats.

The Unification of Italy

The Forces Against Unity in Italy

The settlement after the defeat of Napoleon in 1815 had greatly disappointed those hoping for an Italian nation-state. The Italian peninsula consisted of separate states controlled by powerful enemies of Italian nationalism:

- The Habsburg Dynasty of Austria controlled, either directly or through its vassals, Lombardy and Venetia in the north, and the duchies of Tuscany, Parma, and Modena.
- The pope governed an area known as the Papal States in central Italy.
- A branch of the Bourbon dynasty (which ruled France) controlled the Kingdom of the Two Sicilies in the south.
- An Italian dynasty, the House of Savoy, controlled both the island of Sardinia in the south and Piedmont in the northwest.

In addition to political divisions and foreign interests, the Italian peninsula was also divided by economic and cultural differences. The northern areas of the peninsula benefited from industrialization and, consequently, internal migration of southerners looking for work. The southern areas, and the islands of Sicily and Sardinia, suffered from *latifundismo*, or the control of vast amounts of land by a tiny proportion of the population.

Latifundismo also accounted for the larger numbers of southern Italians immigrating into the Americas—more than four million by the early part of the twentieth century, going primarily to the United States, Argentina, and Brazil in search of "*pane e lavoro*" (bread and work).

Culturally, the peninsula retained use of many dialectical variations on Italian, which hampered unification. Socially and politically, the middle-class merchants and manufacturers, located mostly in the north, wanted a greater degree of unity for easier trade and tended to support liberal reforms; they were opposed by the staunchly conservative, traditional landed elites.

Italian Nationalism to 1850

Italian nationalism had been forged in opposition to Napoleon's rule. After 1815, dreams of a unified Italy were kept alive in secret societies like the *Carbonari*, secret clubs whose members came mostly from middle-class families and from the army. In 1820, the *Carbonari* had briefly succeeded in organizing an uprising that forced King Ferdinand I of the Kingdom of the Two Sicilies to grant a constitution and a new Parliament. But Austrian troops, with the blessing of the Concert of Europe, crushed the revolt. The Austrians put down a similar revolt by the *Carbonari* in Piedmont from 1831 to 1832.

In the 1840s, Giuseppe Mazzini's Young Italy had carried the banner of Italian nationalism. Both a Romantic and a liberal, Mazzini fought for the establishment of an Italian republic that would serve, as he believed ancient Rome had, as a beacon for the rest of humanity. By mid-century, Mazzini had forged a movement known as the *Risorgimento*, which was composed mostly of intellectuals and university students who shared his idealism. From 1834 to 1848, the *Risorgimento* attempted a series of popular insurrections, briefly establishing a Roman Republic in 1848 until it was crushed (like its liberal counterparts throughout Europe) by the forces of reaction. In defeat, it was evident that the *Risorgimento* had failed to win the support of the masses.

Cavour and Victory over Austria

At mid-century, Count Camillo Benso di Cavour, the chief minister of King Victor Emmanuel II of the Kingdom of Piedmont-Sardinia, emerged as the new champion of Italian nationalist hopes. Cavour differed from Mazzini and other leaders of the Italian nationalist movement in several significant ways. He was a conservative aristocrat with ties to the most powerful ruler on the peninsula, King Victor Emmanuel II, and not a middle-class intellectual. He supported the idea of a constitutional monarchy rather than that of a republic. Cavour was, in short, a cautious and practical statesman. Not an idealist, Cavour was an opportunist.

Cavour sought to increase the amount of territory under the control of the Piedmont whenever possible and to weaken the opponents of Italian unification by playing them against each other. Between 1855 and 1860, Cavour took advantage of several such opportunities and managed to unite all of northern Italy under the Piedmont region. In 1855, he brought the Piedmont region and its army into the Crimean War on the side of England and France, who were fighting Russia. This resulted in no immediate gains, but the peace conference afforded Cavour the opportunity to denounce the Austrian occupation of Italian lands. In 1858, Cavour reached a secret agreement with Napoleon III of France and gained the promise of French support should Austria attack the Piedmont region. The following year, Cavour goaded the Austrians into attacking by mobilizing forces and refusing an ultimatum to disarm. French and Piedmontese troops defeated the Austrians at the Battles of Magenta and Solferino, and drove Austrians out of Lombardy. Further gains by the Piedmont region were thwarted by Napoleon III's abrupt signing of the Treaty of Villafranca with the Austrians. By 1860, however, the majority of the northern and north-central duchies shook off their Austrian rulers and voluntarily united with the Piedmont region.

Garibaldi and Victory in the South

The success of northern Italians in throwing off Austrian domination inspired their southern counterparts. A series of peasant revolts, tinged with anti-Bourbon sentiment, arose in the south. Southern Italian nationalists found a different kind of leader in Giuseppe Garibaldi and, in 1860, launched a series of popular uprisings, which put all of southern Italy under his control. The southern nationalist movement differed from its northern counterpart in several significant ways. Garibaldi was a Romantic nationalist who had been an early supporter of Mazzini. The southern nationalist movement was a genuine revolt of the masses, rather than the political maneuverings of a single kingdom. Garibaldi hoped to establish an Italian republic that would respect the rights of individuals and improve the lot of the peasants and workers.

In May 1860, Garibaldi raised an army of 1,000 red-shirted Italian patriots and landed in Sicily to aid a peasant revolt underway there. In a few short months, Garibaldi and his red-shirts provided leadership to a nationalist revolt that took control of most of southern Italy and set its sights on Rome.

The Kingdom of Italy and the Completion of Italian Unification

Cavour publicly condemned Garibaldi's conquests but secretly aided them. When Garibaldi's troops began to threaten Rome, Cavour persuaded Napoleon III, who had sworn to protect the pope, to allow the Piedmontese army to invade the Papal States in order to head off Garibaldi. By September 1860, Piedmont controlled the Papal States and set up a ring around Rome.

When Piedmontese forces, led by King Victor Emmanuel II, met Garibaldi and his forces outside Rome in September 1860, Garibaldi submitted and presented all of southern Italy to Victor Emmanuel; in the end, Garibaldi's dream of a unified Italy was stronger than his commitment to the idea of a republic. In March 1861, the Kingdom of Italy was formally proclaimed. It was a constitutional monarchy under Victor Emmanuel II with a parliament elected by limited suffrage. It consisted of all of the Italian peninsula, except the city of Rome (which was still ruled by the pope and protected by French troops) and the province of the Veneto (which was still occupied by Austrian troops). The Veneto became part of the Kingdom of Italy during the Austro-Prussian War of 1866 and the unification of Italy was completed when Rome (with the exception of Vatican City) followed during the Franco-Prussian War of 1870.

The Unification of Germany

Forces Against Unity in Germany

Unlike Italy, Germany in the middle of the nineteenth century was free of direct foreign domination. It existed as a loose confederation of independent states. Within that loose confederation, several forces worked against national unity. Profound cultural differences existed between the rural, conservative, Protestant north and the urban, liberal, Roman Catholic south. The individual German states each had a long history of proud independence.

Habsburg Austria continued to exert a powerful influence on, or controlled, a large portion of the German confederation.

Prussian Leadership

With the failure of the liberal Frankfurt Assembly in 1848, leadership in the German nationalist movement passed to Prussia. Prussia was a strong northern kingdom ruled by the Hohenzollern dynasty and supported by a powerful class of landed aristocrats known as *Junkers*. Prussia also had the strongest military in Germany, and in 1845, Prussia led the way in establishing the *Zollverein*, a large free-trade zone, consisting of all German states but excluding Austria. This combination of military and economic power led many Germans to look to Prussia for leadership.

Bismarck and War with Denmark and Austria

In 1861, Prussia's new monarch, William I, wanted to reorganize and further strengthen the military, but the liberal legislature resisted, and a power struggle between the monarch and the legislature ensued. William I turned to the conservative *Junker* Otto von Bismarck to be his prime minister. Bismarck forced a showdown, and it quickly became apparent that the support of the Prussian people was with the king, the army, and Bismarck. With the power of the army behind him and the government fully established, Bismarck set out a policy to unify Germany under the Prussian crown, which came to be known as *Realpolitik* and asserted that the aim of Prussian policy would be to increase its power by whatever means and strategies were necessary and useful. Bismarck asserted that the unification of Germany would be accomplished by a combination of "blood and iron."

First, Bismarck isolated France through a series of treaties, including the Three Emperors' League (with Austria and Russia), the Reinsurance Treaty (Russia), and the Triple Alliance (with Austria and Italy). Then he quickly concluded that a war with Austria was inevitable, and he engineered one in an episode that has come to be known as the *Schleswig-Holstein Affair*. He began by enlisting Austria as an ally in a war with Denmark over two duchies, Schleswig and Holstein, which had large German-speaking populations. Once Denmark was forced to cede the two duchies, Bismarck provoked an argument with Austria over control of them. Bismarck's next moves were a perfect illustration of *Realpolitik* in action:

- First, Bismarck obtained Italian support for a war with Austria by promising Italy the province of Venetia.
- Next, he ensured Russian neutrality by supporting Russia's actions against its rebellious Polish subjects.
- Then, he met secretly with Napoleon III of France and persuaded him that a weakening of Austrian power was in the best interests of France.
- Finally, and only after those preparations were in place, he carried out a series of diplomatic and military maneuvers that provoked Austria into declaring war.

In the resulting Austro-Prussian War of 1866, Prussian troops surprised and overwhelmed a larger Austrian force, winning victory in only seven weeks. The result was the expulsion of Austria from the old German Confederation and the creation of a new North German Confederation, which was completely under the control of Prussia.

War with France

All that remained for Bismarck was to draw the south German states into the new Confederation. But the south (which was predominantly Catholic and liberal) feared being absorbed by the Protestant and authoritarian Prussians. Bismarck concluded that only one thing would compel the south Germans to accept Prussian leadership: a war with a powerful foreign enemy. So he set about engineering one.

The opportunity came when both France and Prussia got involved in a dispute over the vacant throne in Spain. Bismarck, with the support of the Prussian military leadership, edited a communication between Napoleon III and William I (a communication now known as the Ems Telegram) to make it seem as though they had insulted one another, which Bismarck then released to the press. Tempers flared, and France declared war. The south German states rallied to aid Prussia. Combined German forces quickly routed the French troops, capturing Napoleon III and taking Paris in January 1871.

The Second Reich

On January 18, 1871, the unification of Germany was completed. The heads of all the German states gathered in the Hall of Mirrors in the Palace of Versailles outside Paris and proclaimed William I kaiser (emperor) of the German Empire (formally the Second Reich, honoring the old Holy Roman Empire as the First Reich). The new empire took the provinces of Alsace and Lorraine from France and billed the French 5 billion francs as a war indemnity.

Mass Politics and Nationalism in the Habsburg Empire

In the dual monarchy of Austria-Hungary, mass politics continued to mean competition between nationalities for greater autonomy and relative supremacy within the empire. In an age of nation-building, the Habsburg Empire, with its Austrian minority dominating an empire consisting of Hungarians (also known as Magyars), Czechs, Serbs, Romanians, and other ethnic groups, was an anachronism. The forces of nationalism, therefore, worked to tear the empire apart. After Austria's defeat by Prussia in 1866, the Austrian Emperor Franz Joseph attempted to deal with what has come to be called "the nationalities problem." By agreeing to the Compromise of 1867, he set up the dual monarchy of Austria-Hungary. Franz Joseph served as the ruler of both Austria and Hungary, each of which had its own parliament. This arrangement essentially set up an alliance between the Austrians and the Hungarians against the other ethnic groups in the empire. The introduction of universal manhood suffrage in 1907 made Austria-Hungary so difficult to govern that the emperor and his advisors began bypassing the parliament and ruling by decree.

Mass Politics and Nationalism in France

Louis-Napoleon Bonaparte had originally been elected president of the Second Republic in 1848. When the National Assembly refused to amend the constitution to allow him to run for a second term, he staged a coup d'état on December 2, 1851. The public overwhelmingly sided with Louis-Napoleon, who granted them universal manhood suffrage. They responded, in two plebiscites, by voting to establish a Second Empire and to make Louis-Napoleon hereditary emperor.

Like his namesake, Louis-Napoleon attempted to increase his popularity by expanding the Empire, but soon his foreign adventures began to erode his popularity. By 1870, the liberal parliament had begun to reassert itself. The humiliating defeat in the Franco-Prussian War brought down both Louis-Napoleon and the Second Empire, and it also set in motion a battle between monarchists and the people of Paris who, having defended Paris from the Germans while the aristocrats fled, now considered themselves to represent the nation of France. When elections in 1871 resulted in a victory for the monarchists, the people of Paris refused to accept the results and set up their own democratic government, which came to be known as the Paris Commune. The Commune ruled the city of Paris in February and March 1871, before being crushed by the French Army.

Monarchists initially controlled the government of the new Third Republic, but they remained divided between factions. By the end of the 1870s, France was governed by a liberal government elected by universal manhood suffrage. However, in the late 1880s, conservative nationalists supported an attempted coup by General George Boulanger. The attempt—which has come to be known as the Boulanger Affair—failed, but it underscored the fragility of French democracy and the volatility of mass politics in France.

Mass Politics and Nationalism in Russia

At mid-century, Russia's government was the most conservative and autocratic in Europe. The peasants of Russia were still bound to the land by serfdom. The Crimean War (1853–1856), in which Russia essentially battled Great Britain and France for control of parts of the crumbling Ottoman Empire, damaged the reputation of both the tsar and the military. Alexander II, who ascended the throne in 1855, was determined to strengthen Russia by reforming and modernizing it. He abolished serfdom, made the judiciary more independent, and created local political assemblies.

However, Russia was plagued by its own nationalities problem. Alexander II attempted to deal with it by relaxing restrictions on the Polish population within the Russian Empire, but this fanned the flames of nationalism and led to an attempted Polish Revolution in 1863. Alexander II responded with increased repression of Poles and other ethnic minorities within the Russian Empire. And after an attempt on his life in 1866, Alexander II gave up all notions of liberal reform and proceeded to turn Russia into a police state. In response, mass politics took the form of terrorism. Radical groups like the People's Will carried out systematic acts of violent opposition, including the assassination of Alexander II with a bomb in 1881. His successor, Alexander III, responded by waging war on liberalism and democracy. Initiating a program of "Russianization," he attempted to standardize language and religion throughout the Russian Empire.

Mass Politics and Nationalism in Great Britain

Mass participation in politics in Great Britain in the nineteenth century (in the form of mass demonstrations and riots) provided the pressure that enabled liberals to force through the Great Reform Bill of 1832. This bill enfranchised most of the adult, male middle class.

In the decades that followed, the liberals seemed satisfied with limited reform. The rise of Chartism (1837–1842) demonstrated the degree to which the lower-middle and working classes desired further reform. Chartists organized massive demonstrations in favor of the People's Charter, a petition that called for the following:

- Universal manhood suffrage
- Annual Parliaments
- Voting by secret ballot
- Equal electoral districts

- Abolition of property qualifications for Members of Parliament
- Payment of Members of Parliament

If enacted into law, the People's Charter would have had the effect of creating a completely democratic House of Commons. But Parliament rejected the Charter on numerous occasions.

In 1867, the new leader of the Conservative (or Tory) Party, Benjamin Disraeli, convinced his party that further reform was inevitable and engineered the passage of the Reform Bill of 1867. The bill doubled the number of people eligible to vote and extended the vote to the lower-middle class for the first time. Additionally, the Conservatives passed a number of laws regulating working hours and conditions, and the sanitary conditions of working-class housing.

In 1884, the Liberals, under William Gladstone, again took the lead, engineering the passage of the Reform Bill of 1884. This bill included the following reforms:

- It extended the right to vote further down the social ladder, thereby enfranchising two-thirds of all adult males.
- It made primary education available to all.
- It made military and civil service more democratic.

The most significant result of the advent of mass politics in Great Britain was competition between Liberals and Conservatives for the newly created votes. In 1879, Gladstone embarked on the first modern political campaign, which came to be known as the Midlothian Campaign, riding the railway to small towns throughout his district to give speeches and win votes. Disraeli and the Conservatives countered with a three-pronged platform of "Church, Monarchy, and Empire."

It is important to bear in mind the context within which these events took place. Nationalism cannot be wholly separated from the forces of industrialism, for it was often through government support of industry that nationalists helped increase their nations' power and influence relative to the rest of the world. To this end, Louis Napoleon (Napoleon III) developed investment banks and encouraged massive railroad construction, and Sergei Witte of Russia imposed protective tariffs, promoted railroad construction, and solicited foreign investment. Bismarck's *Zollverein* used economic policy to simultaneously strengthen Prussia and weaken a potential rival, Austria. This, in turn, gave rise to changes in social class structures, prompting social tensions with nationalists that had to be accommodated (Great Britain), coopted (Italy), or repressed (Russia, at times).

Ireland, or "the Irish Question," provides an interesting case study of the social tensions created, or at least exacerbated, by nationalism and industrialization. The nineteenth century witnessed a rise in both the rights and duties of Great Britain's social classes. The Reform Bills of 1832, 1867, and 1884 gave the vote to the majority of adult males, offering opportunities to participate in the previously socially restricted military, church, and civil service ranks. Elementary education was made universal. Health and housing acts contributed to a sense of well-being, thanks in large part to the benefits of industrialization.

Into this atmosphere of prosperity, however, came the difficulties caused by the gap between grand social advancements and unequal distribution of power and wealth. This imbalance was most visible in the agricultural sector and was worsened by the nationalist divide between English and Irish Protestants and Catholics. The Irish Land League, led by Charles Stuart Parnell, sought a redistribution of land because much of Ireland's territory remained in English hands. English political opposition forces joined to defeat Home Rule, and this would leave Ireland split between Roman Catholic supporters of Home Rule and Protestant landowners.

Political and nationalist concerns brought Great Britain to the edge of civil war. Home Rule was granted in 1912, although not implemented until after World War I.

Review Questions

Multiple Choice

Questions 1–3 refer to the following passage:

I will not, sir, at present express any opinion as to the details of the Bill; but having during the last twenty-four hours given the most diligent consideration to its general principles, I have no hesitation in pronouncing it a wise, noble, and comprehensive measure, skillfully framed for the healing of great distempers, for the securing at once of the public liberties and of the public repose, and for the reconciling and knitting together of all the orders of the State. [The Ministers'] principle is plain, rational, and consistent. It is this, to admit the middle class to a large and direct share in the representation, without any violent shock to the institutions of our country. . . .

I praise the Ministers for not attempting, under existing circumstances, to make the representation uniform. I praise them for not effacing the old distinction between the towns and the counties, for not assigning members to districts, according to the American practice, by the rule of three. They have done all that was necessary for the removing of a great practical evil, and no more than was necessary.

Thomas Babington Macaulay, Speech on the Reform Bill of 1832, March 2, 1831

1. Based on the passage, which best expresses Macaulay's position on the Reform Bill?
   A. He believed the bill would be good for Great Britain.
   B. He thought the bill went too far.
   C. He opposed the bill.
   D. He attempted to amend the bill.

2. According to Macaulay, what was the main purpose of the bill?
   A. The adoption of a constitution for Great Britain
   B. The enfranchisement of the middle class
   C. The enfranchisement of the working class
   D. The creation of democracy in Great Britain

3. Based on the passage and your knowledge of European History, who would be most likely to oppose the bill on the grounds that it was too limited in its scope?
   A. A liberal lawyer
   B. A radical factory worker
   C. A conservative aristocrat
   D. A moderate merchant

Short Answer

4. Briefly explain TWO similarities and ONE difference between the unifications of Italy and Germany.

Answers and Explanations

1. **A** is correct because the passage states Macaulay's belief that the bill was "skillfully framed" for "the reconciling and knitting together of all the orders of the State." B is incorrect because the passage contains no notion that the bill went too far. C is incorrect because the passage states that he would not express an opinion on whether it should be passed. D is incorrect because the passage makes no mention of an amendment.

2. **B** is correct because, in the passage, Macaulay states that he understands the framing principle of the bill is "to admit the middle class to a large and direct share in the representation." A is incorrect because the passage makes no mention of creating a constitution for Great Britain. C is incorrect because the passage makes no mention of the working class. D is incorrect because the passage makes no mention of democracy and because the Reform Bill enfranchised only the middle class.

3. **B** is the correct answer. The passage indicates reform is limited to the middle classes, a liberal position which would exclude a radical factory worker. Both A and D would likely be supporters as they would be members of the middle class, and thus both liberal and likely beneficiaries of the policy. C is incorrect as a conservative aristocrat, though likely to oppose the policy, would probably do so on the grounds that it was too generous, not too restrictive.

4. Suggested answer:

Thesis: The unifications of Italy and Germany were similar in two ways: (1) Both had to overcome significant economic and cultural differences between the north and the south; (2) Both were achieved by, and in the interests of, the aristocratic class. The unifications of Italy and Germany differed in that a genuine class revolt contributed to the unification process only in Italy.

Paragraph Outline:

I. Italy: The northern areas of the peninsula were more industrialized and well developed economically than the still largely rural and agricultural areas of the south; culturally, the people of the more developed northern region felt little connection to the poor people in the south. Extensive use of dialects throughout Italy also hampered unity.

Germany: significant cultural barriers existed between the rural, conservative, Protestant north and the urban, liberal, Catholic south; economically, the powerful influence of Habsburg Austria, which controlled or influenced a large portion of the German Confederation.

II. Italian unification was achieved through the efforts of Count Camillo Benso di Cavour, a conservative aristocrat who united Italy in order to create a constitutional monarchy under Victor Emmanuel II, king of Piedmont-Sardinia. German unification was achieved by Otto von Bismarck, a conservative aristocrat who united Germany under William I, king of Prussia.

III. The southern part of the Italian peninsula was originally unified by the efforts of Giuseppe Garibaldi, a Romantic nationalist who had been an early supporter of Mazzini. The southern movement was a genuine revolt of the masses, rather than the political maneuverings of a single kingdom. Garibaldi hoped to establish an Italian republic that would respect the rights of individuals and improve the lot of peasants and workers, but capitulated when given a choice by Cavour between the fulfillment of Italian unification or civil war.

Rapid Review

In the nineteenth century, increased political participation by the masses supported the growth of nationalist ideology and feeling. The failure of the revolutions of 1848 broke the fragile alliance between liberalism and nationalism. Accordingly, the unifications of Italy and Germany were achieved by and for the conservative aristocracy. Meanwhile, the Habsburg Empire was plagued by a nationalities problem and became Austria-Hungary in 1867. France's defeat led to the fall of the Second Empire in France, and Alexander II turned Russia into a police state. In Great Britain, mass politics provided the impetus for a series of reform bills that would make the country the most democratic of European societies in the nineteenth century.

Further Resources

John Fowles, *The French Lieutenant's Woman*
(Made into a film in 1981)

CHAPTER 21

Mass Politics and Imperialism

IN THIS CHAPTER

Summary: Among the factors leading to the development of European imperialism in the nineteenth century were economic needs created by industrialization, traditional competition between European nations, and the need for European political elites to find ways to win the support of a new political force: the masses. This chapter reviews the growth of European empires beyond Europe, chiefly in Africa, where European powers quickly staked out claims to virtually the entire continent, and Asia, where European control was generally exerted through local elites.

Key Terms:

KEY IDEA

- ✪ **New Imperialism** The expansion of European influence and control in the last decades of the nineteenth century. It was characterized by a shift from indirect commercial influence to active conquest and the establishment of direct political control of foreign lands around the globe, particularly in Africa and Asia.
- ✪ **Scramble for Africa** The rush of European powers to claim interest in and sovereignty over portions of Africa in the first half of the 1880s. It culminated in the Berlin Conference of 1885, at which European powers laid down rules for the official claiming of African territories. As a result, by the end of the 1880s, only Liberia and Ethiopia remained independent African countries.
- ✪ **Suez Canal** A canal opened in 1869, built by a French company with Egyptian labor, that connects the Mediterranean Sea through Egypt to the Red Sea and the Indian Ocean. In 1875, Great Britain took advantage of the Egyptian ruler's financial distress and purchased a controlling interest in the canal. Control of the canal led to British occupation and the annexation of Egypt.

- ✪ **Sepoy Rebellion of 1857 (sometimes known as "the Sepoy Mutiny")**
  A well-organized anti-British uprising led by military units of Indians who had formerly served the British. It resulted in the British government taking direct control of India and a restructuring of the Indian economy to produce and consume products in order to aid the British economy.
- ✪ **Taiping Rebellion** An attempt to overthrow the Manchu rulers of China (1850–1864), whose authority had been undermined by Western interference. Defending their rule from the Rebellion made the Manchus ever more dependent on Western support.
- ✪ **Globalization** Political, cultural, economic interdependence of the world's nations and the global nature of contemporary problems.

Key Individuals:

- ✪ Joseph Conrad
- ✪ Paul Gauguin
- ✪ Vincent Van Gogh
- ✪ Rudyard Kipling (author of "The White Man's Burden")
- ✪ Chinua Achebe

Introduction

In the nineteenth century, the development of mass politics helped to make imperialism the defining characteristic of a vigorous and powerful nation-state. In the first part of the nineteenth century, European imperialism (primarily in Africa and Asia) tended to take the form of indirect commercial influence and was, therefore, generally a continuance of Europe's seventeenth- and eighteenth-century economic activity. In the last decades of the nineteenth century, European powers shifted from indirect commercial influence to active conquest and the establishment of direct political control of foreign lands around the globe, particularly in Africa and Asia. This imperial expansion of European influence and control is often referred to as the "New Imperialism." It can also be regarded as a return to the mercantilist policies of the Age of Discovery and Exploration, or what can be called "old imperialism" (see Chapter 13).

Causes of the New Imperialism

The causes of the New Imperialism are a matter of debate among historians, but all explanations involve, to some degree, the factors summarized here. To accommodate their growing industrial economies, European countries needed increased access to raw materials from around the world. Sustained production relied on global markets for European manufactured goods. In addition, technological innovations in weaponry and transportation encouraged European military adventurism.

Rudyard Kipling's "The White Man's Burden" expresses the sense of historical destiny that allowed the nineteenth-century unification of European nations and led to the growth of strong European national identities. It also shows the traditional European elites' political beliefs as these elites competed for fame and glory through conquest. All these elements enabled European political elites to win support of newly politicized and enfranchised masses that they needed in order to stay in power.

The direct effects and devastating side effects of the New Imperialism are poignantly and tragically portrayed in Chinua Achebe's classic novel *Things Fall Apart*. The rivalries among European powers that developed with the New Imperialism also anticipate the events and characteristics that would lead Europe into World War I.

The Scramble for Africa

Two developments spurred an unprecedented "scramble" on the part of European powers to lay claim to vast areas of the African continent. They were the British takeover of the Suez Canal in Egypt and Belgium's aggressive expansion into the Congo.

The Suez Canal, connecting the Mediterranean Sea through Egypt to the Red Sea and the Indian Ocean, was built by a French company and opened in 1869. In 1875, Great Britain took advantage of the Egyptian ruler's financial distress and purchased a controlling interest in the canal. By the early 1880s, anti-British and anti-French sentiment was building in the Egyptian army. In the summer of 1882, the British launched a preemptive strike, landing troops in Egypt, defeating Egyptian forces, and setting up a virtual occupation of Egypt. Supposedly temporary, the occupation lasted 32 years. Great Britain's control of Egypt led to further European expansion in Africa in two ways:

- In order to provide greater security for Egypt, Great Britain expanded farther south.
- In return for France's acceptance of the British occupation of Egypt, Great Britain supported French expansion into northwest Africa.

A new competition for imperial control of sub-Saharan Africa was initiated by the expansion of Belgian interests in the Congo. In 1876, King Leopold II of Belgium formed a private company and sent explorer Henry Stanley to the Congo River basin to establish trading outposts and sign treaties with local chiefs. Alarmed by the rate at which the Belgians were claiming land in central Africa, the French expanded their claims in western Africa, and Bismarck responded with a flurry of claims for Germany in eastern Africa. This sudden burst of activity led to the Berlin Conference of 1885. There, representatives of European powers established free-trade zones in the Congo River basin and established guidelines for the partitioning of Africa. No African representatives were present at the conference. The guidelines essentially set up two principles:

- A European nation needed to establish enough physical presence to control and develop a territory before it could claim it.
- Claimants must treat the African population humanely.

After the Berlin Conference, European nations completed the Scramble for Africa until nearly the entire continent was, nominally at least, under European control. Unfortunately, the principle of humane treatment of Africans was rarely followed. European control in Africa resulted in a distinct lack—indeed, a blocking—of native economic and political development.

Dominance in Asia

In the era of the New Imperialism, European powers also exerted control over Asia. Here, however, the general method was to rule through local elites.

India: Ruled by Great Britain

In India, the British dominated, initially through the British East India Company, a private trading company that used its economic and military power to influence local politics.

Following the Sepoy Rebellion of 1857 (sometimes known as the Sepoy Mutiny), an organized anti-British uprising led by military units of Indians who had formerly served the British, the British government took direct control, naming Queen Victoria Empress of India, and restructured the Indian economy to produce and consume products in order to aid the British economy.

A sense of Indian nationalism began to develop as a response to the more intrusive British influence, resulting in the establishment of the Indian National Congress in 1885. The Congress, though really an organization of Hindu elites, promoted the notion of a free and independent India.

Southeast Asia: Dominated by France

In Southeast Asia, the French emulated the British strategy of ruling through local elites and fostering economic dependence. During the 1880s and early 1890s, France established the Union of Indochina, effectively dominating in the areas that would become Vietnam, Laos, and Cambodia. The Union lasted until the definitive defeat of French armies at Dien Bien Phu in 1954.

China: Under Increasing European Control

China had been infiltrated by British traders in the 1830s. The British traded opium grown in India to Chinese dealers in exchange for tea, silk, and other goods that were highly prized in Great Britain. When the Chinese government attempted to end the trade, Great Britain waged and won the Opium War (1839–1842) and forced the Chinese to sign the Treaty of Nanking. The treaty ceded Hong Kong to Great Britain, established several tariff-free zones for foreign trade, and exempted foreigners from Chinese law.

The humiliation of the Manchu rulers and the undermining of the Chinese economy that resulted from foreign interference led to the Taiping Rebellion (1850–1864). Defending their rule from the Rebellion made the Manchus ever more dependent on Western support. Chinese nationalism and resistance to foreign influence again manifested itself in the Boxer Rebellion (1899–1900). The combined forces of the European powers were able to suppress the rebellion, but in 1911, a revolution led by Sun Yat-sen succeeded in overthrowing the Manchu dynasty, and a Chinese republic was established.

Japan: Westernization

Japan had been forcibly opened to Western trade by an American fleet commanded by Commodore Matthew J. Perry in 1853–1854. The Japanese government signed a number of treaties granting Western powers effective control of foreign trade. The result was civil war and revolution, which culminated in the Meiji Restoration, during which modernizers, determined to preserve Japanese independence, restored power to the emperor and reorganized Japanese society along Western lines. By 1900, Japan was an industrial and military power. In 1904, the country quarreled with Russia over influence in China and stunned the world with its victory in the Russo-Japanese War (1905).

Russia: Expansion

Russia had reached the Pacific Coast by the seventeenth century; 200 years later it controlled Siberia, Central Asia, Turkestan, Manchuria, and everything leading south to the Black Sea (in part, thanks to the ailing Ottoman Empire). Russia divested itself of Alaska, selling it to the United States in 1867. Russia agreed with Great Britain to use Afghanistan as a buffer state between the two powers and to partition Persia. In 1905, Russia's attempt to take over Korea brought about a confrontation with Japan, and Russia lost the subsequent war.

Review Questions

Multiple Choice

Questions 1–3 refer to the following passage:

This is the entire issue of empire. A people limited in number and energy and in the land they occupy have the choice of improving to the utmost the political and economic management of their own land, confining themselves to such accessions of territory as are justified by the most economical disposition of a growing population; or they may proceed, like the slovenly farmer, to spread their power and energy over the whole earth, tempted by the speculative value or the quick profits of some new market, or else by mere greed of territorial acquisition, and ignoring the political and economic wastes and risks involved by this imperial career.

It must be clearly understood that this is essentially a choice of alternatives; a full simultaneous application of intensive and extensive cultivation is impossible. A nation may either, following the example of Denmark or Switzerland, put brains into agriculture, develop a finely varied system of public education, general and technical, apply the ripest science to its special manufacturing industries, and so support in progressive comfort and character a considerable population upon a strictly limited area; or it may, like Great Britain, neglect its agriculture, allowing its lands to go out of cultivation and its population to grow up in towns, fall behind other nations in its methods of education and in the capacity of adapting to its uses the latest scientific knowledge, in order that it may squander its pecuniary and military resources in forcing bad markets and finding speculative fields of investment in distant corners of the earth, adding millions of square miles and of unassimilable population to the area of the Empire. . . .

No remedy will serve which permits the future operation of these forces. It is idle to attack Imperialism or Militarism as political expedients or policies unless the axe is laid at the economic root of the tree, and the classes for whose interest Imperialism works are shorn of the surplus revenues which seek this outlet.

John A. Hobson, *Imperialism*, 1902

1. Hobson understood imperialism to result from which of the following?
    A. The strategic requirements of national defense
    B. Economic decisions
    C. Political necessities
    D. A religious mission

2. Hobson believed that imperialism was not inevitable and argued which of the following positions?
    A. It was necessary for a country to thrive economically.
    B. It was beneficial in the long run to industrialized countries.
    C. It was beneficial in the long run for the countries being conquered.
    D. It was detrimental to the long-term economic health of the imperialist country.

3. According to the passage, who benefited the most from imperialism?
    A. The country being conquered
    B. The imperialist country
    C. Only certain classes within the imperialist country
    D. Only certain classes within the conquered country

Short Answer

4. Identify TWO causes of the New Imperialism and briefly explain how those causal factors might be used to explain the Scramble for Africa.

Answers and Explanations

1. **B** is correct because the passage refers to the economic choice of domestic investment versus quick profits through imperial expansion. A is incorrect because the passage does not refer to the strategic requirements of national defense. C is incorrect because the passage does not refer to politics. D is incorrect because the passage does not refer to any religious mission.

2. **D** is correct because the passage argues that the practice of imperialism produces short-term profits for some classes within the imperialist country, but leads to the neglect of investment necessary for the country's long-term economic health. A is incorrect because the essay does not refer to imperialism as an economic necessity. B and C are incorrect because the passage argues that, in the long term, imperialism is economically harmful.

3. **C** is correct because the passage is analyzing the roots of imperialism (and thus the actions of the imperialist country, not the conquered country) and because the passage refers to "the classes for whose interest Imperialism works." A and D are incorrect because the passage is analyzing the roots of imperialism (and thus the actions of the imperialist country, not the conquered country). B is incorrect because the passage states that there are "classes for whose interest Imperialism works," and argues that, more generally, imperialism is bad for all countries concerned.

4. Suggested answer:

    Thesis: Two causes of the New Imperialism that help to explain the Scramble for Africa are the need for new raw materials in the expanding industrial economy of Europe and technological innovations in weaponry and transportation.

    Paragraph Outline:

    I. The need for new raw materials in the expanding industrial economy of Europe helps to explain the Scramble for Africa by providing a *motive* for European expansion into Africa, for example, diamonds in South Africa.

    II. Technological innovations in weaponry (such as the breech-loading rifle) and transportation (such as the steam-powered gunboat) help to explain the Scramble for Africa by providing the *means* that encouraged European economic and military adventurism.

Rapid Review

The New Imperialism was the result of a complex set of impulses, which included economic needs created by industrialization, competition among European nations fueled by nationalism and militarism, and the need for political elites to find ways to win the support of a new political force—the masses. The New Imperialism resulted in the Scramble for Africa, in which European powers laid claim to the entire continent in the last two decades of the nineteenth century. In Asia, the New Imperialism generally took the form of indirect European control exerted through local elites.

Further Resources

Chinua Achebe, *Things Fall Apart* (and be sure to read the Yeats poem "The Second Coming")

Kamala Markandaya, *Nectar in a Sieve*

J. G. Farrell, *The Siege of Krishnapur*

Mariano Azuela, *The Underdogs*

Enrique Rodó, *Ariel*

Graham Greene, *The Quiet American*

CHAPTER > 22

Politics of the Extreme and World War I

IN THIS CHAPTER

Summary: This chapter describes how political parties on both the extreme left and right of the political spectrum gained ground at the turn of the twentieth century, as the gradual reform of liberalism lost its appeal. Also included in this chapter is an explanation of how the great powers of Europe constructed an alliance system that divided Europe into two armed camps, leading to a total war of attrition (World War I) with disastrous consequences.

Key Terms:

- ✪ **Ultranationalists** Political parties which argued that political theories that put class solidarity ahead of loyalty to a nation threatened the very fabric of civilization. Thus, they vowed to fight liberalism and socialism (see Chapter 20 for nationalism).
- ✪ **Zionism** A movement for the creation of an independent state for Jews, which came into being in 1896 when Theodor Herzl published *The Jewish State*, a pamphlet that urged an international movement to make Palestine the Jewish homeland.
- ✪ **Triple Alliance** A military alliance among Germany, Austria-Hungary, and Italy, forged by Otto von Bismarck after the unification of Germany in 1871.
- ✪ **Triple Entente** A military alliance among Great Britain, France, and Russia, which countered the Triple Alliance.

⬢ **Bolsheviks** A party of revolutionary Marxists, led by Lenin, who seized power in Russia in November 1917.

⬢ **Treaty of Versailles (also Peace of Paris)** The name given to the series of five treaties that made up the overall settlement following World War I.

⬢ **Ottoman Empire** Successor to the Byzantine Empire with the taking of Constantinople in 1453, the Ottoman Empire would remain the center of trade and cultural interactions between East and West (or between Christian Europe and Muslim Middle East) until 1922, when the Republic of Turkey was proclaimed.

Key Individuals:

⬢ Anna Maria Mozzoni

⬢ Otto von Bismarck

⬢ Emmeline Pankhurst

⬢ Karl Marx

⬢ Lenin

⬢ Friedrich Engels

⬢ Alfred Dreyfus

Introduction

By the beginning of the twentieth century, more people were participating in politics than ever before, but the majority of them were dissatisfied. For those on the left, the pace of reform was too slow and the nature of reform too limited. For those on the right, reforms were unsettling and threatened valued traditions. As a result, political activism on both the left and the right became more extreme. Meanwhile, the great powers of Europe divided themselves into two armed camps and fought what came to be known as World War I, a war of attrition that permanently transformed Europe.

Labor Unions Begin in Britain, Then Spread to Other Countries

Europe's working-class population fell into the category of individuals who believed that liberal reform was too slow and too limited; they turned instead to labor unions and socialist parties. In Great Britain, workingmen formed the national Trades Union Congress, an organization that united all the labor unions of the country together for political action, and supported the newly formed Labour Party, a political party that ran working-class candidates in British elections. The working classes of other European countries followed Great Britain's lead, forming unions and supporting socialist parties.

Socialist Parties in Britain, France, and Germany

As Europe's labor movement turned political, it turned to socialists like Karl Marx for leadership. In 1864, Marx helped union organizers found the International Workingmen's Association, often referred to as the First International. The loose coalition of unions and political parties fell apart in the 1870s but was replaced by the Second International in 1889.

While Marx and his communist associates argued for the inevitability of a violent revolution, the character and strength of socialist organizations varied from country to country. In Great Britain, the socialist organization, known as the Fabian Society, counseled against revolution but argued that the cause of the working classes could be furthered through political solutions. The Fabian Society's ultimate goal was a society in which the parts of the economy that were crucial to people's survival and comfort, such as heat and water, should be owned by the state and regulated by experts employed by the government. In France, socialist parties banded together to join the French Socialist Party under the leadership of Jean Jaurès. The fortunes of the French Socialist Party in elections improved steadily in the first years of the twentieth century, and by 1914, it was a major power in French politics.

In Germany, the Social Democrats, led by August Bebel, were the most successful socialist party in Europe. The Social Democrats espoused the "revisionist socialism" of Eduard Bernstein, who urged socialist parties to cooperate with bourgeois liberals in order to earn immediate gains for the working class. By 1914, the Social Democrats were the largest political party in Germany.

Women's Suffrage Movements and Feminism

Always left out of liberal reforms and sometimes excluded from labor unions, women of the late nineteenth and early twentieth centuries formed political movements of their own. Feminist groups campaigning for women's rights united in 1878 to convene in Paris for the International Congress of Women's Rights.

In Great Britain, the movement focused mostly on the issue of women's suffrage, or voting rights. The movement went through three distinct phases. The first was a pioneering phase, lasting from 1866 to 1870, during which suffrage agitation focused on the Reform Act of 1867 and won a number of successes at the level of local government through petitioning and pamphleteering. The second was a long period of relative dormancy, from 1870 to 1905. The third was a period of militancy, lasting from 1905 to 1914, during which the National Union of Women's Suffrage Societies, headed by Millicent Garrett Fawcett, campaigned vigorously for women's voting rights, and the Women's Social and Political Union, led by Emmeline Pankhurst and her daughters, Christabel and Sylvia, campaigned, often violently, for a broader notion of women's rights.

In France and Germany, feminists such as Louise Michel in France and Clara Zetkin in Germany folded their movements into the broader cause of workers' rights and politically supported socialist parties.

Meanwhile, in Italy, there was a history of feminism dating back to the Renaissance, though it remained confined primarily to the upper classes until the mid-nineteenth century, which witnessed the spread of literacy and education to include women. The Casati law of 1859 established a system that trained women as teachers, and it resulted in women organizing to protect working conditions and wages. Not until 1876, however, were women admitted to universities. Anna Maria Mozzoni spurred awareness of social injustices against women, and inspired changes that were embodied in Italy's Civil Code following unification. Her work led to legal majority for unmarried women and equal inheritance rights. However, in Italy, women achieved the right to vote only in 1945.

Across the Mediterranean, in Spain, many of these same rights, though inspired by eighteenth- and nineteenth-century Enlightenment ideas, came about only in the 1930s. Women's suffrage there dates from 1945.

Anarchist Activity

People under the more oppressive regimes, where even liberal reform was resisted, turned to anarchism. Theoreticians like Mikhail Bakunin and Pyotr Kropotkin urged the elimination of any form of state authority that oppressed human freedom, and ordinary people enacted the doctrine, first through the method of the "general strike" (massive work stoppages designed to bring the economy to a halt) and later, and more often, through assassination attempts on the lives of government officials. Political assassinations in the first years of the twentieth century included King Umberto I of Italy and President William McKinley of the United States.

Ultranationalism and Anti-Semitism

The international quality of the socialist movement was in direct opposition to the ideology of nationalism that had dominated the second half of the nineteenth century. At the end of the nineteenth and at the beginning of the twentieth centuries, a harder, more extreme version of nationalism came into being. Ultranationalists argued that political theories and parties that put class solidarity ahead of loyalty to a nation threatened the very fabric of civilization, and they vowed to fight them to the death.

Nineteenth-century nationalism had always had a racial component, and ultranationalism quickly merged with the age-old European suspicion of the Jewish people, known as anti-Semitism. The most notorious example of ultranationalist and anti-Semitic political power was the Dreyfus Affair. In 1894, a group of bigoted French army officers falsely accused Alfred Dreyfus, a young Jewish captain, of treason. Dreyfus was convicted and sent to Devil's Island prison. The evidence was clearly fabricated, and liberals and socialists quickly came to Dreyfus's defense. Novelist Émile Zola published an open letter, "J'Accuse," accusing the army of covering up evidence that would have exonerated Dreyfus. (Dreyfus spent five years on Devil's Island, but was not exonerated until 1906.) His numerous trials (he was eventually exonerated) divided the nation, illustrating how strong ultranationalist and anti-Semitic feelings were in the French establishment.

Zionism

In the face of anti-Semitism, a movement for the creation of an independent state for the Jewish people, known as Zionism, came into being. In 1896, Theodor Herzl published *The Jewish State*, a pamphlet that urged an international movement to make Palestine the Jewish homeland. Herzl also distinguished between political Zionism, which referred to the creation of a Jewish state, and practical Zionism, which called for philanthropic support of Jewish settlement in the land of Israel. A year later, the World Zionist Organization was formed, and by 1914, nearly 85,000 Jews, primarily from Eastern Europe, had emigrated to Palestine.

The Causes of World War I

The causes of World War I are still debated by historians, but all explanations include the following to varying degrees. It is useful to remember the mnemonic MANIA (Militarism, Alliance System, Nationalism, Industrialization, Assassination of the Archduke Franz Ferdinand) when recalling the causes of World War I.

- **Militarism:** In general, this refers to the creation and maintenance of standing armies. Germany was convinced that war with the Triple Entente countries was inevitable.

Accordingly, it devised a strategy, known as the Schlieffen Plan, for a two-front war that called for a military thrust westward toward Paris at the first sign of Russian mobilization in the east. The hope was to knock the French out of the war before the Russians could effectively mobilize.

- **Alliance System:** After unification in 1871, Bismarck sought security in the Triple Alliance (Germany, Austria-Hungary, Italy); Great Britain, France, and Russia countered with the Triple Entente. The Alliance System was supposed to make war between the major powers too costly; instead, its assurance of military reprisal limited diplomatic options.
- **Nationalism:** This refers to an intense pride in one's nation and its people. Ten distinct linguistic and ethnic groups lived within the border of Austria-Hungary, and all were agitating for either greater autonomy or independence.
- **Industrialization/Imperialism:** Germany's rise as an industrial and military power generated a heated rivalry with Great Britain. Industrialization promoted imperialism in that it called for the acquisition of colonies to supply the raw materials necessary to same.
- **Assassination:** The June 28, 1914, assassination of the Austrian Archduke, heir to the Habsburg throne, by a young Bosnian patriot, brought the nationalism problem to a crisis point. The subsequent ultimatum issued by Austria-Hungary, and backed by Germany, led to the involvement of secondary allies, particularly Russia, in a series of steps that would lead to declarations of war.

The Beginning of the War: 1914–1915

Within weeks of the assassination of the Austrian Archduke, the lines of World War I would be drawn, thanks in large part to the Alliance System. Austria-Hungary (backed by Germany) issued unpalatable ultimatums to Serbia; Serbia asked for help; the Russians responded and mobilized the army (in part because it needed to keep access to cold-weather ports for its shipping industry); Germany declared war on Russia; and so the allied groups were drawn into war.

Key events leading to the beginning of the war and an early stalemate included the following:

- On July 23, 1914, Austria, at Germany's urging, moved to crack down on Serbian nationalism by imposing demands that Serbia could not meet (Austrian control of media and police entities), after the assassination of Austrian Archduke Franz Ferdinand.
- On July 28, 1914, Austria declared war on Serbia. Russia began military mobilization as a show of support for Serbia; that mobilization triggered the Schlieffen Plan.
- On August 4, 1914, the German army invaded Belgium, heading for Paris. In the first sixteen months of combat, France suffered roughly half of all its war casualties. Two-thirds of one million men were killed.
- Belgian resistance gave time for British troops to join the battle in late August, but they joined a retreat.
- Russian troops mobilized faster than expected and invaded East Prussia. On August 26, 1914, German Commander Helmuth von Moltke transferred troops from the Western Front to the Eastern Front. The victory by the Germans at the Battle of Tannenberg led to the liberation of East Prussia and began a slow steady German advance eastward. However, the timetable of the Schlieffen Plan was altered, and the Germans were doomed to fight a two-front war.
- On September 6, 1914, French troops met the Germans at the First Battle of Marne.

- October and November 1914 saw a series of local engagements aimed at outflanking the enemy, sometimes known as the Race for the Sea, which extended the front line west until it reached the English Channel.
- The British determination to hold on to the entire French coast stretched the front north through Flanders. In the First Battle of Ypres in October and November 1914, the German advance was halted for good, leading to a stalemate and the beginning of trench warfare.
- The Alliance system pulled six countries (and their allies) into the war initially, with Russia, Great Britain, and France on one side, and Germany, Austria-Hungary, and Italy on the other. Because Italy's membership in the Triple Alliance called for aid to Austria only in the case of Austria's being attacked, Italy quickly left to join the Triple Entente forces, in hopes of regaining the northeastern part of the country under Austrian control.

Total War

When war was declared in 1914, it was met with a joyous enthusiasm all across Europe. Explanations for this reaction include the following:

- A fascination with militarism that pervaded European culture.
- Feelings of fraternity or brotherhood that a war effort brought out in people who lived in an increasingly fragmented and divided society.
- A sense of Romantic adventurism that cast war as an alternative to the mundane, working life of industrial Europe.

Additionally, there were several shared expectations among Europeans as they went to war:

- Recent experience, such as the Franco-Prussian war of 1871, suggested that the war would be brief; most expected it to last about six weeks.
- Each side was confident of victory.
- Each side expected a war of movement, full of cavalry charges, and individual heroism.

The reality was a war of nearly five years of trench warfare and the conversion of entire economies to the war effort. As both sides literally dug in, soldiers fought from a network of trenches up to 30 feet deep, often flooded with water and infested with rats and lice. Military commanders, who commanded from rear-guard positions, continued to launch offensive attacks, ordering soldiers "over the top" to the mercy of the machine guns that lined enemy trenches. Trench warfare, the use of mustard gas, tanks, water-cooled machine guns, and aircraft primarily for reconnaissance were some of the innovations of World War I. They marked the beginning of thoroughly modern warfare characterized by impersonal and efficient killing.

Total war also meant changes on the home front, some of which would have lasting consequences:

- Governments took direct control of industries vital to the war effort. Governments also imposed price, wage, and rent controls; rationed food and material goods; regulated imports and exports; and took over both transportation systems and industry. England's Defence of the Realm Act and France's imposition of the same, curtailed civil liberties. Journalists who wrote negative reports were drafted. Protesters were arrested as traitors. A literature of opposition appeared in the works of writers like Siegfried Sassoon and Wilfred Owen.
- Labor unions worked with businesses and government to relax regulations on working hours and conditions.

- Class lines were blurred as people from all walks of life worked side by side to aid the war effort.
- Women were drawn into the industrial workforce in greater numbers and gained access to jobs that had traditionally been reserved for men.

1916: "The Year of Bloodletting"

In 1916, a war of attrition was fought in trenches in France and Belgium. Each side tried to exhaust the resources of the other.

- In February 1916, French troops, led by Marshall Petain, repulsed a German offensive at the Battle of Verdun; 700,000 men were killed.
- From July to November 1916, the British attempted an offensive that has come to be known as the Battle of the Somme; by its end, 400,000 British soldiers; 200,000 French soldiers; and 500,000 German soldiers lay dead.
- On April 6, 1917, America declared war on Germany. Several factors triggered the American entry, including the sinking of American vessels by German U-boats and the Zimmermann Note (a diplomatic correspondence of dubious origin, purporting to reveal a deal between Germany and Mexico).

Russian Revolution and Withdrawal

In March 1917, food shortages and disgust with the huge loss of life (more than a million soldiers dead) exploded into a revolution that forced the tsar's abdication. The new government, dominated by a coalition of liberal reformers and moderate socialists (sometimes referred to as "Mensheviks"), opted to continue the war effort.

In November 1917, a second revolution brought the Bolsheviks to power. A party of revolutionary Marxists—led by Vladimir Ilyich Ulyanov, who went by the name of Lenin—the Bolsheviks saw the war as a battle between two segments of the bourgeoisie fighting over the power to exploit the proletariat. Accordingly, the Bolsheviks decided to abandon the war and consolidate their revolutionary gains within Russia. They signed the Treaty of Brest-Litovsk with Germany in March 1918, surrendering Poland, Ukraine, Finland, and the Baltic provinces to Germany.

Shortly after the signing of the treaty, Russia was engulfed by civil war. Anticommunist groups, generally called "the Whites" in contrast to the communist Reds, were led by members of the old tsarist elite intent upon defending their privileges. Both sides received support from foreign governments, and for more than three years, from December 1917 to November 1920, the Bolshevik regime was engaged in a life-and-death struggle, which it ultimately won.

Germany's Disintegration and the Peace Settlement

Germany launched one last great offensive in March 1918 through the Somme toward Paris. The "Allies," as the French, British, and American coalition came to be known, responded by uniting their troops under a single commander, the French General Ferdinand Foch, for the first time. French troops were reinforced by fresh British conscripts and 600,000 American troops. By July 1918, the tide had turned in the Allies' favor for good. German forces retreated slowly along the whole Western Front. By early September, the German high command informed their government that peace had to be made at once. On November 9, 1918, German Kaiser William II abdicated, and two days later—at the eleventh hour of the eleventh day of the eleventh month—representatives of a new German government agreed to terms that amounted to unconditional surrender.

Peace negotiations began in Paris in January 1919 and were conducted by the victors; Germany was forced to accept the terms dictated to it. The French delegation was led by Georges Clemenceau, whose desire was to make sure that Germany could never threaten France again. The U.S. delegation was led by President Woodrow Wilson, who approached the peace talks with bold plans for helping to build a new Europe that could embrace the notions of individual rights and liberty, which he believed characterized the United States. Great Britain was led by Prime Minister David Lloyd George, who tried to mediate between the vindictive Clemenceau and the idealistic Wilson.

The result was a series of five treaties that have, collectively, come to be known as the Treaty of Versailles. The overall settlement, sometimes also referred to as "the Peace of Paris," contained much that was unprecedented and much that would sow the seeds of further conflict. Among the more significant aspects of the settlement were the following:

- Germany was forced to pay $5 billion annually in reparations beginning in 1921, with no guarantee as to the total amount (the final amount was set at $33 billion in 1921). Germany made its final reparation payment in October 2010.
- New independent nations were established in Eastern Europe as Hungary, Czechoslovakia, and Yugoslavia were created out of the old Austria-Hungary; Finland, Estonia, Latvia, and Lithuania were created out of the western part of the old Russian Empire; and Poland was created out of lands formerly part of Russia, Germany, and Austria-Hungary.
- Germany, in what came to be known as "the war guilt clause," was forced to accept full blame for the war. This along with the imposition of reparations would cripple both the post-war economy and the Weimar Republic's ability to govern legitimately.
- Germany was stripped of all its overseas colonies.
- The territory of Alsace-Lorraine, taken by Germany during the Franco-Prussian War of 1870–1871, was returned to France.
- The Allies were given the right to occupy German territories on the west bank of the Rhine River for 15 years.
- Germany's armed forces were limited to 100,000 soldiers and saddled with armament limitations.

Furthermore, the Treaty provoked long-lasting effects both in and outside of Europe. The Mandate System, sanctioned by the League of Nations, gave the French administrative (in actuality, colonial) control of Syria and Lebanon and the English gained control of Palestine and three Ottoman provinces of Mesopotamia, these latter coming together to form modern-day Iraq.

With the dissolution of the Ottoman Empire (member of the Axis), Turkey was able to continue the elimination of Armenians, who had allied with Russia during the war and who were considered enemies and traitors. The continued Armenian genocide resulted in an estimated 1.5 million Armenians' deaths.

Nations and peoples still in search of self-determination expressed their discontent in rebellions such as the Easter Rebellion in Ireland, the Arab revolt against the Turks, and, even, to some degree, the final stages of the Russian revolution.

Review Questions

Multiple Choice

Questions 1–3 refer to the following passage:

> In the Second International the German "decisive force" played the determining role. At the [international] congresses, in the meetings of the international socialist bureaus, all awaited the opinion of the Germans. Especially in the questions of the struggle against militarism and war. . . . And what did we in Germany experience when the great historical test came? The most precipitous fall, the most violent collapse. Nowhere has the organization of the proletariat been yoked so completely to the service of imperialism. Nowhere is the state of siege borne so docilely. Nowhere is the press so hobbled, public opinion so stifled, the economic and political class struggle of the working class so totally surrendered as in Germany. . . .
>
> The world war is a turning point. . . . The world war has altered the conditions of our struggle and, most of all, it has changed us. Not that the basic law of capitalist development, the life-and-death war between capital and labor, will experience any amelioration. But now, in the midst of the war, the masks are falling and the old familiar visages smirk at us. The tempo of development has received a mighty jolt from the eruption of the volcano of imperialism. The violence of the conflicts in the bosom of society, the enormousness of the tasks that tower up before the socialist proletariat—these make everything that has transpired in the history of the workers' movement seem a pleasant idyll. Historically, this war was ordained to thrust forward the cause of the proletariat. . . . It was ordained to drive the German proletariat to the pinnacle of the nation.

Rosa Luxemburg, "The War and the Workers," *The Junius Pamphlet*, 1916

1. What did European socialists hope to gain at the Second International?
   A. Guidance in political action from German socialists
   B. Guidance in political action from French socialists
   C. Guidance in political action from the German government
   D. Growth in membership

2. When war broke out in 1914, socialist organizations in Germany
   A. attempted revolution.
   B. supported the government and the war effort.
   C. called for widespread work stoppages.
   D. united in opposition to the war.

3. How did Luxemburg view the war?
   A. As a great opportunity for Germany
   B. As the end of European civilization
   C. As an event that would end class antagonism
   D. As a moment that could ultimately help the socialist cause

Short Answer

4. Briefly explain the role that the Alliance System played in causing World War I.

Answers and Explanations

1. **A** is correct because the passage states that, at the Second International meeting of socialist parties, "all awaited the opinion of the Germans." B is incorrect because the passage makes no mention of French socialists. C is incorrect because the passage refers to socialist groups at the Second International, and because European socialist groups

did not look to national governments for guidance. D is incorrect because one cannot tell from the passage how many socialist groups existed in prewar Europe.

2. **B** is correct because the passage indicates that when war broke out, "the organization of the proletariat [joined itself] completely to the service of imperialism," and that "the . . . political class struggle of the working class so totally surrendered . . . in Germany." A is incorrect because the passage makes no reference to any attempt at revolution. C is incorrect because the passage does not refer to a call for work stoppages. D is incorrect because the passage implies that the socialist parties of Germany *failed* to unite in opposition to the war.

3. **D** is correct because the passage says that the "war was ordained to thrust forward the cause of the proletariat. . . . It was ordained to drive the German proletariat to the pinnacle of the nation." A is incorrect because the passage does not refer to an opportunity for Germany. B is incorrect because the passage does not refer to the end of European civilization. C is incorrect because the passage does not predict the end of class antagonism.

4. Suggested answer:

Thesis: The Alliance System, created to make war more costly and, therefore, less likely, actually helped to cause World War I by making neutrality nearly impossible.

Paragraph Outline:

I. Bismarck sought to gain security by creating the Triple Alliance (Germany, Austria-Hungary, and Italy), but this so alarmed Great Britain and its longtime adversaries, France and Russia, that they countered by creating the Triple Entente.

II. The Alliance System was supposed to make war between the major powers too costly; instead its assurance of military reprisal limited diplomatic options and created the specter of a two-front war for Germany, convincing Germany that it had to go to war sooner rather than later. Once Germany attacked, all of the countries of the Alliance were honor-bound to join in.

Rapid Review

At the turn of the twentieth century, political gains were made by parties on the extreme left and right of the political spectrum, as the gradual reform of liberalism lost its appeal. The great powers of Europe constructed an alliance system that divided them into two armed camps. From August 1914 to November 1918, the two camps fought a total war of attrition. In the process, the oppressive police state of the Romanovs fell to Marxist revolutionaries in November 1917. The peace settlement that followed the war sought to weaken and punish Germany.

The ramifications of World War I and the five treaties bringing it to an end are many, varied, and long-lasting; these are what have led historians to call World War I "the defining event of the twentieth century."

Further Resources

J. L. Carr, *A Month in the Country*
Dalton Trumbo, *Johnny Got His Gun*
Pat Barker, *Regeneration*

CHAPTER 23

The Interwar Years and World War II

IN THIS CHAPTER

Summary: In the 1930s, the grim economic conditions of the Great Depression caused the political parties of the center to lose support to socialists on the left and to fascists on the right. Mussolini's fascists took power in Italy. Adolf Hitler came to power in Germany and embarked on a policy of rearmament and expansion that led to World War II. This chapter provides a review of these events and the course of World War II, during which 50 to 60 million people lost their lives, including 6 million Jews murdered in the Holocaust.

Key Terms:

- **Weimar Republic** The name given to the liberal democratic government established in Germany following World War I.
- **Spartacists** Marxist revolutionaries in post–World War II Germany, led by Rosa Luxemburg and Karl Liebknecht, who were dedicated to bringing a socialist revolution to Germany.
- **New Economic Plan (NEP)** A plan instituted by Lenin in the early 1920s that allowed rural peasants and small-business operators to manage their own land and businesses, and to sell their products—a temporary compromise with capitalism that worked well enough to get the Russian economy functioning again.
- **Great Depression** A total collapse of the economies of Europe and the United States, triggered by the American stock market crash of 1929 and lasting most of the 1930s.

- **Blackshirts (*squadristi*)** Italian fascist paramilitary groups, largely recruited from disgruntled war veterans, commanded by Mussolini. They were increasingly relied upon by the Italian government to keep order in the 1920s.
- **National Socialist German Workers' Party (NSDAP, or the Nazi Party)** German political party that began as a small right-wing group—one of the more than 70 extremist paramilitary organizations that sprang up in post–World War I Germany. It was neither socialist nor did it attract many workers; it was a party initially made up of war veterans and misfits. The man responsible for its rise to power was Adolf Hitler.
- ***Anschluss*** The annexation of Austria by Nazi Germany in March 1938.
- **The Holocaust** A genocide in which approximately six million Jews were killed by the Nazi regime and its collaborators.
- **Spanish Civil War 1936–1939** Often referred to as a "dress rehearsal" for World War II. Brought Francisco Franco to power and ended the monarchy.

Key Individuals:

- Adolf Hitler
- Benito Mussolini
- Francisco Franco
- Franklin Delano Roosevelt
- Winston Churchill
- Charles De Gaulle

Introduction

The 1920s were an era of deep uncertainty, as the population of Europe grappled with the experiences and consequences of World War I. In the 1930s, the politics of the extreme flourished, as fascism emerged as an ideology that appealed to the downtrodden. By 1939, Adolf Hitler and his Nazi party controlled Germany, and his systematic repudiation of the Versailles Treaty led to the Second World War, which raged from 1939 to 1945.

Problems and Challenges After World War I

The men who survived the Great War, as World War I was called in the 1920s and 1930s, came home to a world of economic, social, and cultural uncertainty. Governments had borrowed heavily to finance their war efforts, and interest payments were now coming due. The need to pay enormous sums in veteran and widow war benefits and unemployment benefits further burdened the economies. The inability of economies to meet the reviving demand for goods added inflation to an already grim economic mix. For the first ten years following the war, Europe experienced a roller-coaster economy, as recessions followed brief periods of prosperity.

Socially, conditions were equally uncertain. Class deference was a casualty of World War I; lingering notions that the wealthier classes were somehow superior to working people were eroded by the experience of working and fighting side by side. Traditional views on gender had also been challenged by the wartime need to suspend restrictions on where and how women worked. In rapid succession, women across Europe gained the right to vote and fought to hold on to the greater freedom they had enjoyed during the war years. Activists like Marie Stopes in England and Theodore van de Velde in the Netherlands published works emphasizing birth control and sexual pleasure for women in marriage.

Politically, uncertainty fueled continued radicalization. In France, ultraconservative and socialist parties vied for power. Responding to the rise of fascism, French moderate, socialist and communist parties allied to form the Popular Front, which gained control over the government in 1936. Though short-lived, this coalition enacted important reforms including collective-bargaining rights, a 40-hour work week, and a minimum wage. Eventually the alliance fell victim to extremist factions on both the left and right. The Popular Front was less successful in Spain, where it controlled the government for only a few months before falling to a fascist coup led by General Francisco Franco.

In Great Britain, the wartime coalition government led by David Lloyd George stayed intact and won another term in office, but the Labour Party made great gains at the expense of the Liberals. The various subjects of the British Empire, who had supported Great Britain in the war effort, now began to demand that their loyalty and sacrifice be rewarded, and independence movements coalesced in Ireland and India.

In the newly created or reconstituted nations of East-Central Europe—Hungary, Poland, and Yugoslavia—liberal democracy failed to take root, for a variety of reasons. As primarily agrarian societies, these nations lacked the necessary stable, industrial economy; democratic traditions; and experienced politicians. Additionally, arbitrary post–World War I borders were imposed and incorporated minority ethnic groups, resulting in internal conflicts that further eroded the political stability of these states, and ultimately led to right-wing authoritarian regimes coming to power. The social democratic governments of the Scandinavian region fared much better during this period. Generous social services were funded through relatively high taxes, though this didn't seem to hinder economic growth. Several key industries were organized into privately owned cooperatives, which weathered global economic swings better than in other countries.

The cultural developments of the Interwar years also reflected the deep uncertainty of the period. The 1920s have often been referred to as "the Roaring Twenties." The cabaret culture, where men and women mixed easily, seemed to reflect a loosening of social conventions and a pursuit of pleasure after the sacrifices of the war years. But cultural historians have increasingly pointed out that the culture of the Interwar years seemed to reflect a deep anxiety for the future.

This was partly fueled by new scientific theories that exacerbated this uncertainty. During the Industrial Revolution, science seemed to march inexorably forward, improving the human condition, and gradually revealing the mysteries of the universe. However, the horrors of World War I highlighted the destructive aspects of technological progress. Even before World War I, Albert Einstein developed his theory of relativity (1905), demonstrating that space and time do not exist as absolutes, but are relative to the observer. Danish physicist Niels Bohr, together with Ernest Rutherford, proposed an atomic model with electrons orbiting a nucleus. Later Bohr posited that electrons can be both particles and waves, though not at the same time. Building on Bohr's work, Werner Heisenberg argued that one cannot know a single particle's exact position and velocity at the same time. The more precisely one measures the first variable, the less precisely one knows the second, and vice-versa.

Psychology, too, contributed to this sense of uncertainty with Sigmund Freud's psychoanalytic theory of personality that stated that personality was formed through childhood conflicts which were stored in the unconscious mind. Freud introduced psychoanalysis as an attempt to uncover these previously hidden drivers of conscious behavior and thought. Carl Jung extended this idea to include a "collective unconscious," with ancestral memories from our evolutionary past, which expresses itself in dreams through symbolic forms and archetypes. All of these theories seemed to run counter to the previously dominant Newtonian view, that the world was fixed, orderly, and ultimately knowable with careful application of logic and reason.

Social anxiety and uncertainty found expression in Interwar artistic movements. Based on the idea that artistic and cultural norms were meaningless in the wake of the atrocities of World War I, **Dadaists** used elements of chance, absurdity, and incongruity in their work. Examples include Marcel Duchamp's *Fountain* (1917), consisting of an upside-down urinal with a fake signature, and Hans Arp's *Collage with Squares Arranged according to the Laws of Chance* (1917). Dadaism paved the way for other movements like **surrealism**, in which images are changes and juxtaposed in a dream-like way, epitomized by Salvador Dali's painting *The Persistence of Memory* (1931), with its "melting" watches.

Musicians, too, attempted to break with convention during this time. Arnold Schoenberg created **atonal music**, with a new compositional form based on a twelve-note scale, independent of any traditional key.

In architecture, the Bauhaus school in Germany attempted to unite applied arts, like furniture and textiles, with fine arts of painting and sculpture. Led by architect Walter Gropius, the Bauhaus school helped spread **functionalism**, in which the purpose of the building takes precedence over its ornamentation. Sometimes simply concrete and steel boxes with glass windows, these buildings were intended to represent the future.

Though most movies were aimed at pleasing a mass audience, some filmmakers captured the uncertainty of the time. An excellent example is Fritz Lang's film *Metropolis* (1925). Filmmaking became a popular art form in the Interwar years, and film stars became celebrities whose lifestyle seemed to epitomize the Roaring Twenties. However, Lang's *Metropolis* depicted a world in which humans are dwarfed by an impersonal world of their own creation. Similarly, T. S. Eliot's epic poem, *The Waste Land* (1922), depicts a world devoid of purpose or meaning.

The Weimar Republic in Germany

The problems and uncertainties of the Interwar years were felt most keenly in Germany. The new government, known as the Weimar Republic, was a liberal democracy led by a moderate Social Democrat, Friedrich Ebert. It was a government doomed to failure by several factors. First, liberal democracy was a form of government largely alien to the German people, whose previous allegiance had been to the kaiser. Second, the German people perceived the government as having been imposed upon them by vengeful enemies after World War I. Third, the Weimar Republic was blamed for the humiliating nature of the Treaty of Versailles. Fourth, it was faced with insurmountable economic problems, as the general economic difficulties of Interwar Europe were compounded by Germany's need to pay the huge war reparations imposed on it.

Almost immediately, the government of the Weimar Republic was challenged by Marxist revolutionaries, known as Spartacists, led by Rosa Luxemburg and Karl Liebknecht, who were dedicated to bringing a socialist revolution to Germany. In order to defeat them, Ebert turned to the old imperial army officers who formed regiments of war veterans known as the *Freikorps* ("Free Corps"). Once the right-wing forces gained the upper hand, they too tried to overthrow the Weimar government in a coup attempt in 1920 that has come to be known as the *Kapp Putsch*. The government was saved, ironically, by the workers of Germany, who forced the right-wing insurgents to step down by staging a general strike. Just as the Weimar government began to stabilize, it found itself unable to pay the reparations demanded of it. When the French occupied the Ruhr Valley in retaliation, German workers again went on strike. The overwhelming uncertainty caused by the situation triggered hyperinflation, which made German currency essentially worthless.

A weakened Germany would be vulnerable to communism so Western nations attempted to stabilize Germany's economy. The United States proposed the Dawes Plan in 1924 to help Germany with reparations, consisting of U.S. loans and investments to foster economic recovery, with reduced reparations and loan repayments, based on Germany's ability to pay. This was followed by the Locarno Treaty in 1925, a series of agreements reaffirming Germany's western border with France, demilitarization of the Rhineland, and Germany's entry in the League of Nations. While moderate Germans saw the treaty as a positive step, with Germany being treated as an equal partner on the world stage, others perceived it to be a betrayal of Germany and an attempt to validate the hated Treaty of Versailles.

The Soviet Union in Economic Ruins

By the onset of the 1920s, the bloody civil war between the monarchist "Whites" and the Bolshevik-led "Reds" was finally over, and Lenin held uncontested leadership of Russia. But it was a country in ruins, whose people could find neither jobs nor food. In order to deal with the crisis, Lenin launched the New Economic Plan (NEP), which allowed rural peasants and small-business operators to manage their own land and businesses and to sell their products. This temporary compromise with capitalism worked well enough to get the Russian economy functioning again.

In July 1923, Lenin constructed the Soviet Constitution of 1923. On paper it created a federal state, renamed the Union of Soviet Socialist Republics (USSR), but in practice, power continued to emanate from Lenin and the city that he named the capital in 1918, Moscow. Lenin died unexpectedly from a series of strokes in 1924. The man who won the power struggle to succeed him was the Communist Party Secretary Joseph Stalin. From 1924 to 1929, Stalin used a divide-and-conquer strategy combined with his control of the party bureaucracy to gain full control of the party and, thereby, of the Soviet Union. In the autumn of 1924, Stalin announced, in a doctrine that came to be known as "Socialism in One Country," that the Soviet Union would abandon the notion of a worldwide socialist revolution and concentrate on making the Soviet Union a successful socialist state.

In 1928, Stalin ended the NEP and initiated the first of a series of five-year plans, which rejected all notions of private enterprise and initiated the building of state-owned factories and power stations. As an extension of the plan, Stalin pursued the collectivization of agriculture, destroying the culture of the peasant village and replacing it with one organized around huge collective farms. The peasants resisted and were killed, starved, or driven into Siberia in numbers that can only be estimated but that may have been as high as eight million.

Many of Stalin's reforms targeted the Ukraine, which had seen a weakening of Soviet influence. Perhaps because their social class was inconsistent with communist ideals, or perhaps because they were the most likely sources of resistance, *kulaks*, or relatively well-off land-owning peasants, were targeted as enemies of the people. Between forced collectivization and forced relocation to work camps or mines, perhaps a third of them died in deplorable conditions. Still, resistance continued, as farmers stole back their tools from the collectives, or simply refused to harvest the crops. In response, Stalin continually increased the grain quotas Ukraine shipped to the Soviet Union, eliminating any surplus to feed the Ukrainian people. Stalin also sealed Ukraine's borders, effectively denying relief to the Ukrainians and preventing news of the famine from spreading. The Soviet government emphatically denied any famine, the Red Cross was barred from entry, and Westerners were confined to Moscow. A few Westerners were shown "Potemkin villages," artificially constructed villages, populated with party loyalists to create an image of happy and prosperous peasants. Because of this, little was known about the extent of this catastrophe, known as "the Holodomor," until the fall of the Soviet Union uncovered relevant documents. Because of its deliberate, man-made nature, some consider the Holodomor a form of genocide, while others argue that many non-Ukrainians also died as a result of famine.

Between 1935 and 1939, Stalin set out to eliminate all centers of independent thought and action within the party and the government. In a series of purges, somewhere between seven and eight million Soviet citizens were arrested. At least one million of those were executed, while the rest were sent to work in camps known as *gulags*. The end result was a system that demanded and rewarded complete conformity to the vision of the Communist Party as dictated by Stalin.

The Great Depression

The post–World War I European economy was built on a fragile combination of international loans (mostly from the United States), reparations payments, and foreign trade. In October 1929, the New York stock market crashed, with stocks losing almost two-thirds of their value. Unable to obtain further credit, trade dried up. The result was an economic collapse that has come to be known as the Great Depression. Attempts to deal with the problem in traditional ways—by cutting government expenditures, tightening the supply of money, and raising tariffs on imported goods—only made things worse. By 1932, the economies of Europe were performing at levels that were only half those of 1929. Jobs became scarce as the economy contracted, and large segments of the population fell into poverty.

British economist John Maynard Keynes argued that governments needed to increase their expenditures and run temporary deficits in order to "jump-start" the stagnant economy, but his ideas were only slowly accepted. Europe's economies recovered very slowly, and in the interim, parts of Europe succumbed to a new ideology of the desperate and downtrodden—fascism.

The Rise of Fascism

Historians struggle with definitions of fascism because it has no single coherent ideology, and its form varied from nation to nation. But all fascism was a mixture, to one degree or another, of the following ingredients: intense nationalism; emphasis on struggle and shared sacrifice; devotion and obedience to a charismatic leader (sometimes called a cult of personality); glorification of the military and warfare; and expressed hatred of both socialism and liberalism. Motherhood was exalted, with women encouraged to stay home and raise the next generation of "warriors." Both Germany and Italy gave medals to women based on the number of children they had. Fascist regimes in both Germany and Italy used modern media as propaganda to further reinforce the people's obedience. They also used architecture to generate nationalistic pride, as well as demonstrate their strength and power. Fascist architecture typically consisted of large public buildings, similar to a Roman style but without ornamentation, and dedicated to a "mass experience."

Mussolini and Italian Fascism

The birthplace of fascism was Italy, which became the first country in Europe to have a fascist government. Italy, though a member of the Triple Alliance with Germany and

Austria-Hungary, had originally chosen to remain neutral in World War I. But in 1915, Italy entered the war on the side of the Entente in hopes of recovering lands previously taken by Austria-Hungary. Italian war veterans returned home disillusioned, as the war experience had turned out to be a nightmare. One such veteran, a former socialist named Benito Mussolini, founded the National Fascist Party in 1919. The new party began to field candidates for the Italian legislature and to establish itself as the party that could save Italy from the threat of socialism. By 1922, squads of fascist "Blackshirts" (*squadristi*), largely recruited from disgruntled war veterans, were doing battle with bands of socialists "Redshirts," and the Italian government was increasingly unable to keep order. In October 1922, Mussolini organized 20,000 fascist supporters and announced his intention to march on Rome. King Victor Emmanuel III responded by naming Mussolini prime minister of the Italian government.

Mussolini quickly moved to consolidate his power by pushing through a number of constitutional changes. A showdown between Mussolini and what parliamentary forces still existed in Italy came in the summer of 1924, when fascists were implicated in the murder of the socialist member of the Italian parliament, Giacomo Matteotti. The masses supported Mussolini, and by early 1926, all opposition parties had been dissolved and declared illegal, and the king had abdicated, effectively making Mussolini dictator of Italy.

Mussolini acted to limit dissent from the public, too. After Mussolini recognized Vatican City and Catholicism as the state religion, the Catholic Church encouraged Italians to support the new regime. Mussolini also exercised some control over media outlets and organized a secret police, though with mixed results. Though educational institutions did retain some independence, Mussolini's government organized outside youth groups as a way to maintain its ability to indoctrinate Italian youth. The *Dopolovoro* was a national recreation agency, which organized public viewings of films, concerts, athletic events, and even holiday excursions. They were all carefully coordinated and supervised by the State in service to its message.

Hitler and German Nazism

Understanding the rise of Adolf Hitler and the Nazi Party in Germany requires an understanding of the post–World War I context. Wartime propaganda had led the German public to believe that the war was going well. As a result, Germany's surrender came as an inexplicable shock. The peace settlement seemed unfair and unduly harsh, and there was a growing sense among the German people that Germany must have been betrayed. In that context, the Nazis became popular by telling the German people several things they desperately wanted to hear. The Nazis told unemployed youth and displaced veterans that they would form an essential part of a rebuilt Germany. They blamed Germany's World War I defeat on a betrayal by the Jews, and promised to end the payments for war reparations. The Nazis also pledged to restore Germany's military greatness and eliminate socialism. This helped ensure the support of the Church and business interests, both of whom would be weakened by the spread of socialism.

The so-called National Socialist German Workers' Party (NSDAP), or the Nazi Party, began as a small right-wing group and one of the more than 70 extremist paramilitary organizations that sprang up in postwar Germany. It was neither socialist nor did it attract many workers; it was a party initially made up of war veterans and the unemployed. The man responsible for its rise to power was Adolf Hitler, a failed Austrian art student and war veteran.

Hitler used military attitudes and techniques, as well as expert propaganda, to turn the NSDAP into a tightly knit organization with mass appeal. Hitler and the Nazis made their first bid for power in November 1923 in the "Beer Hall Putsch," when they tried to stage a coup to topple the Bavarian government in Munich. It failed, but Hitler gained national attention in the subsequent trial, during which he publicly decried the terms of the Treaty of Versailles and espoused his views of racial nationalism. Years of reorganization and building of grassroots support produced significant electoral gains in the elections of 1930.

In the elections of 1932, the Nazis won over 35 percent of the vote. Hitler refused to take part in a coalition government, and the German president, the aging military hero Paul von Hindenburg, made the crucial decision to appoint Hitler chancellor of Germany (the equivalent of prime minister). Early in 1933, the German parliament building, the *Reichstag*, burned down. Hitler declared a state of emergency and assumed dictatorial powers. He then used them to eliminate socialist opposition to Nazi rule. In the elections of 1933, Nazis won 288 seats out of 647. With the support of 52 deputies of the Nationalist Party, and in the absence of Communist deputies, who were under arrest, the Nazis were able to rule with a majority. By bullying the members of the *Reichstag* into passing the Enabling Act of March 1933, Hitler was essentially free to rule as a dictator.

Manipulation of public opinion through the use of propaganda formed a key part of Hitler's strategy. With a special propaganda ministry headed by Joseph Goebbels, the Nazis used modern communications to consolidate control. Hitler's radio speeches were so effective that public loudspeakers were erected to broadcast his messages to those without radios. Film documentaries also reinforced the Nazi message, the most famous of which was *The Triumph of the Will* (1935) by Leni Riefenstahl, which recorded the Nazi Party Congress in Nuremberg. Riefenstahl used techniques that were cutting edge at the time, like long-lens shots and traveling cameras, to emphasize the grandeur and majesty of the event.

Fascist Dictatorships in Spain and Portugal

In both Spain and Portugal, Western-style parliamentary governments faced opposition from the Church, the army, and large landowners. In 1926, army officers overthrew the Portuguese Republic that had been created in 1910, and gradually António de Oliveira Salazar, an economics professor, became dictator.

In Spain, antimonarchist parties won the election of 1931, and King Alphonso XIII fled as the new Spanish Republic was set up. When a socialist cartel won the election of 1936, General Francisco Franco led a revolt against the Republic from Spanish Morocco, plunging Spain into a bloody civil war. Franco received support from the Spanish monarchy and the Church, while Germany and Italy sent money and equipment. The Republic was defended by brigades of volunteers from around the world (famous writers George Orwell and Ernest Hemingway among them) and eventually received aid from the Soviet Union. The technological might provided by the Germans allowed Franco's forces to overwhelm the defenders of the Republic. A branch of the Luftwaffe was sent, primarily as a means for them to obtain valuable war experience and to evaluate the German aerial capability and strategy. Essentially serving as a trial run for World War II, the destruction of the town of Guernica by German planes was memorialized in Pablo Picasso's 25-foot-long mural *Guernica* (1937), poignantly illustrating the nature of the mismatch. By 1939, Franco ruled Spain as dictator.

Fascism in France

During World War I, France had essentially been administered by the military. At the war's conclusion, Parliament rushed to reassert its dominance, and France became governed by moderate coalitions. But the elections of 1924 swept the *Cartel des Gauches*, a coalition of socialist parties, to power, causing a reaction in the form of a flurry of fascist organizations, with names like *Action française* ("French Action"), the Legion, and the *Jeunesses Patriotes* ("Youth Patriots"). These organizations remained on the political fringe, but they provided extremist opposition and a source of anti-Semitism, which became prominent in the collaboration of the Vichy regime during the German occupation of France in World War II.

Fascism in Great Britain

In Great Britain, small right-wing extremist groups were united in the 1930s under the leadership of Sir Oswald Mosley, who created the British Union of Fascists (BUF). They were united by their hatred of socialism and their anti-Semitism. Although never politically significant in Great Britain, the BUF did mount a serious public disturbance in October 1934 when it battled with socialists and Jewish groups in an incident that has come to be known as the "Battle of Cable Street." More importantly, the existence of the BUF and the initial reluctance of the British government to ban it demonstrate the existence of some sympathy for their authoritarian and anti-Semitic views among powerful people in Britain. Once the war broke out, the BUF was banned and Mosley was jailed.

World War II

Adolf Hitler had come to power by promising to repudiate the Treaty of Versailles. In March 1936, he took his first big step by moving his revitalized armed forces into the Rhineland, the area on the west bank of the Rhine River, which the treaty had deemed a demilitarized zone. When that move provoked no substantive response from France or Great Britain, Hitler embarked on a series of moves to the east that eventually triggered the Second World War:

- In March 1938, Germany annexed Austria without opposition (an event sometimes referred to as the *Anschluss*).
- Hitler then claimed the *Sudetenland*, a region of Czechoslovakia that was home to 3.5 million German speakers.
- Great Britain reacted with what has been called a "policy of appeasement," agreeing in the Munich Agreement of September 1938 to allow Hitler to take the *Sudetenland* over Czech objections in exchange for his promise that there would be no further aggression.
- In March 1939, Hitler broke the Munich Agreement by invading Czechoslovakia.
- As Hitler threatened Poland, the hope of Soviet intervention was dashed by the surprise announcement, on August 23, 1939, of a Nazi–Soviet Non-Aggression Pact, guaranteeing Soviet neutrality in return for part of Poland.
- On September 1, 1939, Germany invaded Poland.
- On September 3, 1939, both France and Great Britain declared war on Germany.

In order to understand why Great Britain followed a policy of appeasement and was slow to recognize the pattern of aggressive expansion in Hitler's actions in 1938 and 1939, one has to take into account the historical context. The Germans, feeling humiliated by their World War I defeat, were eager for the opportunity to avenge themselves, which necessarily involved rebuilding its military. Great Britain and its allies, on the other hand, considered World War I as "the war to end all wars" and had little appetite for renewed hostilities. Great Britain hadn't rebuilt its military at all, and consequently was in no position to back up any ultimatums they might give to Hitler. Many British leaders privately agreed with the Germans that the Treaty of Versailles had been unprecedented and unwarranted. Without support from the public and key leaders, any attempt by the British government to pursue a military response to Hitler's actions would have been political suicide.

Blitzkrieg and the "Phony War" (1939–1940)

As Germany invaded Poland, Great Britain and France were not yet in a military position to offer much help. The Poles fought bravely but were easily overrun by the German *blitzkrieg*, or "lightning war," which combined air strikes and the rapid deployment of tanks and highly mobile units. Poland fell to Germany in a month.

Meanwhile, Great Britain sent divisions to France, and the British and French general staffs coordinated strategy. But the strategy was a purely defensive one of awaiting a German assault behind "the Maginot Line"—a vast complex of tank traps, fixed artillery sites, subterranean railways, and living quarters—which paralleled the Franco-German border but failed to protect the border between France and Belgium. Over the winter of 1939 and 1940, war was going on at sea, but on land and in the air there was a virtual standoff that has come to be termed the "the Phony War." During the lull, however, the Soviet Union acted on its agreement with Hitler, annexing territories in Poland and Eastern Europe, including Estonia, Latvia, and Lithuania, and invading Finland.

The Battles of France and Britain (1940)

In April 1940, the Phony War came to an abrupt end. The German *blitzkrieg* moved into Norway and Denmark to prevent Allied intervention in Scandinavia and to secure Germany's access to vital iron ore supplies, and then into Luxembourg, Belgium, and the Netherlands in preparation for an all-out attack on France.

By early June 1940, the German army was well inside France. The Maginot Line proved useless against the mobility of the German tanks, which skirted the Line by going north through the Ardennes Forest. On June 14, 1940, German troops entered Paris. Two days later, the aging General Marshal Pétain assumed control of France and signed an armistice with Germany, according to which the German army, at French expense, would occupy the northern half of France, including the entire Atlantic coast, while Pétain himself governed the rest from the city of Vichy. Not all of France was happy with the deal. General Charles de Gaulle escaped to Britain and declared himself head of a free French government. In France, many joined a Free French movement, which would provide active resistance to German occupation throughout the remainder of the war.

In Great Britain, Prime Minister Neville Chamberlain, who had been the architect of Great Britain's appeasement policy, resigned. King George VI turned to the 65-year-old Winston Churchill, who had been nearly the lone critic of the appeasement policy. Churchill used his oratory skill throughout the war to bolster moral and strengthen the Allies' resolve. The German *blitzkrieg* now drove to the English Channel, trapping the Allied army at the small seaport of Dunkirk. In an episode that has come to be known as "the Miracle of Dunkirk," more than 338,000 Allied troops (224,000 of them British), surrounded on all sides by advancing German units, were rescued by a motley flotilla of naval vessels, private yachts, trawlers, and motorboats. The episode buoyed British spirits, but Churchill was somber, pointing out that "wars are not won by evacuations."

Hitler, and many neutral observers, expected Great Britain to seek peace negotiations, but Churchill stood defiant. The German High Command began preparing for the invasion of Great Britain, but the invasion never came. Hitler's staff was handicapped by both the lack of time given to them and by their relative lack of experience in mounting amphibious operations. A successful invasion of England required air superiority over the English Channel; a combination of daring fighting by the Royal Air Force and a coordinated effort of civilian defense operations all along the coast foiled German attempts to gain it.

A frustrated Hitler responded by ordering an intensive nightly bombing of London in a two-month attempt to disrupt industrial production and to break the will of the British people. In the end, neither was achieved. In mid-October, Hitler decided to postpone the invasion; the Battle of Britain had been won by the British. As a result, Hitler turned his attentions to the Soviet Union.

The War in North Africa and the Balkans (1941–1942)

Italy already had a presence in North Africa, having colonized Libya since 1912 and having invaded and conquered Abyssinia (now Ethiopia) in 1935. Still, Mussolini longed to recreate the glory of the Roman Empire, a key component of which was British-occupied Egypt. In 1941, the war spread beyond Europe as Italian forces invaded North Africa, attempting to push the British out of Egypt. However, British forces routed the Italians; Germany responded by sending troops into North Africa and the Balkans. Germany had two objectives: It wanted control of the Balkans for their rich supply of raw materials, especially Romanian oil, and also control of the Suez Canal in Egypt, which was the vital link between Great Britain and its resource-rich empire.

The Germans successfully occupied the Balkans, as British efforts to make a last-ditch stand in mainland Greece and on the nearby island of Crete proved in vain. Italian regiments in Libya were reinforced by German divisions under General Erwin Rommel, and the ill-equipped British forces were driven back into Egypt.

German Invasion of the Soviet Union (June to December 1941)

The Nazi–Soviet Non-Aggression Pact had always been a matter of convenience. Both sides knew that war would eventually come; the question was when. Hitler answered the question late in the spring of 1941, launching Operation Barbarossa and sending three million troops into the Soviet Union.

Hitler hoped that by creating a German empire across the entire European continent, Great Britain would simply capitulate, eliminating the need for an invasion of Great Britain. In addition, his army would benefit from the additional resources, specifically Ukrainian wheat and oil from the Caucasus. Because of his racialist view of the world, Hitler believed that the "Slavic" peoples of the Soviet Union might prove an easier target than his "Teutonic cousins," the British.

Germany's eastern army succeeded in conquering those parts of the Soviet Union that produced 60 percent of its coal and steel and almost half its grain, and by December, it was within striking distance of Moscow. But as winter set in, the Russian army launched a counterattack against German forces, who were ill-supplied for a winter war. The Russian army suffered millions of casualties but turned back the German invasion.

Hitler's decision to attack the Soviet Union had one other great consequence: it forged the first link in what would become the Grand Alliance between Great Britain, the Soviet Union, and the United States, as Churchill (despite being a staunch anticommunist) pledged his support to the USSR. Publicly, he announced, "Any man or state that fights against Nazidom will have our aid." Privately, he remarked that if Hitler invaded Hell, it would be desirable to find something friendly to say about the devil. The final link in the Grand Alliance would come through a combination of Churchill's persuasion and a Japanese attack.

The American Entry and Its Impact (1942)

Churchill and the American president, Franklin Roosevelt, met in August 1941 on a battleship off the Newfoundland coast. They composed the Atlantic Charter, a document setting forth Anglo-American war aims. It rejected any territorial aggrandizement for either Great Britain or the United States, and it affirmed the right of all peoples to choose their own form of government.

By 1939, a modernized and militarized Japan had conquered the coastal area of China, and its expansionist aims led it to join Germany and Italy as part of what came to be known as the Axis. When war broke out, Japan occupied the part of Indochina that had been under French control and began to threaten the Dutch East Indies. The United States responded with an economic embargo on all exports to Japan. On December 7, 1941, Japanese air forces launched a surprise attack in Pearl Harbor, Hawaii, hoping to cripple U.S. naval forces in the Pacific Ocean. The United States immediately declared war on Japan, and within a few days, Germany and Italy had declared war on the United States.

Initially, America's impact on the war was through resources rather than soldiers, but its entry provided the third and final turning point (along with the Battle of Britain and Germany's decision to invade the Soviet Union) in the war. Throughout 1942, American productive capacities were being built up, and the American military force kept growing. In the autumn of 1942, American marines landed on the island of Guadalcanal; it was to be the first of many islands to be recaptured from the Japanese at great cost of human lives.

The Holocaust

Under Adolf Hitler, Germany engaged in a systematic campaign of anti-Semitism, which gradually escalated to a horrific degree. Starting in 1935, the Nuremberg Laws denied Jewish Germans the rights to German citizenship, to vote or to hold office, and prohibited Jews from marrying German citizens. Jews were forcibly removed from their homes and segregated in ghettoes. When a low-level German officer was killed by a Jew in November 1938, a night of coordinated violence known as *Kristallnacht* (the Night of Broken Glass) resulted, in which synagogues were burned, Jewish businesses were destroyed, and more than 100 Jews were killed. Later, Jews and others regarded by the Nazis as "undesirables" were transported to concentration camps, like Dachau, in which they were used as forced labor in appalling and inhumane conditions.

In 1942, at the Wannsee Conference, Hitler and his senior officers planned and coordinated the "Final Solution," the deliberate and methodical extermination of Jewish people in Europe. It began when *Schutzstaffel* (SS) troops under Reinhard Heydrich and Heinrich Himmler began executing Jewish and Slavic prisoners, who had been gathered from around Europe and forced into concentration camps. At first, firing squads were used. Next, the process was speeded up through the use of mobile vans of poison gas. Eventually, large gas chambers were constructed at the camps, including Treblinka and Sobibór, so that thousands could be murdered at one time. In the end, an estimated six million Jews were murdered. In addition, an additional seven million other people were murdered; among them were Gypsies, homosexuals, socialists, and political dissidents generally, Jehovah's Witnesses, and other targeted groups.

Outside the Nazi inner circle, people and governments were slow to believe and to comprehend what was happening; they were even slower to respond. Neighbors turned a blind eye when Jews were rounded up and put on trains. Collaborating governments—from Vichy France to Croatia—assisted in various ways with the rounding up and extermination of the Jews. Finally, British and American commanders refused to divert bombing missions from other targets in order to put the camps out of commission. Some brave individuals, though, did act to resist the Nazis. Occupied nations like Poland formed governments-in-exile in London. Resistance movements throughout Europe disseminated anti-Nazi propaganda, sabotaged Nazi facilities, and even engaged in espionage. Women, too, acted as couriers and even assassins for resistance movements. Within Germany, a group of Nazi officers attempted to assassinate Hitler by planting a bomb in his headquarters. It failed to kill Hitler, and several thousand were executed in the ensuing purge.

The Axis in Retreat (1942–1943)

In June and August 1943, the tide turned against the Axis forces in the Soviet Union, the Mediterranean, and the Pacific. In June 1942, the Germans resumed their offensive in the Soviet Union. By August, they were on the outskirts of Stalingrad on the Volga River. The mammoth Battle of Stalingrad lasted six months; by the time it ended in February 1943, the greater part of a German army had died or surrendered to the Russians, and the remainder was retreating westward.

In October 1942, the British Eighth Army under General Bernard Montgomery halted General Rommel's forces at the Battle of El Alamein, 70 miles west of Alexandria, Egypt, and began a victorious drive westward. In May 1943, Germany's Africa Korps surrendered to the Allies. In November 1943, Allied forces under General Dwight Eisenhower's command landed in Morocco and Algeria and began a drive that pushed all Axis forces in Africa into Tunisia. Seven months later, all Axis forces had been expelled from Africa.

Allied victories in Africa enabled them to advance steadily northward from the Mediterranean into Italy and precipitated the overthrow of Mussolini and the signing of an armistice by a new Italian government. Germany responded by treating its former ally as an occupied country. German resistance made the Allied campaign up the Italian peninsula a long and difficult one.

Allied Victory (1944–1945)

On "D-Day," June 6, 1944, Allied forces under General Eisenhower's command launched an audacious amphibious invasion of German-held France on the beaches of Normandy. The grand assault took the form of an armada of 4,000 ships supported by 11,000 airplanes. By the end of July, Allied forces had broken out of Normandy and encircled the greater part of the German army.

By late August, Paris was liberated, and Hitler's forces were on the retreat. Germany seemed on the point of collapse, but German defensive lines held, and the British people were exposed to a new threat: long-range V-2 rockets fired from the German Ruhr rained down on them for seven months more. The last gasp of the German army came in December 1944 with a sudden drive against thinly held American lines in the Belgian sector. In what has come to be known as the Battle of the Bulge, the Allies checked the German attack and launched a counteroffensive.

In early 1945, Allied troops finally crossed the Rhine River into Germany. In May, they successfully defeated German forces in the Battle of Berlin. On May 1, it was announced that Hitler was dead, and on May 7, the German High Command surrendered unconditionally. In the Pacific, the long and deadly task of retaking the Pacific Islands was averted by the dropping of atomic bombs on two Japanese cities: one on Hiroshima on August 6, 1945, and another on Nagasaki on August 9, 1945. Japan surrendered unconditionally on September 2, 1945.

Assessment and Aftermath of World War II

World War II was even more destructive than World War I, and civilian casualties, rather than military deaths, made up a significant portion of the 50 to 60 million people who perished in the conflict. Many of Europe's great cities lay in ruins from repeated aerial bombings.

Vast numbers of Europeans were displaced and on the move. Some were trying to get back to homes they were driven from by the war, while others whose homes were destroyed simply had no place to go. Russian prisoners of war were compelled, many against their will, to return to the Soviet Union, where they were greeted with hostility and suspicion by Stalin's regime; many were executed or sent to labor camps. Between 12 and 13 million Germans were moving west. Some were fleeing the vengeance of Soviet troops, while others were driven from their homes in the newly reconstituted Czechoslovakia and other Eastern European countries, and from East Prussia, which had been handed over to Poland.

The war also produced a new power structure in the world. The traditional European powers of Great Britain, France, and Germany were exhausted. Their overseas empires disintegrated rapidly, as they no longer had the resources or the will to keep their imperial holdings against the desires of local inhabitants. In the years immediately following the war, India gained independence from Britain, Syria and Lebanon broke away from France, and the Dutch were expelled from Indonesia.

More importantly, ideological and pragmatic differences among the Allied Powers, which had been subjugated to the more pressing goal of defeating the Axis Powers, now began to bubble to the surface. Mutual distrust, resentment from differences over wartime strategies, and a fundamental disagreement about the fate of Eastern European countries soured relations between the Soviet Union and the other Allied Powers, setting the stage for a political divide that was to dominate international relations for the next forty years. As the new world order emerged after World War II, it became clear that the United States and the Soviet Union stood alone as great powers.

Review Questions

Multiple Choice

Questions 1–3 refer to the following passage:

Fascism, the more it considers and observes the future and the development of humanity quite apart from political considerations of the moment, believes neither in the possibility nor the utility of perpetual peace. It thus repudiates the doctrine of Pacifism—born of a renunciation of the struggle and an act of cowardice in the face of sacrifice. War alone brings up to its highest tension all human energy and puts the stamp of nobility upon the peoples who have courage to meet it. All other trials are substitutes, which never really put men into the position where they have to make the great decision—the alternative of life or death. . . .

Fascism [is] the complete opposite of . . . Marxian Socialism, [according to which] the materialist conception of [the] history of human civilization can be explained simply through the conflict of interests among the various social groups and by the change and development in the means and instruments of production. . . . Fascism, now and always, believes in holiness and in heroism; that is to say, in actions influenced by no economic motive, direct or indirect. And if the economic conception of history be denied, according to which theory men are no more than puppets, carried to and fro by the waves of chance, while the real directing forces are quite out of their control, it follows that the existence of an unchangeable and unchanging class-war is also denied. . . .

Fascism denies, in democracy, the absurd conventional untruth of political equality dressed out in the garb of collective irresponsibility, and the myth of "happiness" and indefinite progress . . . political doctrines pass, but humanity remains, and it may rather be expected that this will be a century of authority . . . a century of Fascism.

Benito Mussolini, *What Is Fascism?*, 1932

1. How did fascists view war?
   A. As a necessary evil
   B. As a path to greatness for a nation
   C. As the cause of Europe's troubles
   D. As motivated by economic concerns

2. Which of the following most precisely defines fascism?
   A. A party that was another type of socialism
   B. A party that believed that class conflict is inevitable
   C. A party that believed that people are no more than puppets
   D. A party that rejected the Marxist understanding of history

3. How did fascists view the state?
   A. As the supreme authority in a nation
   B. As the protector of individual liberty
   C. As rightful owner of the means of production
   D. As the guarantor of the equality of citizens

Short Answer

4. Briefly describe TWO of the problems facing European countries in the Interwar years, and explain how ONE of the problems you identified helps to explain the causes of World War II.

Answers and Explanations

1. **B** is correct because the passage says that war "puts the stamp of nobility upon the peoples who have courage to meet it." A is incorrect because the passage indicates that war is beneficial to a people, not evil. C is incorrect because the passage does not state that war is the source of Europe's troubles. D is incorrect because the passage rejects the notion that people are motivated by economic concerns.

2. **D** is correct because the passage states that fascism is the "complete opposite of . . . Marxian Socialism," and goes on to reject the materialist contention that history is explained through class conflict. A is incorrect because the passage asserts that fascism is the opposite of Marxian socialism and contends that individuals act in ways undetermined by economic and class interest. B is incorrect because the passage *denies* that class conflict is inevitable. C is incorrect because the passage attributes the notion that people are puppets to socialism, not fascism.

3. **A** is correct because the passage indicates that a century of fascism is a century of authority, and because it denies the liberal notions of individual liberty and equality. B is incorrect because the passage does not refer to the protection of individual liberty. C is incorrect because the passage does not refer to a seizure of the means of production. D is incorrect because the passage explicitly denies the liberal notion of equality.

4. Suggested answer:

   Thesis: During the Interwar years, European countries faced severe economic uncertainty and political radicalization. The political radicalization brought to power governments that desired a second military conflict.

   Paragraph Outline:

   I. The post–World War I European economy was built on a fragile combination of international loans (mostly from the United States), reparations payments, and foreign trade. In October 1929, the New York stock market crashed, with stocks losing almost two-thirds of their value. Unable to obtain further credit, trade dried up. The result was an economic collapse that has come to be known as the Great Depression.

   II. Politically, the economic and cultural uncertainty fueled continued radicalization. In France, ultraconservative and socialist parties vied for power. In Italy and Germany, fascist parties came to power.

   III. The fascist ideology was predicated on militarization and a belief that war tested and ennobled a people. Such an ideology was one factor causing World War II.

Rapid Review

Europe in the 1920s was characterized by a fluctuating economy built on debt and speculation. With the Stock Market Crash of 1929, credit dried up, and the Great Depression ensued. The economic problems added to a climate of social and cultural uncertainty and disillusionment. Political parties of the center lost support to socialists on the left and fascists on the right.

In the late 1930s, Adolf Hitler came to power in Germany and embarked on a policy of rearmament and expansion. France and Great Britain responded initially with a policy of appeasement, but when Hitler invaded Poland in September 1939, the Second World War began. Initial German success in the war was reversed in stages by three crucial turning points:

- Great Britain's victory in the Battle of Britain in 1940
- Hitler's decision to abandon an invasion of Great Britain and invade the Soviet Union instead
- The entry of the United States into the war following the Japanese attack on Pearl Harbor on December 7, 1941

Germany surrendered on May 7, 1945. Japan surrendered on September 2, 1945, following the dropping of two atomic bombs on the cities of Hiroshima and Nagasaki in August. In the end, between 50 and 60 million people lost their lives in the Second World War, including 6 million Jews, who were murdered in the Holocaust. The traditional powers of Europe—Great Britain, France, and Germany—gave way to two new superpowers: the United States and the Soviet Union.

Further Resources

J. L. Carr, *A Month in the Country*

Dalton Trumbo, *Johnny Got His Gun*

Pat Barker, *Regeneration*

Ken Follett, *The Fall of Giants*

John Hersey, *Hiroshima*

Louis de Bernières, *Corelli's Mandolin* (the book, *not* the movie)

Lawrence of Arabia (the film) (1962)

A. J. Liebling, *World War II Writings* and *The Road Back to Paris* (journalism at its best)

CHAPTER **24**

The Cold War, Integration, and Globalization

IN THIS CHAPTER

Summary: Following World War II, the Soviet Union solidified its control of Eastern Europe, creating an "Iron Curtain" that divided East and West. The two superpowers, the United States and the Soviet Union, engaged in a global conflict, called "the Cold War." This chapter provides a review of the important events of the Cold War and describes the growing economic integration in Western Europe that culminated in the creation of the European Union. This chapter also reviews the sudden end of the Cold War, including the rapid disintegration of the Soviet Union, the destruction of the Iron Curtain, and the reunification of Germany.

Key Terms:

KEY IDEA

- ✪ **Truman Doctrine** A U.S. doctrine (named after President Harry Truman), created in 1947, which established a system of military and economic aid to countries threatened by communist takeover.
- ✪ **Marshall Plan** A plan (named after U.S. Secretary of State George Marshall), launched in 1947, which provided billions of dollars of aid to help the Western European powers rebuild their infrastructures and economies following World War II.
- ✪ **Council for Mutual Economic Assistance** The Soviet Union's response to the Marshall Plan, whereby the Soviet Union offered economic aid packages for Eastern European countries.

- **North Atlantic Treaty Organization (NATO)** A military alliance, formed in 1949, which united the Western powers against the Soviet Union.
- **Warsaw Pact** The Soviet Union's response, in 1949, to the formation of NATO, which established a military alliance of the communist countries of Eastern Europe.
- **Détente** An era of warmer diplomatic relations between the United States and the Soviet Union, for a period lasting from the 1960s into the 1980s. It was characterized by a number of nuclear test ban treaties and arms-limitation talks between the two superpowers.
- **Prague Spring** An episode in 1968 when Czechoslovakian communists, led by Alexander Dubcek, embarked on a process of liberalization. Under Dubcek's leadership, the reformers declared that they intended to create "socialism with a human face." Dubcek tried to proceed by balancing reforms with reassurances to the Soviet Union, but on August 21, 1968, Soviet and Warsaw Pact troops invaded and occupied the major cities of Czechoslovakia.
- **Velvet Revolution** The name for the nearly bloodless overthrow of Soviet communism in Czechoslovakia in 1989.
- **Globalization** A term that refers to the increasing integration and interdependence of the economic, social, cultural, and even ecological aspects of life in the late twentieth and early twenty-first centuries. The term refers not only to the way in which the economies of the world affect one another, but also to the way that the experience of everyday life is becoming increasingly standardized by the spread of technologies that carry with them social and cultural norms.

Key Individuals:
- Alexander Dubcek
- Alexander Solzhenitsyn
- Helmut Kohl
- Ho Chi Minh
- Josef Stalin
- Lech Walesa
- Mikhail Gorbachev
- Margaret Thatcher
- Nikita Khrushchev
- Václav Havel

Introduction

Following World War II, the Cold War developed between the two new superpowers: the Soviet Union and the United States. In response, Western European nations followed a course of economic integration that culminated in the creation of the European Union. In the decades that followed the collapse of the Soviet Union, Europe experienced both a revival of nationalism and the emergence of globalization.

The Development of Nuclear Weapons

In 1942, Enrico Fermi, an Italian immigrant who fled Fascist Italy with his Jewish wife, built the first nuclear reactor in Chicago, producing the first self-sustaining nuclear chain reaction. Drawing on Fermi's work, in 1944, German physicists Otto Hahn and Fritz Strassman published a paper (based on work they had done with Lise Meitner, a Jewish physicist who was forced to emigrate due to increasing anti-Semitism in Nazi Germany) that purported to show that vast amounts of energy would be released if a way could be found to split the atom. As World War II raged, the American government secretly funded an effort, known as the Manhattan Project, to build an atomic bomb. In 1945, the project's international team of physicists, led by American physicist Robert Oppenheimer, succeeded in building three atomic bombs. After testing one, the remaining bombs were dropped on two Japanese cities: Hiroshima (on August 6, 1945) and Nagasaki (on August 9, 1945). The advent of these nuclear weapons forced Japan's unconditional surrender and created a nuclear arms race between the United States and the Soviet Union.

The Settlement Following World War II

There was no formal treaty at the conclusion of the Second World War. The postwar shape of Europe was determined by agreements reached at two wartime conferences in Tehran, Iran (in December 1943), and Yalta, Crimea, then part of the Soviet Union (in February 1945), and, where agreement could not be reached, by the realities of occupation at the war's end.

Franklin Roosevelt and Joseph Stalin both preferred to end the war with the United States and British forces advancing through France and Soviet forces pushing into Germany from the east, leaving the Soviet Union to liberate and occupy Eastern Europe. Stalin harbored some resentment against the Allies, particularly the United States, for failing to extend the lend-lease program to the Soviets, for delaying the opening of a second front to relieve pressure on Soviet troops, and (later) for failing to commit funds for Soviet reconstruction after the war. In addition, the United States did not inform the Soviet Union of the atomic bomb's development, though they did tell Great Britain. These conditions, together with the Soviet Union's desire for buffer zones to protect them from invasion and the need for strategic resources, set the stage for post-war conflict.

In the eventual settlement, Germany was disarmed and divided into sectors with Western powers controlling the western sector and the Soviet Union controlling the eastern sector. Though Berlin was in the eastern sector, it was also divided into Western-controlled West Berlin and Soviet-controlled East Berlin. Poland lost territory to the Soviet Union in the east, somewhat offset by Polish gains in the west, at Germany's expense.

Although the agreement called for self-determination and democratic elections in Eastern Europe, the Soviets had already begun installing pro-communist governments in the occupied countries, beginning with Poland (despite Poland's government-in-exile in London). Eastern European nations dominated by the Soviet Union eventually included East Germany, Poland, Romania, Czechoslovakia, Hungary, and Bulgaria. Yugoslavia, under Marshal Tito, was communist yet "nonaligned" with the Soviets.

Despite the creation of the United Nations (UN) in 1945 to promote international peace and cooperation, by 1946 an "Iron Curtain" (a term used by Winston Churchill in a speech given in the United States) had descended over Eastern Europe. The Iron Curtain stretched from the Baltic Sea in the north to the Adriatic Sea in the south, and divided Europe between a communist East and a capitalist West.

The Cold War

The Cold War in Europe

The phrase *Cold War* refers to efforts of the ideologically opposed regimes of the United States and the Soviet Union to extend their influence and control of events around the globe, without engaging in direct military conflict with one another. The first showdown between the superpowers occurred from June 1948 until May 1949, when Soviet troops cut off all land traffic from the west into Berlin in an attempt to take control of the whole city. In response, the Western Powers, led by the United States, mounted what has come to be known as the Berlin Airlift, supplying West Berlin and keeping it out of Soviet control. In 1949, the Western-controlled zones of Germany were formally merged to create the independent German Federal Republic. One month later, the Soviets established the German Democratic Republic in the eastern zone.

In 1947, the United States established the Truman Doctrine, offering military and economic aid to countries threatened by communist takeover. That same year, President Harry Truman's secretary of state, George Marshall, launched what has come to be known as the Marshall Plan, contributing billions of dollars of aid to help the Western European powers to rebuild their infrastructures and economies. The thinking was that economically vibrant economies were better able to resist communist movements. Although financial assistance was offered to the Soviet Union and Eastern European countries, it came with a degree of independent oversight that was unacceptable to Stalin and was thus rejected (as Truman anticipated). The Marshall Plan is often given credit for the "economic miracle" of Western Europe's economic recovery. Whatever the reason, Western Europe experienced a period of economic growth after World War II that allowed for the establishment of generous welfare programs. The Soviet Union soon countered with the Council for Mutual Economic Assistance (COMECON), an economic aid package for Eastern European countries.

In 1949, the United States established the North Atlantic Treaty Organization (NATO), uniting the Western powers in a military alliance against the Soviet Union. The Soviet Union countered with the Warsaw Pact, a military alliance of the communist countries of Eastern Europe. The one great military imbalance of the postwar period, the United States' possession of the atomic bomb, was countered by the development of a Soviet atomic bomb in 1949. From then on, the two superpowers engaged in a nuclear arms race that saw each develop an arsenal of hydrogen bombs by 1953, followed by huge caches of nuclear warheads mounted on intercontinental ballistic missiles (ICBMs). The overarching strategy of amassing nuclear weapons became appropriately known by its acronym MAD, which stood for "mutual assured destruction." This strategy "reasoned" that neither side would use its nuclear weapons if its own destruction by a retaliatory blast was assured.

The Global Cold War

Once the two superpowers had done what they could to shore up their positions in Europe, their competition spread across the globe. For example, the Cuban Missile Crisis of October 1962, in which Soviet attempts to install nuclear missiles in Cuba, were met with a U.S. blockade of the island, and brought the world to the brink of nuclear war. Eventually the Soviets backed down and removed the missiles. But, in general, the nuclear capabilities of the United States and the Soviet Union precluded a direct confrontation. Instead the tensions played out in a series of limited or "proxy wars," in which the two countries supported opposite sides of existing conflicts in other parts of the world. Many major world events during the second half of the twentieth century were directly related to the Cold War.

In Asia, the Chinese Civil War (1945–1949) pitted Soviet-backed communist forces, who were led by Mao Zedong, against the Nationalist forces of Jiang Jieshi (often known as Chiang Kai-Shek), who were backed by the United States. The Korean War (1950–1953) involved North Korean communists, supported by the Soviet Union and China, and the South Koreans, supported by the United Nations and the United States. This produced a stalemate near the 38th parallel (the original post–World War II dividing line between North and South Korea) at the cost of some 1.5 million lives. Later, during the Vietnam War, communist forces led by Ho Chi Minh battled an authoritarian, anticommunist government, increasingly reliant on U.S. military aid for its existence (throughout the 1960s until U.S. withdrawal in 1973). In the Afghanistan conflict, Soviet troops invaded to support a faltering pro-Soviet regime. They engineered a coup and installed a new pro-Soviet leader. Rebel "mujahideen" groups pursued a guerilla war, with funding and training provided by the United States, Pakistan, and Saudi Arabia.

The Middle East was also the scene of U.S.–Soviet conflict. When the United States backed out of an agreement in the mid-1950s to help Egypt build the Aswan Dam, Egypt retaliated by nationalizing the British-controlled Suez Canal. Egypt subsequently benefited from Soviet support in the ensuing battles against Great Britain, France, and Israel. Pressured by the United States to withdraw, Great Britain relinquished the Suez Canal; this event marked the decline of British influence in international relations. Moreover, the Soviets then helped Egypt build the Aswan Dam when the United States would not, improving the Soviet Union's standing in the Middle East. In 1973, the United States and the Soviet Union again clashed during the Yom Kippur War, in which Soviet-supplied Arab forces attempted to retake the Sinai Peninsula and Golan Heights from U.S.–backed Israel.

Despite conflicts, the West allowed the Soviet Union a great deal of latitude within its "sphere of influence" in Eastern Europe. For example, in 1956, a popular uprising broke out in Hungary, encouraged by Nikita Khrushchev's speech denouncing Stalinist policies. Though Hungary asked for Western support, none was forthcoming for fear of a nuclear confrontation, allowing the Soviets to violently crush the rebellion. Though Khrushchev's speeches had seemed to indicate a softer position, his actions in Hungary proved otherwise.

Although it was less in the world news headlines, the Cold War also had devastating effects in Latin America and Africa, where, for the better part of three decades, local and regional disputes were shaped by the intervention of Soviet and American money, arms, and covert operations. Many of the difficulties faced by these regions today can be traced back to the Cold War.

Détente with the West, Crackdown in the East

Beginning in the late 1960s and lasting into the 1980s, U.S.–Soviet relations entered into a new era that has come to be known as the era of *détente*. In this period, both sides backed away from the notion of a struggle only one side could win. The era of *détente* was characterized by a number of nuclear test-ban treaties and arms-limitation talks between the two superpowers.

However, while Soviet–U.S. relations were thawing during this period, the Soviet Union demonstrated on several occasions that it still intended to rule the Eastern Bloc with a firm hand. The most dramatic of these events occurred in 1968 in an episode that has come to be known as the Prague Spring. Czechoslovakian communists, led by Alexander Dubcek, embarked on a process of liberalization, stimulated by public demand for greater freedom, economic progress, and equality. Under Dubcek's leadership, the reformers declared that they intended to create "socialism with a human face." Dubcek tried to proceed by balancing reforms with reassurances to the Soviet Union. But on August 21, Soviet and Warsaw Pact troops invaded and occupied the major cities of Czechoslovakia; it was the largest military operation in Europe since the Second World War.

The Soviet regime also continued to demand conformity from its citizens and to punish dissent. A good example is the case of Aleksandr Solzhenitsyn, the acclaimed author who wrote novels that attempted to tell the truth about life in the Soviet Union. For writing novels like *The Cancer Ward* (1966) and *The First Circle* (1968), Solzhenitsyn was expelled, in November 1969, from the Russian Writers' Union. Much to the irritation of the Soviet government, his work was highly acclaimed in the West, and he was awarded the Nobel Prize in Literature in 1970. Following the 1973 publication of his novel *The Gulag Archipelago*, he was arrested. But in a sign that some concessions were being made to Western opinion, he was deported to West Germany rather than exiled to Siberia.

The totalitarian regimes associated with the Eastern Bloc countries, and earlier with Nazism, spurred many in the Christian community into action. The Second Vatican Council of the Catholic Church (1962–1965) took the remarkable step of affirming Catholicism's roots in Judaism, Jews' covenant with God, and the idea that disparate faiths worshipped the same God. An important corollary in the wake of the Holocaust was the rejection of civil discrimination based on religion. Like Lutheran pastors Martin Niemöller and Dietrich Bonhoeffer, both of whom opposed many of Hitler's actions, Pope John Paul II spoke out against totalitarianism and in favor of human rights. One of his first acts as Pope was to travel to his homeland Poland, emphasizing human dignity and urging the Polish people to maintain their faith. When thousands turned out to see him, it galvanized the Solidarity movement (discussed later in this chapter in the "Poland and Solidarity" section) by demonstrating that they were not alone.

The European Union

The leaders of Western Europe realized almost immediately following World War II they were going to need to function as a whole in order to rival the economic and military power of the two superpowers. Throughout the second half of the twentieth century, Europe embarked on a process of economic integration that occurred in several stages. In 1950, France and West Germany removed tariffs and cooperated in the coal and steel industry, and later included Italy, Belgium, Luxembourg, and the Netherlands. By 1957, those six countries had established the European Economic Community (EEC), sometimes called the Common Market, to reduce tariff barriers and restrictions on the flow of capital and labor. Eventually the EEC incorporated other public functions, becoming the European Community (EC) in 1967.

Over the next 20 years, the EC added Denmark, the United Kingdom, Ireland, Greece, Portugal, and Spain. With the signing of the Maastricht Treaty in 1992, Europe moved towards closer political and economic integration with the creation of the European Union (EU), adopting a common currency (the euro) and forming the world's largest trading bloc. Following the breakup of the Soviet Union, the EU underwent a massive expansion, welcoming countries either newly freed or newly constituted after the breakup of the Soviet Union. The addition of Cyprus, the Czech Republic, Estonia, Hungary, Latvia, Lithuania, Malta, Poland, Slovakia, and Slovenia in 2004, Bulgaria and Romania in 2007, and Croatia in 2013 brought the total membership to 28 countries.

These fledgling democracies had more fragile economies than their Western European counterparts, which strained relations among the members. Freedom of movement within the European Union meant that Eastern Europeans could freely travel to Western countries for work. Additionally, when those nations adopted the euro as their currency, their economies became intertwined with other EU nations. When certain members were unable to pay or refinance their debts (for example, Greece, Ireland, Spain, and Portugal) around 2009, the stability of the euro was threatened. Though EU members intervened to stabilize the currency, the conditions they imposed required drastic cuts in government spending and sparked protests, especially in Greece.

The growing importance of the European Union has also prompted some concerns about a loss of national identity and sovereignty, particularly in Great Britain. After Britons voted to leave the European Union in a referendum in 2016, Prime Minister Theresa May invoked Article 50 of the Treaty on the European Union, declaring the United Kingdom's intent to withdraw. Negotiations for the "divorce" have been complex and contentious, though, and waning support among the British public for withdrawal leaves the outcome in some doubt.

The Disintegration of the Iron Curtain and the Soviet Union

Between 1985 and 1989, the world was stunned as it witnessed the rapid disintegration of the Soviet Union, the destruction of the Iron Curtain, and the reunification of Germany. The causes of these dramatic events were rooted in the nature of the Soviet system, which had for decades put domestic and foreign politics ahead of the needs of its own economy and of its people. The result was an economic system that could no longer function. The trigger for its disintegration was the ascension of a new generation of Soviet leaders.

Gorbachev and the "New Man"

While Western Europe was creating the European Community and dreaming of economic and political power that could match those of the superpowers, the big lie of the Soviet economy was coming home to roost. While the Soviet Union had continued with a command economy after World War II and initially experienced strong industrial growth, its economy was undermined by corruption, excessive military spending at the expense of other sectors, and an extensive black market. In 1985, Mikhail Gorbachev succeeded a long line of aging Stalinist leaders. At the age of 54, Gorbachev represented a younger and more sophisticated generation that had spent significant time in the West. Gorbachev believed that the Soviet Union's survival required a restructuring (*perestroika*) of both its economy and its society, and an openness (*glasnost*) to new ideas. Accordingly, Gorbachev challenged the people of the Soviet Union and its satellite countries to take on a new level of responsibility. But such an invitation quickly fanned the fires of autonomy in satellite states.

Poland and Solidarity

There had been growing agitation in Poland since 1980, when workers under the leadership of an electrician named Lech Walesa succeeded in forming a labor union known as "Solidarity." Pressured by numerous strikes, the Polish government recognized the union despite threats of Soviet intervention. By 1981, the movement had become more political, as some of Solidarity's more radical members began calling for free elections. As tensions grew, the Polish military, led by General Wojciech Jaruzelski, responded to the crisis by imposing martial law and a military dictatorship. But with Gorbachev calling for reform,

Jaruzelski tried, in November 1987, to gain legitimacy for his rule through a national referendum. However, the majority of voters either voted against or abstained. In August 1988, Jaruzelski ended his military dictatorship and set up a civilian government.

The new government attempted to retain the political monopoly of the Communist Party while simultaneously opening Poland up for Western business. This proved to be impossible, and Walesa and Solidarity took advantage of the new openness to push for political freedom. In January 1989, Solidarity was legalized, and in April, the Communist Party gave up its monopoly on political power. In the first free election in Poland since before World War II, Solidarity triumphed and a noncommunist government was established in September. In December 1990, Walesa was elected president, and Poland began to face the hard task of learning how to live in an unruly democratic society and how to deal with the economic ups and downs of capitalism.

Czechoslovakia and the Velvet Revolution

Seeing Poland and Hungary (which held free elections in the summer and fall of 1989) shed their communist governments without Soviet intervention energized Czech resistance to communist rule. Student-led demonstrations in the fall of 1989 were met with the tear gas and clubs of the police, but the students were soon joined by workers and people from all walks of life. Leading dissidents, like the playwright Václav Havel, began a movement known as the Civic Forum, which sought to rebuild notions of citizenship and civic life that had been destroyed by the Soviet system. Soon Havel and other dissidents were jailed, but they became symbols of defiance and moral superiority.

What followed has come to be known as the Velvet Revolution. Faced with massive demonstrations in Prague (shown around the world on television), and urged by Gorbachev himself to institute democratic reform, Czechoslovakia's communist leaders resigned on November 24. After negotiations and maneuvers by both the Communist Party and the Civic Forum, Havel was chosen president on December 25, 1989. Alexander Dubcek, who had led the revolt of 1968, was brought home from exile and named chairman of the Czechoslovakian Parliament.

German Reunification

West Germans had never accepted the division of Germany. The constitution of the German Federal Republic provided legal formalities for reunification. How the East Germans felt about the society of their Western relatives was hard to know. When reunification came, it came suddenly. East German dissidents organized themselves along the lines of the Civic Forum model pioneered in Czechoslovakia. In response to the pressure for reform, the communist regime rescinded its traditional order to shoot anyone trying to escape to West Berlin, and shortly thereafter issued "vacation visas" to those wishing to see their families in the West. There was little expectation of their return.

On November 9, 1989, protesters moved toward the Berlin Wall, and meeting almost no resistance from the soldiers, started to hammer it down. East Germans streamed into West Berlin, where they were embraced by tearful West Germans who gleefully gave them handfuls of cash. The West German chancellor, conservative Helmut Kohl, moved quickly toward reunification. It was a reunification that amounted to East Germany being annexed by the West. Completely swept away in the pace of reunification were the original Civic Forum leaders who were not at all sure that they wished to be reunified with West Germany and its capitalist economy. Nevertheless, beginning in March 1990, reunification proceeded quickly with East German elections, the drafting and ratification of a reunification treaty, and the first unified national election all completed before the end of the year.

Helmut Kohl, "the Reunification Chancellor," and his Christian Democrat party would remain in power until 1998.

The Soviet Union Comes Apart

Caught between the hardliners who wished to slow down reform and a population that wanted it to come faster, Gorbachev's popularity began to slip. Determined to go forward, Gorbachev persuaded the Communist Party to give up its monopoly on political power and called for free elections. Sensing collapse, Party members resigned in large numbers.

The various "republics" that made up the Soviet Union now emulated the satellite states and began to agitate for independence. Lithuania led the way, declaring the restoration of Lithuanian independence in March 1990. Others soon followed suit, including the Russian Republic, led by the charismatic deputy, Boris Yeltsin. Gorbachev was faced with a crisis. In the spring of 1991, Gorbachev proposed a compromise. He suggested that all the republics sign a Treaty of the Union, declaring them all to be independent but also members of a loose confederation. In August 1991, just as the treaty was about to take effect, hardliners tried to oust Gorbachev. For three days, there was confusion about who was in charge and what the military would do. Yeltsin seized the moment, positioning himself between the parliament building and military tanks. The military backed off and the coup attempt failed, but it was Yeltsin who was now the favorite. Gorbachev resigned late in 1991, and the Soviet Union, as the world had known it, disintegrated. Most of the republics chose to join a loose confederation known as the Commonwealth of Independent States (CIS), whereas a few, especially the Baltic states, opted for independence.

The Rise of Nationalism in Eastern Europe

Following the collapse of the Soviet Union, nationalism, which had been driven underground, again came to the surface in Eastern Europe. In Czechoslovakia, resurgent nationalism split the country in half; the Slovak region formed the republic of Slovakia and the Czechs formed the Czech Republic. Meanwhile, in the former Soviet republic of Azerbaijan, traditional tensions with Armenians reemerged, with alleged violence against Armenians. This caused Armenians to declare an autonomous state in the Nagorno-Karabakh region of Azerbaijan. In the Russian Republic, Chechens began a guerrilla war against Russian troops when their demands for independence were refused.

Yugoslavia: Fragmentation

During the Cold War, Yugoslavia was composed of six ethnically self-conscious member "republics" held together by the Communist Party. As the communist regime began to collapse, the ethnic rivalries of Yugoslavia quickly reasserted themselves. The fragile multiethnic system fell apart as Slovenia and then Croatia declared independence in 1991. Serbia, the largest "republic" of Yugoslavia, tried to hold the union together but war erupted between Serbia and Croatia and, at about the same time, the Serbian province of Kosovo revolted against Serbian rule. In Bosnia-Herzegovina, the situation degenerated into a vicious, multisided war with acts of genocide committed on all sides. In the end, Yugoslavia split into seven independent nations—the six former republics of Yugoslavia plus Kosovo (although the independence of Kosovo is not recognized by Serbia and some other countries, including Russia).

Social, Economic, and Political Changes in post–Cold War Europe

Globalization

While politics in the post–Cold War era often seemed to regress, the unity of the world's economies, societies, and cultures continued to move forward. Near the end of the twentieth century, the term *globalization* became prominent to describe the increasing integration and interdependence of the economic, social, cultural, and even ecological aspects of life. The term *globalization* refers not only to the way in which the economies of the world affect one another, but also to the way that the experience of everyday life is becoming increasingly standardized by the spread of technologies that carry with them social and cultural norms.

During this time, improvements in transportation, communication, and automation intensified, which reduced the cost of producing and distributing goods internationally and created a truly global economy, with both multinational and transnational corporations. As Europe transitioned from an industrial, factory-based economy to a post-industrial, service economy, social class structures changed, most notably with an expansion of the middle class. In addition to typical middle-class occupations, an educated class of professional managers and administrators emerged. The expansion of a prosperous middle class further encouraged a culture of mass consumerism, begun earlier in the twentieth century.

Student Revolts

During the 1960s, philosophers, like Herbert Marcuse, contended that capitalist societies encouraged materialism and consumerism because they eroded the dissatisfaction of the proletariat, which was necessary to advance communism. However, small groups of committed students could overthrow the ruling classes. Partly driven by theories like these, partly reacting to international events like the Vietnam War, and partly driven by frustrations over outdated and overburdened university systems, a series of student revolts erupted around Western Europe. In France in 1968, student movements and worker movements combined, which resulted in student takeovers of university buildings and widespread strikes. Germany, too, experienced student protests. In both countries, police quashed the student violence, though the issues prompting them remained unresolved.

Green Party Movements

The increase in scope and pace of global post-industrial economies, in conjunction with technological advances, has given rise to environmental movements in Europe. Beginning in the 1970s, the ecological consequences of industrial and post-industrial economies became all too apparent. Air quality suffered due to vehicle and factory emissions, which caused health concerns and even damaged buildings. Waterways became polluted with runoff from pesticides and fertilizers, as well as chemicals dumped by industrial concerns. As populations expanded, wildlife habitats like forests contracted.

Challenges to the Welfare State

The concept of the cradle-to-grave welfare state came under increasing pressure in the latter quarter of the twentieth century, squeezed by twin pressures of changing demographics and shrinking budgets. Improved medical technologies extended life expectancies; at the same time, people gained more control over their own fertility than at any other time in history, reducing the birth rate. An aging population led to imbalances between those drawing welfare state benefits and those contributing to the system. Governments have responded by scaling back benefits or even shifting government-controlled industries to the private sector. An example of privatization occurred during the 1980s in Great Britain under Prime Minister Margaret Thatcher, who sold off British Telecom, British Steel, and the water industry, among others. Frequently, attempts to increase working hours or to scale back benefits have been met with protests and strikes by workers, who charge that governments are reneging on promises made.

Additionally, Western European governments have attempted to address declining birth rates by supporting families with children through a range of policies including subsidized or free childcare, generous parental leave, tax breaks to families, or even cash payments to couples for a second child (Italy). Though the policies vary from country to country, most have made efforts in this regard.

Belief Systems

Medical advances in areas like fertility, abortion, genetic engineering, and end-of-life treatments challenged established definitions of life and death. This led to political and social conflicts over the ethical and moral implications of these issues. Vatican II, discussed earlier, also attempted to address the apparent contradictions between the literal interpretation of the Bible and new scientific theories regarding things like origins of the universe and man. Vatican II clarified that scientific discovery, so long as it does not override moral laws, does not conflict with faith, as they are both derived from God. Although Vatican II addressed Catholic practices in the modern world, it continued with traditional doctrines of rejecting female clergy and divorce.

Immigration

Immigration, which has reshaped many traditionally homogeneous European nations into diverse cultures, is another source of social tension. Fears of a weakening national identity, concerns about competition for jobs, and anxiety over national security have sometimes led to a backlash against immigrant communities. In addition, particularly with respect to Muslim immigrants, European governments struggle to balance their commitment to secularism with religious freedom (in the case of Muslim girls wearing the hijab headscarf in French schools, for example) and to individual rights with national security. Anti-immigrant sentiment has taken political shape in the form of right-wing political parties such as the National Front in France, that advocate economic protectionism and restricted immigration. Recent attacks by followers of the Islamic State of Iraq or Syria (ISIS) or the Islamic State of Iraq and the Levant (ISIL), terrorist organizations advocating an extremist version of Islam, have further inflamed these tensions.

Women

One demographic group that made great gains in the second half of the twentieth century was women, particularly in the political arena. In the early 1950s and 1960s, women typically married young and had children early. Advances like the contraceptive pill helped women control their own fertility rates, a factor in declining birth rates. Smaller families meant women had more free time to gain an education and to seek employment. Postwar economic growth contributed to this trend, as did the growing white-collar employment sector. Economic complexity made two incomes more desirable or even a necessity for families. In addition, the social landscape was changing, including growing numbers of single women of working age due to divorce or to delayed marriage. The combination of these factors led to unprecedented numbers of women in the workplace where they often were subject to discrimination in the form of limited opportunities for promotion and disparities in pay with their male counterparts. This gave rise to a new feminist movement in the

1970s, which found inspiration in earlier feminist writers like Simone de Beauvoir, whose book *The Second Sex* argued that patriarchal society had relegated women to second-class status as "Other," but that women could choose to free themselves from such roles. Women sought change in the political arena, eventually winning such victories as the abolition of laws restricting divorce and abortion in Italy. Women also gained political office in Europe during this time period; most notable was Margaret Thatcher, who served as Great Britain's Prime Minister from 1979 to 1990. Mary Robinson led Ireland from 1990 to 1997, and many Scandinavian countries like Norway and Iceland had female leaders during the 1980s. In the twenty-first century, this trend has continued with Angela Merkel in Germany and Teresa May in Britain, among others.

Review Questions

Multiple Choice

Questions 1–3 refer to the following passage:

> In a great number of countries, far from the Russian frontiers and throughout the world, Communist fifth columns are established and work in complete unity and absolute obedience to the directions they receive from the Communist center. Except in the British Commonwealth and in the United States where Communism is in its infancy, the Communist parties or fifth columns constitute a growing challenge and peril to Christian civilization. . . .
>
> I do not believe that Soviet Russia desires war. What they desire is the fruits of war and the indefinite expansion of their power and doctrines. But what we have to consider here today while time remains, is the permanent prevention of war and the establishment of conditions of freedom and democracy as rapidly as possible in all countries. . . . From what I have seen of our Russian friends and allies during the war, I am convinced that there is nothing they admire so much as strength, and there is nothing for which they have less respect than for weakness, especially military weakness. For that reason the old doctrine of a balance of power is unsound.
>
> Winston S. Churchill, "Iron Curtain" speech, March 5, 1946

1. What was Churchill's belief regarding communism?
   A. Communism was an immediate threat in the United States.
   B. The Russian frontier was in danger of falling to communist forces.
   C. Communists in European countries were obedient to the communist government of the Soviet Union.
   D. Communism posed a growing challenge to Asia.
2. What did Churchill believe to be the goal of the Soviet Union?
   A. The expansion of its power and influence wherever possible
   B. A global revolution of the proletariat
   C. A third world war
   D. Control of all of Asia
3. Which statement best represents Churchill's argument?
   A. A third world war was inevitable.
   B. Securing the rule of democratic governments in Europe required a strong military presence throughout Europe.
   C. A balance of power must be created between the West and the Soviet Union.
   D. The United States should join the British Commonwealth in order to prevent the spread of communism.

Short Answer

4. Briefly explain TWO ways in which people were able to reconstruct civic life in the police-states that had been formed under Soviet-style communism, and illustrate each with an example.

Answers and Explanations

1. **C** is correct because the passage states the belief that "Communist fifth columns are established and work in complete unity and absolute obedience to the directions they receive from the Communist center" (that is, the Soviet Union). A is incorrect because the passage states that communism was "in its infancy" in the United States. B is incorrect because the Russian frontier was already a part of the Soviet Union at the time of the speech, and because the reference in the passage is to places *far from* the Russian frontier. D is incorrect because the passage states that communism posed a growing threat "to Christian civilization," that is, to Europe and the United States.

2. **A** is correct because the passage states Churchill's belief that the government of the Soviet Union wanted "the indefinite expansion of their power and doctrines." B is incorrect because the passage makes no mention of a global revolution of the proletariat. C is incorrect because the passage says that Churchill does *not* believe that the Soviet Union wants war. D is incorrect because the passage makes no mention of Asia.

3. **B** is correct because the passage implies that military weakness would encourage the expansionist aims of the Soviet Union. A is incorrect because the passage does not refer to the inevitability of war. C is incorrect because the passage states Churchill's belief that "the old doctrine of a balance of power is unsound." D is incorrect because the passage does not urge the United States to join the British Commonwealth.

4. Suggested answer:

Thesis: During the 1980s, people within the police-states of Soviet-dominated Eastern Europe were able to reconstruct spaces for normal civic life in several ways, including the development and expansion of a labor union movement and the development of "civic forums."

Paragraph Outline:

I. In Poland in the 1980s, workers under the leadership of an electrician named Lech Walesa succeeded in forming a labor union known as Solidarity. Pressured by numerous strikes, the Polish government recognized the union despite threats of Soviet intervention.

II. In Czechoslovakia in the 1980s, people from all walks of life created a movement that became known as the Civic Forum, which, by commandeering public spaces like libraries and churches for town meetings, began to rebuild notions of citizenship and civic life that had been destroyed by the Soviet system.

Rapid Review

Following World War II, the Soviet Union solidified its control of Eastern Europe, creating an "Iron Curtain" that divided East from West. The two superpowers, the United States and the Soviet Union, engaged in a conflict, called the Cold War, which had global implications. The advent of nuclear weapons forced Japan's unconditional surrender but subsequently created a nuclear arms race between the United States and the Soviet Union. Meanwhile, Western European nations followed a course of economic integration that culminated in the creation of the European Union. Between 1985 and 1989, systemic economic problems and a bold attempt at reform led to the rapid disintegration of the Soviet Union, the destruction of the Iron Curtain, and the reunification of Germany. In the decades that followed, two major trends affected life in Europe: the revival of nationalism and the emergence of globalization.

Further Resources

Eugene Burdick and William J. Lederer, *The Ugly American*

Tom Clancy, *The Hunt for Red October*

Ian Fleming, *From Russia with Love*

William Golding, *The Lord of the Flies*

Graham Greene, *The Quiet American*

John le Carré, *The Spy Who Came In from the Cold*

Richard Condon, *The Manchurian Candidate*

CHAPTER 25

Science and Culture

History cannot be studied in a vacuum. The twentieth century will be remembered as a century of wars—world wars, civil wars, wars of independence, and imperialism. It may also be called "the century of arts and letters," given the vast production of both, often in reaction to the chaos and flux of the world. What is especially interesting, moreover, is the role of scientific and technological advances, and of the interactions between culture and science.

World War I (1914–1918) saw the last use of the cavalry and the first use of tanks, mustard gas, airplanes (though mainly for reconnaissance), and water-cooled machine guns. In a sense, it used modern technology to perfect impersonal and efficient killing, changing the nature of warfare forever. World War I redefined the map of Europe and left a "lost generation" of disillusioned and cynical people. The Spanish Civil War (1936–1939), a "dress rehearsal" for World War II, served as a testing ground for saturation bombing. World War II (1939–1945) used new technologies to destroy a generation of German and Russian men, and much of European Jewry. World War II displaced vast numbers of people and weakened societal hierarchies.

Wars for independence from imperial overlords—in Indochina, Algeria, and other emerging nations in Asia and Africa—occupied much of the 1950s, 1960s, and 1970s. Wars during the twentieth century, however, produced remarkable cultural responses, changed gender roles across the board, and refined industry so that in peacetime its mass production capabilities coupled with the rise of advertising created a consumerist society.

Just as the development of the moveable-type printing press by Johannes Gutenberg in the early Renaissance (about 1450) contributed to the spread of literacy, education, and humanistic thought, and eventually to the Reformation and the Counter-Reformation, the creation of mass media (radio, television, computers, the Internet) and mass transport (the automobile, airplanes) led to irreversible globalization. Nowhere were continuity, causes and effects, connections, and synergy between arts and sciences more visible than during the twentieth century.

Culture and science are, above all, cumulative, with the whole frequently being greater than the sum of the parts. Purpose helps to determine this synergy. From earliest times, for example, art had a purpose: It progressed from being ritualistic or being used to keep records of events to becoming decorative as well. All these elements came together during the Classical era, when art also served propagandistic and political goals. Monumental architecture and art became ever more prevalent, and they reflected the ideals of an era. During the Middle Ages, artwork was often instructional—used to educate a primarily illiterate populace. With the Renaissance focus on humanism, art became realistic and the purview of not just the upper classes, but of a growing middle class. The content of painting, for example, shifted from large-scale religious, mythological, and historical images to smaller scenes of still-life, portraits, and people involved in everyday activities.

While there is evidence of decorative artwork (specifically, of jewelry) during nomadic prehistory, it would take settlement, the result of, among other things, the Agricultural Revolution in the Neolithic and following periods, to witness permanent decorative arts, made for dwellings and ritualistic or religious sites. Settlement itself gave rise to specialization and division of labor; that is, it promoted the production of surplus goods, like foodstuffs. Surplus food meant that not everyone in a community had to participate in the production of food; they could follow a different path. This allowed the development of an artistic "class," supported by farming and governing classes.

The use of various metals, particularly of bronze, gave rise to better weaponry and permanent art. Roman discovery of concrete led to durable architecture. By medieval times, art had become both *dulce et utile* ("pleasing and instructive," a phrase Horace coined to describe literature). During this period, the performing arts—almost entirely under the sway of the Roman Catholic Church—served to entertain and educate. Due to the advances in mathematics and engineering, the intertwining of art, philosophy, religion, and science let churches evolve into beautiful, colorful, tall, Gothic structures, which were aimed at showing that contemplation of beauty led to contemplation of the divine.

In addition, Renaissance advances in mathematics; patronage from the upper classes, the church, and the merchant class; and the use of new techniques (linear perspective, for example) made possible the creation of realistic artwork. Art and performing arts became accessible to larger numbers of people through the creation of public theaters and museums, and the use of professional actors.

By the twentieth century, advances in science inspired artists to not just use everything that had developed in the preceding millennia, but to go beyond traditional techniques and purposes, and to use them in new ways and for new ends. Perhaps most famous is the impact of Albert Einstein's Theory of General Relativity on art. The ideas of all points of view being possible, of a four-dimensional space-time continuum, and of "modernism" as recasting our view of reality led to radical interpretations by artists. In a world in which war became "normal," artists used art to express politics. Artists objected to growing nationalism and imperialism, most notably in the works of Expressionists (Henri Matisse) and Cubists (Pablo Picasso), and in Futurist and Bauhaus architecture. The opposite also occurred. Art was used to express pro-war politics, in the form of the propagandistic art that supported World War I and World War II war efforts. In the second half of the twentieth century, art, especially that of Pop Culture, set about to portray human existence, both cynically and realistically.

How does one "read" a work of art? What is the medium, and how does it reflect scientific innovations? What subject or theme is represented, and what is its historical, social, religious, or political significance? How does a work of art reflect the culture or philosophy of the era in which it was produced? What recognizable symbols, stereotypes, or archetypes are present in a work? What is the artist's purpose? Is it:

- to produce a realistic image?
- to record a historical event?
- to make use of new techniques that might well reflect scientific theories?
- to serve as propaganda or satire?
- to express feelings about social or political issues?

To understand literature in the twentieth century, it is useful to look at the development of the novel. The Renaissance, with its considered human center, allowed for realistic narrative, using characters taken from the real, or contemporary, world. It was written in prose and in the vernacular. In short, it was accessible. By the 1700s and into the late 1800s, the historical novel dominated the literary landscape; it portrayed characters realistically and began to have protagonists who were not royalty. Novelists began to take a moral stance; authors like Charles Dickens, Gustave Flaubert, Thomas Hardy, and Henry James contended that novelists could construct an entire civilization, but needed to do so with an eye to demonstrating a sense of justice and commitment.

As the twentieth century unfolded, authors like Ernest Hemingway, Marcel Proust, Franz Kafka, Luigi Pirandello, Virginia Woolf, and James Joyce continued to feel a sense of commitment (Joyce added a sense of alienation and absurdity)—often combining traits of the historical novel with their personal perceptions of the world about them. Leonard Woolf, husband of Virginia Woolf, wrote: "In 1914 in the background of one's life and one's mind there were light and hope; by 1918 one had unconsciously accepted a perpetual public menace and darkness and had admitted into the privacy of one's mind or soul an iron fatalistic acquiescence in insecurity and barbarism." There is a vast war literature that clearly shows this climate of opinion. (Perhaps the most famous work of this nature is Erich Maria Remarque's *All Quiet on the Western Front*.)

The twentieth-century novel, in general, took on a pessimistic, dramatic narrative tone and was notably self-centered. Following World War I and II, however, novelists began to demonstrate a sense of social obligation and a belief in the power of the individual to effect change. Once again, art-as-politics became the norm. As a result, literature became a means to express the ideas and ideals of various movements: feminism, equal rights, independence from colonial or imperial powers, and pacifism, for example.

The value and use of fiction as a historical resource is much debated among historians. Deciphering an author's purpose, intent, and even ideology is important in evaluating works of fiction that react to historical events or eras. It is worth bearing in mind this quotation of professor and author Lynn Hunt: "It may seem that the past is by definition over, but the past is always changing because historians and the purposes of history are changing too. . . . Every new age looks for an understanding of its place in time, and without history it would not have one."

To think about:

- How do you "read" art? Choose a painting, piece of sculpture, photograph, building, or public work (a bridge, for example) and explain how it reflects an idea or an era.
- Why do novels get banned?
- Is film noir a reflection of the modern world?
- How has mass communication affected our perceptions of other cultures?
- Which scientific advance of the twentieth century would you consider most useful?
- Which scientific advance of the twentieth century would you consider most destructive?

STEP **5**

Build Your Test-Taking Confidence

AP European History Practice Exam 1
AP European History Practice Exam 2

AP European History Practice Exam 1

SECTION I, PART A

ANSWER SHEET

1 (A) (B) (C) (D)
2 (A) (B) (C) (D)
3 (A) (B) (C) (D)
4 (A) (B) (C) (D)
5 (A) (B) (C) (D)
6 (A) (B) (C) (D)
7 (A) (B) (C) (D)
8 (A) (B) (C) (D)
9 (A) (B) (C) (D)
10 (A) (B) (C) (D)
11 (A) (B) (C) (D)
12 (A) (B) (C) (D)
13 (A) (B) (C) (D)
14 (A) (B) (C) (D)
15 (A) (B) (C) (D)
16 (A) (B) (C) (D)
17 (A) (B) (C) (D)
18 (A) (B) (C) (D)
19 (A) (B) (C) (D)

20 (A) (B) (C) (D)
21 (A) (B) (C) (D)
22 (A) (B) (C) (D)
23 (A) (B) (C) (D)
24 (A) (B) (C) (D)
25 (A) (B) (C) (D)
26 (A) (B) (C) (D)
27 (A) (B) (C) (D)
28 (A) (B) (C) (D)
29 (A) (B) (C) (D)
30 (A) (B) (C) (D)
31 (A) (B) (C) (D)
32 (A) (B) (C) (D)
33 (A) (B) (C) (D)
34 (A) (B) (C) (D)
35 (A) (B) (C) (D)
36 (A) (B) (C) (D)
37 (A) (B) (C) (D)
38 (A) (B) (C) (D)

39 (A) (B) (C) (D)
40 (A) (B) (C) (D)
41 (A) (B) (C) (D)
42 (A) (B) (C) (D)
43 (A) (B) (C) (D)
44 (A) (B) (C) (D)
45 (A) (B) (C) (D)
46 (A) (B) (C) (D)
47 (A) (B) (C) (D)
48 (A) (B) (C) (D)
49 (A) (B) (C) (D)
50 (A) (B) (C) (D)
51 (A) (B) (C) (D)
52 (A) (B) (C) (D)
53 (A) (B) (C) (D)
54 (A) (B) (C) (D)
55 (A) (B) (C) (D)

AP European History Practice Exam 1

SECTION I, PART A

Multiple-Choice Questions
Recommended Time—55 minutes

Directions: The multiple-choice section consists of 55 questions to be answered in a recommended time of **55 minutes**. The sets of questions below refer to the attached primary source, secondary source, or historical issue. For each question, select the one answer that best answers or completes the question and fill in the letter that corresponds to your choice on the answer sheet supplied.

Questions 1–3 relate to the following passage:

At last it seems to me that I have come to understand why man is the most fortunate of all creatures and consequently worthy of all admiration. . . . The nature of all other beings is limited. . . . Imagine! The great generosity of God! The happiness of man! To man it is allowed to be whatever he chooses to be!

Pico della Mirandola, *Oration on the Dignity of Man*, 1486

1. Pico della Mirandola was participating in which cultural movement?

   A. The Renaissance
   B. The Reformation
   C. The Scientific Revolution
   D. The Enlightenment

2. Pico della Mirandola believed that humankind was unique in what way?

   A. Human beings have a soul.
   B. Human beings know that they will die.
   C. It is possible for human beings to go to heaven.
   D. The potential of the human being is unlimited.

3. Pico della Mirandola rejected which of the following notions?

   A. Man was a unique kind of creature.
   B. God intended man to strive to achieve.
   C. Man is unworthy of admiration.
   D. Humans are God's equals.

Questions 4–6 relate to the following petition:

The Scribbling-Machines have thrown thousands of your petitioners out of employ, whereby they are brought into great distress, and are not able to procure a maintenance for their families, and deprived them of the opportunity of bringing up their children to labour. . . . The number of Scribbling-Machines extending about seventeen miles south-west of Leeds exceed all belief, being no less than *one hundred and seventy!* And as each machine will do as much work in twelve hours, as ten men can in that time do by hand, . . . [And, as the machines do] as much work in one day as would otherwise employ twenty men, . . . [a] full four thousand men are left to shift for a living how they can, and must of course fall to the Parish, if not timely relieved. . . . How are those men, thus thrown out of employ to provide for their families; and what are they to put their children apprentice to, that the rising generation may have something to keep them at work, in order that they may not be like vagabonds strolling about in idleness? . . . Many more evils we could enumerate, but we would hope, that the sensible part of mankind, who are not biased by interest, must see the dreadful tendency of their continuance; a depopulation must be the consequence; trade being then lost, the landed interest will have no other satisfaction but that of being *last devoured*.

Leeds Woolen Workers Petition, 1786

4. This document can be used as evidence for which of the following?

   A. The spread of revolutionary ideas among the British working class in the eighteenth century
   B. The rise of the Luddite movement in Britain in the eighteenth century
   C. The replacing of traditional laborers by machines in the industrialization of Britain in the eighteenth century
   D. An increase in the use of child labor in eighteenth-century Britain

5. The sentiments expressed by the Leeds woolen workers illustrate which of the following historical trends?

   A. The social effects of industrialization
   B. The rise of nationalism
   C. Imperial expansion
   D. Cultural changes in a material age

6. The authors of this document made which of the following assumptions?

   A. The introduction of machines did not increase economic productivity.
   B. The economic well-being of the city and region was tied to its inhabitants having employment.
   C. Having large families was economically advantageous.
   D. The working class was lazy and tended toward idleness.

Questions 7–9 relate to the following excerpt from a poem:

Take up the White Man's burden—
Send forth the best ye breed—
Go bind your sons to exile
To serve your captives' need;
To wait in heavy harness,
On fluttered folk and wild—
Your new-caught, sullen peoples,
Half-devil and half-child.

. . .

Take up the White Man's burden—
The savage wars of peace—
Fill full the mouth of Famine
And bid the sickness cease;
And when your goal is nearest
The end for others sought . . .
Watch sloth and heathen Folly
Bring all your hopes to naught.

Rudyard Kipling, *The White Man's Burden*, 1899

7. Based on this poem, Kipling's conception of the British imperial mission could best be summed up as which of the following?
   A. A difficult but necessary task
   B. A ruthless exercise of power
   C. A glorious, religious responsibility
   D. A hopeless task with no purpose

8. The poem describes which kind of attitude toward the native peoples who were under the rule or influence of the British Empire?
   A. They are "exiled sons" of the British race.
   B. While "savage," they fight wars for the sake of a lasting peace.
   C. They are ready for conversion to Christianity.
   D. They are the product of a less-civilized and less-developed civilization.

9. It is generally acknowledged that Kipling fashioned *The White Man's Burden* to address the subject of the American colonization of the Philippines, which the United States had recently won from Spain in the Spanish-American War. With that information in mind, what message can Kipling be said to be offering the Americans in this excerpt?
   A. A reminder of the responsibility of advanced civilizations to bring the benefits of modern civilization to less-developed peoples
   B. A warning to avoid the war and hardships of imperialism
   C. An exhortation to Christianize the heathen peoples of the world
   D. An ironic presentation of the sheer folly of imperialism

Questions 10–12 refer to the engraving below:

William Hogarth, *Marriage à la Mode (The Marriage Contract), Plate 1*, 1745

10. The scene depicted in the engraving refers to which manifestation of social change in the eighteenth century?

    A. The marriage of older men to younger women
    B. The liquidation of art collections by a cash-poor aristocracy
    C. The combining, through marriage, of aristocratic status and bourgeois wealth
    D. The movement to allow Protestant churchmen to marry

11. The engraving is an example of which of the following developments in eighteenth-century art?

    A. Artists' abandonment of realistic representation
    B. Artists' criticism of social practices through satire
    C. Artists' creation of flattering portraits for rich patrons
    D. The continued development of landscape

12. Which of the following is an accurate summation of the kind of commentary Hogarth was attempting?

    A. The practice of selling art to foreigners leads to cultural bankruptcy.
    B. The practice of painting flattering portraits of the rich will be the death of true art.
    C. The practice of economically motivated marriages of convenience is morally repugnant and bound to bring misery.
    D. The marrying of aristocratic status to bourgeois wealth will solidify the future of the realm.

Questions 13–14 refer to the following quotation:

The various modes of worship which prevailed in the Roman world were all considered by the people as equally true; by the philosopher as equally false; and by the magistrate as equally useful.

Edward Gibbon, *The Decline and Fall of the Roman Empire*, 1776–1788

13. The interpretation of the state of religious belief in ancient Rome by the eighteenth-century English historian Edward Gibbon might be offered as evidence for which of the following?

    A. The clergy's monopoly on academic scholarship in eighteenth-century Britain
    B. The hatred of all things Roman by British scholars in the eighteenth century
    C. The spread of religious skepticism among the educated elite of Britain in the eighteenth century
    D. The lack of sources available to the eighteenth-century scholar for the study of ancient Roman civilization

14. Gibbon's interpretation of the state of religious worship in ancient Rome could be best summarized how?

    A. In ancient Rome, religious worship was decentralized and tended to vary with one's social position.
    B. In ancient Rome, religious worship was the source of much social tension and turmoil.
    C. In ancient Rome, religious worship was homogeneous and highly centralized.
    D. In ancient Rome, religious worship was revolutionized by the introduction of Christianity.

Questions 15–17 refer to the following map:

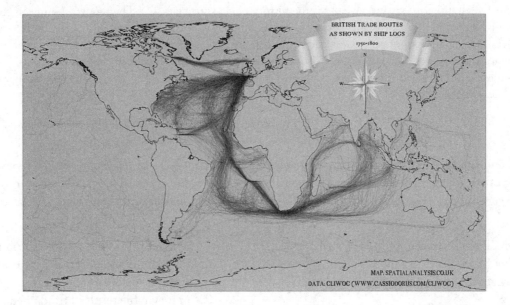

15. The map above was constructed by drawing a thin line for each voyage recorded in British trade ship logs between 1750 and 1800. As a result, the darker shaded areas record the most heavily traveled routes. Which of the following conclusions could be drawn from the evidence provided by this map?

    A. British ships did not sail along the west coast of Africa during this period.
    B. British ships did not sail the Atlantic Ocean during this period.
    C. British ships did not sail the Pacific Ocean during this period.
    D. British ships did not sail in the Indian Ocean during this period.

16. The information provided by the map could be used as evidence to support which of the following assertions?

    A. British ships frequented a northwest passage through North American waters into the Pacific Ocean.
    B. China was a frequent destination of British trade ships.
    C. British trade ships frequented the Mediterranean Sea during this period.
    D. A Triangle of Trade connected Britain, North America, and the west coast of Africa.

17. The information provided by the map could be used as evidence to support which of the following assertions?

    A. British trade ships of this period reached trade ports in India by sailing southward around the horn of Africa and into the Indian Ocean.
    B. British trade ships of this period transported slaves from western Africa to the New World.
    C. British trade ships of this period reached India by sailing west through the Mediterranean Sea and through the Suez Canal into the Indian Ocean.
    D. British trade ships of this period did not travel to India.

Questions 18–20 refer to the following passage:

The history of all hitherto existing societies is the history of class struggles. . . . The modern bourgeois society that has sprouted from the ruins of feudal society has not done away with class antagonisms. It has but established new classes, new conditions of oppression, new forms of struggle in place of the old ones. Our epoch, the epoch of the bourgeoisie, possesses, however, this distinctive feature: it has simplified the class antagonisms. Society as a whole is more and more splitting up into two great hostile camps, into two great classes, directly facing each other: Bourgeoisie and Proletariat.

Karl Marx and Friedrich Engels, *The Communist Manifesto*, 1848

18. Marx and Engels would be most inclined to view which of the following developments as a significant event in European history?

   A. The War of the Roses
   B. The French Revolution of 1789 to 1793
   C. The Seven Years' War
   D. Britain's Glorious Revolution of 1688

19. *The Communist Manifesto* can be understood as an example of the influence of which mode of modern European thinking?

   A. The Oxford Movement
   B. Materialism and economic determinism
   C. Hegelian idealism
   D. The rationalism of the Scottish Enlightenment

20. A follower of Marx and Engels's view of history would argue that an all-out war between the bourgeoisie and the proletariat classes was

   A. a destructive development that could be avoided through the study of philosophy.
   B. a possibility that should be encouraged in order to foster progress.
   C. an inevitable result of fundamental economic change.
   D. an example of history repeating itself.

Questions 21–23 refer to the following quotation:

1848 was the decisive year of German, and so of European, history: it recapitulated Germany's past and inspired Germany's future. . . . Never has there been a revolution so inspired by a limitless faith in the power of ideas; never has a revolution so discredited the power of ideas in its result. The success of the revolution discredited conservative ideas; the failure of the revolution discredited liberal ideas. After it, nothing remained but the idea of Force, and this idea stood at the helm of German history from then on. For the first time since 1521, the German people stepped on to the centre of the German stage only to miss their cue once more. German history reached its turning-point and failed to turn. This was the fateful essence of 1848.

A. J. P. Taylor, *The Course of German History*, 1945

21. What is the subject of Taylor's analysis?

   A. The Industrial Revolution in the context of German history
   B. The failure of the revolutions of 1848
   C. The rise of the Nazi Party in Germany
   D. The importance of the revolutions of 1848 in modern German history

22. Taylor argues that the most important effect of the political revolutions of 1848 was

   A. the failure to bring about a change in the ruling class.
   B. the demonstration of the power of ideas.
   C. the discrediting of both conservative and liberal political ideology.
   D. the creation of the idea of a modern police force.

23. Why might it be important to note that Taylor was writing his analysis in 1945?

  A. A historian writing at the end of World War II might be inclined to look for, and find, the origins of perceived German belligerence.
  B. A historian writing in 1945 would be dead now, and therefore, his analysis is irrelevant.
  C. Historical analysis written in 1945 is "out of date," and one should look for a more recent book.
  D. A historian writing at the end of World War II would be looking for the origins of the Cold War.

Questions 24–26 refer to the following passage:

Perestroika [Restructuring] is an urgent necessity arising from the profound processes of development in our social-ist society. This society is ripe for change. It has long been yearning for it. Any delay in beginning *perestroika* could have led to an exacerbated internal situation in the near future, which, to put it bluntly, would have been fraught with serious social, economic, and political crises.

Mikhail Gorbachev, *Perestroika: New Thinking for Our Country and the World*, 1987

24. What was Gorbachev's primary justification for *perestroika*?

  A. A restructuring of the socialist society of the Soviet Union was inevitable.
  B. A restructuring of the socialist society of the Soviet Union would exacerbate the current situation.
  C. A restructuring of the socialist society of the Soviet Union was necessary in order to avoid a crisis.
  D. A restructuring of socialist society was nec-essary in order to avoid the collapse of the Soviet Union.

25. Gorbachev believed that

  A. the problems that required *perestroika* were the fault of capitalist enemies of socialism.
  B. the problems that required *perestroika* were internal to the development of socialist society.
  C. a socialist society could not work.
  D. a socialist society could not coexist with capitalism.

26. Gorbachev argued that which of the following was true?

  A. The need for *perestroika* had come upon Soviet society suddenly.
  B. The need for *perestroika* had been exaggerated.
  C. The need for *perestroika* was long in the making.
  D. The time for *perestroika* had passed.

Questions 27–29 refer to the following passage:

"It's come! It's posted at the district mayor's office," a passerby shouted at me as he ran. I reached the *Rue Drout* in one leap. . . . I read the message at a glance. . . . "The First Day of Mobilization Will Be Sunday, August 2 [1914]." . . . It was an announcement to a million and a half Frenchmen. . . . War! . . . Dead tired but exhilarated, I got back to [my newspaper's office] and burst into the office of Georges Clemenceau, our chief. "What is Paris saying?" he asked me. "It's singing, sir!" "It will be all right then," [Clemenceau replied].

Roland Doregelès, *After 50 Years*, c. 1965

27. According to Doregelès, how did people react to mobilization?

   A. Mobilization for war in 1914 was greeted with great skepticism in Paris.
   B. Mobilization for war in 1914 was greeted with great skepticism all across Europe.
   C. Mobilization for war in 1914 was greeted with great enthusiasm all across Europe.
   D. Mobilization for war in 1914 was greeted with great enthusiasm in Paris.

28. From the passage, one may infer that Doregelès

   A. shared Paris's excitement about the advent of war.
   B. was disgusted that his city should be excited about the advent of war.
   C. was frightened that his city should be excited about the advent of war.
   D. had grave doubts about France's ability to win the coming war.

29. According to the passage, Clemenceau

   A. was disgusted to hear that Paris was reacting with joy at the advent of war.
   B. had grave doubts about France's ability to win a war against Germany.
   C. would one day serve as prime minister of France.
   D. was relieved to hear that Paris was reacting with joy at the advent of war.

Questions 30–31 refer to the following passage:

For the catastrophe of 1914 the Germans are responsible. . . . Germany, in this matter, was unfortunate enough to allow herself (in spite of her skill at dissimulation) to be betrayed into an excess of candour by her characteristic tendency to go to extremes. *Deutschland über alles. Germany above everything!* . . . There you have the ultimate framework of an old but childish race.

Georges Clemenceau, *Grandeur and Misery of Victory*, 1930

30. Clemenceau demonstrated what feelings toward the Germans?

   A. He blamed Germany for the Great Depression.
   B. He blamed Germany for World War I.
   C. He blamed Germany for World War II.
   D. He blamed Germany for the Franco-Prussian War.

31. Clemenceau, referring to the German national anthem, concluded which of the following?

   A. The Lyrics from the popular song *Deutschland über alles* (which eventually became the German national anthem) showed the reason Germany started the war.
   B. The Lyrics from the popular song *Deutschland über alles* (which eventually became the German national anthem) were evidence of Germany's aggressive attitude.
   C. The reason Germany lost the war was that it was betrayed from within.
   D. Germany provided the ultimate framework for modern warfare.

Questions 32–33 refer to the following quotation:

What is tolerance? . . . We are full of weakness and errors; let us mutually pardon our follies. This is the last law of nature. . . . Of all religions, the Christian ought doubtless to inspire the most tolerance, although hitherto the Christians have been the most intolerant of all men.

Voltaire, *Philosophic Letters on the English*, 1733

32. Voltaire was participating in what cultural movement?

    A. The Scientific Revolution
    B. The Reformation
    C. The Enlightenment
    D. The Romantic Movement

33. From the quotation, what becomes clear about Voltaire?

    A. Voltaire was an atheist.
    B. Tolerance was a value of the Enlightenment.
    C. Voltaire believed tolerance violated the laws of nature.
    D. Voltaire believed tolerance was uniquely English.

Questions 34–36 refer to the following passage:

For a long time, educated Germans answered it in the positive, initially by laying claim to a special German mission, then, after the collapse of 1945, by criticizing Germany's deviation from the West. Today, the negative view is predominant. Germany did not, according to the now prevailing opinion, differ from the great European nations to an extent that would justify speaking of a "unique German path." And, in any case, no country on earth ever took what can be described as the "normal path."

Heinrich August Winkler, *Germany: The Long Road West*, Volume 1, 2006

34. What does the passage indicate about the author's point of view?

    A. The notion of a unique German path in history has never been the prevailing public opinion in Germany.
    B. Winkler advocates a Marxist view of German history.
    C. There has been a long-standing debate in Germany about the existence of a unique German path in history.
    D. The question of a unique German path in history has been answered once and for all.

35. Before 1945,

    A. there was significant belief in a unique German mission in history.
    B. almost no one believed in a unique German mission in history.
    C. the historian Heinrich August Winkler argued that there was a unique German mission in history.
    D. the historian Heinrich August Winkler opposed the notion that there was a unique German mission in history.

36. The belief that Germany had a unique mission in history

    A. resulted from Germany's defeat in World War II.
    B. was unaffected by Germany's defeat in World War II.
    C. was proven correct by Germany's defeat in World War II.
    D. was discredited by Germany's defeat in World War II.

Questions 37–39 refer to the following poster from Great Britain during World War II:

38. What change does the poster reflect?

    A. Women were put in charge of factories in Great Britain during World War II.
    B. Women made up a significant portion of the British military during World War II.
    C. Women were happy to join the industrial workforce in Great Britain during World War II.
    D. Women were involved in the production of munitions during World War II.

39. What was the purpose or focus of propaganda in Great Britain during World War II?

    A. It focused predominately on minority groups.
    B. It had the same goals as German propaganda.
    C. It aimed at making women feel like they were an important part of the war effort.
    D. It gave an unrealistic picture of the opportunities open to women.

37. What is the overall message of this poster?

    A. The wartime needs of Britain led to the conscription of women into the military.
    B. The wartime economy of Britain required women to do factory work.
    C. Women working in factories with men led to social change in Britain.
    D. Wartime needs led to women joining the industrial workforce of Great Britain for the first time.

Questions 40–42 refer to the following passage:

Having by our late labours and hazards made it appear to the world how high a rate we value our freedom, and God having so far owned our cause, as to deliver the enemies thereof into our hands: We do now hold ourselves bound in mutual duty to each other, to take the best care we can for the future, to avoid both the danger of returning into a slavish condition, and the chargeable remedy of another war. . . . In order whereunto we declare:

1. That matters of Religion, and the ways of God's worship are not at all entrusted by us to any human power . . .

2. That the matter of [compelling] and constraining any of us to serve in the wars is against our freedom . . .

3. That in all laws made, or to be made, every person may be bound alike. . . .

Leveller Army Officers, *An Agreement of the People,* 1647

40. According to the passage, one may infer that the authors of the passage recently fought in which of the following?

    A. The Seven Years' War
    B. The American War for Independence
    C. The English Civil War
    D. The Battle of Agincourt

41. What were the officers fighting for?

    A. They were fighting for religious freedom.
    B. They were defending the monarchy in the English Civil War.
    C. They were fighting to establish a republic.
    D. They were fighting for independence from England.

42. According to the authors, what was the end goal of the war?

    A. To form a ruling body of England
    B. To establish equality under the law in England
    C. An end to hostilities
    D. Abolition of slavery

Questions 43–45 refer to the following passage:

We have, by this perpetual and irrevocable edict, established and proclaimed:

"First, that the recollection of everything done be one party or the other . . . during all the preceding period of troubles, remain obliterated and forgotten, as if no such things had ever happened. . . .

"We ordain that the Catholic Apostolic and Roman religion shall be restored and reestablished in all places and localities of this our kingdom and countries subject to our sway, where the exercise of the same has been interrupted, in order that it may be peaceably and freely exercised, without any trouble or hindrance. . . .

"And in order to leave no occasion for troubles or differences between our subjects, we have permitted, and herewith permit, those of the said religion called Reformed to live and abide in all the cities and places of this our kingdom and countries of our sway, and without being annoyed, molested, or compelled to do anything in the matter of religion contrary to their consciences. . . ."

Henry IV of France, *The Edict of Nantes*, 1598

43. From the passage, one may infer that

   A. Henry IV was a Catholic.
   B. Henry IV was a Protestant.
   C. before 1598, France had been free of religious conflict.
   D. before 1598, France was stricken with religious conflict.

44. *The Edict of Nantes* proclaimed which of the following?

   A. The Catholic Church in France was banned.
   B. The Catholic Church could exist in France.
   C. The Catholic Church is the one true Church.
   D. The Catholic Church caused too much trouble and hindrance in France.

45. Henry IV proposed which of the following?

   A. Banning Protestants from France
   B. Allowing Protestants to be able to live peacefully in his kingdom
   C. His own conversion to Roman Catholicism
   D. His own conversion to Protestantism

Questions 46–48 refer to the following passage:

The assumption by a government of the office of Reliever-general to the poor is necessarily forbidden by the principle that a government cannot rightly do anything more than protect. In demanding from a citizen contributions for the mitigation of distress . . . the state is . . . reversing its function. . . . To enforce the fundamental law—to take care that every man has freedom to do all that he wills, provided he infringes not the equal freedom of any other man. . . . [But that] is quite a separate thing from insuring him satisfaction. . . .

  The poverty of the incapable, the distresses that come upon the imprudent, the starvation of the idle, and those shoulderings aside of the weak by the strong . . . are the decrees of a large, farseeing benevolence. . . . When regarded not separately, but in connection with the interests of universal humanity, these harsh fatalities are seen to be full of the highest beneficence.

Herbert Spencer, *Social Statistics: Survival of the Fittest Applied to Humankind*, 1851

46. Spencer was an advocate of which nineteenth-century political philosophy?

    A. Conservatism
    B. Anarchism
    C. Liberalism
    D. Socialism

47. Which of the following best represents Spencer's underlying belief?

    A. He opposed the use of tax money to provide aid to the poor.
    B. He challenged the government's right to tax the people.
    C. He believed that the government should do more than merely protect its people.
    D. He believed that working people should unite for a common cause.

48. Spencer supported which social philosophy?

    A. Utopian socialism
    B. Social conservatism
    C. Romanticism
    D. Social Darwinism

Questions 49–52 refer to the following passage:

The principle which regulates the existing social relations between the two sexes—the legal subordination of one sex to the other—is wrong in itself, and now one of the chief hindrances to human improvement. . . . The masters of all other slaves rely, for maintaining obedience on fear. . . . The masters of women wanted more than simple obedience, and they turned their whole force of education to effect their purpose. All women are brought up from the very earliest years in the belief that their ideal of character is the very opposite of that of men; not self-will and government by self-control, but submission and yielding to the control of others. . . . If the general principle of social and economic science is . . . true, we ought to act as if we believed it, and not to ordain that to be born a girl instead of a boy . . . shall decide the person's position through all life."

John Stuart Mill, *The Subjection of Women*, 1869

49. Mill was an advocate of which nineteenth-century political philosophy?

    A. Socialism
    B. Conservatism
    C. Anarchism
    D. Liberalism

50. Mill also advocated which of the following?

    A. The abolition of slavery
    B. The maintenance of a patriarchal social organization
    C. The reform of women's education
    D. An end to arranged marriages

51. Mill subscribed to which view of human nature?

  A. People are born evil and corrupt.
  B. People are generally good and will do the right thing most times.
  C. Men and women have natures that are substantially different from one another.
  D. People are born *tabula rasa*—a blank slate.

52. According to the passage, Mill advocated which of the following?

  A. The abolition of marriage
  B. Equal opportunity for women
  C. Social engineering of a better society
  D. Social Darwinism

Questions 53–55 refer to the following passage:

As with a Commander of the Army, or leader of any enterprise, so it is with the mistress of the house. Her spirit will be seen through the whole establishment; and just in proportion as she performs her duties intelligently and thoroughly, so will her domestics follow in her path. Of all of those acquirements, which more particularly belong to the feminine character, there are none which take a higher rank, in our estimation, than such as enter into a knowledge of household duties; for on these are perpetually dependent the happiness, comfort, and well-being of the family.

Isabella Beeton, *Book of Household Management*, 1861

53. Beeton's book treats which subject?

  A. The role of women in army regiments
  B. The running of a school for domestic servants
  C. The running of a school for girls
  D. The role of a woman in running her own domestic household

54. Beeton believed that

  A. women were better suited than men for the task of household management.
  B. women were better suited than men to run schools.
  C. men were better suited than women for the task of household management.
  D. men were better suited than women to run schools.

55. Beeton was prompted to write the book because of which of the following situations?

  A. Women held considerable power and responsibility in the public sphere of social life.
  B. Women were denied power and responsibility in the public sphere of social life.
  C. Women held considerable power and responsibility within the domestic sphere of social life.
  D. Women were denied power and responsibility within the domestic sphere of social life.

Go on to Section I, Part B. ➔

AP European History Practice Exam 1

SECTION I, PART B

Short-Answer Questions
Recommended Time—40 minutes

Directions: The short-answer section consists of three questions to be answered in a recommended time of **40 minutes**. Briefly answer ALL PARTS of three of the following four questions. Answer Questions 1 and 2; then choose to answer either Question 3 or Question 4. Be sure to write in complete sentences; outlines, phrases, and bullets will not be accepted.

Answer all parts of the following question.

1. In history, science and society are intertwined.

a) Identify ONE factor that contributed to the development of the Scientific Revolution; explain how it contributed to the development of the Scientific Revolution.

b) Identify ONE key figure in the Scientific Revolution and describe how he or she challenged traditional thought about the world.

c) Identify ONE effect that the Scientific Revolution had on later European political thought; explain how it affected European political thought.

Answer all parts of the following question.

2. Historians have frequently compared the French Revolution (1789–1799) and the Russian Revolution (1917–1924), arguing that they are fundamentally similar.

a) Briefly identify TWO pieces of evidence that support this comparison, and explain how they support the comparison.

b) Briefly identify ONE piece of evidence that undermines this argument, and explain how it undermines this argument.

Use the passages below to answer either Question 3 or Question 4.

By moon or star-light, thus, from my first dawn
Of childhood, did ye love to intertwine
The passions that build up our human soul
Not with the mean and vulgar works of man,
But with high objects, with eternal things,
With life and Nature, purifying thus
The elements of feeling and of thought
And sanctifying by such discipline
Both pain and fear, until we recognize
A grandeur in the beatings of the heart.

      William Wordsworth, *The Prelude*

There is a pleasure in the pathless woods,
. . . a rapture on the lonely shore.
There is a society where none intrudes
By the deep sea, and music in its roar;
I love not man the less, but nature more.

      George Gordon Lord Byron, *Childe Harold*

3. Answer Parts A and B.

a) Briefly explain ONE aspect of Romantic thought as shown in the poetic excerpts.

b) Briefly explain TWO reasons for the rise of the Romantic Movement.

Use the passage below to answer all parts of the question that follows.

It is a truth which admits not a doubt, that the comforts and well-being of the poor cannot be permanently secured without some regard on their part, or some effort on the part of the legislature, to regulate the increase of their numbers, and to render less frequent among them early and improvident marriages. The operation of the system of poor laws has been indirectly contrary to this. They have rendered restraint superfluous, and have invited imprudence, by offering it a portion of the wages of prudence and industry.

David Ricardo, *Principles of Political Economy and Taxation*, 1817

4. Answer Parts A and B.

a) Briefly explain ONE reason that the passage can be identified with classical liberalism.

b) Briefly describe TWO factors that explain the rise to prominence of classical liberalism at the time at which the passage was written.

STOP. End of Section I.

AP European History Practice Exam 1

SECTION II, PART A

Document-Based Question
Recommended Time—60 minutes

Directions: The document-based section consists of one question to be answered in a recommended time of **60 minutes**. The following question is based on documents 1–7 provided below. (The documents have been edited for the purpose of this exercise.) The historical thinking skills that this question is designed to test include contextualization, synthesis, historical argumentation, and the use of historical evidence. Your response should be based on your knowledge of the topic and your analysis of the documents.

Write a well-integrated essay that does the following:

- States an appropriate thesis that addresses all parts of the question
- Supports that thesis with evidence from at least six of the seven documents and your knowledge of European history beyond these documents
- Analyzes most of the documents in terms of their purpose, point of view, argument, limitations, format, intended audience, and/or social context
- Places your argument in the context of appropriate broader regional, national, or global developments

Question: Compare and contrast the ideologies presented below concerning the proper form and role of government in society.

Document 1

Source: Samuel Smiles, *Self-Help*, 1859

"Even the best institutions can give man no active aid. Perhaps the utmost they can do is to leave him free to develop himself and improve his individual condition. But in all times men have been prone to believe that their happiness and well-being were to be secured by means of institutions rather than by their own conduct. Hence the value of legislation as an agent in human advancement has always been greatly over-estimated."

Document 2

Source: Joseph de Maistre, *Essay on the Generative Principle of Political Constitutions*, 1809

"One of the greatest errors of a century which professed them all was to believe that a political constitution could be created and written *a priori*, whereas reason and experience unite in proving that a constitution is a divine work and that precisely the most fundamental and essentially constitutional of a nation's laws could not possibly be written."

Document 3

Source: John Stuart Mill, *On Liberty*, 1859

". . . [T]he sole end for which mankind are warranted, individually or collectively, in interfering with the liberty of action of any of their number, is self-protection. That the only purpose for which power can be rightfully exercised over any member of a civilised community, against his will, is to prevent harm to others."

Document 4

Source: Prince Clement von Metternich, secret memorandum to Emperor Alexander I of Russia, 1820

"Presumption makes of every man the guide of his own belief, the arbiter of laws according to which he is pleased to govern himself, or to allow someone else to govern him and his neighbors; it makes him, in short, the sole judge of his own faith, his actions and the principles according to which he guides them. . . . Placed beyond the passions which agitate society, it is in the days of trial chiefly that [monarchs] are called upon to despoil realities of their false appearances, and to show themselves as they are, fathers invested with the authority belonging by right to the heads of families, to prove that, in the days of mourning, they know how to be just, wise, and therefore strong, and that they will not abandon the people whom they ought to govern to be the sport of factions, to error and its consequences, which must involve the loss of society."

Document 5

Source: Karl Marx and Friedrich Engels, *The Communist Manifesto*, 1848

"The proletariat will use its political supremacy to wrest, by degrees, all capital from the bourgeoisie, to centralize all instruments of production in the hands of the State, i.e., of the proletariat organized as the ruling class; and to increase the total productive forces as rapidly as possible."

Document 6

Source: Eduard Bernstein, *Evolutionary Socialism*, 1909

"I set myself against the notion that we have to expect shortly a collapse of the bourgeois economy, and that social democracy should be induced by the prospect of such an imminent, great, social catastrophe to adapt its tactics to that assumption. . . . [T]he conquest of political power necessitates the possession of political rights; and the most important problem of tactics which German social democracy has at this moment to solve, appears to me to be to devise the best way for the extension of the political and economic rights of the German working classes."

Document 7

Source: Peter Kropotkin, *Anarchism: Its Philosophy and Ideal*, 1898

"When we ask for the abolition of the State and its organs we are always told that we dream of a society composed of men better than they are in reality. But no; a thousand times no. All we ask is that men should not be made worse than they are."

Go on to Section II, Part B. ➜

AP European History Practice Exam 1

SECTION II, PART B

Long-Essay Question
Recommended Time—40 minutes

Directions: The long-essay section consists of one question to be answered in a recommended time of **40 minutes**. Write an essay that responds to ONE of the following three questions.

Question 1: Analyze the major social effects of the Industrial Revolution.

Question 2: Explain the ways in which the development of mass politics contributed to the New Imperialism of the late nineteenth century.

Question 3: Identify and explain two examples of the contributing role of the arts in determining a "climate of opinion."

End of Practice Exam

› Answers and Explanations

Section I, Part A: Multiple-Choice Questions

1. **A.** The reference to the pride and confidence in the abilities of man and the date of publication both tell you that this is a passage from a Renaissance thinker. B is incorrect because such pride would be frowned upon by advocates of the Protestant Reformation. C is incorrect because the passage does not refer to knowledge about the natural world and because the Scientific Revolution was a seventeenth-century phenomenon. D is incorrect because the Enlightenment was an eighteenth-century development.

2. **D.** The passage says that humans are the most fortunate creatures because, unlike other creatures whose nature is limited, a man is "allowed to be whatever he chooses to be!" A is incorrect because the passage does not mention a soul. B is incorrect because the passage does not mention man's foreknowledge of death. C is incorrect because the passage does not mention heaven.

3. **C.** The passage explicitly says that man is worthy of admiration, thus one can easily infer that Pico rejects the notion that man is *un*worthy of admiration. A is incorrect because the passage states that man alone has an unlimited potential; thus, one may infer that Pico accepts, rather than rejects, the notion that man is unique. B is incorrect because one may infer from the passage that God, having given man an unlimited nature, intended him to strive to achieve, and because striving to achieve is a value of Renaissance humanists like Pico. D is incorrect because one cannot infer anything from the passage about humans' ability to become the equal of God.

4. **C.** The petitioners are clearly objecting to the elimination of their traditional laboring jobs by the introduction of machines. A is incorrect because the petitioners are asking for a return to *traditional* modes of work. B is incorrect because there is no evidence in this document that the Leeds woolen workers were resorting to the violent destruction of machines that characterized the Luddite movement. D is incorrect because there is no evidence in the document for an increase in the use of child labor; rather, the document expresses concern about the loss of apprenticeship opportunities.

5. **A.** The replacing of workers and traditional labor techniques by machines was a prominent social effect of industrialization. B is incorrect because the document makes no reference to nationalist concerns. C is incorrect because the document makes no reference to the empire or its expansion. D is incorrect because the concerns of the document are about a specific social effect—the elimination of jobs, not broader cultural issues.

6. **B.** The document makes the argument that unemployment would lead to the depopulation of the region, which in turn would cause the collapse of the local economy. A is incorrect because the document explicitly acknowledges that productivity is increased by the introduction of machines. C is incorrect because the document makes no reference to the size of families. D is incorrect because the document is an appeal for continued work and mentions "idleness" only as an undesirable outcome of unemployment.

7. **A.** The metaphor of a burden and images of a "heavy harness" and "savage wars of peace" all indicate difficult but necessary work. B is incorrect because none of the images in the poem implies ruthlessness. C is incorrect because the excerpt contains no images that are glorious or religious. D is incorrect because, though the excerpt does refer to hopes coming to naught, the overall theme of a burden implies an important purpose that justifies the effort.

8. **D.** Phrases like "half-devil, half-child," and "sloth and heathen" imply that these are peoples of a backward or less-developed civilization. A and B are incorrect because both of the lines they refer to are describing the British imperialists, not the people over whom the British are ruling. C is incorrect because nothing in the excerpt suggests that the natives are "ready" for conversion.

9. **A.** The excerpt contains both a message of responsibility and a warning about great costs. B is incorrect because the excerpt exhorts the Americans to "take up the . . . burden," not avoid it. C is incorrect because the excerpt does not call for the Christianizing of other civilizations. D is incorrect because the poem is devoid of irony; it considers the burden of imperial rule to be heavy but not folly.

10. **C.** Hogarth was commenting on the phenomenon of cash-strapped aristocrats marrying their sons to daughters of wealthy bourgeois businessmen in order to ensure a combination of wealth and status in the next generation of the family. A is incorrect because the engraving depicts two fathers haggling over the details of marrying their son and daughter. B is incorrect because the subject of the engraving is not the sale of art. D is incorrect because the subject of the engraving is not churchmen marrying.

11. **B.** Hogarth was criticizing the practice of economically motivated marriage through a satirically humorous depiction. A is incorrect because the scene is depicted realistically. C is incorrect because the depiction of the aristocrats in the scene is not flattering. D is incorrect because the image is not a landscape.

12. **C.** The sight of two fathers treating their children as economic assets while the clergyman leers at the bride-to-be shows Hogarth's moral repugnance. The mutual lack of interest shown by the future bride and groom foreshadows the misery that will follow (and which Hogarth depicts in the rest of this series of engravings). A is incorrect because the subject of the engraving is not the sale of art to foreigners. B is incorrect because portrait painting and patronage are not the subject of the engraving. D is incorrect because the scene depicted does not inspire confidence in the future of the realm.

13. **C.** There was a spread of religious skepticism among the educated elite in Britain in the eighteenth century, and the possibility of a skeptical and flexible attitude toward religion is implied in Gibbon's interpretation. A is incorrect because Gibbon was not a clergyman, and the clergy did not have a monopoly on scholarship in eighteenth-century Britain. B is incorrect because the excerpt implies no hatred of Roman religious attitudes. D is incorrect because one can tell nothing about the sources available from the excerpt.

14. **A.** Gibbon's interpretation refers to various attitudes toward religious worship that correlated with the social position of the worshipper. B is incorrect because Gibbon makes no reference to social tension or turmoil. C is incorrect because Gibbon refers to various kinds of religious worship, which implies the opposite of homogeneity and centralization. D is incorrect because Gibbon makes no reference to the introduction of Christianity in this excerpt.

15. **C.** There are no lines on the map that indicate British sailing routes in the Pacific Ocean. A, B, and D are incorrect because there are lines on the map that indicate British sailing routes along the west coast of Africa, in the Atlantic Ocean, and in the Indian Ocean.

16. **D.** The dark shaded lines connecting Britain, North America, and the west coast of Africa indicate the existence of such a Triangle of Trade. A is incorrect because no lines travel through North American waters to the Pacific Ocean. B is incorrect because there are very few lines connecting Britain and China. C is incorrect because there are no lines indicating British trade voyages in the Mediterranean during this period.

17. **A.** The heavy blue shading shows a high frequency of British trade ship voyages southward, around the horn of Africa, and to India via the Indian Ocean. B is incorrect because the map offers no evidence for assertions about the cargo that ships carried. The map shows that no British trade ships sailed west through the Mediterranean Sea, and because the map indicates that there is no Suez Canal during this period. D is incorrect because the map clearly

provides evidence for numerous voyages to India by British ships during this period.

18. **B.** Marx and Engels viewed the French Revolution as a significant effect of the economic change that created a powerful bourgeoisie. A, C, and D are incorrect because they are merely political struggles between members of a stable ruling aristocracy.

19. **B.** Marx and Engels's belief that all history is the struggle of economic classes is materialist, and their belief in the inevitability of historical events as a reaction to economic change is an example of economic determinism. A is incorrect because the Oxford Movement was a movement of High Church Anglicans in England whose members argued for the return to lost Christian traditions of faith. C is incorrect because, while Marx makes use of the Hegelian dialectic, he turns it on its head, emphasizing materialist, economic causes, instead of the role of ideas, in history. D is incorrect because the economic ideas of the thinkers of the Scottish Enlightenment, such as Adam Smith, emphasized the importance of individual self-interest and action, whereas Marx emphasized the importance of economic classes.

20. **C.** Marx and Engels's view of history was that class conflict and the events that manifested from it were the inevitable consequences of economic change. A and B are incorrect because the economic determinism that characterized Marx and Engels's thought convinced them that class warfare was inevitable, not a possibility which could be avoided. D is incorrect because the excerpt does not say anything about history repeating itself, and because Marx and Engels did not believe that history repeated itself.

21. **D.** The quotation is discussing the discrediting of political ideology in modern German history as a result of the revolutions of 1848 and their failure to bring about significant change. A is incorrect because the quotation does not discuss industrialization. B is incorrect because the quotation is not offering an analysis of the reasons why the revolutions failed but of the effects of that failure on modern German history. C is incorrect because the quotation does not analyze

the rise of the Nazi Party in Germany (even though there is an implied connection).

22. **C.** The quotation suggests that the most important long-term effect was the rise of "Force" as the only viable option in German political history, due to the discrediting of both the conservative and liberal political ideologies in the course of the revolutions of 1848. A is incorrect because, although the quotation notes that no change in who ruled was brought about *in* 1848, the thrust of the quotation is about the long-term effects of the revolutions of 1848 on German history. B is incorrect because, although the quotation notes that the early stages of the revolutions demonstrated the power of ideas, it argues that the long-term effect is a discrediting of that power. D is incorrect because the "Force" alluded to in the quotation is not a police force.

23. **A.** It is important to note the post–World War II context of a historical analysis that purports to find the roots of a German fascination with "Force" as a political ideology. B is incorrect because it is not the status of the historian, but the quality of his logic and evidence that one should consider. C is incorrect because, although the statement is in some general sense true, it is not particularly important to the reading of Taylor's analysis. D is incorrect because, although the statement may be true, it is not at all relevant to Taylor's analysis, which does not purport to find the roots of the Cold War.

24. **C.** The passage quotes Gorbachev as saying that *perestroika* (restructuring) was urgently necessary because delay would have exacerbated (worsened) the situation and led to crises. A is incorrect because the passage does not say that restructuring was inevitable. B is incorrect because the passage does not say that restructuring would exacerbate the situation, but rather that *delay* in restructuring would. D is incorrect because the passage does not go as far as to say that delay in restructuring would have caused the collapse of the Soviet Union.

25. **B.** In the passage Gorbachev states that the need for *perestroika* arose from the process of development in the socialist society in which he and his audience lived. A is incorrect because the passage

makes no mention of capitalist enemies. C is incorrect because *perestroika* was meant to allow a socialist society to develop successfully, and because the passage makes no mention of the failure of socialism. D is incorrect because the passage makes no mention of capitalism.

26. **C.** The passage quotes Gorbachev as saying that the time for *perestroika* was ripe and that people had yearned for change for a long time. A is incorrect because the passage says that people had yearned for change for a long time, and because it says nothing about a sudden crisis. B is incorrect because the document says nothing about the need for *perestroika* being exaggerated. D is incorrect because the document says the time for *perestroika* is ripe, not that it has passed.

27. **D.** Doregelès recalled that the people of Paris (thereby indicating that it is the reaction of the people of that city) were singing (a sign of enthusiasm). A is incorrect because Doregelès recalled that the people of Paris were singing (a sign of enthusiasm, not skepticism). B and C are incorrect because Doregelès recalled that the people of *Paris* were singing; one can infer nothing, therefore, about the rest of Europe.

28. **A.** Doregelès says that he was "exhilarated" (excitedly happy) by what he had seen and experienced. B is incorrect because nothing in the passage indicates that Doregelès was disgusted. C is incorrect because nothing in the passage indicates that Doregelès was frightened. D is incorrect because the passage gives no indication about how Doregelès thought France would fare in the war.

29. **D.** The passage tells us that Clemenceau reacted by saying, "It will be all right then," indicating that Clemenceau had some concern that the French public would react poorly. A is incorrect because nothing in the passage indicates that Clemenceau was disgusted. B is incorrect because there is nothing in the passage that indicates what Clemenceau thought of France's chances in the war. C is incorrect because nothing in the passage indicates that Clemenceau would serve as Prime Minister of France.

30. **B.** World War I began in 1914, and the passage clearly states that Clemenceau blames Germany for it. A is incorrect because the Great Depression began in 1929. C is incorrect because World War II began in 1939. D is incorrect because the Franco-Prussian War began in 1870.

31. **B.** The passage indicates that Clemenceau believes that the chauvinistic lyrics of *Deutschland über alles* reveal the German aggressiveness that caused the war. A is incorrect because the passage does not offer an argument or an opinion about the *reasons* Germany started the war. C is incorrect because the meaning of *betrayed* in the passage is "unwittingly revealed" and refers to Germany's intentions, not the outcome of the war. D is incorrect because the phrase *ultimate framework* refers to the German "race," not to modern warfare.

32. **C.** The date locates the passage in the eighteenth century (the century of the Enlightenment), the phrase *law of nature* is a key phrase from the Enlightenment, and Voltaire is a famous Enlightenment *philosophe*. A is incorrect because the Scientific Revolution was a seventeenth-century phenomenon, and because Voltaire is associated with the Enlightenment. B is incorrect because the Reformation was a sixteenth-century phenomenon, and because Voltaire is associated with the Enlightenment. D is incorrect because the Romantic Movement was an eighteenth-century phenomenon, and because Voltaire is associated with the Enlightenment.

33. **B.** Voltaire is known to be an Enlightenment *philosophe*, and the quotation asserts the necessity of tolerance. A is incorrect because, although it criticizes the behavior of Christians, it says nothing about Voltaire's religious beliefs (or lack thereof). C is incorrect because the quotation asserts that the imperfection of men is a natural law; it does not say that tolerance violates the laws of nature. D is incorrect because, although the quotation is from a letter praising English society, it does not say that tolerance is uniquely English.

34. **C.** The passage indicates that German public opinion on the existence of a unique German path in history shifted in 1945 and has shifted again "today" (when Winkler was writing in 2006); all of that indicates a long-standing debate. A is incorrect because the passage indicates that

the prevailing public opinion until "today" held that there was some sort of unique German path in history. B is incorrect because there is nothing Marxist about the existence of public belief in a unique German path in history. D is incorrect because the passage says nothing to indicate that Winkler believed that the question has been answered "once and for all."

35. **A.** In the first sentence of the passage, Winkler asserts that there was significant public belief in a special German mission. B is incorrect because, in the first sentence of the passage, Winkler asserts that there was significant public belief in a special German mission. C and D are incorrect because Winkler was not asserting or opposing anything in 1945; he wrote in 2006.

36. **D.** The passage indicates that Germany's defeat in World War II ("the collapse of 1945") led to a shift from asserting that Germany had a unique mission in history to a claim that Germany was unique in the way it had "deviated" from the rest of Western civilization. A is incorrect because the passage clearly indicates that public opinion on the existence of a unique German mission was changed by the collapse of 1945. B is incorrect because the passage clearly indicates that German public opinion on the question of its uniqueness was substantively affected by the collapse of 1945. C is incorrect because the passage indicates that public opinion was changed by the collapse of 1945, not "proven to be correct."

37. **B.** One can infer from this World War II–era poster that the wartime economy required women to do factory work. A is incorrect because the poster does not indicate that women were being conscripted. C is incorrect because the poster indicates nothing about the consequences of women and men working together in factories. D is incorrect because nothing in the poster indicates that this was the first time that women were part of Great Britain's industrial workforce.

38. **D.** The prevalence of tanks and aircraft seeming to emanate from the factory in the poster allow you to infer that women were used in the production of munitions in Great Britain during World War II. A is incorrect because one may infer nothing from the poster about who is "in

charge" of the factories. B is incorrect because one may infer nothing from the poster about the proportions of men and women in the military. C is incorrect because one may infer nothing from the poster about the emotional state of the women working in factories.

39. **C.** It is clear that the goal of the poster was to make women feel like they were important to the war effort. A is incorrect because women were not a minority group in Great Britain during World War II. B is incorrect; although its assertion that British and German propaganda had similar goals is probably true, it cannot be inferred from this British poster alone. D is incorrect because factory work during the war was available to women (and because the poster asserts nothing more than that).

40. **C.** The phrase "late labours and hazards," the reference to the delivering of the enemies of God into their hands, the date (1647), and the term "Leveller" all allow one to infer that the authors recently fought in the English Civil War. A is incorrect because the Seven Years' War was fought from 1756 to 1763. B is incorrect because the American War for Independence was fought from 1775 to 1782. D is incorrect because the Battle of Agincourt was fought in 1451.

41. **A.** The demand articulated by the passage, "That matters of Religion, and the ways of God's worship are not at all entrusted by us to any human power," allows one to infer that the authors of the passage fought for religious freedom. B is incorrect because the Levellers fought on the Parliamentary side, not the side of the monarchy, and because supporters of the monarchy would not be demanding any of the things the Levellers do in the passage. C is incorrect because nothing in the passage mentions the establishment of a republic. D is incorrect because the Levellers were English, and because the passage mentions nothing about independence.

42. **B.** The phrase, "That in all laws made, or to be made, every person may be bound alike," allows one to infer that the authors of the passage meant to establish equality under the law in England. A is incorrect because nothing in the passage indicates that the Levellers were

demanding to form a ruling body of England. C is incorrect because, at the time the passage was written, hostilities in the English Civil War had already ceased, and because nothing in the passage indicates a demand for the cessation of hostilities. D is incorrect because the authors were army officers, not slaves (the word *slavish* in the phrase, "the danger of returning into a slavish condition," is used as an analogy).

43. **D.** One can infer from the phrase, "the recollection of everything done by one party or the other . . . during all the preceding period of troubles," that Henry is trying to put an end to religious conflict in France. A and B are incorrect because one can infer nothing about Henry IV's own religion from the document. C is incorrect because the phrase, "the recollection of everything done by one party or the other . . . during all the preceding period of troubles," clearly indicates that there had been religious conflict in the period prior to 1598.

44. **B.** The reference to the restoration of the Catholic Church anywhere where it had been interrupted allows one to infer that Henry IV was assuring the existence of the Catholic Church in France. A is incorrect because the reference to the restoration of the Catholic Church anywhere where it had been interrupted shows that Henry IV was not abolishing the Catholic Church. C is incorrect because nothing in the passage allows one to infer that Henry IV believed or asserted that the Catholic Church was the one true Church. D is incorrect because nothing in the passage allows one to infer that Henry IV believed or asserted that the Catholic Church had caused too much trouble and hindrance.

45. **B.** The phrase, "herewith permit, those of the said religion pretended Reformed to live and abide in all the cities and places of this our kingdom and countries of our sway," allows one to infer that Henry IV intended for Protestants to be able to live peacefully in his kingdom. A is incorrect because the phrase, "herewith permit, those of the said religion pretended Reformed to live and abide in all the cities and places of this our kingdom and countries of our sway," shows that Henry IV

intended for Protestants to be able to live peacefully in his kingdom, not be banned from it. C and D are incorrect because nothing in the passage allows one to infer anything about Henry IV's religious conversion.

46. **C.** The statement in the passage, "To enforce the fundamental law—to take care that every man has freedom to do all that he wills, provided he infringes not the equal freedom of any other man," allows one to infer that Spencer was an advocate of nineteenth-century liberalism. A is incorrect because the passage makes no reference to the nineteenth-century conservative belief in the value of traditional customs and institutions. B is incorrect because nothing in the passage refers to the nineteenth-century anarchist belief that the government was the enemy of liberty. D is incorrect because nothing in the passage makes reference to the nineteenth-century socialist belief that competition should be replaced by cooperation.

47. **A.** The passage makes it clear that Spencer believed that to use tax money to aid the poor exceeded the bounds of the proper role of government and would do harm to the "universal interests of humanity." B is incorrect because the passage does not challenge the right of the government to tax its people. C is incorrect because the passage explicitly says that the government "cannot rightly do anything more than protect." D is incorrect because the passage makes no reference to people uniting.

48. **D.** The last paragraph of the passage articulates the basic belief of social Darwinism, that weeding out of the weak makes for a stronger, more prosperous society. A is incorrect because nothing in the passage makes any reference to the creation of the cooperative society called for by utopian socialism. B is incorrect because nothing in the passage refers to the upholding of traditional social customs called for by social conservatism. C is incorrect because nothing in the passage refers to the cultivation of emotion and sentiment called for by Romanticism.

49. **D.** The passage's reference to "hindrances to human improvement" allows one to infer that

Mill was an advocate of nineteenth-century liberalism. A is incorrect, because nothing in the passage makes reference to the nineteenth-century socialist belief that competition should be replaced by cooperation. B is incorrect because the passage makes no reference to the nineteenth-century conservative belief in the value of traditional customs and institutions. C is incorrect because nothing in the passage refers to the nineteenth-century anarchist belief that the government was the enemy of liberty.

50. **C.** The passage indicates that the cause of women's submission to men is the nature of women's early education; thus, one may infer that Mill advocated educational reform to reverse the condition. A is incorrect because the subject of the passage is the subjection of women; the word "slavery" is used metaphorically. C is incorrect because a patriarchal social hierarchy is based on the subjection of women; Mill's passage is dedicated to ending the subjection of women. D is incorrect because there is no reference to the institution of marriage in the passage.

51. **D.** The passage's notion that early education determines a person's character is consistent with a *tabula rasa*, or blank slate, theory of human nature. A is incorrect because nothing in the passage refers to a corrupt or evil nature of human beings. B is incorrect because nothing in the passage implies that people are generally good or will do the right thing most of the time. C is incorrect because the passage indicates that the differences between the nature of women and men are a product of differing early educations.

52. **B.** Mill's call, in the last sentence of the passage, for an end to a system by which gender decides a person's opportunity in life allows one to infer that Mill advocated for equal opportunity for women. A is incorrect because the passage does not refer to the institution of marriage. C is incorrect because the passage does not mention social engineering. D is incorrect because the passage does not advocate the benefits of unbridled competition the way a social Darwinist passage would.

53. **D.** The references to the "mistress of the house" and "household duties," along with the title, allow one to infer that the subject is the role of a woman in running her own domestic household. A is incorrect because the reference to a commander of the army is a metaphor. B is incorrect because the "domestics" referred to are household servants. C is incorrect because the topic of the passage is clearly the management of a household, not a school.

54. **A.** The passage's reference to the importance of "acquirements, which more particularly belong to the feminine character" allow one to infer that Beeton believed that women were better suited than men for the task of household management. B and D are incorrect because the topic of the passage is not the running of a school. C is incorrect because the passage's reference to the importance of "acquirements, which more particularly belong to the feminine character" allow one to infer that Beeton believed that women, not men, were better suited than men for the task of household management.

55. **C.** The reference in the passage to a mistress of the house being the "leader" of an establishment, and her assertion that the "happiness, comfort, and well-being of the family" were dependent on her doing her job well, allow one to infer that Beeton believed that women held considerable power and responsibility within the domestic sphere of social life (within the confines of the household). A and B are incorrect because the passage makes no reference to the public sphere of life (outside the confines of the household). D is incorrect because the reference in the passage to the mistress of the house being the "leader" of an establishment and her assertion that the "happiness, comfort, and well-being of the family" were dependent on her doing her job well allow one to infer that Beeton believed that women held considerable power and responsibility within the domestic sphere of social life (within the confines of the household), not that they were denied such power and responsibility.

Section I, Part B: Short-Answer Questions

Strategies

Remember the strategies discussed in Chapter 6 for the short-answer questions:

Step 1. Compose a topic sentence that responds to the question and gives you something specific to support and illustrate.

Step 2. Support and illustrate the assertion in the topic sentence with specific examples.

Question 1

In history, science and society are intertwined.

a) A good response will provide one factor that contributed to the development of the Scientific Revolution AND an explanation of how it contributed to the development of the Scientific Revolution, such as:
  - Renaissance humanists who sought out classical Greek and Roman texts discovered variations in translations, as well as works by other thinkers who contradicted classical philosophers such as Aristotle. Attempts to reconcile these contradictions led to more systematic methods of inquiry. It also resulted in a shift in thinking from the spiritual world to the natural world, as well as an emphasis on observation and logical inquiry.
  - The "Age of Discovery" and the concomitant commercial revolution also fueled the Scientific Revolution. Better understanding of astronomy for navigational purposes, as well as the need for careful and accurate design and measurement in ship design, all spurred scientific discovery.
  - Renaissance artists emphasized realism in the natural world and sought to study its workings so as to portray the world more accurately. This led to the study of geometry (for perspective), as well as botany, biology, and anatomy. Many artists also applied their ideas to technology.

b) A good response will identify ONE major figure in the Scientific Revolution, as well as explain how he or she challenged a traditional theory about the world, such as:
  - Copernicus or Galileo who both were instrumental in developing (Copernicus) and proving (Galileo) heliocentric theory, which challenged the traditional geocentric view of the world articulated by Ptolemy and supported by the Catholic Church.

  - William Harvey or Andreas Vesalius, both of whom challenged Galen's traditional humoral views of human anatomy and physiology. William Harvey demonstrated that blood circulates around the body via the heart, that there is only one circulatory system (not two, as Galen hypothesized). Vesalius studied human anatomy by actually dissecting bodies to observe their structures firsthand.
  - Sir Isaac Newton, in his book *Principia*, changed understanding of astronomy by providing a new framework for understanding planetary motion, including the law of gravitation. This challenged traditional thought by demonstrating that the natural world has universal laws which govern its behavior, like those of a giant machine.

c) A good response will identify ONE way in which the Scientific Revolution affected political thought, such as:
  - Enlightenment philosophers sought to apply similar methods of rationalism, reason, and empiricism to determine the "natural laws" of human behavior and society, including the "natural" form of government. For example, John Locke, in his *Two Treatises of Government*, used logic to determine that men are capable of cooperating to form governments, and that those are created with the consent of the governed. Montesquieu used the scientific method to identify perfect conditions for different types of governments (republics for small states, etc.). He determined that separation of powers into three branches provided the ideal way to prevent concentration of power.
  - Utilitarians, such as John Stuart Mill or Jeremy Bentham, attempted to use empiricism to quantify ethics in political and social policy. They advocated that policies be evaluated based on their results, and that the best were those that effected the greatest good for the greatest number.
  - Female philosophers in the Enlightenment, especially Mary Wollstonecraft, used logic and reason to argue for political equality for women. She used reason and logic to compare arbitrary systems of domination of some groups over others, like slavery or monarchy, to the arbitrary political subordination of women.

Question 2

Historians have frequently compared the French Revolution (1789–1799) and the Russian Revolution (1917–1924), arguing that they are fundamentally similar.

a) A good response will identify how TWO pieces of evidence support the argument that the French and Russian Revolutions were similar, such as:

- Both countries were deeply in debt from wars. In France, these were due to earlier wars of Louis XIV, whereas in Russia, they were due to the burden of participating in World War I. Both countries responded to these debts by increasing the tax burden on lower classes like peasants and the bourgeoisie.
- Radicals in both nations were inspired by new political theories that seemed to justify transforming the political regime. French revolutionaries were inspired by the ideas of the *philosophes* in the Enlightenment, whereas in Russia, they were inspired by the ideas of Marxism.
- Women played pivotal roles early on in both revolutions. In France, women protested the shortage of bread by marching on Versailles and escorting King Louis XVI into Paris. In Russia, female factory workers, angry at having to stand in line for bread rations after long factory shifts, protested and encouraged a general workers' strike.
- Both revolutions had middle-class factions that attempted to form moderate governments, before being taken over by more radical elements. In France, this was seen in the National Assembly, whose goal was establishment of a constitutional monarchy. In Russia, it took the form of the provisional government formed in March 1917, which embarked on a series of liberal reforms but intended to fulfill Russia's wartime commitments.
- In both nations, revolutionary tensions were exacerbated by weak leadership in the form of Louis XVI in France and Nicholas II in Russia.

b) A good response will identify ONE piece of evidence undermining the comparison that the Russian and French Revolutions were similar, such as:
- The French Revolution ultimately resulted in few permanent political changes, including return of hereditary monarchy in the 1800s. In Russia, the political landscape was permanently changed with the execution of the entire royal family. Russia never again had a monarchy.
- A second difference can be seen in the attitudes toward foreign conflicts. In France, war with other countries like Austria was encouraged by some revolutionaries as a means of uniting the nation, whereas in Russia, the war turned people against the government.

Question 3

One aspect of the Romantic Movement was its insistence on the importance of the cultivation of the senses, sentiment, and emotion.

Two examples of that aspect of the Romantic Movement are seen in the works of William Wordsworth and Lord Byron. The roots of Romanticism are often traced back to the works of Rousseau, who argued that humans are born essentially good and virtuous but are easily corrupted by society. Both Wordsworth and Byron refer to the purity of Nature as opposed to the corrupt and "vulgar" experiences of society.

Part B: Briefly explain TWO reasons for the rise of the Romantic Movement.

Two reasons for the rise of the Romantic Movement are the emphasis on reason that dominated the writings of the Enlightenment *philosophes* and the changes wrought by the process of industrialization.

The works of Rousseau and Goethe explicitly assert the need for the cultivation of the senses, sentiment, and emotion as a remedy for the ruthless and soulless rationalism of the Enlightenment. Meanwhile, many of the Romantics explicitly offered the solace of nature as a remedy for the dehumanizing effects of factory work and urban living conditions, both of which they saw as arising from the excessive emphasis on reason in European society. For example, the works of the English poets William Wordsworth and Samuel Taylor Coleridge extolled the almost mystical qualities of the lake country of northwest England. Lord Byron and Mary Shelley concentrated on the corrupting effects of society on pure souls, again stressing the importance of Nature.

Question 4

Ricardo's notion that state intervention on behalf of the poor ("the poor laws") would only serve to increase the number of poor people identifies the passage with classical liberalism.

Classical liberalism asserted that there were laws of nature that governed economic markets and that any attempt by the state or society to interfere with the workings of those laws would only make matters worse. Specifically, Ricardo is writing in the tradition of Adam Smith, who argued in *Wealth of Nations* (1776) that there was an "invisible hand" that guided the economic activity of societies.

Two factors that help explain the rise to prominence of classical liberalism in 1817 are the wide-ranging influence of the Enlightenment and the emergence of a fully commercial economy in Great Britain (where Ricardo wrote).

By 1815, Enlightenment works such as John Locke's *Essay on Human Understanding* and *Second Treatise of Government* (both 1689) and Adam Smith's

Wealth of Nations (1776), which propounded the existence of laws of nature and the need for constitutions that synchronized human law with natural law, provided a treasure trove of ideas that could be applied to new economic questions. By the second decade of the nineteenth century, such ideas were mined by a new generation of thinkers who were confronted both by the world's most productive economy and a whole set of unprecedented social problems that came with it. Thinkers like Ricardo and Jeremy Bentham (who espoused utilitarianism, a strain of liberalism that argued that all human laws and institutions ought to be judged by their usefulness in promoting "the greatest good for the greatest number" of people) saw in classical liberalism an approach to social problems that embraced a tradition of rational scientific thought that could be adapted to new problems.

Section II, Part A: Document-Based Question (DBQ)

Strategies

Remember the five steps to a history essay of high quality described in Chapter 7:

Step 1. As you read the documents, determine what they have in common and how they reveal different points of view.

Step 2. Compose a thesis that explains how these documents are linked in the way you have chosen.

Step 3. Compose your topic sentences and make sure that they add up logically to your thesis.

Step 4. Support and illustrate your thesis with specific examples that contextualize the documents.

Step 5. *If you have time*, compose a one-paragraph conclusion that restates your thesis.

Grouping the Documents

A question about politics or political ideology almost always lends itself to the construction of a spectrum. Begin by grouping the documents according to ideology. Outline the shared aspects of each group of documents and explain how those shared characteristics identify a particular ideology. Construct a spectrum and organize the groups along it. Finally, note the differences in the documents within each group to note

the variation possible in each ideology. For speed and brevity, refer to the documents by their number.

Creating Your Outline

A possible outline to an answer to this DBQ looks like this:

Thesis: The documents illustrate a spectrum of political ideologies that run from conservatism through liberalism to socialism.

Topic Sentence A: Documents #2 and #4 are examples of conservatism.

Specific Examples: In #2, de Maistre illustrates the conservative belief that written constitutions are unnatural. In #4, Metternich illustrates the conservative belief that traditional monarchy is the natural, time-tested and, therefore, proper form of government, and that monarchs must not yield to calls for reform.

Topic Sentence B: Documents #1 and #3 are examples of liberalism.

Specific Examples: In #1, Smiles illustrates the early liberal belief that only individual effort can better a person's social and economic position. In #3, Mill illustrates the liberal position that the only legitimate role for government is to protect individual liberty. (Note: later in his career, Mill would speak for the utilitarian position that there is a role for government in improving social conditions.)

Topic Sentence C: Documents #5 and #6 are examples of socialism.

Specific Examples: In #5, Marx and Engels establish the position of scientific socialism, which argues that capitalism demands the exploitation of the working class, will inevitably crash, and that the workers should seize political power through violent revolution. In #6, Bernstein provides a corrective in the form of revisionism, arguing that capitalism's collapse is not imminent and that the workers should participate in politics.

Topic Sentence D: Document #7 is an example of anarchism and does not fit well on the spectrum.

Specific Example: Kropotkin illustrates the position of anarchism that government corrupts humanity and must be disrupted and if possible destroyed. Because it is anti-political, it does not fit neatly on a political spectrum.

Conclusion: The documents form a political spectrum from conservatism through liberalism to socialism, with anarchism rejecting the notion of a political spectrum.

Section II, Part B: Long-Essay Question

Strategies

Choose the question for which you can quickly write a clear thesis and three topic sentences that you can illustrate and support with several specific examples. Then follow the formula to constructing a history essay of high quality.

Step 1. Find the action words in the question, and determine what the question wants you to do.

Step 2. Compose a thesis that responds to the question and gives you something specific to support and illustrate.

Step 3. Describe a broader historical context relevant to the prompt.

Step 4. Compose your topic sentences, and make sure that they add up logically to your thesis.

Step 5. Support and illustrate your thesis with specific examples.

Step 6. *If you have time,* compose a one-paragraph conclusion that restates your thesis.

And remember the pitfalls to avoid:

- **Avoid long sentences with multiple clauses.** Your goal is to write the clearest sentence possible; most often the clearest sentence is a relatively short sentence.
- **Do not get caught up in digressions.** No matter how fascinating or insightful you find some idea or fact, if it doesn't directly support or illustrate your thesis, don't put it in.
- **Skip the mystery.** Do not ask a lot of rhetorical questions, and do not go for a surprise ending. The readers are looking for your thesis, your argument, and your evidence; give it to them in a clear, straightforward manner.

Creating Your Outline: Question 1

Question 1: Analyze the major social effects of the Industrial Revolution.

Thesis: The Industrial Revolution produced a western European society that was more urban, less family oriented, and filled with uncertainty.

Topic Sentence A: The rise of the centralized factory system that characterized the Industrial Revolution produced a western European society that was much more urban.

Specific Examples: In the eighteenth century, the majority of the British population lived in the countryside. By the end of the nineteenth century, the majority of the British population lived in cities. Examples include the rise of Manchester, Sheffield, and Birmingham from small villages to industrial cities.

Topic Sentence B: The Industrial Revolution created a western European society that was less family oriented.

Specific Examples: Eldest sons and daughters moved to cities to seek factory work. With the rise of industrial cities came the rise of working-class slums. Fathers, wives, and children often worked in different factories.

Topic Sentence C: The Industrial Revolution destroyed the certainties of traditional society.

Specific Examples: In the agricultural economy, there was no such thing as unemployment. As more and more machines were introduced, the demand for labor went down, and unemployment became a cyclical phenomenon. The rise of the workhouses and poor houses in Great Britain were responses to that unemployment.

Conclusion: The Industrial Revolution replaced the traditional, rural, family-oriented society of certainty with a new urban, individualized society of uncertainty.

Creating Your Outline: Question 2

Question 2: Explain the ways in which the development of mass politics contributed to the New Imperialism of the late nineteenth century.

Thesis: The development of mass politics contributed to the development of the New Imperialism of the late nineteenth century by creating a large group of nationalistic voters whose support had to be won by political elites.

Topic Sentence A: The second half of the nineteenth century saw a development of a large group of new voters.

Specific Examples: In Great Britain, reform bills of 1867 and 1884 created nearly universal manhood suffrage. In France, Louis-Napoleon granted universal manhood suffrage in 1848. In Germany, Bismarck promised universal manhood suffrage (though he never provided it) in return for popular support of his policies.

Topic Sentence B: The newly politicized masses were enthusiastically nationalist.

Specific Examples: Support for the Crimean War and the occupation of Egypt in Great Britain. Plebiscites for the Second Empire, making Louis-Napoleon emperor in France. Support for the Franco-Prussian War in Germany.

Topic Sentence C: Politicians discovered that imperialism appealed to the newly politicized masses.

Specific Examples: Disraeli made the Conservatives the party of "Church, monarchy, and *empire*" in Great Britain. Louis-Napoleon's decision to end the republic and proclaim the Second Empire in France. Bismarck's "blood and iron" unification of Germany. The popularity of the Scramble for Africa.

Conclusion: The rise of a large, nationalistic constituency that politicians had to win over contributed to the New Imperialism of the late nineteenth century.

Creating Your Outline: Question 3

Question 3: Identify and explain two examples of the contributing role of the arts in determining a "climate of opinion."

Thesis: The arts as a whole reach a broad public and influence, if indirectly, the public's reactions to current events.

Topic Sentence A: Visual arts—posters, editorial cartoons, paintings—are examples of artwork directed often at a public, and designed to elicit a reaction.

Specific Examples: War posters geared to promoting nationalistic fervor and patriotism. Editorial cartoons, often reflective of policy concerns, direction, and plans. Paintings that both show events, frequently from a particular point of view, and ideals.

Topic Sentence B: The performing arts—plays or films, for example—can reflect current events and policy concerns.

Specific Examples: Movies and plays can reach a broad audience and bring topics of current and ongoing interest to life. War is a topic common to both genres: The portrayal of the Battle of Agincourt in which a small English force defeated a larger and better equipped French force is portrayed as "glorious" in a 1940s film designed to whip up patriotic fever and in the 1980s film, which demonstrated a distinct post-Vietnam antipathy to war.

Conclusion: The arts can portray society as it is and society as it should be, giving audiences topics for common conversation and concern. They can serve as inspiration for subsequent policy movements.

AP European History Practice Exam 2

SECTION I, PART A
ANSWER SHEET

1 Ⓐ Ⓑ Ⓒ Ⓓ
2 Ⓐ Ⓑ Ⓒ Ⓓ
3 Ⓐ Ⓑ Ⓒ Ⓓ
4 Ⓐ Ⓑ Ⓒ Ⓓ
5 Ⓐ Ⓑ Ⓒ Ⓓ
6 Ⓐ Ⓑ Ⓒ Ⓓ
7 Ⓐ Ⓑ Ⓒ Ⓓ
8 Ⓐ Ⓑ Ⓒ Ⓓ
9 Ⓐ Ⓑ Ⓒ Ⓓ
10 Ⓐ Ⓑ Ⓒ Ⓓ
11 Ⓐ Ⓑ Ⓒ Ⓓ
12 Ⓐ Ⓑ Ⓒ Ⓓ
13 Ⓐ Ⓑ Ⓒ Ⓓ
14 Ⓐ Ⓑ Ⓒ Ⓓ
15 Ⓐ Ⓑ Ⓒ Ⓓ
16 Ⓐ Ⓑ Ⓒ Ⓓ
17 Ⓐ Ⓑ Ⓒ Ⓓ
18 Ⓐ Ⓑ Ⓒ Ⓓ
19 Ⓐ Ⓑ Ⓒ Ⓓ

20 Ⓐ Ⓑ Ⓒ Ⓓ
21 Ⓐ Ⓑ Ⓒ Ⓓ
22 Ⓐ Ⓑ Ⓒ Ⓓ
23 Ⓐ Ⓑ Ⓒ Ⓓ
24 Ⓐ Ⓑ Ⓒ Ⓓ
25 Ⓐ Ⓑ Ⓒ Ⓓ
26 Ⓐ Ⓑ Ⓒ Ⓓ
27 Ⓐ Ⓑ Ⓒ Ⓓ
28 Ⓐ Ⓑ Ⓒ Ⓓ
29 Ⓐ Ⓑ Ⓒ Ⓓ
30 Ⓐ Ⓑ Ⓒ Ⓓ
31 Ⓐ Ⓑ Ⓒ Ⓓ
32 Ⓐ Ⓑ Ⓒ Ⓓ
33 Ⓐ Ⓑ Ⓒ Ⓓ
34 Ⓐ Ⓑ Ⓒ Ⓓ
35 Ⓐ Ⓑ Ⓒ Ⓓ
36 Ⓐ Ⓑ Ⓒ Ⓓ
37 Ⓐ Ⓑ Ⓒ Ⓓ
38 Ⓐ Ⓑ Ⓒ Ⓓ

39 Ⓐ Ⓑ Ⓒ Ⓓ
40 Ⓐ Ⓑ Ⓒ Ⓓ
41 Ⓐ Ⓑ Ⓒ Ⓓ
42 Ⓐ Ⓑ Ⓒ Ⓓ
43 Ⓐ Ⓑ Ⓒ Ⓓ
44 Ⓐ Ⓑ Ⓒ Ⓓ
45 Ⓐ Ⓑ Ⓒ Ⓓ
46 Ⓐ Ⓑ Ⓒ Ⓓ
47 Ⓐ Ⓑ Ⓒ Ⓓ
48 Ⓐ Ⓑ Ⓒ Ⓓ
49 Ⓐ Ⓑ Ⓒ Ⓓ
50 Ⓐ Ⓑ Ⓒ Ⓓ
51 Ⓐ Ⓑ Ⓒ Ⓓ
52 Ⓐ Ⓑ Ⓒ Ⓓ
53 Ⓐ Ⓑ Ⓒ Ⓓ
54 Ⓐ Ⓑ Ⓒ Ⓓ
55 Ⓐ Ⓑ Ⓒ Ⓓ

AP European History Practice Exam 2

SECTION I, PART A

Multiple-Choice Questions
Recommended Time—55 minutes

Directions: The multiple-choice section consists of 55 questions to be answered in a recommended time of **55 minutes**. Each set of questions below refers to the written passage or figure that precedes it. Select the best answer for each question, and fill in the corresponding letter on the answer sheet supplied.

Questions 1–3 refer to the passage below.

Albeit the king's Majesty justly and rightfully is and ought to be the supreme head of the Church of England, and so is recognized by the clergy of this realm in their convocations, yet nevertheless, for corroboration and confirmation thereof, and for increase of virtue in Christ's religion within this realm of England, and to repress and extirpate all errors, heresies, and other enormities and abuses heretofore used in the same, be it enacted, by authority of this present Parliament, that the king, our sovereign lord, his heirs and successors, kings of this realm, shall be taken, accepted, and reputed the only supreme head in earth of the Church of England, called *Anglicans Ecclesia*; and shall have and enjoy, annexed and united to the imperial crown of this realm, as well the title and style thereof, as all honors, dignities, preeminences, jurisdictions, privileges, authorities, immunities, profits, and commodities to the said dignity of the supreme head of the same Church belonging and appertaining; and that our said sovereign lord, his heirs and successors, kings of this realm, shall have full power and authority from time to time to visit, repress, redress, record, order, correct, restrain, and amend all such errors, heresies, abuses, offenses, contempts, and enormities, whatsoever they be, which by any manner of spiritual authority or jurisdiction ought or may lawfully be reformed, repressed, ordered, redressed, corrected, restrained, or amended, most to the pleasure of Almighty God, the increase of virtue in Christ's religion, and for the conservation of the peace, unity, and tranquility of this realm; any usage, foreign land, foreign authority, prescription, or any other thing or things to the contrary hereof notwithstanding.

English Parliament, Act of Supremacy, 1534

1. The English Parliament argued that the Act of Supremacy would do which of the following?

   A. Give the English king a new position of authority

   B. Give the position of head of the Church of England to Henry VIII alone and exclude his heirs

   C. Establish Calvinism as the one true theology in England

   D. End various forms of corruption plaguing the Church in England

2. The passage can be used as evidence for which of the following historical trends of the time period?

   A. The consolidation of the power of the monarchy

   B. The increased power of the Catholic Church

   C. The increased piety of the nobility

   D. The increasing religiosity of the masses

3. The Act was, in part, a way to do what?

   A. An attempt to prevent the spread of Protestantism in England

   B. An attempt to resolve Henry VIII's financial difficulties

   C. An attempt to legitimize Henry VIII's only heir

   D. An attempt to ally England with the Holy Roman Emperor

Questions 4–6 refer to the passage below.

Florence is more beautiful and five hundred forty years older than your Venice. . . . We have round about us thirty thousand estates, owned by nobleman and merchants, citizens and craftsman, yielding us yearly bread and meat, wine and oil, vegetables and cheese, hay and wood, to the value of nine thousand ducats in cash. . . . We have two trades greater than any four of yours in Venice put together—the trades wool and silk. . . . Our beautiful Florence contains within the city . . . two hundred seventy shops belonging to the wool merchant's guild, from whence their wares are sent to Rome and the Marches, Naples and Sicily, Constantinople . . . and the whole of Turkey. It contains also eighty-three rich and splendid warehouses of the silk merchant's guild.

Benedetto Dei, "Letter to a Venetian," 1472

4. How was wealth in Renaissance Italy measured?

   A. The size of landed estates
   B. The number of estates owned by an individual
   C. The monetary value of goods
   D. The amount of gold held

5. The economy of Renaissance Florence was primarily based on which of the following?

   A. Banking
   B. The export of agricultural goods
   C. War and conquest
   D. The manufacture and export of wool and silk products

6. The passage may be used as evidence for the existence of which of the following Renaissance cultural characteristics?

   A. Pride in the mastery of the military arts
   B. Chivalry
   C. Civic pride
   D. Patronage of the arts

Questions 7–9 refer to the passage below.

First we must remark that the cosmos is spherical in form, partly because this form being a perfect whole requiring no joints, is the most complete of all, partly because it makes the most capacious form, which is best suited to contain and preserve everything; or again because all the constituent parts of the universe, that is the sun, moon and the planets appear in this form; or because everything strives to attain this form, as appears in the case of drops of water and other fluid bodies if they attempt to define themselves. So no one will doubt that this form belongs to the heavenly bodies. . . .

That the earth is also spherical is therefore beyond question, because it presses from all sides upon its center. Although by reason of the elevations of the mountains and the depressions of the valleys a perfect circle cannot be understood, yet this does not affect the general spherical nature of the earth. . . .

As it has been already shown that the earth has the form of a sphere, we must consider whether a movement also coincides with this form, and what place the earth holds in the universe. . . . The great majority of authors of course agree that the earth stands still in the center of the universe, and consider it inconceivable and ridiculous to suppose the opposite. But if the matter is carefully weighed, it will be seen that the question is not yet settled and therefore by no means to be regarded lightly. Every change of place which is observed is due, namely, to a movement of the observed object or of the observer, or to movements of both. . . . Now it is from the earth that the revolution of the heavens is observed and it is produced for our eyes. Therefore if the earth undergoes no movement this movement must take place in everything outside of the earth, but in the opposite direction than if everything on the earth moved, and of this kind is the daily revolution. So this appears to affect the whole universe, that is, everything outside the earth with the single exception of the earth itself. If, however, one should admit that this movement was not peculiar to the heavens, but that the earth revolved from west to east, and if this was carefully considered in regard to the apparent rising and setting of the sun, the moon and the stars, it would be discovered that this was the real situation.

Nicolas Copernicus, *The Revolutions of the Heavenly Bodies*, 1543

7. What belief distinguished Copernicus from the traditional, Aristotelian natural philosophers of his day?

   A. The cosmos is spherical.
   B. The Earth is spherical.
   C. The cosmos is geostatic.
   D. The Earth is not stationary.

8. Copernicus's argument for a spherical cosmos was based on

   A. observation and induction.
   B. ancient textual authority.
   C. experimentation.
   D. deduction from first principles.

9. In which tradition was Copernicus working?

   A. The Aristotelian tradition
   B. The natural magic tradition
   C. The skeptical tradition
   D. The Platonic/Pythagorean tradition

Questions 10–11 refer to the passage below.

About the year 1645, while I lived in London . . . I had the opportunity of being acquainted with diverse worthy persons, inquisitive into natural philosophy, and other parts of human learning; and particularly of what has been called the "New Philosophy" or "Experimental Philosophy." We did by agreements . . . meet weekly in London on a certain day, to treat and discourse of such affairs. . . . Our business was (precluding matters of theology and state affairs), to discourse and consider of Philosophical Enquiries, and such as related thereunto: as physics or physic[s], anatomy, geometry, astronomy, navigation, statics, magnetics, chemics, mechanics, and natural experiments; with the state of these studies, as then cultivated at home and abroad. We then discoursed of the circulation of the blood, the valves in the veins, the *venae lactae*, the lymphatic vessels, the Copernican hypothesis, the nature of comets and new stars, the satellites of Jupiter, the oval shape (as it then appeared) of Saturn, the spots in the sun, and its turning on its own axis, the inequalities and selenography of the moon, the several phases of Venus and Mercury, the improvement of telescopes, and grinding of glasses for that purpose, the weight of air, the possibility, or impossibility of vacuities, and nature's abhorrence thereof, the Torricellian experiment in quicksilver, the descent of heavy bodies, and the degrees of acceleration therein; and diverse or divers[e] other things of like nature. Some of which were then but new discoveries, and others not so generally known and embraced, as now they are. . . .

   We barred all discourses of divinity, of state affairs, and of news, other than what concerned our business of Philosophy. These meetings we removed soon after to the Bull Head in Cheapside, and in term-time to Gresham College, where we met weekly at Mr. Foster's lecture (then Astronomy Professor there), and, after the lecture ended, repaired, sometimes to Mr. Foster's lodgings, sometimes to some other place not far distant, where we continued such enquiries, and our numbers increased.

Dr. John Wallis, *Account of Some Passages of his Life*, 1700

10. The passage shows evidence for the development of which of the following?

    A. An independent society for the study of natural philosophy in the seventeenth century
    B. The study of natural philosophy in the royal courts in the seventeenth century
    C. New universities for the study of natural philosophy in the seventeenth century
    D. The study of natural philosophy in the Church in the seventeenth century

11. Wallis's group was primarily interested in

    A. undermining the traditional worldview.
    B. creating a secular science to challenge the Church.
    C. ascertaining the state of the New Philosophy in England and abroad.
    D. the regulation of new knowledge so as not to undermine traditional values.

Questions 12–14 refer to the passage below.

[T]he the end and measure of this power, when in every man's hands in the state of nature, being the preservation of all of his society, that is, all mankind in general, it can have no other end or measure, when in the hands of the magistrate, but to preserve the members of that society in their lives, liberties, and possessions, and so cannot be an absolute, arbitrary power over their lives and fortunes, which are as much as possible to be preserved, but a power to make law, and annex such penalties to them, as may tend to the preservation of the whole by cutting off those parts, and those only, which are so corrupt that they threaten the sound and healthy, without which no severity is lawful. And this power has its original only from compact, and agreement, and the mutual consent of those who make up the community. . . .

Whensoever, therefore, the legislative shall transgress this fundamental rule of society; and either by ambition, fear, folly or corruption, endeavor to grasp themselves, or put into the hands of any other, an absolute power over the lives, liberties, and estates of the people; by this breach of trust they forfeit the power the people had put into their hands for quite contrary ends.

John Locke, *Two Treatises of Government*, 1690

12. According to Locke, how did society and its legitimate government hold power over the members of society?

   A. Divine right
   B. The consent of those members of society
   C. A covenant between the members of society
   D. Conquest

13. Locke was an advocate of which political system?

   A. Divine right monarchy
   B. Absolutism
   C. Constitutionalism
   D. Socialism

14. According to Locke, how did a government lose its legitimacy?

   A. When it is weak and can be overthrown
   B. When the people wish to change governors
   C. When it becomes corrupt
   D. When it tries to exercise absolute power

Questions 15 and 16 refer to the image below.

"England is not a free people, till the poor that have no land,
have a free allowance to dig and labour the commons . . ."
Gerrard Winstanley, 1649

15. Who were Gerrard Winstanley and his Diggers resisting?

    A. The king in the English Civil War
    B. Parliament in the English Civil War
    C. The enclosure movement
    D. The institution of the three-field agricultural system

16. What actions did the Parliamentarian regime that was victorious in the English Civil War in 1649 take?

    A. Parliament supported the efforts of Winstanley and the Diggers to return to old customs.
    B. Parliament was determined to drive Winstanley and the Diggers off of all common land.
    C. Parliament rewarded Winstanley and the Diggers for their previous support by awarding them use of the commons.
    D. Parliament was indifferent to Winstanley and his movement.

Questions 17–19 refer to the passage below.

In a word, whoever will deign to consult common sense upon religious opinions, and will bestow on this inquiry the attention that is commonly given to any objects we presume interesting, will easily perceive that those opinions have no foundation; that Religion is a mere castle in the air. . . .

Savage and furious nations, perpetually at war, adore, under diverse names, some God, conformable to their ideas. . . . Madmen everywhere be seen who, after meditating upon their terrible God, imagine that to please him they must do themselves all possible injury. . . . The gloomy ideas more usefully formed of the Deity, far from consoling them under the evils of life, have everywhere disquieted their minds, and produced follies destructive to their happiness.

How could the human mind make any considerable progress, while tormented with frightful phantoms, and guided by men interested in perpetuating its ignorance and fears? . . . Occupied solely by his fears, and by unintelligible reveries, he has always been at the mercy of his priests, who have reserved for themselves the right of thinking for him and directing his actions. . . .

Let men's minds be filled with true ideas; let their reason be cultivated. . . . To discover the true principles of morality, men have no need of theology, of revelation, or of gods.

Baron Paul d'Holbach, *Good Sense*, 1772

17. Which of the following best characterizes d'Holbach's theological stance?

   A. Atheist
   B. Deist
   C. Protestant
   D. Catholic

18. d'Holbach was participating in which movement?

   A. The later stages of the Protestant Reformation
   B. The new political ideas of the early Enlightenment
   C. The phase of the Enlightenment that called for "enlightened despotism"
   D. The later, radical phase of the Enlightenment

19. Why can the passage be identified as part of the eighteenth-century cultural movement known as the Enlightenment?

   A. It defends atheism.
   B. It affirms the core Enlightenment ideals of reason and freedom of thought.
   C. It offers a rational proof of the existence of God.
   D. It uses satire to undermine orthodox ideas.

Questions 20 and 21 refer to the passage below.

The National Assembly, after having heard the report of the ecclesiastical committee, has decreed and do decree the following as constitutional articles:

Title I

    IV. No church or parish of France nor any French citizen may acknowledge upon any occasion, or upon any pretext whatsoever, the authority of an ordinary bishop or of an archbishop whose see shall be under the supremacy of a foreign power, nor that of his representatives residing in France or elsewhere. . . .

Title II

    I. Beginning with the day of publication of the present decree, there shall be but one mode of choosing bishops and parish priests, namely that of election.

    II. All elections shall be by ballot and shall be decided by the absolute majority of the votes.

    III. The election of bishops shall take place according to the forms and by the electoral body designated in the decree of December 22, 1789, for the election of members of the departmental assembly.

    XXI. Before the ceremony of consecration begins, the bishop elect shall take a solemn oath, in the presence of the municipal officers, of the people, and of the clergy, to guard with care the faithful of his diocese who are confided to him, to be loyal to the nation, the law, and the king, and to support with all his power the constitution decreed by the National Assembly and accepted by the king.

Civil Constitution of the Clergy, July 12, 1790

20. According to the passage, what was the goal of the authors?

    A. To reform the church of France along Protestant lines

    B. To make the clergy of France subservient to the French government

    C. To ensure that the clergy of France would be completely abolished

    D. To make the clergy of France subservient to the Pope in Rome

21. Which of the following groups in France in 1790 would have been most likely to oppose the proclamations of this document?

    A. Members of the National Assembly

    B. Supporters of the king

    C. Existing archbishops

    D. Simple parish priests who cared deeply about their parishioners

Questions 22–24 refer to the passage below.

From this moment until that in which the enemy shall have been driven from the soil of the Republic, all Frenchmen are in permanent requisition for the service of the armies. The young men shall go to battle; the married men shall forge arms and transport provisions; the women shall make tents and clothing and shall serve in the hospitals; the children shall turn old linen into lint; the aged shall betake themselves to the public places in order to arouse the courage of the warriors and preach the hatred of kings and the unity of the Republic. . . .

The Committee of Public Safety is charged to take all necessary measures to set up without delay an extraordinary manufacture of arms of every sort which corresponds with the ardor and energy of the French people. It is, accordingly, authorized to form all the establishments, factories, workshops, and mills which shall be deemed necessary for the carrying on of these works, as well as to put in requisition, within the entire extent of the Republic, the artists and workingmen who can contribute to their success.

The representatives of the people sent out for the execution of the present law shall have the same authority in their respective districts, acting in concert with the Committee of Public Safety; they are invested with the unlimited powers assigned to the representatives of the people to the armies.

The Levée en Masse, August 23, 1793

22. This passage refers to the establishment of which of the following?

    A. The French Republic
    B. The Committee of Public Safety
    C. War against the Coalition
    D. Mass conscription

23. The passage is one example of the way in which the Committee of Public Safety

    A. revamped the economy of the new French Republic.
    B. successfully harnessed the human resources of the new French Republic.
    C. reformed the religious rituals of the Church in the new French Republic.
    D. brought about its own destruction.

24. Why could it be argued that what is discussed in the passage represents a turning point in the history of warfare in modern European history?

    A. It represented the introduction of weaponry produced by large-scale industrialization.
    B. It advocated the total extinction of a nation's enemies.
    C. It was war run by a committee.
    D. It advocated total war.

Questions 25–27 refer to the passage below.

Many things combine to make the hand spinning of wool, the most desirable work for the cottager's wife and children. A wooden wheel costing 2 s[hillings] for each person, with one reel costing 3 s[hillings] set up the family. The wool-man either supplies them with wool by the pound or more at a time, as he can depend on their care, or they take it on his account from the chandler's shop, where they buy their food and raiment. No stock is required, and when they carry back their pound of wool spun, they have no further concern in it. Children from five years old can run at the wheel, it is a very wholesome employment for them, keeps them in constant exercise, and upright; persons can work at it till a very advanced age.

But from the establishment of the [mechanical] spinning machines in many counties where I was last summer, no hand work could be had, the consequence of which is the whole maintenance of the family devolves on the father, and instead of six or seven shillings a week, which a wife and four children could add by their wheels, his weekly pay is all they have to depend upon. . . .

I then walked to the Machines, and with some difficulty gained admittance: there I saw both the Combing Machine and Spinning Jenny. The Combing Machine was put in motion by a Wheel turned by four men, but which I am sure could be turned either by water or steam. The frames were supplied by a child with Wool, and as the wheel turned, flakes of ready combed Wool dropped off a cylinder into a trough, these were taken up by a girl of about fourteen years old, who placed them on the Spinning Jenny, which has a number of horizontal beams of wood, on each of which may be fifty bobbins. One such girl sets these bobbins all in motion by turning a wheel at the end of the beam, a wire then catches up a flake of Wool, spins it, and gathers it upon each bobbin. The girl again turns the wheel, and another fifty flakes are taken up and Spun. This is done every minute without intermission, so that probably one girl turning that wheel, may do the work of One Hundred Hand Wheels at the least. About twenty of these sets of bobbins, were I judge at work in one room. Most of these Manufactories are many stories high, and the rooms much larger than this I was in. Struck with the impropriety of even so many as the twenty girls I saw, without any woman presiding over them, I enquired of the Master if he was married, why his Wife was not present? He said he was not a married man, and that many parents did object to send their girls, but that the poverty of others, and not having any work to set them to, left him not at any loss for hands. I must do all the parties the justice to say, that these girls appeared neat and orderly: yet at best, I cannot but fear the taking such young persons from the eyes of their parents, and thus herding them together with only men and boys, must bring up a dissolute race of poor.

Observations . . . on the Loss of Woollen Spinning, c. 1794

25. What changes are described in the passage?

    A. The shift from cottage industry organization to the mill system
    B. The shift from agricultural work to industrial manufacturing
    C. The shift from single country markets to international trade
    D. The shift from individual labor to labor organized into trade unions

26. What does this passage say about spinning wool?

    A. The work took very little time.
    B. A family could make enough spinning to support the entire household.
    C. The initial investment in equipment was quickly recouped.
    D. The work was done only by girls.

27. What was one of the moral objections to mill work in the wool spinning industry?

    A. That religious instruction was not provided to the young workers in the mills
    B. That it promoted petty theft by desperate workers
    C. That it broke down traditional gender roles by employing women and girls in a trade
    D. That large numbers of young girls worked for unmarried men without parental supervision

Questions 28–30 refer to the passage below.

After as careful an examination of the evidence collected as I have been enabled to make, I beg leave to recapitulate the chief conclusions which that evidence appears to me to establish. As to the extent and operation of the evils which are the subject of this inquiry [the results indicate]:

That the various forms of epidemic, endemic, and other disease caused, or aggravated, or propagated chiefly amongst the labouring classes by atmospheric impurities produced by decomposing animal and vegetable substances, by damp and filth, and close and overcrowded dwellings prevail amongst the population in every part of the kingdom, whether dwelling in separate houses, in rural villages, in small towns, in the larger towns—as they have been found to prevail in the lowest districts of the metropolis. . . .

That the ravages of epidemics and other diseases do not diminish but tend to increase the pressure of population. . . . [In] the districts where the mortality is greatest the births are not only sufficient to replace the numbers removed by death, but to add to the population.

That the younger population, bred up under noxious physical agencies, is inferior in physical organization and general health to a population preserved from the presence of such agencies.

That the population so exposed is less susceptible of moral influences, and the effects of education are more transient than with a healthy population.

That these adverse circumstances tend to produce an adult population short-lived, improvident, reckless, and intemperate, and with habitual avidity for sensual gratifications.

Sir Edwin Chadwick, *Inquiry into the Sanitary Condition of the Poor*, 1842

28. According to the passage, what was one of the chief sources of disease in the poor areas of mid-nineteenth-century Britain?

    A. A diet deficient in important nutrients and vitamins
    B. Overcrowded living conditions and poor sanitation
    C. A new wave of the Black Death
    D. Unsafe working conditions

29. According to Chadwick's report, what was the effect of rampant epidemic and disease on population pressure?

    A. A decrease in population pressure was due to high mortality rates
    B. No effect, because high mortality rates balanced out high birth rates
    C. An increase in population pressure was due to higher birth rates
    D. No effect, because population pressure and rates of epidemic and disease are unrelated

30. Mid-nineteenth-century reformers in Britain believed that unsanitary living conditions

    A. produced a population of poor moral quality.
    B. had no effect on the morality of the population.
    C. caused disease.
    D. improved moral values, as people had to struggle harder in their daily lives.

Questions 31 and 32 refer to the image below.

THE LIFE

AND

HISTORY OF SWING,

THE

KENT RICK-BURNER.

WRITTEN BY HIMSELF.

See page 21.

LONDON:
PRINTED AND PUBLISHED BY R. CARLILE,
62, FLEET-STREET.
1830.

Price Threepence.

31. The image most likely refers to which of these events in 1830?

    A. The death of King George IV of England and the ascension of William IV

    B. The Swing Riots in Britain

    C. The July Revolution in France

    D. The Irish Potato Famine

32. What is the conflict depicted in the image?

    A. One between factory owners and industrial workers

    B. One between naval officers and sailors

    C. One between agricultural and industrial interests

    D. One between landlords and agricultural laborers

Questions 33 and 34 refer to the passage below.

Europe no longer possesses unity of faith, of mission, or of aim. Such unity is a necessity in the world. Here, then, is the secret of the crisis. It is the duty of every one to examine and analyze calmly and carefully the probable elements of this new unity. . . .

It was not for a material interest that the people of Vienna fought in 1848; in weakening the empire they could only lose power. It was not for an increase of wealth that the people of Lombardy fought in the same year; the Austrian Government had endeavored in the year preceding to excite the peasants against the landed proprietors, as they had done in Gallicia; but everywhere they had failed. They struggled, they still struggle, as do Poland, Germany, and Hungary, for country and liberty; for a word inscribed upon a banner, proclaiming to the world that they also live, think, love, and labor for the benefit of all. They speak the same language, they bear about them the impress of consanguinity, they kneel beside the same tombs, they glory in the same tradition; and they demand to associate freely, without obstacles, without foreign domination, in order to elaborate and express their idea; to contribute their stone also to the great pyramid of history. It is something moral which they are seeking; and this moral something is in fact, even politically speaking, the most important question in the present state of things. It is the organization of the European task. . . . The nationality of the peoples . . . can only be founded by a common effort and a common movement; . . . nationality ought only to be to humanity that . . . of a human group called by its geographical position, its traditions, and its language, to fulfil a special function in the European work of civilization.

Giuseppe Mazzini, *On Nationality*, 1852

33. According to Mazzini, what was the proper definition of a nation?

   A. A kingdom with longstanding borders
   B. A people with shared geography, language, and traditions
   C. A people strong enough to avoid foreign domination
   D. A people with a unified political ideology

34. Mazzini could best be described as influenced by which two ideological movements of the mid-nineteenth century?

   A. Conservatism and nationalism
   B. Socialism and nationalism
   C. Romanticism and nationalism
   D. Anarchism and socialism

Questions 35–37 refer to the passage below.

Yesterday Deputy Bamberger compared the business of government with that of a cobbler who measures shoes, which he thereupon examines as to whether they are suitable for him or not and accordingly accepts or rejects them. I am by no means dissatisfied with this humble comparison. . . . The profession of government in the sense of Frederick the Great is to serve the people, and may it be also as a cobbler; the opposite is to dominate the people. We want to serve the people. But I make the demand on Herr Bamberger that he act as my co-shoemaker in order to make sure that no member of the public goes barefoot, and to create a suitable shoe for the people in this crucial area. . . .

For it is an injustice on the one hand to hinder the self-defense of a large class of our fellow citizens and on the other hand not to offer them aid for the redress of that which causes the dissatisfaction. That the Social Democratic leaders wish no advantage for this law, that I understand; dissatisfied workers are just what they need. Their mission is to lead, to rule, and the necessary prerequisite for that is numerous dissatisfied classes. They must naturally oppose any attempt of the government, however well-intentioned it may be, to remedy this situation, if they do not wish to lose control over the masses they mislead. . . .

The whole problem is rooted in the question: does the state have the responsibility to care for its helpless fellow citizens, or does it not? I maintain that it does have this duty. . . . It would be madness for a corporate body or a collectivity to take charge of those objectives that the individual can accomplish; those goals that the community can fulfill with justice and profit should be relinquished to the community. [But] there are objectives that only the state in its totality can fulfill. . . . Among the last mentioned objectives [of the state] belong national defense [and] the general system of transportation. . . . To these belong also the help of persons in distress and the prevention of such justified complaints. . . . That is the responsibility of the state from which the state will not be able to withdraw in the long run.

Otto von Bismarck, "Reichstag Speech on the Law for Workers' Compensation," 1884

35. This passage most clearly shows the influence of which of the following trends in Europe in the second half of the nineteenth century?

   A. The birth of constitutionalism
   B. The blending of nationalism with liberalism
   C. The birth of popular nationalism
   D. The blending of nationalism with conservativism

36. In the passage, how is Bismarck attempting to portray his government?

   A. As servants of the people
   B. As absolute rulers
   C. As leaders who deserve to be followed
   D. As loyal opposition to the party in power

37. According to Bismarck, what was the role of the state?

   A. To fulfill all social objectives that are worthy of being fulfilled
   B. To fulfill no social objectives but rather leave them to private individuals and the community
   C. To fulfill social objectives that have been demanded by the people
   D. To fulfill social objectives that it alone can fulfill

Questions 38–40 refer to the image below.

38. In the image, Giuseppe Garibaldi is depicted as fitting the "boot of Italy" onto the leg of King Victor Emmanuel II of Piedmont-Sardinia. What does this say about the cartoonist's beliefs?

    A. He opposed Italian unification.
    B. He favored Italian unification.
    C. He believed Garibaldi to have had a significant role in bringing about the unification of Italy.
    D. He believed that Count Cavour was most responsible for Italian unification.

39. What is the most likely date of the image?

    A. Before June 1848
    B. After June 1848
    C. After October 1860
    D. Before October 1860

40. How does the cartoonist view the unification of Italy generally?

    A. He viewed the unification of Italy as coming to fruition.
    B. He viewed the unification of Italy as doubtful.
    C. He viewed the unification of Italy as a positive development.
    D. He viewed the unification of Italy as a negative development.

Questions 41 and 42 refer to the passage below.

Confidential—For Your Excellency's personal information and guidance

The Austro-Hungarian Ambassador yesterday delivered to the [German] Emperor [Wilhelm II] a confidential personal letter from the Emperor Francis Joseph [of Austria-Hungary], which depicts the present situation from the Austro-Hungarian point of view, and describes the measures which Vienna has in view. A copy is now being forwarded to Your Excellency. . . .

His Majesty desires to say that he is not blind to the danger which threatens Austria-Hungary and thus the Triple Alliance as a result of the Russian and Serbian Pan-Slavic agitation. . . . His Majesty will, furthermore, make an effort at Bucharest, according to the wishes of the Emperor Franz Joseph, to influence King Carol to the fulfillment of the duties of his alliance, to the renunciation of Serbia, and to the suppression of the Romanian agitations directed against Austria-Hungary.

Finally, as far as concerns Serbia, His Majesty, of course, cannot interfere in the dispute now going on between Austria-Hungary and that country, as it is a matter not within his competence. The Emperor Franz Joseph may, however, rest assured that His Majesty will faithfully stand by Austria-Hungary, as is required by the obligations of his alliance and of his ancient friendship.

> Theobald von Bethmann-Hollweg (chancellor of Germany),
> telegram to the German ambassador at Vienna, July 6, 1914

41. Which of the following best describes the context of Bethmann-Hollweg's telegram?

    A. Germany's collaboration with Austria-Hungary during Germany's unification process
    B. The Balkan Question and the Triple Alliance
    C. Germany's rearmament in violation of the Treaty of Paris
    D. Germany's negotiations with Austria-Hungary and Italy to create the Triple Alliance

42. Why is Bethmann-Hollweg's telegram often referred to as Germany's "blank check"?

    A. It pledged Germany to join the Triple Alliance and support Austria-Hungary against the Triple Entente.
    B. It was understood to give Austria an unlimited scope of response to the assassination of Franz Ferdinand, to Serbia, and to Pan-Slavism within the Austro-Hungarian Empire.
    C. It pledged Germany's unlimited support to Franz Joseph in his efforts to succeed the recently assassinated Franz Ferdinand.
    D. It offered nothing in terms of real support to Franz Joseph and Austria-Hungary.

Questions 43–45 refer to the passage below.

How has the war affected women? How will it affect them? Women, as half the human race, are compelled to take their share of evil and good with men, the other half. The destruction of property, the increase of taxation, the rise of prices, the devastation of beautiful things in nature and art—these are felt by men as well as by women. Some losses doubtless appeal to one or the other sex with peculiar poignancy, but it would be difficult to say whose sufferings are the greater, though there can be no doubt at all that men get an exhilaration out of war which is denied to most women. . . .

Men and women must take counsel together and let the experience of the war teach them how to solve economic problems by co-operation rather than conflict. Women [drawn into the workforce] have been increasingly conscious of the satisfaction to be got from economic independence, of the sweetness of earned bread, of the dreary depression of subjection. They have felt the bitterness of being "kept out"; they are feeling the exhilaration of being "brought in." They are ripe for instruction and organization in working for the good of the whole. . . .

It would be wise to remember that the dislocation of industry at the outbreak of the war was easily met . . . because there was an untapped reservoir of women's labor to take the place of men's. The problems after the war will be different, greater, and more lasting. . . .

Because it will obviously be impossible for all to find work quickly (not to speak of the right kind of work), there is almost certain to be an outcry for the restriction of work in various directions, and one of the first cries (if we may judge from the past) will be to women: "Back to the Home!" This cry will be raised whether the women have a home or not. We must understand the unimpeachable right of the man who has lost his work and risked his life for his country, to find decent employment, decent wages and conditions, on his return to civil life. We must also understand the enlargement and enhancement of life which women feel when they are able to live by their own productive work, and we must realize that to deprive women of the right to live by their work is to send them back to a moral imprisonment (to say nothing of physical and intellectual starvation), of which they have become now for the first time fully conscious. And we must realize the exceeding danger that conscienceless employers may regard women's labor as preferable, owing to its cheapness and its docility. . . . The kind of man who likes "to keep women in their place" may find he has made slaves who will be used by his enemies against him.

Helena Swanwick, "The War in Its Effect upon Women," 1916

43. Which of the following best describes the context for Swanwick's essay?

    A. Possible social changes likely to occur with the coming of World War II
    B. The effects of social changes that had occurred over a decade of warfare
    C. The effects of social change being felt during the so-called Interwar Years
    D. The social changes that were being experienced during World War I

44. According to the author, what would happen to women drawn into the workforce at the war's conclusion?

    A. Women would never be able to readjust to life at home.
    B. Women would revolt against traditional social rules.
    C. Women would face pressure to return to the home.
    D. Women would be paid better than men because of the experience they had gained.

45. Swanwick surmised that some employers would be tempted to see women in what way?

    A. As cheap and manageable alternatives to returning male labor
    B. As unsuitable for a return to home life
    C. As fair game for military service in the next war
    D. As willing and able to work alongside men

Questions 46–47 refer to the passage below from the Treaty of Brest-Litovsk.

ARTICLE I: Germany, Austria-Hungary, Bulgaria and Turkey for the one part, and Russia for the other part, declare that the state of war between them has ceased. They are resolved to live henceforth in peace and amity with one another. . . .

ARTICLE III: The territories lying to the west of the line agreed upon by the contracting parties, which formerly belonged to Russia, will no longer be subject to Russian sovereignty; the line agreed upon is traced on the map submitted as an essential part of this treaty of peace. The exact fixation of the line will be established by a Russo-German commission.

Treaty of Brest-Litovsk, March 14, 1918

46. How can the Treaty of Brest-Litovsk best be described?

    A. As the result of the Bolsheviks' need to end the Russian war effort in order to consolidate their revolutionary gains
    B. As the result of corruption on the part of Bolshevik leaders and collaboration with Russian business interests
    C. As the result of the breaking up of the Triple Entente
    D. As the result of French and British aid being given to the so-called White Russians who opposed the Bolshevik government

47. What was the result of Article III of the treaty?

    A. The surrender of the western part of the German Empire to the Russian Empire
    B. The surrender of the eastern part of the German Empire to the Russian Empire
    C. The surrender of the western part of the Russian Empire to the German Empire
    D. The surrender of the eastern part of the Russian Empire to the German Empire

Questions 48 and 49 refer to the passage below.

Apart from the desire to produce beautiful things, the leading passion of my life has been and is hatred of modern civilization. What shall I say of it now, when the words are put into my mouth, my hope of its destruction—what shall I say of its supplanting by Socialism?

What shall I say concerning its mastery of and its waste of mechanical power, its commonwealth so poor, its enemies of the commonwealth so rich, its stupendous organization—for the misery of life! Its contempt of simple pleasures which everyone could enjoy but for its folly? Its eyeless vulgarity which has destroyed art, the one certain solace of labor? All this I felt then as now, but I did not know why it was so. The hope of the past times was gone, the struggles of mankind for many ages had produced nothing but this sordid, aimless, ugly confusion; the immediate future seemed to me likely to intensify all the present evils by sweeping away the last survivals of the days before the dull squalor of civilization had settled down on the world.

This was a bad lookout indeed, and, if I may mention myself as a personality and not as a mere type, especially so to a man of my disposition, careless of metaphysics and religion, as well as of scientific analysis, but with a deep love of the earth and the life on it, and a passion for the history of the past of mankind.

William Morris, *How I Became a Socialist*, 1896

48. By 1896, Morris had dedicated himself to what goal?

    A. The spread of mechanical power in industry
    B. The transformation of Britain into a commonwealth
    C. The triumph of socialism
    D. The spread of liberal democracy

49. What was Morris's relationship to socialism?

    A. He chose to become a socialist because he was appalled by the great waste of resources and general misery caused by modern society.
    B. He chose to become a socialist because of the persuasiveness of Marx's arguments.
    C. He rejected socialism because it produced nothing but ugly confusion.
    D. He rejected socialism because of a deep love of the earth and the life on it.

Questions 50 and 51 refer to the passage below.

The situation is critical in the extreme. In fact it is now absolutely clear that to delay the uprising would be fatal.

With all my might I urge comrades to realize that everything now hangs by a thread; that we are confronted by problems which are not to be solved by conferences or congresses (even congresses of Soviets), but exclusively by peoples, by the masses, by the struggle of the armed people. . . .

Who must take power? That is not important at present. Let the Revolutionary Military Committee do it, or "some other institution" which will declare that it will relinquish power only to the true representatives of the interests of the people, the interests of the army, the interests of the peasants, the interests of the starving.

All districts, all regiments, all forces must be mobilized at once and must immediately send their delegations to the Revolutionary Military Committee and to the Central Committee of the Bolsheviks with the insistent demand that under no circumstances should power be left in the hands of Kerensky [and his colleagues], . . . not under any circumstances; the matter must be decided without fail this very evening, or this very night.

Vladimir Ilyich Ulyanov, known as Lenin, "Call to Power," 1917

50. What was the immediate context of Lenin's "Call to Power"?

   A. Russia's entrance into World War I
   B. The onset of the February Revolution
   C. Russia's exit from World War I
   D. The onset of the October Revolution

51. Which of the following did Lenin believe necessary?

   A. The Russian military had to launch a new offensive.
   B. Kerensky had to move immediately against the Bolsheviks.
   C. The Bolshevik faction could wait no longer to seize power.
   D. Only the Russian military could effectively govern Russia.

Questions 52 and 53 refer to the passage below.

In order to make the title of this discourse generally intelligible, I have translated the term "Protoplasm," which is the scientific name of the substance of which I am about to speak, by the words "the physical basis of life." I suppose that, to many, the idea that there is such a thing as a physical basis, or matter, of life may be novel—so widely spread is the conception of life as something which works through matter. . . . Thus the matter of life, so far as we know it (and we have no right to speculate on any other), breaks up, in consequence of that continual death which is the condition of its manifesting vitality, into carbonic acid, water, and nitrogenous compounds, which certainly possess no properties but those of ordinary matter.

Thomas Henry Huxley, "The Physical Basis of Life," 1868

52. According to the passage, how did Huxley define "life"?

   A. A force that works through matter
   B. Essentially a philosophical notion
   C. Merely a property of a certain kind of matter
   D. A supernatural phenomenon

53. Huxley's view is representative of which nineteenth-century ideology?

   A. Anarchism
   B. Materialism
   C. Conservatism
   D. Romanticism

Questions 54 and 55 refer to the passage below.

As a Jew, I have never believed in collective guilt. Only the guilty were guilty.

Children of killers are not killers but children. I have neither the desire nor the authority to judge today's generation for the unspeakable crimes committed by the generation of Hitler.

But we may—and we must—hold it responsible, not for the past, but for the way it remembers the past. And for what it does with the memory of the past. In remembering, you will help your own people vanquish the ghosts that hover over its history. Remember: a community that does not come to terms with the dead will continue to traumatize the living.

We remember Auschwitz and all that it symbolizes because we believe that, in spite of the past and its horrors, the world is worthy of salvation; and salvation, like redemption, can be found only in memory.

Elie Wiesel, "Reflections of a Survivor," 1987

54. What did Wiesel believe about the current generation of Germans?

   A. They shared their ancestors' guilt for the Holocaust.
   B. They had a responsibility to remember the Holocaust.
   C. They shared in the responsibility for the Holocaust.
   D. They had no responsibility where the Holocaust was concerned.

55. Why did Wiesel assert that remembering the Holocaust was important?

   A. It was necessary for the German people to become reconciled to their own history.
   B. It hindered the healing process for the German people.
   C. It would ensure that it never occurred again.
   D. It would allow the Jews to forgive the German people.

Go on to Section I, Part B. ➜

AP European History Practice Exam 2

SECTION I, PART B

Short-Answer Questions
Recommended Time—40 minutes

Directions: The short-answer section consists of three questions to be answered in a recommended time of **40 minutes**. You must answer questions 1 and 2, but you may choose to answer **either** question 3 or question 4. Briefly answer ALL PARTS of each question. Be sure to write in complete sentences; outlines, phrases, and bullets will not be accepted.

1. Answer Parts A, B, and C.

   a) Identify ONE change in agricultural practices during the seventeenth century that contributed to the Industrial Revolution, and explain how it contributed to the Industrial Revolution.
   b) Describe ONE social problem caused by the growing urbanization.
   c) Explain ONE way in which governments tried to address the social problem.

2. Answer Parts A and B

   a) Identify ONE factor that contributed to the New Imperialism in the late nineteenth and early twentieth centuries, and explain how it contributed to the New Imperialism.
   b) Identify and describe TWO ways in which indigenous populations resisted or attempted to resist Western European imperialism during this period.

Answer either question 3 or 4.

3. Answer Parts A and B.

   a) Briefly explain TWO effects that the development of the separate spheres ideology had on women in the nineteenth century.
   b) Briefly explain ONE reason for the emergence of the separate spheres ideology in the nineteenth century.

Use the passage below to answer the question that follows.

Détente does not and cannot abolish the class struggle. No one can expect that under conditions of détente the communists will reconcile themselves to capitalist exploitation or that the monopolists will become revolutionaries. Thus the strict observance of the principle of non-interference in the affairs of other states, respect for their independence and sovereignty—this is the indispensable condition for détente.

   We do not hide the fact that we see in détente the road to the creation of more favorable conditions of peaceful socialist and communist construction. This only goes to show that socialism and peace are inseparable.

Leonid Brezhnev, excerpts from a speech at the CPSU Congress, February 29, 1976

4. Answer Parts A and B.

   a) Briefly explain ONE reason why the passage can be identified with developments in the Cold War.
   b) Briefly describe TWO factors that explain Brezhnev's willingness to enter into détente with the United States during this period.

STOP. End of Section I.

AP European History Practice Exam 2

SECTION II, PART A

Document-Based Question
Recommended Time—60 minutes

Directions: The following question is based on documents 1–7 provided below. (The documents have been edited for the purpose of this exercise.) The historical thinking skills that this question is designed to test include contextualization, synthesis, historical argumentation, and the use of historical evidence. Your response should be based on your knowledge of the topic and your analysis of the documents.

Write a well-integrated essay that does the following:

- States an appropriate thesis that directly addresses all parts of the question.
- Supports that thesis with evidence from all or all but one of the documents *and* your knowledge of European history beyond or outside of the documents.
- Analyzes the majority of the documents in terms of such features as their intended audience, purpose, point of view, format, argument, limitations, and/or social context as appropriate to your argument.
- Places your argument in the context of broader regional, national, or global processes.

Question: Compare and contrast the views presented below concerning the value of empire in the nineteenth century.

Document 1

Source: William Rathbone Gregg, "Shall We Retain Our Colonies?" 1851

[Formerly,] our colonies were customers who could not escape us, and vendors who could sell to us alone.

But a new system has risen up, not only differing from the old one, but based upon radically opposite notions of commercial policy. We have discovered that under this system our colonies have cost us, in addition to the annual estimate for their civil government and their defense, a sum amounting to many millions a year in the extra price we have paid for their produce beyond that which other countries could have supplied to us. . . . [T]hey yield us nothing and benefit us in nothing as colonies that they would not yield us and serve us were they altogether independent.

Document 2

Source: Benjamin Disraeli, "Crystal Palace Speech," 1872

Gentlemen, there is another and second great object of the Tory party. If the first is to maintain the institutions of the country, the second is, in my opinion, to uphold the empire of England. . . .

[W]hat has been the result of this attempt during the reign of Liberalism for the disintegration of empire? It has entirely failed. But how has it failed? Through the sympathy of the colonies with the mother country. They have decided that the empire shall not be destroyed, and in my opinion no minister in this country will do his duty who neglects any opportunity of reconstructing as much as possible our colonial empire, and of responding to those distant sympathies which may become the source of incalculable strength and happiness to this land. Therefore, gentlemen, with respect to the second great object of the Tory party also—the maintenance of the Empire—public opinion appears to be in favour of our principles. . . .

It cannot be far distant, when England will have to decide between national and cosmopolitan principles. The issue is not a mean one. It is whether you will be content to be a comfortable England, modelled and moulded upon continental principles and meeting in due course an inevitable fate, or whether you will be a great country—an imperial country—a country where your sons, when they rise, rise to paramount positions, and not merely obtain the esteem of their countrymen, but command the respect of the world. . . .

Document 3

Source: William Ewart Gladstone, "England's Mission," 1878

The honour to which the recent British policy is entitled is this: that from the beginning . . . to the end, the representatives of England, instead of taking the side of freedom, emancipation, and national progress, took, in every single point where a practical issue was raised, the side of servitude, of reaction, and of barbarism. . . .

Since [the Tory] accession to office, we have taken to ourselves . . . the Fiji Islands; the Transvaal Republic, in the teeth, it is now alleged, of the wishes of more than four-fifths of the enfranchised population; [and] the island of Cyprus. . . . [W]e have begun to protrude our military garrisons into our Indian frontier: in order to warn Russia how justly indignant we shall be if she should take . . . any corresponding step. . . .

I hold that to . . . overlook the proportions between our resources and our obligations, and above all to claim anything more than equality of rights in the moral and political intercourse of the world is not the way to make England great, but to make it morally and materially little.

Document 4

Source: John G. Paton, "Letter on New Hebrides Mission," 1883

For the following reasons we think the British government ought now to take possession of the New Hebrides group of the South Sea islands, of the Solomon group, and of all the intervening chain of islands from Fiji to New Guinea:

1.   Because she has already taken possession of Fiji in the east, and we hope it will soon be known authoritatively that she has taken possession of New Guinea at the northwest, adjoining her Australian possessions, and the islands between complete this chain of islands lying along the Australian coast.
2.   The sympathy of the New Hebrides natives are all with Great Britain, hence they long for British protection, while they fear and hate the French, who appear eager to annex the group, because they have seen the way the French have treated the native races in New Caledonia, the Loyalty Islands, and other South Sea islands. . . .

3.   All the men and all the money used in civilizing and Christianizing the New Hebrides have been British. Now fourteen missionaries and the Dayspring mission ship, and about 150 native evangelists and teachers are employed in the above work on this group, in which over £6000 yearly of British and British-colonial money is expended; and certainly it would be unwise to let any other power now take possession and reap the fruits of all this British outlay.

Document 5

Source: Jules François Camille Ferry, "Speech before the French Chamber of Deputies," 1884

The policy of colonial expansion is a political and economic system . . . that can be connected to three sets of ideas: economic ideas; the most far-reaching ideas of civilization; and ideas of a political and patriotic sort.

In the area of economics, I am placing before you, with the support of some statistics, the considerations that justify the policy of colonial expansion, as seen from the perspective of a need, felt more and more urgently by the industrialized population of Europe and especially the people of our rich and hardworking country of France: the need for outlets [exports]. . . .

Gentlemen, we must speak more loudly and more honestly! We must say openly that indeed the higher races have a right over the lower races. . . . I repeat, that the superior races have a right because they have a duty. They have the duty to civilize the inferior races. . . .

I say that French colonial policy, the policy of colonial expansion, the policy that has taken us under the Empire [Napoleon III's Second Empire], to Saigon, to Indochina, that has led us to Tunisia, to Madagascar—I say that this policy of colonial expansion was inspired by . . . the fact that a navy such as ours cannot do without safe harbors, defenses, supply centers on the high seas.

Document 6

> Source: German newspaper advertisement, June 24, 1890
>
> The diplomacy of the English works swiftly and secretly. What they created burst in the face of the astonished world on June 18th like a bomb—the German-English African Treaty. With one stroke of the pen—the hope of a great German colonial empire was ruined! Shall this treaty really be? No, no and again no! The German people must arise as one and declare that this treaty is unacceptable!... The treaty with England harms our interests and wounds our honor; this time it dares not become a reality! We are ready at the call of our Kaiser to step into the ranks and allow ourselves dumbly and obediently to be led against the enemy's shots, but we may also demand in exchange that the reward come to us which is worth the sacrifice, and this reward is: that we shall be a conquering people which takes its portion of the world itself!

Document 7

> Source: Captain F. D. Lugard, *The Rise of Our East African Empire*, 1893
>
> It is sufficient to reiterate here that, as long as our policy is one of free trade, we are compelled to seek new markets; for old ones are being closed to us by hostile tariffs, and our great dependencies, which formerly were the consumers of our goods, are now becoming our commercial rivals. It is inherent in a great colonial and commercial empire like ours that we go forward or go backward. To allow other nations to develop new fields, and to refuse to do so ourselves, is to go backward; and this is the more deplorable, seeing that we have proved ourselves notably capable of dealing with native races and of developing new countries at less expense than other nations. . . .
>
> A word as to missions in Africa. Beyond doubt I think the most useful missions are the medical and the industrial, in the initial stages of savage development. A combination of the two is, in my opinion, an ideal mission. . . . The "medicine man" is credited, not only with a knowledge of the simples and drugs which may avert or cure disease, but owing to the superstitions of the people, he is also supposed to have a knowledge of the charms and *dawa* which will invoke the aid of the Deity or appease His wrath, . . . The value of the industrial mission, on the other hand, depends, of course, largely on the nature of the tribes among whom it is located, . . . [W]hile improving the status of the native, [Industrial missions] will render his land more productive, and hence, by increasing his surplus products, will enable him to purchase from the trader the cloth which shall add to his decency, and the implements and household utensils which shall produce greater results for his labor and greater comforts in his social life.

Go on to Section II, Part B. ➜

AP European History Practice Exam 2

SECTION II, PART B

Long-Essay Question
Recommended Time—40 minutes

Directions: Write an essay that responds to ONE of the following three questions.

Question 1: Compare the political effects of nationalism on European civilization from 1789 to 1848 with the political effects of nationalism on European civilization from 1866 to 1945.

Question 2: Compare the context in which scientific work was done in the seventeenth century with the context in which scientific work was done in the nineteenth century.

Question 3: Identify and compare TWO characteristics of traditional imperialism (in the sixteenth and seventeenth centuries) and New Imperialism (in the nineteenth century).

End of Practice Exam

〉 Answers and Explanations

Section I, Part A: Multiple-Choice Questions

1. **D.** The passage refers to forms of corruption when it states that the Act would firmly establish the king's "power and authority . . . to visit, repress, redress, record, order, correct, restrain, and amend all such errors, heresies, abuses, offenses" in the realm. A is incorrect because the passage states that the king is already "justly and rightfully . . . the supreme head of the Church of England," and that the purpose of the Act is "for corroboration and confirmation" of that fact. B is incorrect because the passage clearly states that the position of head of the Church of England is established for both Henry VIII and "his heirs and successors, kings of this realm." C is incorrect because the passage makes no reference to Calvinist theology and because the Church of England under Henry VIII did not espouse a Calvinist theology.

2. **A.** The passage is evidence of a monarch, with the aid of his Parliament, consolidating his power at the expense of the Church and its clergy. B is incorrect because the passage indicates that the Act is establishing power in the English monarchy at the expense of the Catholic Church. C is incorrect because the passage does not refer to any increase in piety on the part of the nobility. D is incorrect because the passage does not refer to any increase in religiosity on the part of the masses.

3. **B.** The passage states that the Act establishes Henry VIII's right to "have and enjoy . . . all . . . profits, and commodities . . . of the same Church," which went a long way toward solving his financial difficulties. A is incorrect because the passage makes no mention of preventing the spread of Protestantism and was, by establishing the Church of England's independence from Rome, advancing the Protestant cause in England. C is incorrect because the passage makes no mention of legitimizing an heir and because Henry VIII had no male heir in 1534. D is incorrect because the passage makes no

mention of an alliance with the Holy Roman Emperor.

4. **C.** The author boasts of the monetary value of the goods ("nine thousand ducats in cash") produced on the estates of Florence. A is incorrect because the passage does not mention the size of the estates in Florence. B is incorrect because the passage does not mention the number of estates owned by any individuals. D is incorrect because the passage does not mention gold.

5. **D.** The passage refers to the large number of exports of wool and silk products. A is incorrect because the passage does not refer to banking. B is incorrect because the passage indicates that the production of agricultural products on the estates of Florence is for local consumption. C is incorrect because the passage does not refer to war and conquest.

6. **C.** The passage illustrates the author's great pride in the achievements of his city. A is incorrect because the passage does not refer to the mastery of military arts. B is incorrect because the passage does not refer to the code of chivalry, which was a characteristic of medieval culture, not Renaissance culture. D is incorrect because, despite the fact that patronage of the arts was a Renaissance value, the passage does not mention it.

7. **D.** The passage argues that perception of motion is relative to the observer, and therefore it is possible that the Earth is in motion. A and B are incorrect because Copernicus's assertion that the cosmos and the Earth are spherical is in agreement with the traditional, Aristotelian natural philosophers. C is incorrect because Copernicus is suggesting that the cosmos might not be geostatic.

8. **A.** The argument in the passage rests on observation (that the sun and moon are spherical and that water droplets are spherical) and an induction (that given the preponderance of bodies that are and strive to be circular, it is reasonable to conclude that the cosmos follows the general rule). B is incorrect because the passage makes no reference to ancient textual authority. C is incorrect because the passage

makes no reference to experimentation. D is incorrect because the argument is inductive rather than deductive.

9. **C.** Copernicus's willingness to question the traditional notion that the Earth was stationary is evidence that he was working in the skeptical tradition. A is incorrect because the passage offers evidence of Copernicus's willingness to question the traditional, Aristotelian notion that the Earth was stationary. B is incorrect because nothing in the passage suggests that Copernicus was working in a tradition that believed in nature's "hidden powers." Though it is true that Copernicus is understood to have worked in the Platonic/Pythagorean tradition of searching for the underlying mathematical laws of the universe, D is incorrect because there is nothing in the passage that could be used as evidence for such an assertion.

10. **A.** The passage makes it clear that the group met outside of, and independent from, traditional institutions like universities, courts, and the Church. B is incorrect because the passage makes it clear that the group was not part of a royal court. C is incorrect because it is evident from the passage that the group was not part of an effort to form a new university. D is incorrect because the passage makes it clear that the group was not under the auspices of any church.

11. **C.** The passage states that the goal of the group was to know "the state of these studies, as then cultivated at home and abroad" and indicates that members helped to make this knowledge more readily available. A is incorrect because the passage makes no reference to the goal of undermining the traditional worldview. B is incorrect because the passage says that the group avoided issues of religion, but not that it was dedicated to challenging the Church. D is incorrect because the passage makes no reference to an attempt to regulate knowledge.

12. **B.** The passage explicitly states that "this power has its original only from compact, and agreement, and the mutual consent of those who make up the community." A is incorrect because the passage does not refer to divine right, a concept that Locke wished to discredit. C is incorrect because the word Locke chooses is *consent,*

which implies the possible withdrawal, rather than Hobbes's word—*covenant*—which implied permanency. D is incorrect because the passage does not refer to conquest.

13. **C.** Locke's expression of the preservation of the "lives, liberties, and possessions" of society's members, of the limited nature of properly derived political power, and of the consent of the members of society as the origin of properly derived political power are all key concepts of constitutionalism. A is incorrect because the passage does not argue in favor of divine right monarchy. B is incorrect because the passage explicitly argues that properly derived political power cannot be arbitrary. D is incorrect because Locke's emphasis on the protection of the property and possessions of society members is more in line with liberal constitutionalism than socialism.

14. **D.** The passage states that a government [legislature] forfeits its legitimacy when it "endeavor[s] to grasp themselves, or put into the hands of any other, an absolute power over the lives, liberties, and estates of the people." A is incorrect because the passage does not state that a government loses legitimacy in moments of weakness. B is incorrect because the passage does not say that a government loses its legitimacy any time the people wish to make a change. C is incorrect because the passage does not say that instances of corruption equate to illegitimacy, only that corruption can be one motivation for a government seeking to exercise absolute power.

15. **C.** The illustration demands that people have access to the commons (common land), a custom that was being denied them through the enclosure of land. While the illustration dates from the era of the English Civil War, A and B are incorrect because the illustration does not indicate that Winstanley and the Diggers supported any particular faction. D is incorrect because the illustration does not refer to a three-field agricultural system.

16. **B.** The illustration shows the military force being used to expel Winstanley and the Diggers from the commons. A, C, and D are incorrect because the illustration shows the military force expelling Winstanley and the Diggers and not supporting them, awarding them lands, or showing indifference, respectively.

17. **A.** The passage expresses the atheist view that "men have no need of theology, of revelation, or of gods." B is incorrect because a deist theology holds that God is necessary. C and D are incorrect because both Protestant and Catholic theologies begin with a belief in a necessary God.

18. **D.** Both the date of the passage and its advocacy of atheism locate it in the later, radical phase of the Enlightenment. A is incorrect because the date of the passage and its atheistic stance show that it is not a passage from the later stages of the Protestant reformation. B is incorrect because the passage offers a critique of religion, not political ideas. C is incorrect because the passage offers a critique of religion, not an argument for the need for an enlightened sovereign.

19. **B.** The passage affirms the core Enlightenment ideals of reason and freedom of thought by arguing for a rational critique of religious belief. A is incorrect because not all of the Enlightenment's thought on religion and faith was atheistic. C is incorrect because the passage does not offer rational proof of the existence of God. D is incorrect because the passage is not satirical.

20. **B.** The passage indicates that the clergy of France are to be elected by the people of France, and that these clergy are to "be loyal to the nation." A is incorrect because the passage makes no reference to Protestant theological reforms. C is incorrect because the passage refers to the election of clergy and their loyalty to the nation, not their complete abolishment. D is incorrect because the passage forbids the French people from recognizing clergy appointed by anyone foreign to France (which includes the pope) and because it commands French clergy to be loyal to the nation.

21. **C.** The existing archbishops owed their position to their contacts in Rome and ultimately to the pope. A is incorrect because the document expresses the will of the National Assembly that the clergy be brought under the auspices of the French state. B is incorrect because the document states that, henceforth, the clergy must be loyal to "the nation, the law, and the king," and because a large number of the king's supporters believed the independent power and wealth

of the clergy needed to be curbed and brought under the authority of the state. D is incorrect because some simple parish priests sided with the National Assembly on this issue, believing that simple people would be given greater attention and care under a clergy that was elected and loyal to the French nation.

22. **D.** The document proclaimed that, by law, "all Frenchmen are in permanent requisition for the service of the armies." A is incorrect because the French Republic was proclaimed to exist on September 22, 1792, nearly a year prior to the publication of the *Levée en Masse*. B is incorrect because the Committee of Public Safety was created in March 1793 by the National Convention and then restructured in July 1793; it was the Committee of Public Safety that authored the *Levée en Masse*. C is incorrect because France had declared war on the Habsburg monarchy of Austria on April 20, 1792, and the kingdom of Prussia joined the Austrian side a few weeks later. The *Levée en Masse* was a response to the needs of France in the face of war with the First Coalition, not a declaration of it.

23. **B.** The *Levée en Masse* is a good example of the way in which the Committee of Public Safety successfully harnessed the human resources of the new French Republic; it succeeded in training an army of about eight hundred thousand soldiers in less than a year, turning the tide of the War of the First Coalition in France's favor. A is incorrect because the *Levée en Masse* does not deal with efforts to reform the economy of the new French Republic. C is incorrect because the *Levée en Masse* does not deal with efforts to reform the religious rituals of the Church. D is incorrect because the *Levée en Masse*, and the military success it brought, actually increased the popularity of the Committee of Public Safety.

24. **D.** It can be reasonably argued that the *Levée en Masse* was the first instance in modern European warfare where all elements of the population and all the reserves of the state were committed to a war effort. A is incorrect because the *Levée en Masse* did not introduce weaponry produced by large-scale industrialization. B is incorrect because the *Levée en Masse*

did not advocate the total extinction of France's enemies. C is incorrect because the War of the First Coalition continued to be run by French generals; the *Levée en Masse* simply increased the size and improved the training of the soldiers available to them.

25. **A.** The passage describes the effects on workers who spun thread in their homes for the textile trade as the mode of production shifted to more mechanized labor in a mill system. B is incorrect because the passage does not describe the effects of shifting from agricultural work to industrial manufacturing. C is incorrect because the passage does not discuss shifts in the textile markets, but rather in the mode of production. D is incorrect because the passage does not describe the effects of trade unions.

26. **C.** The passage indicates that there is an initial investment of "A wooden wheel costing 2 s[hillings] for each person, with one reel costing 3 s[hillings] set up the family," while a wife and four children could add six or seven shillings *a week* "by their wheels." A is incorrect because the passage does not indicate that spinning took very little time. B is incorrect because the passage indicates that spinning done by the wife and children supplemented the husband/father's income rather than replaced it. D is incorrect because the passage indicates that spinning as a cottage industry was done by a wife and all the household children; it was in the mill system that it was done almost exclusively by girls.

27. **D.** The passage indicates the author's concern for the moral effects of taking young girls and "herding them together" with unmarried men and boys. A is incorrect because the passage does not refer to a lack of religious instruction in the mills. B is incorrect because the passage does not refer to theft on the part of workers. C is incorrect because the women and girls were already employed in the spinning trade before the shift to the mill system.

28. **B.** The passage states Chadwick's belief that "the various forms of epidemic, endemic, and other disease [are] caused . . . by atmospheric impurities . . . , by damp and filth, and close and overcrowded dwellings." A is incorrect because the passage does not refer to the diet of the poor. C is incorrect because the passage does not refer to the Black Death. D is incorrect because the passage does not refer to the working conditions of the poor.

29. **C.** Chadwick reported that "the ravages of epidemics and other diseases . . . tend to increase the pressure of population." A is incorrect because Chadwick reported that "the ravages of epidemics and other diseases do not diminish but tend to increase the pressure of population pressure." B and D are incorrect because Chadwick reported that "the ravages of epidemics and other diseases . . . tend to *increase* the pressure of population."

30. **A.** The passage indicates a belief that unsanitary living conditions produce a population that "is less susceptible of moral influences" and therefore "improvident, reckless, and intemperate, and with habitual avidity for sensual gratifications." B is incorrect because the passage indicates that unsanitary living conditions had the effect of producing a population that is "improvident, reckless, and intemperate." C is incorrect because the passage does not examine the physical effects of poor sanitation, but rather the moral effects. D is incorrect because the passage indicates that unsanitary living conditions produce a population that is "improvident, reckless, and intemperate," not one with improved morals.

31. **B.** The title ("History of Swing"), the reputed authorship ("Kent Rick-Burner"); and the burning hayrick in the background all refer to the Swing Riots, the widespread uprising by agricultural workers in response to the use of labor-displacing threshing machines and the threatening notes, usually left at the scene of the crimes, signed "Captain Swing." A is incorrect because the images contain no reference to the English monarchy. C is incorrect because the image contains no references to the July Revolution in France. D is incorrect because the image contains no references to the Irish Potato Famine, and because 1830 is too early for such images.

32. **D.** The image depicts a horse-mounted landlord pointing to his burning hayrick and an agricultural laborer pointing to his starving family because their income has been reduced by the use of threshing machines. A is incorrect because the image does not depict a factory setting. B is incorrect because the image does not depict a naval setting. C is incorrect because the image does not depict any industrial setting or interests.

33. **B.** The passage states that "nationality ought only to be . . . a human group called by its geographical position, its traditions, and its language." A is incorrect because the passage does not argue that a nation must be a kingdom or have longstanding borders. C is incorrect because the passage does not say that a nation is only a nation if its people are strong enough to avoid foreign domination. D is incorrect because the passage does not argue that a nation must be made up of people with a unified political ideology.

34. **C.** The passage reflects Mazzini's nationalist desire for a united Italy and his romantic sense that a united Italy is a "natural" entity and a moral imperative of history. A is incorrect because Mazzini's desire for a new nation of Italy goes against mid-nineteenth-century nationalists' emphasis on tradition, stability, and legitimacy. B is incorrect because there are no expressions of socialist ideas in the passage. D is incorrect because there are no expressions of either anarchism or socialism in the passage.

35. **D.** Bismarck, the conservative chancellor of Germany, is portraying his conservative government as the natural caretaker of the nation and its working people, in contrast to the Social Democrats, whom he depicts as doing the bidding of bourgeois capitalists and splitting the nation by looking to exploit and dominate the working classes. A is incorrect because the passage does not address constitutionalism, an ideology born in seventeenth-century Europe. B is incorrect because Bismarck is a conservative delivering a conservative national message. C is incorrect because popular nationalism came into being in the first half of the nineteenth century.

36. **A.** Bismarck says that the purpose of government "is to serve the people," and that as the governing party, the conservatives "want to serve the people." In contrast, he depicts the Social Democrats as a party whose "mission is to lead, to rule." B is incorrect because Bismarck depicts his government as servants of the people, not as absolute rulers who should lead without opposition. C is incorrect because it is the Social Democrats whom Bismarck characterizes as believing that they are "leaders" who should be followed. D is incorrect because Bismarck is the leader of the governing party in Germany, not the loyal opposition.

37. **D.** The passage says that "there are objectives that only the state in its totality can fulfill," and that fulfilling them is a "responsibility of the state from which the state will not be able to withdraw." A is incorrect because the passage states that it "would be madness for a corporate body or a collectivity to take charge of those objectives that the individual can accomplish." B is incorrect because the passage says that "there are objectives that only the state in its totality can fulfill," and that fulfilling them is a "responsibility of the state," not that of private individuals. C is incorrect because the passage does not say that the state must fulfill any objective demanded by the people.

38. **C.** The cartoonist depicts Garibaldi as one of two men responsible for the unification of Italy, allowing one to infer that the cartoonist believed Garibaldi to have had a significant, if subservient, role in that accomplishment. A and B are incorrect because the cartoon offers no clues as to whether the cartoonist approved or disapproved of Italian unification. D is incorrect because Count Cavour's absence from the cartoon disallows a reliable inference as to his importance.

39. **C.** Garibaldi surrendered the southern lands of the Italian Peninsula to Victor Emmanuel II on the bridge of Teano on October 26, 1860. A and B are incorrect because 1848 is well before Garibaldi's campaign in Italy, which occurred in 1860. D is incorrect because Garibaldi would not have been depicted as aiding Victor Emmanuel II until after he surrendered the

southern lands of the Italian Peninsula to him in October 1860.

40. **A.** The cartoon depicts Garibaldi fitting the entire boot of Italy onto the leg of King Victor Emmanuel II, allowing the inference that the cartoonist viewed the unification of Italy as progressing. B is incorrect because fitting the entire boot suggests that the cartoonist viewed the unification of Italy as progressing, not doubtful. C and D are incorrect because nothing in the cartoon allows an inference as to whether the cartoonist viewed the unification of Italy as either a positive or negative development.

41. **B.** The telegram represents Germany's response, as a fellow member of the Triple Alliance, to Austria-Hungary concerning the scope of action open to them in dealing with the Balkan situation, which came to a head with the assassination of Crown Prince Franz Ferdinand on June 28, 1914. A is incorrect because the telegram was not sent during the process of German unification, which occurred from roughly 1866 to 1871. C is incorrect because the telegram was not sent during Germany's rearmament in violation of the Treaty of Paris, which occurred in the 1930s. D is incorrect because the telegram was not sent during 1882 when the Triple Alliance was created.

42. **B.** Bethmann-Hollweg's telegram is often referred to as Germany's "blank check" because it was understood to give Austria an unlimited scope of response to the assassination of Franz Ferdinand, to Serbia, and Pan-Slavism within the Austro-Hungarian Empire. A is incorrect because the telegram did not pledge Germany to join the Triple Alliance, which was previously created in 1882. C is incorrect because Franz Joseph was already emperor of Austria-Hungary; Franz Ferdinand had been his heir. D is incorrect because the telegram was understood to give Austria an unlimited scope of response.

43. **D.** The passage discusses social changes that were occurring during World War I, which broke out in 1914 and would continue to rage until 1918. A is incorrect because the essay was written in 1916, and World War II did not begin until 1939. B is incorrect because World War I

had only been going on for two years in 1916. C is incorrect because the so-called Interwar Years were between 1918 and 1939.

44. **C.** The passage states that "[b]ecause it will obviously be impossible for all to find work quickly . . . there is almost certain to be an outcry for . . . women [to go] 'Back to the Home!'" A is incorrect because the passage says that forcing women back into the home would be unjust; it does not say that women would never be able to adjust. B is incorrect because the passage does not refer to an outright revolt of the nation's women. D is incorrect because the passage indicates that women could be seen as a cheaper alternative labor source by some employers; it does not say that they would be better paid than men.

45. **A.** The passage states that "conscienceless employers may regard women's labor as preferable, owing to its cheapness and its docility." B is incorrect because the passage does not refer to women being corrupted by the workplace. C is incorrect because the passage does not refer to women in the context of military service. D is incorrect because the passage does not refer to women working alongside men.

46. **A.** The Bolshevik government of Russia agreed to the punitive nature of the treaty with Germany and its allies because Russia needed to end the war effort to consolidate its revolutionary gains. B is incorrect because the treaty was not a result of corruption or of collaboration between Bolsheviks and Russian business interests. C is incorrect because the dissolution of the Triple Entente alliance of Britain, France, and Russia was a *result* of the Treaty of Brest-Litovsk. D is incorrect because French and British aid being given to the so-called White Russians who opposed the Bolshevik government *resulted* from the Treaty of Brest-Litovsk.

47. **C.** In Article III of the treaty, Russia surrendered the western part of its empire (Poland, Ukraine, Finland, and the Baltic Provinces) to Germany. A and B are incorrect because, in Article III of the treaty, Russia ceded territory to the German Empire, not the other way around.

C is incorrect because, in Article III of the treaty, Russia surrendered the *eastern* part of its empire (Poland, Ukraine, Finland, and the Baltic Provinces) to Germany.

48. **C.** The passage indicates that Morris had dedicated himself to his "hope of [modern civilization's] destruction" and "its supplanting by Socialism." A is incorrect because the passage does not refer to a dedication to the spread of mechanical power in industry. B is incorrect because the passage does not refer to transforming Britain into a commonwealth. D is incorrect because the passage does not refer to the spread of liberal democracy.

49. **A.** The passage indicates that Morris turned to socialism because he was deeply disturbed by modern civilization's "waste of mechanical power" and "its stupendous organization—for the misery of life!" B is incorrect because the passage makes no reference to Marx's arguments. C is incorrect because the passage indicates that Morris thought it was the past "struggles of mankind," not socialism, that had produced "nothing but this sordid, aimless, ugly confusion." D is incorrect because the passage indicates that his "deep love of the earth and the life on it" was one reason that he chose to embrace socialism, not reject it.

50. **D.** The passage calls for the removal by force of Alexander Kerensky's provisional government, which was the initial act of the October Revolution in Russia in 1917. A is incorrect because Russia had entered World War I in 1914. B is incorrect because the February Revolution in Russia led to the *establishment* of Kerensky's provisional government, not its fall from power. C is incorrect because Russia withdrew from World War I only after Lenin's Bolsheviks had replaced Kerensky's provisional government.

51. **C.** The passage asserts that the Bolsheviks had to seize power immediately from Kerensky and the provisional government. A is incorrect because the passage makes no reference to a new military offensive. B is incorrect because the passage asserts that the Bolsheviks had to seize power immediately from Kerensky and the provisional government, not that Kerensky had to move against the Bolsheviks. D is incorrect because the passage

makes no reference to military rule and because the concept of military rule was antithetical to Lenin's political beliefs.

52. **C.** The passage asserts that life has a physical basis; that is, it possesses "no properties but those of ordinary matter." A is incorrect because the passage states that "the conception of life as a something which works through matter" is a commonly held but incorrect view. B is incorrect because the passage makes no reference to life as a philosophical notion. D is incorrect because the passage asserts that life has a "physical basis," not a supernatural one.

53. **B.** Huxley's view that life has a physical (that is, a material) basis is representative of the nineteenth-century ideology of materialism, which held that nothing exists except matter. A is incorrect because the passage does not represent the nineteenth-century ideology of anarchism, a political ideology that advocated stateless societies. C is incorrect because the passage also does not represent conservatism, a political ideology that advocated respect for tradition in the face of external forces for change. D is incorrect because the passage does not represent romanticism, which urged the cultivation of sentiment and emotion by reconnecting with nature and the past.

54. **B.** Weisel asserts that his German audience was "responsible, not for the past, but for the way it remembers the past." A is incorrect because the passage indicates that Weisel "never believed in collective guilt." C is incorrect because in the passage Weisel asserts that his German audience was *not* responsible for the past. D is incorrect because Weisel asserts that his German audience *was* responsible "for the way it remembers the past."

55. **A.** The passage asserts that remembering the Holocaust is necessary for "coming to terms" with and finding "redemption" for Germany's past. B is incorrect because the passage intimates that remembering the Holocaust would promote healing among the German people, not hinder it. C is incorrect because the passage does not assert that remembering the Holocaust could ensure that it never happened again. D is incorrect, because the passage does not mention Jewish forgiveness of the German people.

Section I, Part B: Short-Answer Questions

Strategies

Step 1. Compose a topic sentence that responds to the question and gives you something specific to support and illustrate.

Step 2. Support and illustrate your assertion in the topic sentence with specific examples.

Suggested Responses

1. a) A good response will identify ONE change in agricultural practices during the seventeenth century that contributed to the Industrial Revolution, and explain how it contributed to the Industrial Revolution, such as:

    - The enclosure movement was developed in response to new agricultural technologies like seed drills, and supported in England by a Parliament dominated by landed nobility. The movement increased agricultural productivity at the same time it displaced small farmers. The increased efficiency of agriculture further reduced the need for labor, creating a mobile, wage-based workforce that was necessary for the Industrial Revolution.
    - The demise of the village common is a second agricultural change, which would have a similar impact on farmers and the creation of a mobile, wage-based workforce.

    b) A good response will describe ONE social problem caused by the growing urbanization, such as:

    - Housing was insufficient to cope with a huge influx in population, resulting in overcrowding, with multiple families often staying in a single apartment. Overcrowding also led to disease spreading quickly as many people were forced into close contact.
    - The increase on population strained sanitation services, with streets filled with sewage and other waste. This resulted in contamination of water sources and outbreaks of illnesses, such as cholera and dysentery.
    - There was little regulation of food. Consumers were sold food cut with contaminants like alum in bread, or lead in pepper, to increase profits by improving the food's appearance or decreasing the cost to produce it.

    c) A good response will explain ONE way in which cities responded to the social problem, such as:

    - Social investigations were performed by governmental bodies such as the Poor Law Commission in England. Often these advocated for the government to take proactive approaches to the social problems by establishing reforms in things like water and sanitation. While governments, often comprised of industrialists, were initially reluctant to support reforms, fear of diseases like cholera went a long way to securing their support. Ultimately Great Britain passed the Public Health Act in 1848, inspiring governments in Germany, the United States, and France to follow suit.
    - Cities hired urban planners to eliminate slums, widen streets, create open spaces and parks, and implement improvements in sewers and water. An example of this is Georges-Eugène Haussman's redesign of Paris, which began in 1853.
    - Scandals over adulterated foods causing death, together with the increasing risk to exports posed by such negative publicity, prompted eventual passage of laws regulating the quality of food and drugs, such as the Sale of Food and Drug Act in Great Britain.

2. a) A good response will include ONE factor that contributed to the New Imperialism in the late nineteenth and early twentieth centuries, and explain how it contributed to the New Imperialism, such as:

    - The spread and intensification of industrialization created a need for raw materials, many of which European nations did not have. By controlling new territories, they simultaneously gained control over their resources while denying rival nations access to those same materials.
    - Social Darwinism helped make the conquest and domination of other nations more palatable by justifying it as part of the ultimate evolution and improvement of humanity. By framing indigenous cultures as inferior to European cultures, one could then justify their subjugation. Additional social theories, like the idea of the "white man's burden," encouraged Europeans to practice a form of cultural imperialism, suppressing indigenous religions and cultural practices.

- Competition among European nations for dominance led to their seeking colonies abroad, to act as coaling stops or refueling stations for their naval and commercial ships. Acquisition of colonies later became an issue of national pride. A nation's failure to secure overseas colonies was construed in that climate as an unacceptable weakness.

- Technological advances, like steamships, helped Western European powers quickly concentrate their military might across the world. Superior weaponry allowed even smaller European military units to quell any resistance with relatively few European casualties. Quinine allowed Europeans to travel and settle without risk of malaria, an earlier deterrent.

b) A good response will include TWO ways in which indigenous populations resisted or attempted to resist Western European imperialism during this period, such as:

- The India Congress Party was formed in India in 1885. Comprised primarily of Hindu elites who had taken advantage of British liberal educations, and inspired by ideas of self-government and equality, they originally sought economic changes and a larger role in policy-making. A more radical faction later emerged which supported independence from Great Britain. One of their leaders was Mohandas Gandhi, who encouraged followers and gained international attention through his acts of civil disobedience.

- The Zulu first came into conflict with the Boers in southern Africa who migrated into their territory to avoid the encroaching British, and then became vassals of the Boer-controlled Natal. When the British took over the territory, the Zulu resisted. The Zulu were an African tribe emphasizing military discipline and organization, which probably accounts for their early victory against the British in which their army, with only spears and superior numbers, defeated a British force armed with modern weapons. Ultimately, though, the British prevailed and the Zulu lost their independence.

- The Sepoy Rebellion, also called the Indian Mutiny, was started by sepoys, who were Indian soldiers working for the British East India Company. A rumor circulated that the grease used to lubricate the cartridges of the new Enfield rifle contained a mix of cow and pig fat. Loading the rifles required biting the end of the cartridge, violating proscriptions of both Muslim and Hindu religions. This occurred in the broader context of a growing resentment against the British who were transforming Indian ways of life. Thus, sepoys refused to use the Enfield rifles. Their harsh sentences prompted other sepoys to attack their British officers, and later any British, including women and children. The British response was swift and violent.

- The Boxer Rebellion was so called because the rebels believed their boxing exercises would render them impervious to bullets. Formed from members of the Society of the Righteous and Harmonious Fists, their goal was to rid China of all foreigners and foreign influences (in the form of Chinese Christians). Encouraged by the Qing dynasty, the Boxers controlled the area around Beijing, killing both foreigners and Chinese Christians, and destroying their property. Finally an international force, headed by the United States, recaptured Beijing.

3. a) One effect that the development of the separate sphere ideology had on women in the nineteenth century was to make any activity outside the home suspect and, therefore, dangerous to a woman's reputation. The best example of this can be seen in the logic and enforcement of Britain's Contagious Disease Act, first passed in 1864.

  The Act, originally intended to curb the spread of venereal disease in towns with naval ports, allowed police to detain any woman suspected of prostitution and force her to have a gynecological exam. In practice, the Act was enforced over much of Great Britain, and any woman caught alone on the streets at night was subject to arrest and the forced exam because the assumption, enforced by separate sphere ideology, was that the only woman who would be out alone after dark was a prostitute.

  Conversely, the development of a separate sphere ideology in the nineteenth century gave women more power within the household. The existence of this effect is more controversial among historians, but one school of thinking argues that the restriction of women's sphere of action to the home actually increased their power within that sphere, giving them almost total control over their children's education, domestic servants, and certain parts of the household budget.

b) One reason that historians almost always cite for the emergence of a separate sphere ideology in the nineteenth century is the competition for jobs created by the second phase of industrialization.

The initial phases of industrialization, occurring in the late eighteenth and early nineteenth centuries, had been labor-intensive, drawing large numbers of men, women, and children into the factories and mills. But in the second half of the nineteenth century, complex machinery began to make much of that labor unnecessary, creating unemployment and intense competition for jobs. Initially men lost their jobs because women and children were cheaper labor. Hence, men reacted by creating a separate sphere ideology that asserted it was unhealthy and unnatural for women to work outside the home.

4. a) The passage can be identified with developments in the Cold War because of frequent references to détente.

The word *détente* denotes an era of relaxing tensions, especially between the United States and the Soviet Union during the Cold War. When used by Leonid Brezhnev, general secretary of the Central Committee of the Communist Party of the Soviet Union from 1964 to 1982, détente can only refer to the era of the Cold War that was characterized by a number of nuclear test ban treaties and arms-limitation talks between the two superpowers, the Soviet Union and the United States.

b) One reason that explains Brezhnev's willingness to cultivate an atmosphere of détente with the United States during this period is the rethinking of U.S. and Soviet foreign policy that followed the Cuban Missile Crisis in 1962.

After this event, which brought the two superpowers to the brink of nuclear war, a rethinking of positions occurred in which both sides acknowledged that more direct and open communication was necessary to avert such brushes with disaster in the future. Détente was essentially an extension of that notion.

Another reason that explains Brezhnev's willingness to cultivate an atmosphere of détente with the United States during this period was the economic strain that the nuclear arms race put on the Soviet Union.

The constant need to keep its country's nuclear arms arsenal more advanced than its opponent's made great demands on both the U.S. and the Soviet economies. The effects of these demands were felt more acutely in the Soviet Union whose economy was less productive than that of the United States. The cost savings gained from the signing of treaties such as SALT I, SALT II, and the Helsinki Accords, which limited the number of nuclear weapons in each superpower's arsenal, provided a great incentive for Brezhnev to cultivate an atmosphere of détente.

Section II, Part A: The Document-Based Question (DBQ)

Strategies

Remember the five steps to a short history essay of high quality:

Step 1. As you read the documents, decide how you are going to group them.

Step 2. Compose a thesis that explains why the documents should be grouped in the way you have chosen.

Step 3. Compose your topic sentences and make sure they logically present your thesis.

Step 4. Support and illustrate your thesis with specific examples that contextualize the documents.

Step 5. *If you have time*, compose a one-paragraph conclusion that restates your thesis. This question asks you to compare and contrast views of empire offered over time. Begin by identifying their similarities and differences (ask what the authors agree and disagree about) and then see if any trends develop over time.

Outline

A possible outline to the answer for this question looks like this:

Thesis: The documents illustrate arguments over the value of colonies to the colonizing nations and illustrate a tendency over time for arguments of political and strategic necessity to replace arguments of economic profitability and moral duty.

Topic Sentence A: Documents #1 and #3 both make arguments that colonies are unnecessary and undesirable because they are economically unprofitable; document #3 makes the further argument that colonies damage the moral standing of the colonizing nation.

Specific Examples: In #1, Gregg (1851) states that colonies have been rendered economically unprofitable (and therefore unnecessary) by the rise of a system of free trade. In #3, Gladstone (1878) says that colonies are unprofitable in both the material and moral sense, as they must be held by military means against the wishes of those who hold them.

Topic Sentence B: Documents #2 and #4 to #7 make arguments for the economic, moral, and strategic necessity of colonies.

Specific Examples: In #2, Disraeli (1872) argues that colonies are desired by "more primitive civilizations" and necessary for a nation to retain international influence and prestige. In #4, Paton (1883) maintains that colonies are morally profitable and necessary for moral reasons—that is, civilizing and Christianizing missions. In #5, Ferry (1884) states that colonies are economically, morally, and strategically necessary due to the need for economic outlets, to fulfill a Christian civilizing mission, and to establish military defense bases. The 1890 German newspaper advertisement in #6 claims that colonies are necessary for reasons of both economic interest and national honor. Finally, in #7, Lugard (1893) reasons that colonies are economically necessary for new markets and for the "development" of the colonizing nation—to prevent the nation from "falling behind."

Topic Sentence C: Read in chronological order, the documents illustrate a trend over time for arguments of economic and strategic necessity replacing arguments of economic profitability and moral duty.

Specific Examples: No documents in the set argue directly for the economic profitability of colonies (though some argue for their economic necessity); the only evidence that arguments for profitability exist is the need to refute them shown in documents #1 and #3. The dominant chord of argument in all documents after 1884 (documents #5 to #7) is necessity—economic, political, and strategic. There is no reference to moral duty after 1890 (documents #6 and #7).

Section II, Part B: The Long-Essay Question

Strategies

Choose the question for which you can quickly write a clear thesis and three topic sentences that you can

illustrate and support with several specific examples. Then follow the five-step formula to constructing a history essay of high quality:

Step 1. Find the action words in the question and determine what it wants you to do.

Step 2. Compose a thesis that responds to the question and gives you something specific to support and illustrate.

Step 3. Compose your topic sentences and make sure they logically present your thesis.

Step 4. Support and illustrate your thesis with specific examples.

Step 5. *If you have time*, compose a one-paragraph conclusion that restates your thesis.

And remember the traps to avoid:

- **Long sentences with multiple clauses.** Your goal is to write the clearest sentence possible; most often the clearest sentence is a relatively short one.
- **Digressions.** No matter how fascinating or insightful you find some idea or fact, if it doesn't directly support or illustrate your thesis, don't put it in.
- **Mystery.** Don't ask a lot of rhetorical questions, and don't go for a surprise ending. The readers are looking for your thesis, your argument, and your evidence; give these points to them in a clear, straightforward manner.

Outlines

Question 1: Compare the political effects of nationalism on European civilization from 1789 to 1848 with the political effects of nationalism on European civilization from 1866 to 1945.

Thesis: From 1789 to 1848, nationalism tended to support the liberal notion that political sovereignty resided with the people, helping to fuel popular uprisings against traditional governments. From 1866 to 1945, nationalism tended to support the conservative belief in the value of historical traditions, helping to fuel movements of national unification under traditional, conservative monarchies and the rise of totalitarian parties with ultranationalist ideologies.

Topic Sentence A: From 1789 to 1848, nationalism was opposed by conservative forces, and nationalists made common cause with liberal reformers.

Specific Examples:

- The "Representatives of the Nation" rhetoric of the French Revolution from 1789 to 1799
- The wave of Liberal Nationalist revolutions from 1820 to 1848, including Spain (1820–1823), Sicily and Piedmont (1821), Greece (1829), Belgium (1830), France (1830), and all of Europe in 1848

Topic Sentence B: From 1866 to 1945, the conservative tendencies of nationalism came to the fore and beliefs in the value of historical traditions and heavily mythologized dreams of past national glories fueled conservative-led movements of national unification and empire building.

Specific Examples:

- The unification of Italy under Cavour and King Victor Emmanuel II
- The unification of Germany under Otto von Bismarck and Kaiser Wilhelm I of Prussia
- The rise of fascist movements in the 1920s and 1930s
- The NSDAP's rise to power in Germany and the popularity of Hitler's ultranationalist rhetoric

Question 2: Compare the context in which scientific work was done in the seventeenth century with the context in which scientific work was done in the nineteenth century.

Thesis: In the seventeenth century, scientific work was done in the context of both the Church and new, secular institutions that were just beginning to offer greater intellectual freedom. In the nineteenth century, scientific work was done almost exclusively in secular institutions that tended to foster materialist theories.

Topic Sentence A1: In the seventeenth century, scientific work was done in both the traditional Church-related institution and in new secular institutions.

Specific Examples:

Science in Church institutions:

- Jesuit astronomers in Italian universities
- Isaac Newton in Cambridge

Science in new secular institutions:

- Royal courts, such as the Court of Cosimo de Medici in Florence
- Royal societies and academies, such as the Royal Society of London
- Smaller, independent academies, such as the Neoplatonic Academy in Florence

Topic Sentence A2: The kind of scientific work (or natural philosophy, as it was termed in the seventeenth century) that was produced in the tension between Church and secular institutions tended to be a blend of traditional thinking in terms of God's purpose and newer thinking that emphasized natural laws and quantifiable, mechanical forces.

Specific Examples:

- Galileo's retention of the traditional, Aristotelian concept of uniform circular motion, combined with his emphasis on direct observation of heavenly bodies and the quantification of their orbits.
- Newton's introduction of the concept of force and his quantification of the force of universal gravitation, together with his retention of a belief in an active God in the universe.

Topic Sentence B1: In the nineteenth century, scientific work was done almost exclusively in secular institutions.

Specific Examples:

- Secular universities, such as the University of Edinburgh and the University of London replaced Cambridge and Oxford as hubs of science in Britain.
- The British Association for the Advancement of Science displaced the Royal Society of London.

Topic Sentence B2: In the new secular context of the nineteenth century, materialist theories replaced more orthodox theories of divine forces and plans.

Specific Examples:

- Charles Darwin theory of evolution by natural selection replaced William Paley's theory of natural theology and divine design.
- Thomas Henry Huxley's On the *Physical Basis of Life* supplanted vital force theories.

Question 3: Identify and compare TWO characteristics of traditional imperialism (sixteenth and seventeenth century) and the New Imperialism (nineteenth century).

Thesis: Imperialism of the sixteenth and seventeenth century is called "traditional" to distinguish it from the New Imperialism of the nineteenth century. Traditional imperialism was primarily based on economics. The more modern version, New Imperialism, frequently demonstrated an ideologically based reason for its existence.

Topic Sentence A: "God, gold, and glory" were the motives behind much of the conquest of the New World by the Spaniards. While conversion of native peoples to Christianity was certainly an important goal of establishing the New World empire, the original motivation for "discovery" and conquest was "gold," or the search for goods available only from Asia and Asia Minor.

Specific Examples: Traditional imperialism was demonstrated as a money-making endeavor by the acquisition of territories during the Golden Age of Exploration and Discovery. Conquerors of the New World immediately put into place controls that allowed the conqueror to make major profits via the system of mercantilism and to keep those conquered peoples from developing (or retaining) their own economic systems. This was direct imperialism, as it accounted not only for control of the economics of a colony, but also for political and social control. Native leaders were not left in place, though some of their institutions did survive conquest.

Topic Sentence B: A more indirect imperialism was characterized by the French and Dutch conquests, which occurred mainly in Africa and Asia, and at least initially mainly along coastal regions.

Specific Examples: The trip to acquire the fabled riches of Asia and Asia Minor was long, and often required ships to stop along the way to restore supplies. Thus, merchants financed farming communities along the coasts of Africa for this very reason. Investor-financed companies, like the Dutch East India Company, allowed eventual control of other people's economies, but without the political control characteristics of more direct imperialism.

Topic Sentence C: The New Imperialism of the nineteenth century was both direct—involving political, social, and economic control—and it was ideologically inspired.

Specific Examples: The "white man's burden" of civilizing the rest of the world, or of making it conform to European ideas and ideals of civilization, was characteristic of this new form of imperialism. The Berlin Conference of 1884–1885, for example, divided up Africa without regard for tribal or governmental boundaries and loyalties, and it imposed governments that took over all aspects of daily life: religion, education, and society generally. Still, the underlying motivation behind much of New Imperialism was economic. The gold, diamonds, tea, rubber, and other resources and products made conquest and control all the sweeter for the New Imperialists.

Conclusion: Imperialism in all its forms seems to be more economically than ideologically driven. A lasting result was the destruction of native economic infrastructures and the marginalization of conquered countries in today's world.

Resource Guide

Using Literary Works in European History
General Websites
General Background
Resources by Historical Period

USING LITERARY WORKS IN EUROPEAN HISTORY

Literary works—novels, poetry, plays, even movies—or pieces that are dependable (i.e., historically accurate) are often more interesting than textbooks. The following suggestions are works that can supplement, though not supplant, your text. The choices are often personal, but also included are general websites that give you a broad array of material. As you consider these alternate resources, bear in mind the content you have studied in class, making connections as appropriate.

What's the point? Certainly, you have enough on your plate already. Perhaps a study group could pick a literary work, an artist or an artistic movement, or a piece of music and have members present one every few weeks. Everyone in the group would benefit without having to do all the work alone.

What to look for: Examples that make clear the importance of points of view and climates of opinion or that flesh out a particular period or event. Two samples follow. Each is meant to be a starting point for AP European History; that is, each makes you consider how history is written, by whom, and to what end.

Example 1

Josephine Tey, *The Daughter of Time*, a novel. This book, a mystery, serves as an introduction to historiography and to effective analysis and communication skills. A discussion or essay topic might include these *prompts*: (1) Use examples from the novel to support the following quotation: "The truth of anything at all doesn't lie in someone's account of it. It lies in all the small facts of the time. An advertisement in a paper. The sale of a house. The price of a ring. The real history is written in forms not meant as history." What examples of true history can you find in the novel? (2) Using *The Daughter of Time* as your frame of reference, give examples of four historical biases regarding King Richard III [England]. Two must be positive and two must be negative. If you like reading Shakespeare, or watching a production of a play, consider comparing Tey and Shakespeare's portrayals of King Richard III. Keep in mind each author's purpose.

Example 2

Watch the two most famous film versions of Shakespeare's *Henry V*—one with Laurence Olivier and one with Kenneth Branagh. Each deals with the same historical events, but the Olivier version was made during World War II and has propagandistic purposes, and the Branagh version, made in the post-Vietnam era, demonstrates modern antipathy to war. How does each film—through its version and vision of historical events—demonstrate authorial (or in this case, directorial) voice or intent?

GENERAL WEBSITES

Novels

- http://www.abebooks.com/books/features/50-essential-historical-fiction-books.shtml
  This site contains brief annotations of novels (primarily); the comments that follow have suggestions of other possibilities.

- http://www.historicalnovels.info
  This site is enormous and a tad overwhelming, citing more than 5,000 works. It is broken down by era.

- https://www.theguardian.com/culture/gallery/2012/may/13/ten-best-historical-novels
  This site focuses on ten novels. It is annotated.

Art

For general information about art, see the book by John Berger, *Ways of Seeing.* This is an art history "text," but it is very short. It will help you with how to analyze and interpret art and how to put it into historical context.

To understand art as propaganda, check out war recruiting and general patriotic posters. See the book by J. Darracott and B. Loftus, *First World War Posters.*

An alternative would be to search the Web for "propaganda WWI posters" and "propaganda WWII posters."

- http://arthistoryresources.net/ARTHLinks.html
  The most complete site available, produced by Christopher L. C. E. Witcombe.

- https://smarthistoryblog.org
  This amazing site offers evaluations of artworks. It has a YouTube channel as well. It is best used to search for specific works, artists, and eras.

Movies

- https://europeisnotdead.com/video/movies-of-europe/european-historical-movies/
  The focus is on twentieth-century Europe and its wars.

Music

There are two sites that start with the Billy Joel song "We Didn't Start the Fire." They flash names and events across the screen. They are useful for finding out what you need to know.

- https://www.youtube.com/watch?v=Swt1Vc0Lc00

This covers the years 1949–1989. Some things are out of chronological order, but this is useful nonetheless.

- https://www.youtube.com/watch?v=c24kzS-UX3k
This covers the years 2000–2009. It's a little heavy on U.S. history but is still useful.

- https://www.youtube.com/watch?v=cL9Wu2kWwSY
This is a piece on information technology.

Novels

Michael Crichton, *Timeline*
Ildefonso Falcones, *The Cathedral of the Sea*
Ken Follett, *Pillars of the Earth*
Edith Pargeter, *A Bloody Field by Shrewsbury*
Various mysteries, including *Sister Fidelma* by Peter Tremayne and The Chronicles of
Brother Cadfael series by Ellis Peters. The latter is available on BBC productions.

Films

Becket (1964)
The Lion in Winter (1968)
Henry V (with Laurence Olivier, 1944; with Kenneth Branagh, 1989)

RESOURCES BY HISTORICAL PERIOD

1450–1648

Machiavelli, *La Mandragola* (*The Mandrake Root*). This play is the source of the line "the end justifies the means."

Irving Stone, *The Agony and the Ecstasy*, which is also a stunning film.

A Season of Giants, a made-for-television movie about the life of Michelangelo.

Michelangelo and Petrarch, various poems

Boccaccio, *Decameron* (excerpts)

1648–1815

Victor Hugo, *Les Misérables*

Mary Shelley, *Frankenstein*

Charles Dickens, *A Tale of Two Cities*

Mary Wollstonecraft, *Maria, or the Wrongs of Woman*

Any of the Romantic poets, but especially Shelley's "To a Skylark," Byron's "Childe Harold" and "Don Juan," and Wordsworth's "The Prelude"

For satire, look at the works of William Hogarth (1697–1764) and James Gilray (1792–1810), caricaturists who specialized in political and social satire. Later, but perhaps better known, is Honoré Daumier (1808–1879). All gave rise to political and editorial cartooning.

1815–1914

Charles Dickens, *Oliver Twist*

Jane Austen, *Pride and Prejudice*

Novels about imperialism/colonialism:

   Africa: Chinua Achebe, *Things Fall Apart*, and be sure to read the Yeats poem "The Second Coming"

   India: Kamala Markandaya, *Nectar in a Sieve*, and J. G. Farrell, *The Siege of Krishnapur*

1914–Present

J. L. Carr, *A Month in the Country*

Dalton Trumbo, *Johnny Got His Gun*

Pat Barker, *Regeneration*

Ken Follett, *The Fall of Giants*

John Hersey, *Hiroshima*

Louis de Bernières, *Corelli's Mandolin* (the book, *not* the movie)

Lawrence of Arabia (the film) (1962)

A. J. Liebling, *World War II Writings* and *The Road Back to Paris* (journalism at its best)